Vivian Charles Sorensen (1916-1993)

In the Service of My Lord

Memoirs of a Missionary

by

Vivian Charles Sorensen

Edited by
Gwendoline D. Sorensen
and
Trevor C. Sorensen

ISBN 0-89697-501-0

Available from these bookstores:

RESTORATION BOOKSTORE
915 E. 23rd Street
Independence, MO 64055

SCHOOL OF SAINTS
520 W. Maple
Independence, MO 64050

TREE OF LIFE BOOKSTORE
210 W. White Oak
Independence, MO 64050

This book is dedicated to my beloved and faithful wife Gwen, without whose support and prayers and loyalty my life would have been different altogether. Thank you, Gwen, dear. May God be with you.

Table of Contents

Foreword

Vivian Charles Sorensen spent 34 years under full-time appointment as a missionary in the Reorganized Church of Jesus Christ of Latter Day Saints (RLDS). Even after his official "retirement," he continued to work as hard as ever to provide ministry to the Saints and nonmembers alike in Australia, New Zealand, French Polynesia, and America.

These memoirs chronicle his life from his boyhood in Australia until his death in Missouri. But even more importantly, they describe the unique challenges, severe tribulations, and exciting adventures of a missionary dedicated to the service of his Lord.

The primary sources for these memoirs are nine audio cassettes that Vivian recorded during the last weeks of his life and the letters he had written almost weekly to his mother (she faithfully safeguarded more than 2,000 of them). After she passed away, the less frequent letters to his sister Mavis supplied additional information. The chapter describing his journey to Europe was taken from microcassettes that Vivian recorded during the trip.

The material has been checked and supplemented as necessary by his wife and son, where possible. We apologize for any facts that are incorrect and for any omissions.

Many memories were left out to avoid making the book too large. For example, a long chapter of spiritual insights and essays on various religious topics was removed. We hope to share these writings of Vivian along with some of his sermons at a later date.

It is anticipated that most readers of these memoirs will be in the United States of America, therefore American spelling and wording have been used predominantly. We ask that the Australian readers will understand.

—Gwen and Trevor Sorensen, 1998

Preface

I am writing my memoirs for my family—my son and daughters, my grandsons and granddaughter—and for anyone else who might be interested.

These memoirs are associated with the people to whom I have ministered. However, I must pay tribute to my own family, especially to my wife, who has been so loyal and patient and helpful through all the years of our marriage, and to our two lovely daughters and our son, who have remained loyal to their covenant to the Lord and who have tried to order their lives in a way which would not bring reproach to their parents. Of course, all of us have made mistakes; nevertheless, we realize that God has truly blessed us. He has allowed us to suffer sometimes, but it has all been for our own good. At this juncture, I salute my family.

I know I have not supplied all these particular subjects in proper order; but I have been very sick while making these tapes. It has been a prodigious task to go through hundreds and hundreds of letters to try and find the tidbits and to try to remember things that have passed from my memory.

As I think of various things that have occurred, I will record them—they can be sorted out later if need be. However, I think that in reading someone's memoirs the unexpected is often the part of it that is so nice—you never know what you are going to get next!

I want to cover as much in these memoirs as possible about life in the islands, because most people who will be reading this have never been there or may never go there.

As I wrote to my parents from Tahiti in 1945, "The Kingdom first" is still my motto—and I hope it always will be!

—Vivian C. Sorensen, 1992

Acknowledgments

We sincerely thank the many people who have helped make the publication of these memoirs possible—from transcribing the audio cassettes, to reviewing, to proofreading. We truly appreciate all who encouraged us to complete this monumental task. But at the risk of leaving someone out, we will not list the names of all these wonderful people. However, without their help, this book could not have been possible.

Tokyo
China
San Francisco
Los Angeles
Midway I.
TROPIC OF CANCER
Philippines
Wake I.
Johnson I.
Hawaii
Guam
PACIFIC OCEAN
Palmyra
Fanning
EQUATOR
Christmas
Gilbert I.
Solomon I.
New Guinea
Marquesas
New
Hebrides
Fiji
Samoa
Australia
New
Caledonia
Roratonga
Tahiti
TROPIC OF CAPRICORN
Pitcairn
N
W
E
S
Sydney
New Zealand

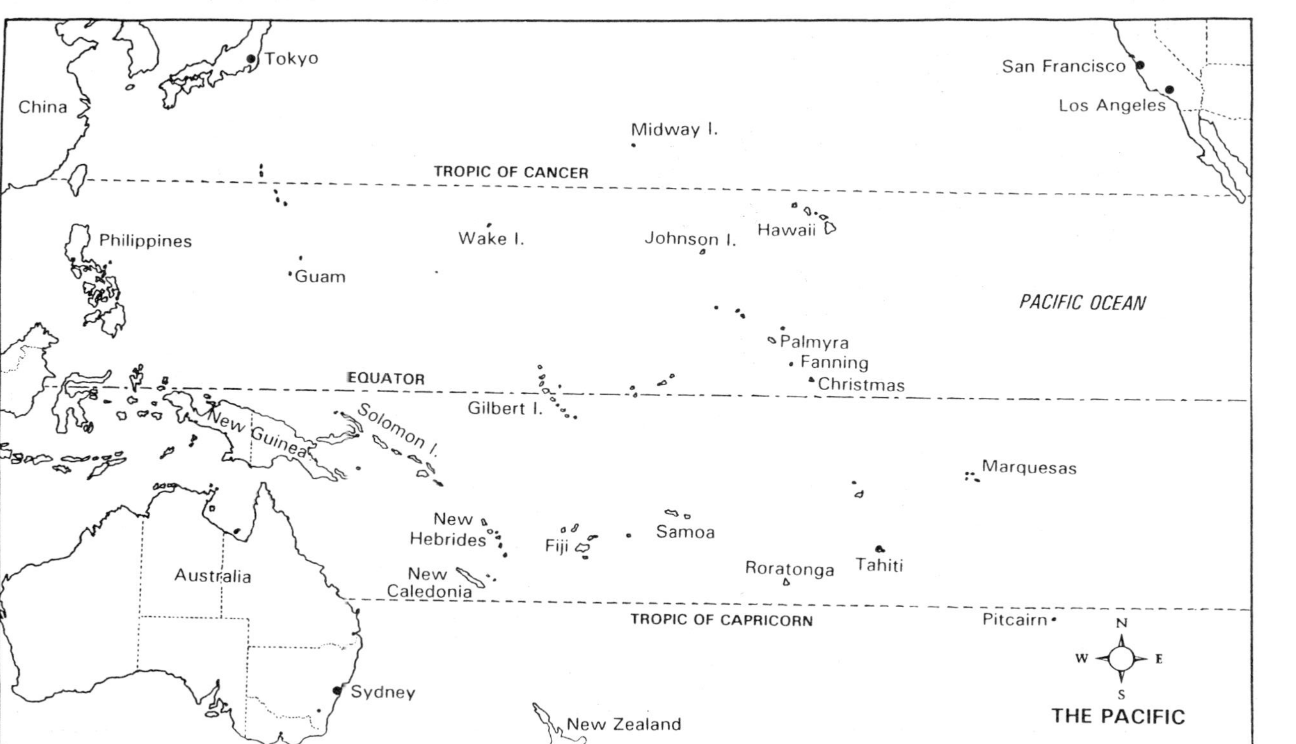

THE PACIFIC

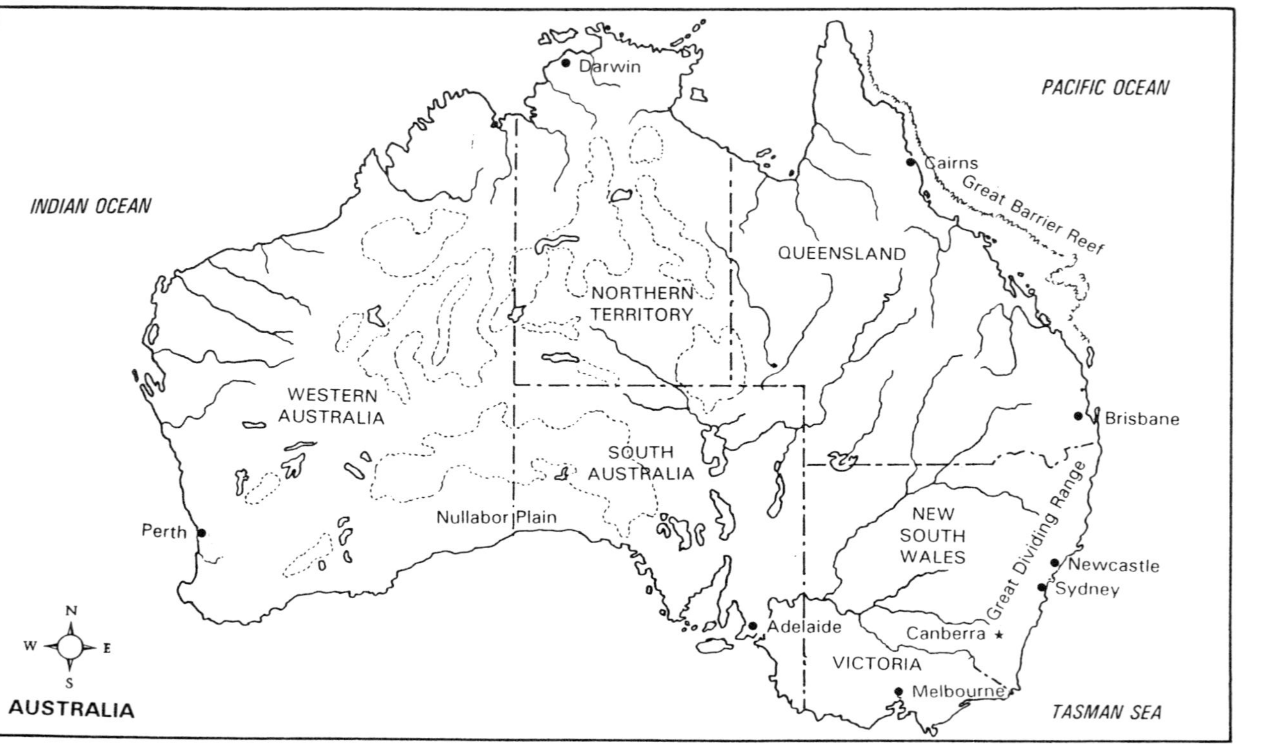
PACIFIC OCEAN
INDIAN OCEAN
Darwin
Cairns
Great Barrier Reef
QUEENSLAND
NORTHERN TERRITORY
WESTERN AUSTRALIA
SOUTH AUSTRALIA
Brisbane
Nullabor Plain
Perth
NEW SOUTH WALES
Great Dividing Range
Newcastle
Sydney
Adelaide
Canberra
VICTORIA
Melbourne
N
W
E
S
AUSTRALIA
TASMAN SEA

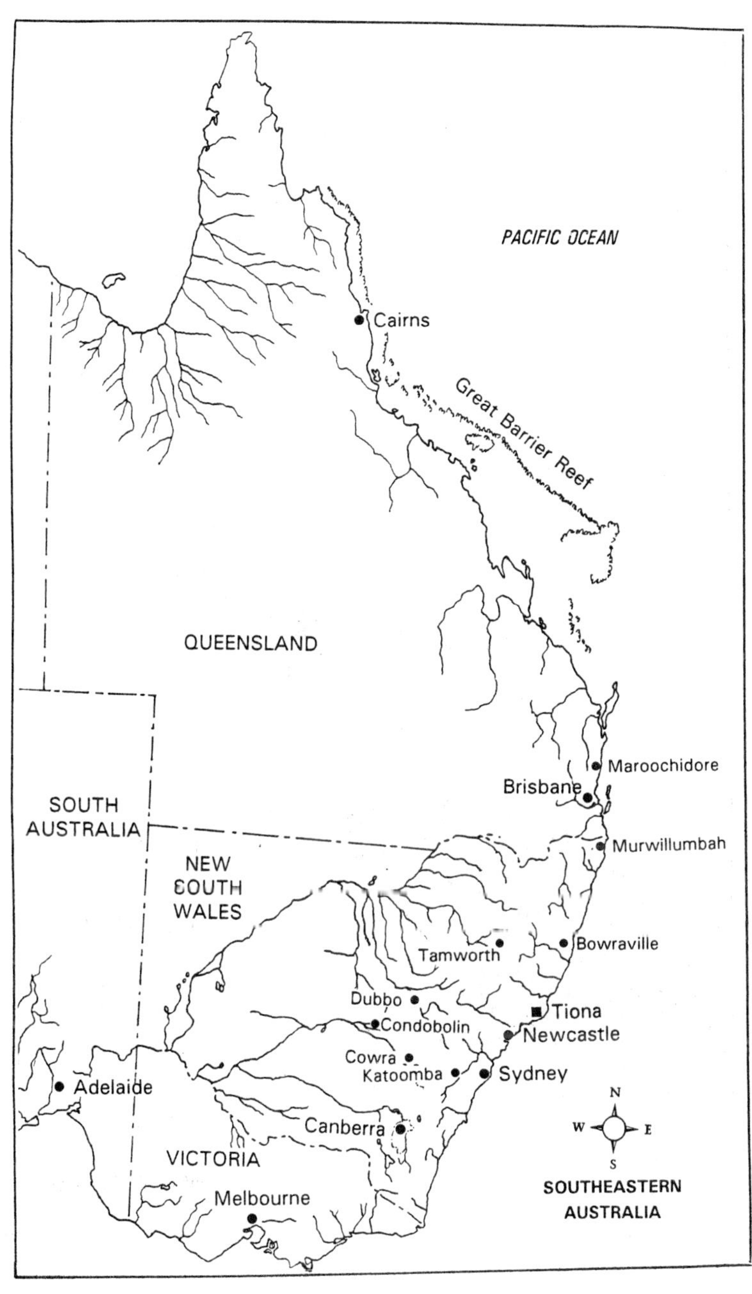
PACIFIC OCEAN
Cairns
Great Barrier Reef
QUEENSLAND
Maroochidore
Brisbane
SOUTH AUSTRALIA
Murwillumbah
NEW SOUTH WALES
Tamworth
Bowraville
Dubbo
Tiona
Condobolin
Newcastle
Cowra
Katoomba
Sydney
Adelaide
Canberra
VICTORIA
Melbourne
N
W
E
S
SOUTHEASTERN AUSTRALIA

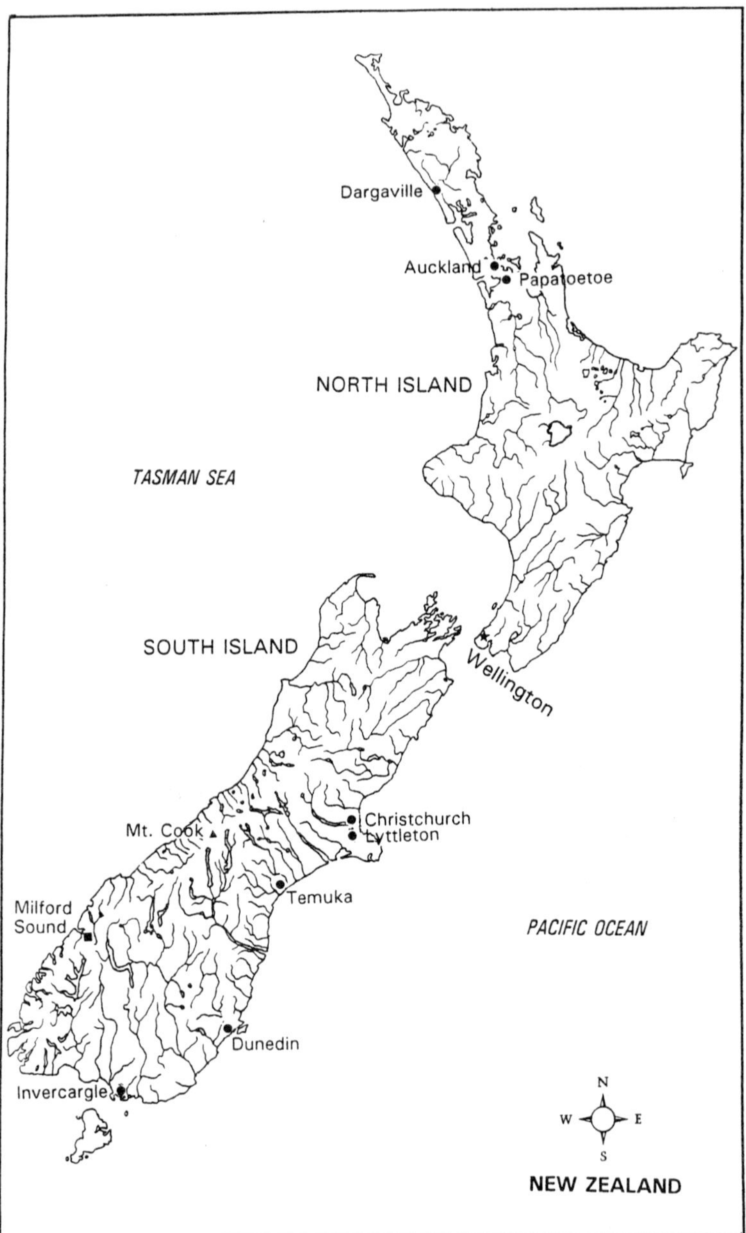
Dargaville
Auckland
Papatoetoe
NORTH ISLAND
TASMAN SEA
SOUTH ISLAND
Wellington
Christchurch
Lyttleton
Mt. Cook
Temuka
Milford
Sound
PACIFIC OCEAN
Dunedin
Invercargle
N
W
E
S
NEW ZEALAND

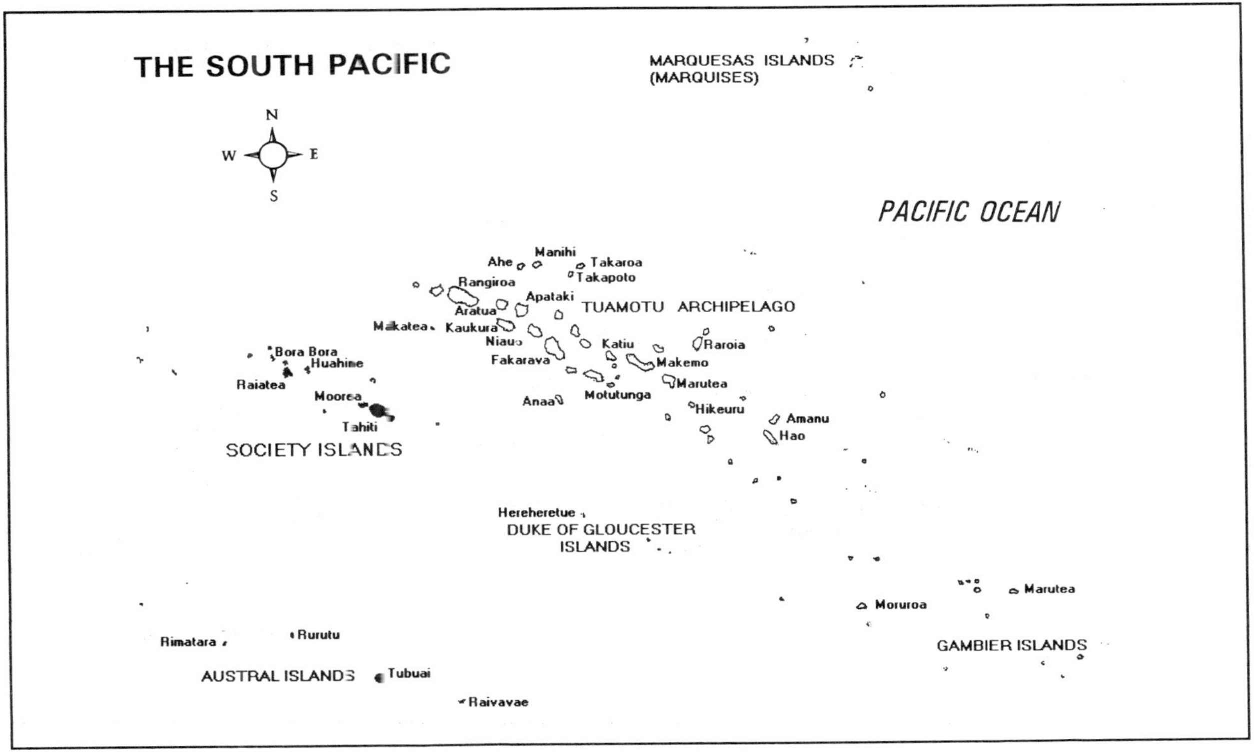

THE SOUTH PACIFIC

N
W E
S

MARQUESAS ISLANDS
(MARQUISES)

PACIFIC OCEAN

Manihi
Ahe
Takaroa
Takapoto
Rangiroa
Apataki
TUAMOTU ARCHIPELAGO
Aratua
Makatea
Kaukura
Niau
Katiu
Raroia
Fakarava
Makemo
Marutea
Anaa
Motutunga
Hikeuru
Amanu
Hao

Bora Bora
Huahine
Raiatea
Moorea
Tahiti
SOCIETY ISLANDS

Hereheretue
DUKE OF GLOUCESTER
ISLANDS

Marutea
Moruroa
GAMBIER ISLANDS

Rimatara
Rurutu
AUSTRAL ISLANDS
Tubuai
Raivavae

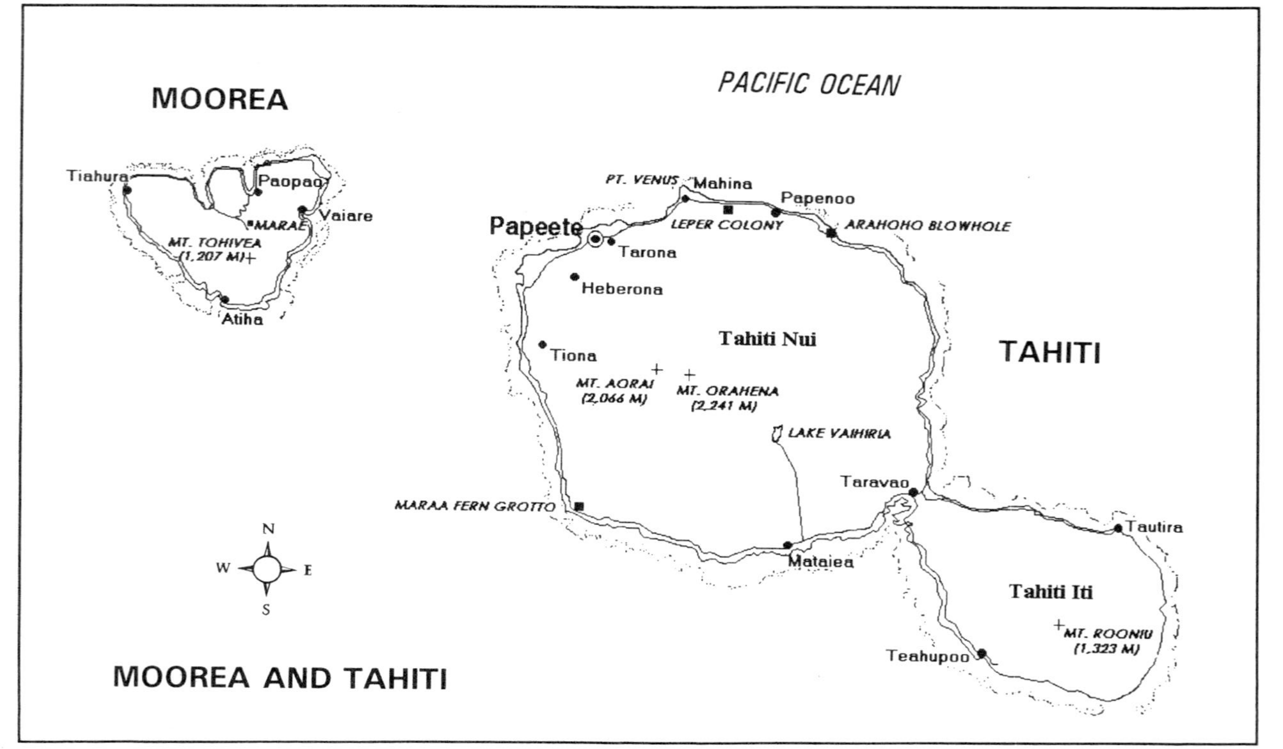

MOOREA
PACIFIC OCEAN
Tiahura
Paopao
Vaiare
MARAE
MT. TOHIVEA
(1,207 M)
Atiha
PT. VENUS
Mahina
Papenoo
Papeete
LEPER COLONY
ARAHOHO BLOWHOLE
Tarona
Heberona
Tahiti Nui
TAHITI
Tiona
MT. AORAI
(2,066 M)
MT. ORAHENA
(2,241 M)
LAKE VAIHIRIA
Taravao
MARAA FERN GROTTO
Tautira
N
W
E
S
Mataiea
Tahiti Iti
MT. ROONIU
(1,323 M)
Teahupoo
MOOREA AND TAHITI

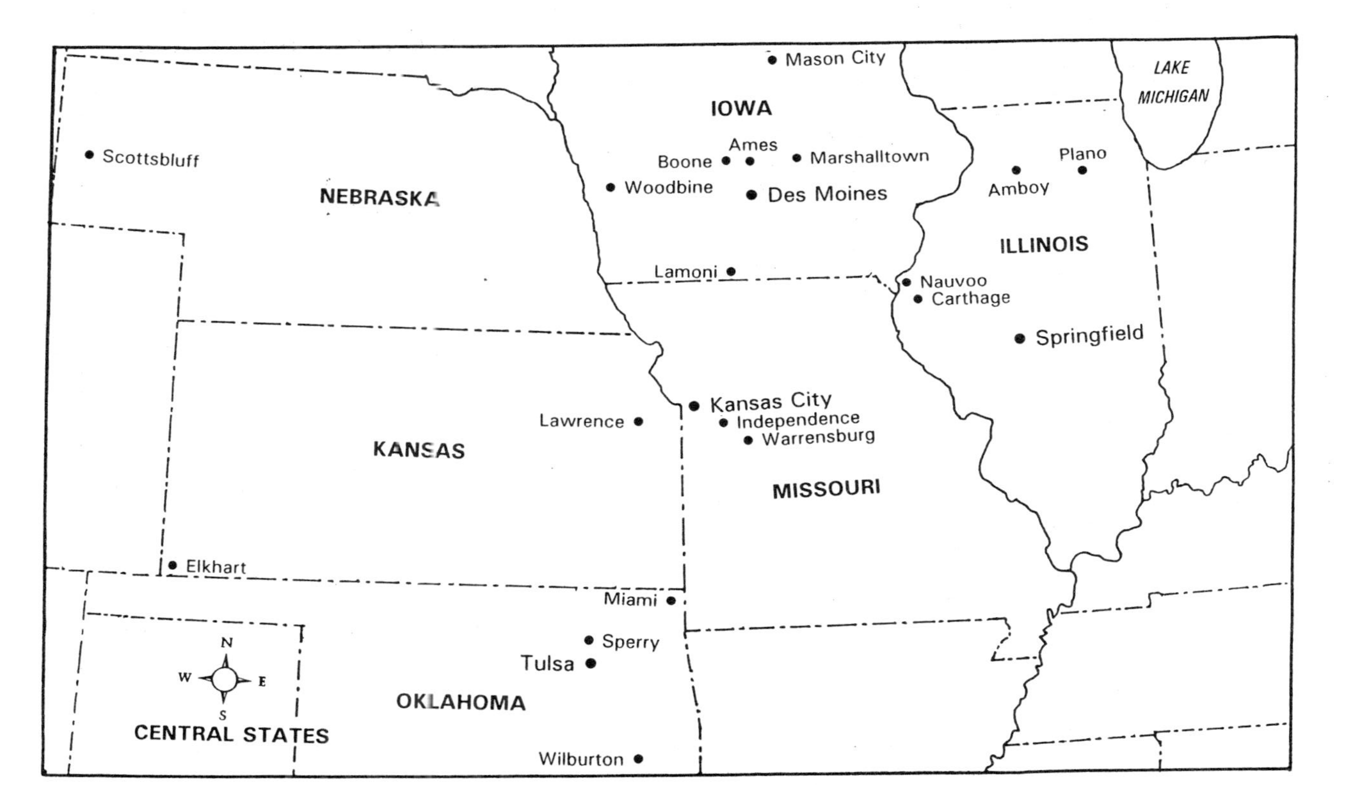
LAKE MICHIGAN
Mason City
IOWA
Ames
Boone
Marshalltown
Woodbine
Des Moines
Lamoni
ILLINOIS
Plano
Amboy
Nauvoo
Carthage
Springfield
Scottsbluff
NEBRASKA
KANSAS
Lawrence
Kansas City
Independence
Warrensburg
MISSOURI
Elkhart
Miami
Sperry
Tulsa
OKLAHOMA
Wilburton
N
W
E
S
CENTRAL STATES

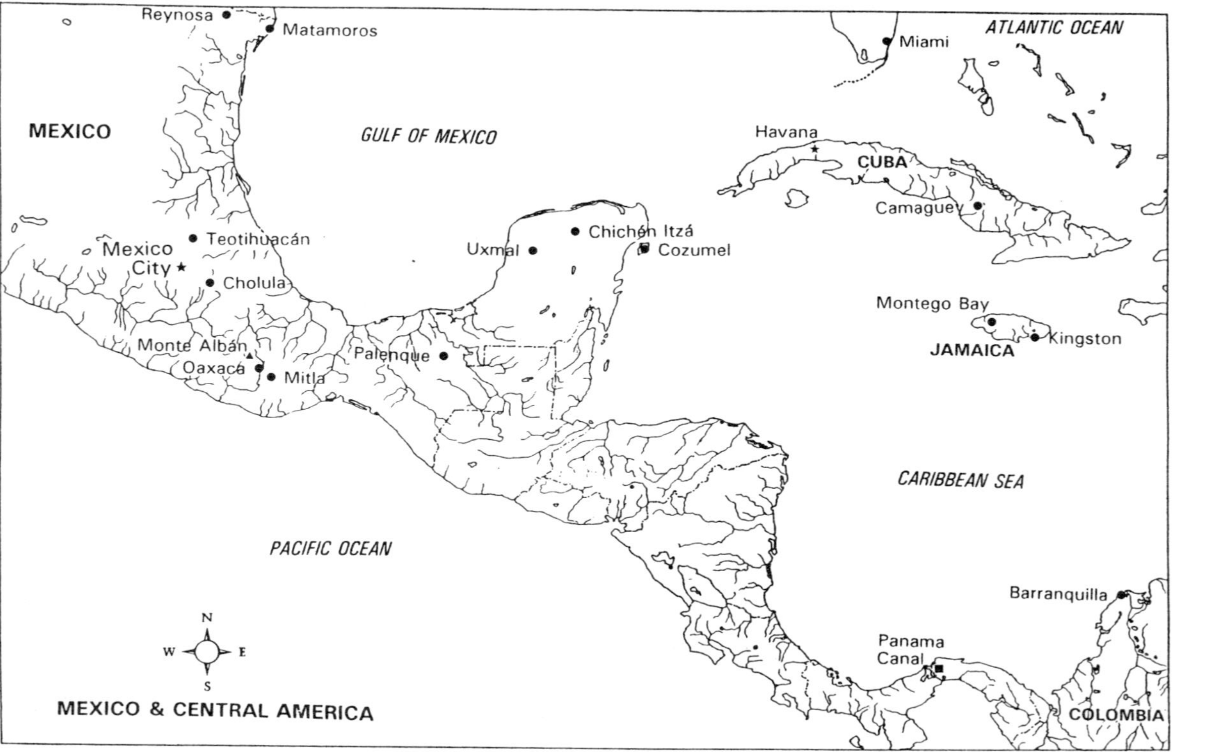

MEXICO & CENTRAL AMERICA

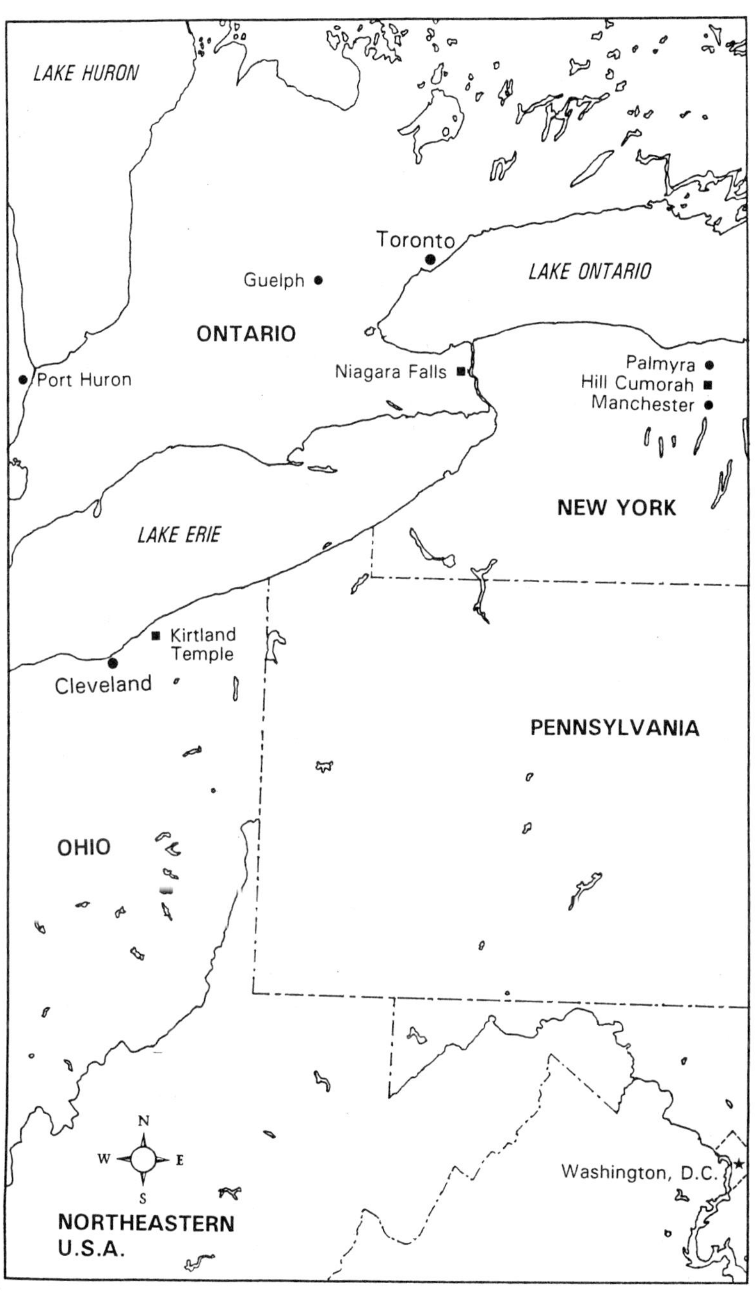

LAKE HURON
Toronto
Guelph
LAKE ONTARIO
ONTARIO
Port Huron
Niagara Falls
Palmyra
Hill Cumorah
Manchester
NEW YORK
LAKE ERIE
Kirtland
Temple
Cleveland
PENNSYLVANIA
OHIO
N
W
E
S
Washington, D.C.
NORTHEASTERN
U.S.A.

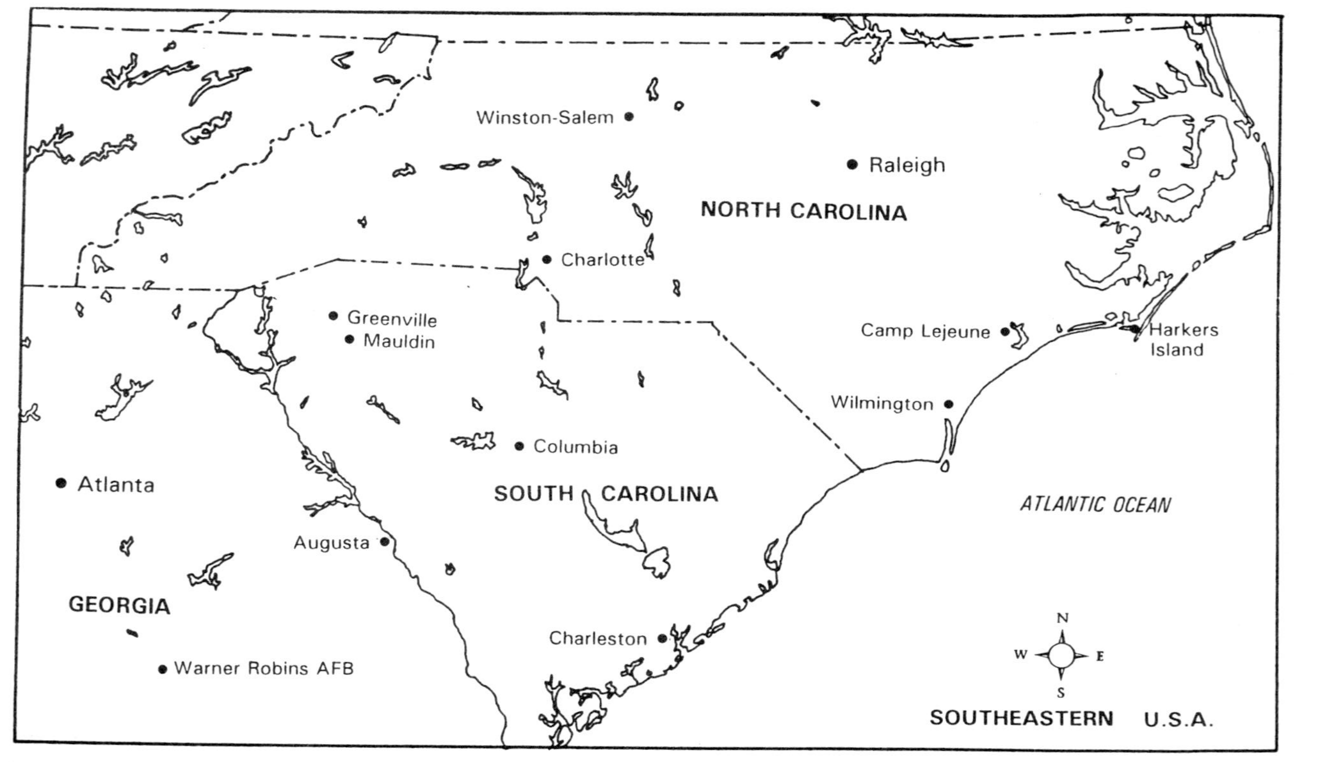

Winston-Salem
Raleigh
NORTH CAROLINA
Charlotte
Camp Lejeune
Harkers Island
Greenville
Mauldin
Wilmington
Columbia
Atlanta
SOUTH CAROLINA
ATLANTIC OCEAN
Augusta
GEORGIA
Charleston
Warner Robins AFB
N
W
E
S
SOUTHEASTERN U.S.A.

CHAPTER 1

My Youth and Early Church Life

What a privilege it has been to minister in the service of my Lord to the people of Australia, New Zealand, French Polynesia, and many states in the U.S. The Lord has guided and protected me all the days of my life, for which I am truly thankful. As I look over my life, I am led to exclaim, "How marvelously Thou hast blessed me, O Lord God Almighty!"

My father, Jens Carl Sorensen, was known as Charlie. His parents were Danish; his father, Christian, was brought from Denmark to Queensland, Australia, by the government to work on its buildings. His mother, Antoinette Christiansen, came by sailing ship from Denmark to Australia when she was 12 years old. During the voyage, her family was saddened by the death of their middle daughter, who was buried at sea. Christian and Antoinette met each other in Australia and were married in Brisbane. My father, born in 1890, was their fifth child.

My mother's maiden name was Ruby Roles, and she was of English descent. She was born in 1894. When she was eleven years old, her family came to live next door to the Sorensen family in Sherwood, a suburb of Brisbane. Many years later my father confided to my sister that when he was fifteen years old he knew Ruby would one day become his wife. They were married in 1914.

My father was a carpenter, but he also learned the trade of applying ornate metal ceilings in big city buildings.

I was born in Sherwood on February 13, 1916—the first of three children. When I was about seven months old, my father was persuaded to move to a banana plantation at Yandina. The price of bananas at that time was very high. So off he went with Mother and me to Yandina, where he labored growing bananas. I think it was fairly successful at the start, but then the price of bananas fell. I remember he said that one time he sent a whole truckload of bananas to market and got a bill back for freight—they did not realize enough money to pay the freight. That was the end of Dad's sojourn on the banana plantation. While we were living there, my sister Silvia was born on September 25, 1918. Today this farm lies submerged under the waters of the Wappa Dam.

My dad liked farming, so we moved to some land where the owner built a house for us. I can remember it quite well. Dad cleared about 25 acres of virgin scrub and jungle rain forest and planted sugar cane, which grew very well. It was almost a model farm with the beautiful Maroochy River running through it. It was there that my younger sister Mavis was born on September 27, 1921, and where I first went to school.

A motorboat went up and down the river taking us school children to and from school. While we lived at the sugar plantation, my father taught me to swim in the Maroochy River. In that hot climate we almost lived in the water. Trees leaned out over the river, and from the hanging "monkey vines" we swung way out into the water. We really had a wonderful time. Every day a mail boat brought mail, food, and all sorts of merchandise.

An old fisherman named Mr. Braydon showed me the first platypus I ever saw along the banks of this river. The duckbill platypus is the only animal in the world that has a bill and webbed feet like a duck, that has fur like a fur-bearing mammal, that lays eggs, and yet suckles its young. It was a challenge for every pupil in Australia to learn to spell its scientific name, O-r-n-i-t-h-o-r-h-y-n-c-h-u-s!

My dad was a hard worker. On really hot summer days while he was felling timber, his boots sometimes were so full of sweat that the water ran out of the eyelets. But it appears that he had labored in vain in the heat. The time came when the owner had to sell the sugar cane plantation to pay his debts.

We then moved quite a long way away to a dairy farm at Tairo. By then I was old enough that I had to pull my weight. It was there that I learned to milk cows and do other farm chores.[1]

At Tairo, Silvia and I walked about three miles to a little one-teacher school. The teacher was a Mrs. Ludlow. It was very difficult to learn with only one teacher and two or three different classes because she could not give us much individual attention. I had some good experiences there, however.

Through the farm ran a beautiful, crystal-clear river, which had a rather unique fish with lungs, called a lung-fish. Some friends and I often went down to swim in the river and catch fish. A man who worked for Dad had a rifle. If a nice school of mullet was swimming around, he

---

[1] Many years later in Illinois an old gentleman had a cow that really needed milking, but he was too sick to milk it. I said, "I'll milk it for you."

He replied, "You couldn't milk a cow; you're a missionary."

I said, "Well, give me a try."

His wife's mouth dropped open when she saw me squirt a big stream of milk in the bucket. I explained that I had learned to milk when I was a boy.

fired into the middle of them to stun them. Then we boys grabbed the stunned fish before they recovered.

My mates and I also robbed many a native beehive of delicious honey, which we sometimes shared with my sisters. Those were all part of my boyhood experiences which I enjoyed very much.

After one year we again moved—that time to return to my birthplace, Sherwood in Brisbane. Dad found work as a general carrier (truck driver). My sisters and I went to Sherwood School. There I first met Gwen Peisker—who was to have such an effect on my life in the years to come as my wife! At that time, however, she was only eight or nine years old, a playmate of my sisters. Her family and ours were the only RLDS Church families within miles.

Soon I was ready for high school. I passed a scholarship exam and gained entrance to the Brisbane State High School. The headmaster there was Mr. Isaac Waddle. He signed his name "I. Waddle," so naturally we called him "The Duck"—but not to his face, of course!

The Great Depression of the 1930s hit, and my father was without work again. In 1930 we decided to go to Windra, where my Uncle Neil Sorensen had a dairy farm. There I milked my share of cows. Uncle Neil also grew cotton, so between milkings I picked cotton. That was not an easy job. The farmers did not have mechanical cotton pickers like they do today, and I remember my fingers being raw and painful from the boles of the cotton sticking into my skin.

From there we went to Uncle Win's farm. Uncle Win had recently died, and we were able to help his widow, Aunt Silvia. I helped Dad clean the brush away. We planted bananas and five acres of sugar cane. The land was so productive that we had a tremendous crop.

Early one morning before sunrise I had a unique experience there. I was up, ready to start my chores, when I saw a ring of koala bears playing. It was so unusual that I awakened my sisters, and we watched them play. When the sun arose, each koala scampered up its own particular eucalyptus tree.

My Uncle Fred Sorensen, Dad, and I also went sugar cane cutting in season, which was terribly hard work. Uncle Fred was fearless when it came to snakes. While cutting cane, I saw him grab a deadly taipan snake by the tail and whip it so that its neck snapped.

After a couple of moves around the Maroochy district, it was decided that my father and I should go to Brisbane to look for work. We started to walk the 70 miles because we were too poor to go by train. But after we had gone about 20 miles, Dad's feet gave out. His boots had rubbed his heels raw. We beckoned a man in a little old truck, and he gave us a ride to the nearest railway station. Since a train to Brisbane was about due, we bought tickets with the little money we had. In Brisbane we stayed with relatives while we looked for work.

Dad obtained work on the Hornibrook Highway, a huge causeway, a mile and three quarters long, which was being built to join two peninsulas over Moreton Bay, a beautiful bay by the city of Brisbane. He also got me a job there, and our family rented a house on ten acres of ground at Aspley, a suburb of Brisbane.

Dad and I drove to work in my uncle's Model T Ford. After several months of work, Dad had a gastric ulcer which hemorrhaged, and he had to be rushed to the hospital in an ambulance. He was quite some time convalescing, so I then had to buy a bicycle and pedal several miles to work.

My cousin Allan Roles came to live with our family about that time, when he was four years old. He was not officially adopted, but he was accepted and brought up as a son, living with my parents until he was 21 years old.

When the job at Moreton Bay was finished, I applied for work with the same company, which was then building the Story Bridge, a huge steel suspension bridge across the Brisbane River. At that time I was about 20 years old. I asked Mr. Hornibrook if they would accept me as an apprentice in engineering (fitting, turning, and welding). I knew I could not start at the beginner's wages.

Mr. Hornibrook said, "You're a good worker, so I'll start you off at fourth-year rate instead of first-year."

The wages were not quite comparable to what I had been getting on the causeway, but Dad also worked there as a bridge carpenter, so our fortunes began to improve.

Three nights a week I attended college. About 5 o'clock I finished work, went across the river on a ferry, walked through the botanical gardens to the university, and did my class work. Then I had to walk a couple of miles to the railway station, ride six or seven miles on the train, and walk another mile and a half before I got home. I rather enjoyed it and did very well with my college studies.

Before the Story Bridge was finished, I took my camera and climbed to the top of the great girders that supported the whole bridge. It was fairly easy going until I got near the top. Then I almost lost my nerve. Right at the top, 200 feet above the river, was a platform only about six feet square—with no guardrails. However, I was able to take some excellent pictures.

I had helped get the air locks all set up, and I knew a good deal about them. So I asked the chief engineer with whom I worked if I could go down to the very bottom of the structure. He told me that I could, but it would be necessary to get a medical certificate because we would be subjected to extreme pressure of about 54 pounds to the square inch.

One evening, in trepidation, I entered the air lock chamber in company with some men who were going down to work. They closed the lid over the top of us and began to increase air pressure. It took us only 20 minutes to go under pressure, and we had to keep poking our chins out and popping our ears. We went down more than 100 feet to the bottom. The men were using jackhammers, and the noise just about broke our eardrums. I wondered if I would come out of it deaf.

While I was down there, I could not pronounce the letter *S*. It was impossible for me to make that hissing sound. Some of the men could do it a bit, those who had a lot of practice. One of the men showed me that we could not blow out a match because of the excessive oxygen in the air. He struck a match, which burned with a flame about six inches long!

The workers could only stay one hour in the air lock because of the high nitrogen content. When we came up into the decompression chamber, the door below us locked. We had to sit in the chamber for 90 minutes. The pressure was reduced to about 25 pounds per square inch fairly quickly, but the remainder had to be let out very slowly.

If anyone got the "bends," caused by nitrogen bubbles in the blood, he was quickly taken to the "air lock hospital" and put in the decompression chamber. I have seen huge strapping men crying like babies from those terrible "jags," as they called them, in these chambers.

A tragedy happened on the bridge to one worker, who thought he could climb anywhere. Sometimes he went to the top of a big crane, got some "spag" on his hands, and slid down the wire rope of the crane rather than taking the time to crawl down. But he became the victim of someone's carelessness. He was 140 feet in the air, running along the steel structure like a monkey until he reached a plank, which was not secured at one end. I heard the clatter when it tipped up. The next minute he hit the ground and was killed instantly.

One day we looked up and saw the chief surveyor of the bridge, a man named Chris, walking on a narrow girder. He walked along quite smartly to one end, turned on his heel almost, and walked back with a 150-foot drop beneath him. Chris was virtually mesmerized by the height. His nerves had become quite frayed because of the tremendous strain of his job. It was his responsibility to ensure that the two halves of that bridge met perfectly so the workers could slip in huge pins—thus joining the bridge forever. Finally someone plucked up enough courage to crawl up, gain his attention, and get him down without mishap.

A week or two later at a certain hour on a certain day when the temperature was just right, the workers were ready to put in the big pins. I was there and watched while the pins were slid in effortlessly. It was a terrific feat of engineering—to build a bridge from each side of a river and to have the spans meet exactly as planned.

The Brisbane River was not only the focus of my employment while I worked on the Story Bridge; it was also significant to my spiritual life since I was baptized in its waters (as I will later relate). The river was also important because of my love of adventure and exploration. My father and I built a small canoe out of waterproofed canvas attached to a wooden frame. We rigged the canoe so that we could add a sail to it when desired.

I spent many happy hours during the late 1930s and early war years exploring several miles of the Brisbane River in my canoe—and had many adventures. One time when I was going along under sail, I heard a rifle shot followed by a whistling sound. I ducked! When I finally looked up, I saw a bullet hole in my sail. Apparently someone had been using it for target practice.

Another time, not long after Gwen and I were married, I persuaded my bride to join me on a canoe ride. It started to rain, so we sought shelter under the pier of a nearby power station. We had barely arrived when an armed guard at the power station began yelling at us to leave. He was not taking any chances. It was wartime, and there was always the threat of sabotage. We were probably the most unlikely looking terrorists that you could imagine!

☼ ☼ ☼

The main purpose of this book is to make known to my friends and relatives my ultimate and complete belief in God and in Jesus Christ, His Son.

My religious training began at the feet of my mother. She was originally a Methodist; but because of the testimony of her Aunt Amber, she was converted and baptized into the Reorganized Church of Jesus Christ of Latter Day Saints shortly before I was born. It broke her heart to be on the various farms and away from the church with no possibility of attending except perhaps once a year. She had the gospel quarterlies and read them to us. She also read the Scriptures and explained many of the wonderful things of the gospel.

Mother often sang hymns to us, which included these inspirational words:

"Through the furnace, through the heat, there beneath the hammer's beat, through temptations manifold, comes my soul like burnished gold."

"I hear thee speak of a better land, they call its children a happy band...."

"Come, O my soul to Calvary, and see the man who died for me, upon the accursed tree...."

"When my life's work is ended, and I cross the swelling tide, a bright and glorious morning I shall see."

All of these had a profound impression on my life, and I tell today's young mothers to sing the songs of Zion to their children. While memory lasts, I shall not forget this heritage that my mother gave to me.

When we moved back to Brisbane, I went to church with my mother and sisters; my father was not a member. We still had a very long way to go to church. From Sherwood we took a train, a streetcar, and then another streetcar until finally we arrived at the street where the church was located.

On November 2, 1929, my two younger sisters and several others, including my wife-to-be, Gwen Peisker, were baptized in a creek not far from the church. I was 13 at the time and very anxious to be baptized, but I was extremely shy and refused to be baptized with the others. Brother N. Wallace Peisker, my future father-in-law, baptized me in the Brisbane River at Indooroopilly in a private service on February 1, 1930, just before my 14th birthday. I was confirmed by Brother Wallace Peisker and his father, Brother E. A. H. Peisker.

The servants of God who came to our home branch in Brisbane influenced me a great deal in my young days. Walter Haworth, A. J. Corbett, Herman Peisker, J. H. N. Jones, and others came from Sydney. Also influential were local priesthood, such as Dolph Loving, N. Wallace Peisker, and others. I drank in the words that fell from their lips. They really ministered to me and had a great influence on my life, encouraging me to seek a personal witness of Christ and the truth of His everlasting gospel. I later came to realize that I could have an influence on others as well.

I was so shy that I would not go to a church social or young people's meeting, even when we returned to Brisbane in 1935 after several years in the country. Finally my mother persuaded me to go to the Zion's League, which was just starting in those days. Very reluctantly I went. I was 19 at the time. The Leaguers were generally 16 to 25 years old. I am very glad that Mother encouraged me, for in Zion's League the Spirit of God began to work in me.

Six months later I was the president of that Zion's League. We had about 40 members at the peak of our membership. It just shows what can happen when one opens his heart to God. I overcame my own timidity and placed my hand in His. He was standing at the door and knocking. When I finally opened the door and let Him in, it was not long before my life was transformed. On November 13, 1935, C. A. Davies and A. J. Corbett ordained me to the office of priest, which was my first priesthood office in the church.

We had a marvelous Zion's League for several years. It was not because I was the leader, but rather because of the caliber of the young people. Some of them were soldiers; and others were devoted young people, who came to the open-air preaching services which we held in the city.

Nearly every Sunday afternoon the Zion's League went into the hospitals in the big city of Brisbane and tried to visit those patients who never had any visitors. Gwen Peisker worked in one of these hospitals before our marriage, and she was often able to point out people who never had visitors. We gave them *Saints' Herald* magazines and talked to them about Christ. I am sure the ministering not only helped them—it helped our young people, too. Of course, not all the young people went. But the most spiritually minded did, and they were much richer for it. We cannot do things for God except He blesses us.

In September of 1940, I was ordained to the priesthood office of elder. My first administration to the sick was to a lady in my home branch who had been ill for a long time. She had some woman's complaint like the woman in the Bible who was afflicted for 12 years. Two other elders put their hands on her head first, and I put my hands on top of their hands. But only the index finger of my right hand was touching her head. As I began to pray, I felt something like an electrical discharge going through my finger from my body into hers. There was no imagination about the electricity with me. She was healed immediately and had no more of that issue of blood. That also consolidated my faith. To God be the glory!

The young people from our Zion's League sometimes went down to Murwillumbah, just over the border in New South Wales, to provide ministry to our small branch there.

The first such trip occurred in 1939 or 1940. On Saturday we climbed to the top of Mount Warning, which is a prominent mountain near the coast. It was named by Captain James Cook when he first discovered the east coast of Australia in 1770. When we arrived at the top, we were met by a breathtaking panorama. Below us was the lush green of the banana plantations on the hillsides and the fields of sugar cane. Beyond this scene of green stretched the beautiful azure blue of the Pacific Ocean. Inspired by this splendor of God's creation, we naturally joined together in a service of worship and prayer. That was truly a mountaintop experience! On the following day, our group of young people provided the Sunday program for the small congregation of the Murwillumbah branch.

Before long, World War II was raging in the Pacific. The Japanese were bombing Darwin, a city in northern Australia; and emotions were running high. We had some wonderful experiences preaching in the streets. On Friday nights we preached on cordoned-off parts of a street in the center of Brisbane. Gasoline was rationed, and there was practically no motor traffic.

One night I was preaching in the center of a circle formed by the sisters and brethren, when a drunken Australian soldier came right up to me—within a foot of my face—and started to blaspheme and swear. Since I was a very new priesthood member, I could not keep going. But our pastor, Dolph Loving, who was a veteran preacher, pulled my coattail. I stepped back, and he walked right into my place. Ignoring the soldier, he carried on with my sermon. It was amazing, really, how the Lord blessed him.

When I stepped back, I steadied the Coleman lantern that illuminated our music books and made a light around us to draw the people. The soldier, not getting any success from harassing the pastor, made a lunge toward the light. He said, "Let's smash their —— light!" But as he reached to grab the light, his arm froze in midair. He could not move it; and a strange, silly look came over his face as though he did not know where he was!

When he had said, "Let's smash their light," some of his mates—who were also somewhat drunk—surged forward. They had just about reached the circle of the ladies, who were becoming frightened because of what was going on. All of a sudden, the men stopped as though restrained by a great chain. Then a tall and well-built American sailor, in his white uniform and gob cap, excused himself to the ladies. He came into the circle, picked up that drunken soldier by the seat of his pants and the scruff of his neck, hoisted him out into the street, and went on his way. The American was there right at the time when he was needed, but we did not see any sign of him again. I often wondered who he was.

A few weeks later, on a sacrament Sunday, the Lord used me for the first time to speak in prophecy—to tell the Saints that the Lord had witnessed their faithfulness and if they preached on the streets, He would never allow that sort of thing to happen again. Well, I was pretty much on the spot. How was I to know except by the Holy Spirit that it was not going to happen again? But it never did; the Lord kept His word. All of this strengthened my faith.

At that time I was still living at home. After the completion of the Story Bridge, I worked as a fitter and turner at the Mars Machine Tool Company. I helped make components for submarine engines and Norden bombsights in support of our war effort. Because of my engineering skills, I did not get into active military service. The government told me to stay where I was—and a good boy does as he is told! I tried to join the Royal Australian Air Force. But I was told if I did, I would be doing the same job as I was doing at the tool company. So I chose to be free to preach the gospel and yet do a good work for my country.

One night as I was preaching on the street, a number of Australian soldiers came and started criticizing me, calling me all sorts of names and saying, "Why aren't you out with our men fighting in the trenches?" The criticism became severe.

Brother Loving, an excellent orator, stepped forward and gave them a tongue lashing. He said, "This man is working at a very essential and secret work for the governments of Australia and America. Then in his spare time he comes out and preaches to men like you who need to repent, and he stands in front of you unafraid. How many of you would be willing to get up here and preach the gospel? I'm sure none of you." They slunk away like whipped dogs. It is wonderful what the power of oratory can do, especially when it is combined with the power of the Holy Spirit.

We then changed from an inner-city street at nighttime to another city street on Sunday afternoon. There we stood under the awning of a large men's outfitters and preached the gospel. My sister Mavis had made a big chart for me, and we suspended it from poles held up by two men. The caption on this chart was "The New Order." You hear people speaking about a new order today as though it were something new. But during World War II, in Australia anyway, everyone was talking about the New Order—"A war to end wars." I wanted to capitalize on the interests of the day, so I thought that was a good caption for my chart.

One Sunday afternoon we sang a couple of hymns while Brother Loving played his trumpet. I noticed a large group of soldiers coming down the street. They heard me commencing to preach and saw the big sign. Most of them stopped and sat down in the street right on the asphalt and listened. The soldiers were a horrible yellow color because of the tablets they had been taking to combat malaria. I also saw two high-ranking officers, one an American and one an Australian. They stood and listened to the entire discourse. Many nonmembers were listening to me, and the Lord gave me great liberty.

After I had finished speaking, the Australian officer beckoned me over to where he was standing. He put out his hand and said, "Young man, I want to congratulate you on those remarks. What you have done today could not have been done in any other way. You see these men? They have just come out of hell—out of the jungles of New Guinea, where there's a sniper in every tree. Their nerves are on edge all the time, wondering whether the next bullet will be for them." He continued, "You've given these men hope, and that's the greatest blessing they can have."

Then the American officer stepped forward and said, "Those are my sentiments also." Just imagine how I felt. I was really in service to these men who needed so much the reassurance and hope of the gospel of the Lord Jesus Christ.[1]

---

[1] In November, 1983, I preached at the South Crysler congregation in Independence, Missouri, where I included this wartime experience in my sermon. A man came to me at the end of the service and told me that he had been present that day on Albert Street in Brisbane, on furlough from New Guinea. He said that I probably had no idea just how much that reassurance helped him and others at that time. What a small world it is!

The street meetings gave me great strength and help in being able to speak my thoughts directly without notes. The people who listened to street preachers in Australia disdained the use of notes. You had to speak "off the cuff." Sometimes we had a good audience, and sometimes we did not. We ended up by baptizing only three men. Two were American soldiers, Laurie Malone and Leon Mote; and the other was an Australian wharf laborer. I met Leon Mote in Alabama many years later.

During the war years we met a large number of American soldiers, sailors, and airmen. Some were members of our church, and some were not; but we tried to make everyone welcome. Thomas Thatcher, originally of Independence, Missouri, one of the American servicemen who were church members, is now the uncle of my daughter-in-law, Lori (Thatcher) Sorensen. Of course, we did not know it at the time, since neither she nor my son had yet been born. Again, what a small world!

About the same time, I made myself a diving helmet. It was a rather crude apparatus, but the helmet fit over the head and shoulders with a big glass window in the front. It tied under the arms and had lead weights to hold it on. Tire pumps pumped air in through a long hose to displace the water. People told me it would not work, but I felt it would. To try it out, I went down an old, unused well that had about eight or ten feet of water in it; and lo and behold, it worked!

At Easter time we had a camp for our Zion's League. One or two Americans were able to get leave for that weekend. A whole crowd of us Australians, including some servicemen, went to Young's Crossing. We pitched two large tents, one for the boys and one for the girls. The campsite was on a lovely river. Several of the young men (those who were courageous enough) tried out my diving helmet, but we had a bit of trouble persuading the young ladies. I think my younger sister Mavis went down first. Some of the others then took courage—it was their first time in any kind of diving gear.[1]

Another thing I made in Australia was a refrigerator, which was a luxury in the 1940s, when most people had the iceman deliver a block of ice each day for the icebox. I also built a charcoal-burning gas producer on my car, since gasoline was rationed and very scarce. It worked very well. It was not as powerful as gasoline (it gave about 70% of the power output of gasoline), but it enabled us to get to destinations as required. The car ran on charcoal, and we had a free supply of fuel by simply stopping at the side of country roads and getting charcoal from burnt trees. One drawback to this type of propulsion was that it often threw sparks everywhere when the motor stopped—with some interesting results.

In 1942 Apostle George Mesley, my sister Mavis, my fiancée Gwen, and I were driving to Murwillumbah along the Gold Coast of Queensland in my old car with the charcoal-burning gas producer. We were awed by a gorgeous rainbow over the ocean, so we pulled the car to the side of the road to better appreciate the beautiful scene.

However, when the motor was stopped, it backfired and

---

[1] Many years later, I made a diving helmet in Tahiti and had some natives take me out in their canoe. I tried it in the crystal-clear water of the harbor. I went down about 20 or 30 feet. The natives were amazed. They called it an *opupu*, which is their word for diving gear. Then I took it to the pearl shell diving islands. You were not allowed to dive for pearl shells with an *opupu*—you had to be skindiving. But they did not mind my going down in the contraption just to sightsee. My *opupu* worked very well! I often used it to look at the colorful coral and fish and other marine life.

sent a shower of sparks over the dry grass, which immediately caught fire! Fortunately I had some gunny sacks in the car. All of us, including the apostle, used them and some green bushes to extinguish the fire. Brother Mesley was greatly amused by the whole incident.

On the return trip, the gas producer again caused some excitement. We stopped in the coastal town of Southport for refreshments. When I turned off the motor, it backfired again with a large shower of sparks, which made the people walking nearby jump and scatter with fright. There was a war on, after all!

My first missionary endeavor away from Brisbane consisted of flying to Kingaroy and visiting at the farm of the Nugent family. Little did I know that that short flight in a twin-engine plane would be the first of dozens of flights as a missionary for the Lord Jesus Christ.

I want to share a love story with you now. I was coming to that stage in my life when I knew it would be wise for me to have a companion. Often I wondered who it would be. I was extremely shy of girls my own age. I drove an old Essex and took my sisters and their friends around to Zion's League outings—the boys had to follow on bicycles! We went swimming on Saturday afternoons, played volleyball games at different places, and often went to the seaside. Although I was very shy, the Lord knew that. He made preparations long before—for me and for the one I was to marry.

When Gwen Peisker was 16 years old and entering her junior year in high school, she had an extraordinary experience. The principal was interviewing the students one by one and asking them what vocations they intended to pursue. As she was waiting her turn, she thought, "Shall I take up nursing or school teaching? It is to be one or the other."

While she was trying to decide, a power or voice spoke to her and said, "Take up nursing because someday you'll be nursing colored people." That was very pronounced in her mind, and she wondered who they would be. She thought they might be the Australian aborigines, who are black.

Not long after that, she had another experience in which she felt that same power tell her that someday she would marry Viv Sorensen. She never told a soul, except for Hazel Pratten, a nonmember girl who boarded with Gwen's family. Hazel just laughed and said, "Don't be silly!" I went blissfully onward—I did not know this had happened, of course, until about six years later.

After Gwen completed her nurses' training in Brisbane, she went to work in Sydney. My sister and I saw her off at the railroad station. Gwen stayed in Sydney for several months doing private nursing. It was during World War II, and she felt conscience-stricken because some of her friends had joined the army as nurses. Consequently, she came back to Brisbane also planning to join the army.

The Lord, however, then began to intervene. The Zion's League had a little social the evening of the very day she arrived from Sydney. When I saw her coming (and I can see her right to this moment—how she was dressed and how beautiful she looked), I thought, "Well, what's wrong with you? You let a lovely young lady like this escape without trying to interest her in any way!" During the evening we were playing a game that had partners. One moment she had one partner, and the next moment I had replaced him.

It had been quite a few years since Gwen had the experience about marrying Viv Sorensen. By that time her faith was wavering. She thought, "Was that experience really from God?" Then there I was, making a move to get her interest. Well, to make a long story short, she did not join the army. Instead, she was invited by my mother and sisters to go with us to the Tiona Reunion during Christmas week of 1941. Very few people could get there in those days because of the gasoline restrictions. We traveled by train. Although the troops occupied most of the seats on the trains, there was some space available for other passengers.

At that reunion I really realized just how much I needed this young woman. Very timidly I went to her at the beautiful Green Cathedral on the reunion grounds, and I asked her if I could be her boyfriend. She was nearly past caring about me because she thought I had let her down years before. But she said, "I suppose so." We soon found that we were meant for each other. Our friendship blossomed from courtship into love and from love into marriage.

Our courtship was somewhat difficult. Both of us had shift work and were sleeping irregular hours, and it was very hard to find time to be together. I sometimes met Gwen at the hospital, and we then went on long walks or sat on a bench in the park near the hospital. There we made plans for our future.

I really loved her and wanted her to be my wife. But before I asked Gwen to marry me, I went to her father and asked his approval. That was not really necessary because Gwen was 23 years old, but I wanted to do it. Brother Peisker replied, "There is no one I would rather she marry!"

I will never forget the night that I proposed to Gwen, May 30, 1942. We went down to a beautiful seaside resort at Lota, a few miles out of Brisbane, a place where we could be alone. Looking out over the ocean with the full moon shining on it, I asked her if she would be my wife. When she said she would, I gave her the first kiss that I had ever given her. I had very high standards—and so did she.

In January Gwen had commenced a course in obstetric nursing at the Brisbane Women's Hospital. She gained her midwifery certificate in October. She finished her training one Saturday in October, and we were married the next.

October 17, 1942, finally arrived with beautiful sunshine—just the way we felt. Gwen had stayed with her parents for a week before the wedding. My sister Mavis decorated the Buranda church, and it was crowded for the ceremony. My sister Silvia was Gwen's bridesmaid, and Dolph Kerswell was my best man. Three-year-old Gwendoline Kerswell was the flower girl, and Brother Dolph Loving performed the ceremony.

The branch gave us a Royal Dolton tea set, which ended up traveling almost around the world with us. Directly after the wedding, Brother Edgar Miles took us in his new car to a photography studio in town. After we were honored with a wedding breakfast held on the large verandah of Gwen's parents' home, Brother Miles drove us to our first little home.

Because of the war, we were not able to have a honeymoon at that time. Still, our marriage lasted—in 1992 we celebrated our 50th wedding anniversary!

A few months before the wedding, I had purchased a house in the Brisbane suburb of Fairfield. Gwen and I and our families spent many hours furnishing and preparing it for our life together. Gwen's father was a professional cabinetmaker and made our bedroom furniture. My father, who was a carpenter, made a kitchen cabinet for us.

We really had some enjoyable times in our first home. Frequently we entertained American servicemen as well as Australians. We got to know Archie Gatrost from San Antonio, Texas, who was in the U.S. Army Air Force. He was very sad because he had just left his beautiful young wife and little daughter.

During one of his visits, we were talking about the ruins of ancient America. Archie said, "If ever you come to my country, I'll give you a trip down there." Many years later he kept that promise.

☼ ☼ ☼

After Christmas Gwen and I went to Tiona to attend our first reunion as a married couple.

On New Year's Day, 1943, when two young men were baptized at the Tiona reunion, a ray of sunlight shone down and illuminated the spot in the lake. Their confirmation was later in the week during a young people's prayer service. I assisted with the first confirmation and then was the spokesman for the confirmation of Dolph Roth from Brisbane. I had proceeded nicely with my confirmation prayer and was about to say, "Receive ye the gift of the Holy Ghost." Just then someone caught hold of my left arm—I thought Apostle George Mesley was warning me that my prayer was becoming too long. He had taught us not to try to make the confirmation prayers into "patriarchal blessings." I finished the prayer without saying the words that I had planned to say.

The rest of the service was outstanding. The apostle stood and said that Jesus Christ was walking the shore of the lake that morning, just as He had done at Galilee 2,000 years ago. Under the influence of the Spirit of God, he said that some young people there would remain loyal to Christ and uphold His name; some would even go to foreign lands. But others would forsake the Lord—for which He sorrowed deeply. Because of the outpouring of the Spirit of God, every one of us was in tears.

After the meeting, the young people were loathe to leave to go to their various classes. But I wanted to get away because I was still smarting inside. When Brother Mesley went to his tent, I went to apologize to him for making the confirmation prayer too long.

He said, "Long? It was rather short, and I wondered why."

When I told him what had happened, he said, "I never touched you, but angels were present this morning. It must have been an angel that caught hold of your arm." Then he suggested that I go and see Dolph.

When I got near Dolph's tent, I heard him crying. I asked what was wrong, and he told me that during his confirmation he had doubted the veracity of the church. He said, "Every bit of faith that I had in it had disappeared. I thought I did wrong in leaving my old church."

Because at that moment Dolph was a nonbeliever, I could see why the Lord did not allow me to bestow the blessing of the Holy Ghost. I told him that he should pray to get his faith back.

I then asked Apostle Mesley if we should confirm Dolph again. He said, "No, the hands of the elders were on him, and their prayers were uttered to God. God has the right to say to whom He will give the gift of the Holy Ghost and to whom He won't. The time wasn't correct to give it, and you were restrained; but when the man is in the right spiritual condition, the Lord will bless him."

After reunion we returned to Brisbane. At a prayer meeting several weeks later, Dolph stood up. With tears streaming down his cheeks, the young brother said, "Tonight I have been born of the Holy Ghost." Because Dolph repented in his heart, the Lord gave him that special gift. That made me understand how important it is to give the confirmation prayers much attention and preparation. That was one of the most remarkable experiences I have had.

☼ ☼ ☼

One day I was riding my bicycle home from work, when an army truck drove past and crowded me off the road. My bike skidded on the gravel, and I went flying off onto the hard ground. My shoulder was badly scraped, and it hurt terribly. An X ray later revealed that my shoulder bone had suffered some damage. This must have been the source of any "chip on my shoulder"!

Shortly after we were married, I earned extra income by repairing General Electric Roundtop refrigerators. It was important to get all the moisture out of the coils before working on the machines, so I often lit a fire beneath them to help speed up the evaporation. One night I mistakenly left one of those fires going when I went to bed. In our bedroom, our bed was placed such that Gwen slept near the window; I slept nearer the door.

After we had fallen asleep, Gwen woke up and noticed through the open window a flickering orange glow reflecting off the house next door. She realized that there must be a fire under our house, so she urgently tried to wake me. Being in a deep sleep, I did not rouse. To save time she pushed me out of the bed and onto the floor, where I immediately awoke. After she told me that there was a fire under the house, I raced downstairs and extinguished it before it had spread too far, although the paint work on the refrigerator was ruined and a rafter was blackened.

Memories of that little home are very dear to us. It was to this home that we brought our first baby, Beth, who was born on November 22, 1943. And it was in this house that I received my first knowledge of my call to the missionary arm of the RLDS Church.

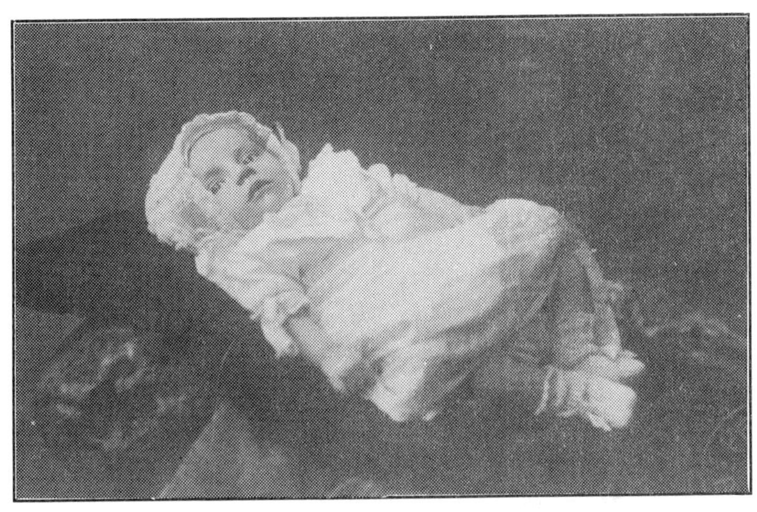

▲ Vivian as a baby in 1916

▸ Vivian and Silvia in 1919

▲ Sugar cane cutters near the Maroochy River

▼ Newspaper photo of Vivian working on the Hornibrook Highway

▲ View of Brisbane from atop the Story Bridge (Vivian in the foreground, 220 feet above the Brisbane River)

▼ Joining the two halves of the Story Bridge

▲ The Brisbane River under the Indooroopilly Bridge, where Vivian was baptized in 1930 (photo taken in 1988)

▼ Street preaching in Brisbane during World War II ▼

▲ Young people in Green Cathedral at Tiona Reunion, 1941 —Silvia, Gwen, and Vivian (first row starting third from right)

▼ Brisbane Zion's League in 1943—Gwen (back row, third from right) and Vivian (third row, fourth from right)

▲ Gwen and Vivian, Brisbane, Australia, October 17, 1942

▲ First home of Gwen and Vivian after marriage—Aylesford Street, Fairfield, Brisbane

▼ Sorensen family in 1940s—Silvia, Mavis, Ruby, and Charlie

CHAPTER 2

To New Zealand on a Journey of Faith

In December of 1943 at the Tiona Reunion, Apostle George Mesley spoke with Gwen in the Green Cathedral. He said, "I feel that your husband has a call to work in the Society Islands. But I decided that I should speak to you before I said anything to him or to the First Presidency. Sometimes a missionary's ministry can fail if his wife cannot adapt to his appointed field. I need to know if you would be comfortable working among colored people."

Gwen then shared her high school experience—when she was contemplating her career and she was told to take up nursing because someday she would be working among colored people. Both she and Brother Mesley felt this was confirmation that the Lord was preparing us for missionary work in the islands. Brother Mesley was then able to recommend me for church appointment.

I had been pastor of the Brisbane Branch for a year when the call came in April, 1944, to go into the mission field. It was something I had longed for, although I had never said anything to anyone about it. Then there it was, opening up before me—a call to go as a missionary to the Society Islands. I always had a great interest in the people of the Pacific islands, having read such books as *Robinson*

Crusoe and *Coral Island.* To go there was beyond my wildest dreams.

I was still doing essential war work at the time, making parts for Norden bombsights as well as experimental gadgets for American submarines. The Mars Machine Tool Company where I worked was under contract to the Americans. I had to get permission from my employer and from the Manpower Authority to leave my employment.

When I approached Mr. Marsh, the manager of the company, he was quite emphatic and said, "No, I will not give permission. There are a lot of bad Australians. Why don't you preach to them?" Well, of course, he did not understand the situation.

I went to the Manpower Authority, which placed men in various positions of importance, and told the authorities what I wanted to do. They said, "Well, we can't go against your employer."

Brother Dolph Loving had been pastor before me and probably would be again. I took him to meet my manager. Brother Loving pleaded, but Mr. Marsh was adamant and would not listen. I can remember Brother Loving saying quite emphatically, "Mr. Marsh, this man has been called by almighty God to minister to His people in the islands of the sea. There is nothing you or anyone else on the face of this earth can do to prevent this coming about, so you might as well give in gracefully." Mr. Marsh became quite angry and still refused.

I went back to the Manpower Authority and told them of the obstinacy of Mr. Marsh. Finally the head man there said, "Clear off. Say nothing about it. Just go to Sydney where you told me you were going and say nothing about it. The less you say the better."

We packed our belongings. On Sunday, July 8, 1944, the branch gave us a send-off party and presented us with a few things, including a fine leather suitcase, a beautiful woolen rug, and a baby's table set for Beth. On Wednesday the Saints came to the railway station to see us off.

We arrived in Sydney, where we stayed with Floyd and Lorna Burdekin at Haberfield. Apostle Mesley took me to the Manpower Authority in Martin Place, where my termination of employment was officially approved. Then we went to the Union Steamship Company to see the editor of the *Pacific Islands Monthly*, a magazine which I knew would be helpful to me in Tahiti. We also looked (unsuccessfully) for a tutor to teach us the Tahitian language.

Very early in August, Brother Mesley and I visited the French Consulate in Sydney, where the workers were celebrating the liberation of Paris. Finally we learned that Gwen and I first had to obtain British passports, with Beth going on her mother's passport. When we subsequently presented these British passports to the French consul, he said that he would cable the governor of Tahiti for a visa.

During our stay in Sydney, I attended a missionary training school. Our studies included English, a very succinct and yet wonderful course taught by Sister Blanche Mesley, and classes on priesthood and missionary methods taught by Brother George Mesley. Brother Alan Frater had us for religious education, teacher training, study of the Three Standard Books, and church history. Brother C. A. Davies gave us a study in psychology, and Brother Herman Peisker taught doctrine. He gave us wonderful insight into the Church of Jesus Christ.

Brother Mesley asked me to teach a class on street meetings and to instruct the others on epidiascope work. I was always experimenting with means of projecting our message onto screens, and an epidiascope (projector) I had made worked quite well.

During the month of October, I got the chicken pox. It was so bad and thick on my head that Gwen had to cut off all my hair. Beth did not recognize me, and she wondered who on earth I was. Brother Mesley took a look at me and said, "Your own mother wouldn't recognize you!"

While we were in Sydney, we had opportunity to go to the nearby beaches. One beastly hot day, Floyd and Lorna Burdekin and Gwen and I and the children went to Bronte. At first we wondered why so few were in the surf. But when we entered the water, we knew—it was just as though we were swimming near Antarctica! We were told that really cold currents come up from the Antarctic at times. Although at Sydney the air might be 100° outside, the water temperature might be only about 40° or 50°. My goodness, it was terribly cold!

We went to Newcastle, where I did some preaching. Gwen and Beth continued on to Brisbane to see our relatives one last time before we left for Tahiti. I returned to Sydney shortly before Gwen and Beth. Beth started walking on the very day they returned. She was about 12 months old.

I felt that I did very well on the examination in the church missionary school. While we were waiting for visas, I browsed around Sydney and bought some things that we would need. Brother Eddie Butterworth was the missionary in Tahiti. On his recommendation we bought two Tahitian Bibles and two brand-new bicycles because they were the main means of getting around the island.

We also bought a five-burner kerosene stove and put an ad in the paper for a secondhand piano for the Tahitian Saints. A lady saw the ad, learned what the instrument was to be used for, and sold her piano to us for a very low price. We also really needed a sewing machine, but the Singer Sewing Machine Company was limited to selling two machines a month because of the war. Although there was a long waiting list, somehow we got a machine immediately! The Lord was indeed taking care of us.

It had been eight months since the last ship had left

Australia for Tahiti. We definitely did not want to wait in Sydney for another eight months. Then we received a letter from Floyd Potter in New Zealand, who said that phosphate boats went from New Zealand to Tahiti about every two months.

It was decided that we would have a much better chance of getting to Tahiti from New Zealand than we would from Australia. About every two or three months, ships loaded with phosphate sailed from the island of Makatea to New Zealand. They returned empty and in ballast to Makatea, passing Tahiti on their way. They were not passenger ships, but occasionally a sympathetic captain made an exception, knowing how difficult things were because of the war.

To travel from Sydney to New Zealand, we secured a berth on a large ship that was taking soldiers, their brides, and other military people back to New Zealand. The name of the ship was the *Rimutaka*, which is a Maori word.

We left Sydney on February 12, 1945, one day before my 29th birthday. We managed to get a first-class suite and had the best food we had eaten for a long time. It was quite an experience.

I remember taking Beth up on deck late in the evening just as the shore of Australia was fading away. Farewell, Australia! It gave me an odd feeling in the heart to say good-bye to my mother country, not knowing how long until—or if ever—I would see it again.

It took us four days to reach New Zealand—1,200 miles away. The ship was zigzagging because of Japanese submarines in the Tasman Sea. There was also a danger from the many Japanese mines. Crossing the Tasman can be very, very rough; but we had a calm voyage to Wellington.

The evening of arrival, we left Wellington by train for Auckland, where we were going to stay. A dirty steam engine pulled us on a miserable, cold trip through the highlands of New Zealand. We arrived in Auckland about 8:30 in the morning. The Potters, the missionary family there, were thrilled to see us.

We found that they were in very poor health—but were so devoted that they did not report it. I wrote to the apostle and told him about their physical condition. He wrote back as much as to say, "Mind your own business!" After all, it was not my business—it was theirs. But Gwen, who was a trained nurse, wrote the apostle quite a letter. Soon thereafter a cable arrived telling Gertie Potter to take the next ship or flying boat home and get medical attention, which she did. My diary shows that in March, 1945, air service from Australia to New Zealand began with big four-engine, British-made Sunderland flying boats.

As it was necessary for us to speak French to get the visas to Tahiti, we hired a French count, Etienne Micard, to teach us. He was a really unusual fellow. He knew perfect Parisian French, but that was not the ideal thing for us since Tahitians spoke their own dialect of French. Gwen and I had studied French in high school, but it was not adequate for daily use.

On Easter Sunday the count attended our church. He was an accomplished pianist, and he played two numbers on the piano. My goodness, what a player! It almost took our breath away. When Floyd Potter preached, the old count listened very intently. He said Floyd was inspired. I told him that our men are called of God, and he seemed to be interested. I later shared the gospel with him.

The count had been to Tahiti recently, and he told me that I should not take my lovely wife there. He said the people in Tahiti were either all mad, bad, or sad. We had heard such stories, but we knew that God was in charge. Our going was in the faith that God would protect us. And He most certainly did!

At that time Gwen was helping a lady who was going to

be a missionary in the Belgian Congo. The lady also needed to learn French, but she was hesitant to be alone in the count's presence. So I went by myself to the count for classes, and Gwen went with this lady. Imagine Gwen helping a Belgian Congo missionary.

Floyd Potter had stayed for a couple of months to complete his work; then he also returned to Australia. We were able to carry on the mission work in New Zealand until the Lord opened the way for us to go to Tahiti.

To get from New Zealand to Tahiti was a nightmare. We had all the difficulty in the world—enough to try the faith of anyone. To write it all down would take volumes, but I will try to include some of the pertinent parts.

We were sending cables, cablegrams, telegrams, and letters to the French authorities, to Eddie Butterworth in Tahiti, and even to F. M. Smith, president of the RLDS Church—trying to get visas for Tahiti. The French authorities (especially the governor) stated that there were too many "Mormon" missionaries, and they did not need any more. However, he said that if we were only replacing two missionaries, he might consider it.

There is no doubt that we exercised faith in our appointment to Tahiti. In May, 1945, I received a letter from Don Alberts, who was a bishop in Sydney, saying that our belongings had been shipped to Tahiti from Sydney. That had been done purely in faith because we did not know for certain when we were going to get there. We did not see our possessions for 18 months from the time we packed them.

While we were waiting in New Zealand, I had my first experience with an evil spirit. A woman was attacked by a spirit and was in a very, very severe depression. We administered, and immediately peace and normality came to her. We knew that God had cast the evil spirit out. This was a wonderful help to me, for in the islands in years to come I would meet this sort of thing fairly often.

In early May "Victory in Europe Day" was celebrated in Auckland. We went to a thanksgiving service at the town hall, where a huge crowd was gathered. When they cheered, Beth cheered with the rest.

We attended a Maori concert at the city hall and enjoyed it very much. The singers wore national costumes and did native dances. One Maori returned soldier had a very beautiful tenor voice.

We still heard nothing from the French consul. We met a man and wife who had returned after 30 years in Tahiti. They knew our missionary, J. Charles May, and gave us some information about our mission homes.

At long last we received a letter from the French consul which said we had to pay 49,000 francs each in order to enter Tahiti. That was about 600 Australian pounds for both of us.

I had to make a trip to Christchurch and even farther south on the South Island to visit some Saints who had not been visited by a missionary for years. I traveled by train to Wellington. It was a very cold trip, but I enjoyed seeing the beautiful snow-capped mountains near Wellington. I visited the French consul in Wellington for a test on my French, which he evaluated as satisfactory. That was a big relief. He said the French officials were investigating our record in Australia.

On the ferry from Wellington, many passengers were sick, but I was not. The next morning we arrived at Lyttleton, which is the port for Christchurch on the South Island. I had a glorious view of the Southern Alps. A heavy frost, almost like snow, covered the roofs of houses. The Saints in Christchurch welcomed me. I went south the next day by train to Temuka, where the isolated Saints lived, and gave some much-needed ministry.

When I returned to Auckland, I discovered that a ship

had called in after leaving Sydney with some 500 war brides bound for the United States.

The French were still willing to consent to our going to Tahiti only if we were replacing others. Brother and Sister May, who were leaving Tahiti for the USA, were waiting for a ship. We were told that when they left, we might be given visas. The French vice consul in Auckland told us that Tahiti was getting a new governor, who was likely to be a more sympathetic man. I certainly hoped so. It was early July, and we had been waiting in New Zealand since the beginning of the year.

In July I was elected pastor of the Auckland Branch "pro tem." Don Alberts appointed me bishop/solicitor for the mission also. We had a fine sacramental service, and the Spirit of God spoke to the people with a message exhorting them to greater diligence.

Shortly after I received a license to perform marriages in New Zealand, I had the privilege of marrying Stan Fulker, a young Australian living in New Zealand, to Sister Peggy Lewis. Just six days prior to the wedding, I had baptized Peggy, which was also my first baptism in New Zealand. A beautiful Spirit was present; some nonmember girls were overcome by the Spirit and wept like children. Stan presented us with a beautiful short-wave radio to use when we got to our home in Tahiti.

We were still hoping to leave for Tahiti in October, so we continued French lessons. We could read the French Bible, which Gwen and I used for evening worship. We also hired a new Tahitian teacher. I was learning a little speech of welcome for Tahiti.

A letter from Eddie Butterworth said that the Mays might leave in September. He wanted us to bring certain items for the mission. I bought a secondhand organ for Tahiti. We had been told the natives loved music, but they had hardly any organs or pianos available.

On August 20 we heard that the Japanese were going to surrender. There was to be peace at last—World War II had finally ended!

In September I was called away to minister to some sick Saints at the far northern end of the North Island of New Zealand. I had a slow train journey from Auckland along the west coast to Dargaville and thence on to Hokianga Harbour just below the Ninety-Mile Beach. On this trip I passed through typical New Zealand farming country—rolling, hilly grasslands that were a rich green in color, studded here and there with hedges and red-roofed cottages. Much of the country was covered with hedges and sometimes wild gorse, an evergreen which at that time of year was covered with pretty yellow flowers.

New Zealand is very mountainous; and on that trip, as with others, I saw rugged timber-clad mountains and hills. As I went farther north, I saw more tree ferns (punga ferns) and scrub country through which ran many streams of clear water; their beds were lined with water cress. From Dargaville I traveled by bus to Opononi, my final destination. It was a wonderful trip because we went through the beautiful Waipeau Forest. The bus wound through miles of magnificent kauri trees and semi-jungle growth studded with innumerable tree ferns, babbling brooks, and rushing torrents. The kauris are a mottled gray, white, and green color with great trunks measuring up to ten feet in diameter. Kauri gum, which was used in paints and varnishes, came from the roots of these trees. There were thousands of them, and they formed an imposing spectacle.

The church family I visited, the Johnstones, lived near the sea on a dairy farm. After living and working on a dairy farm in Queensland for a period, I always said that I had enough of them. Going to the Johnstones' farm made me more emphatic about my decision.

I never saw so much mud in my life as I saw there. I could not go out of the house without gum boots, and the approaches to the cow bails (milking stalls) were quagmires. The cows had to wade through mud almost up to their bellies to enter the yard, and often they had to be pulled out of the mud by a horse. With all the rain and lack of sun in the winter, the place just became impossible. To walk from the house to the bails you had to hop from one tuft of grass to another. If you missed, it was just too bad—for you were likely to go down to your knees in mud!

I administered to the Johnstones' baby, who had a persistent cold, and to their son, who had complications with a broken arm. Brother Johnstone, a priest, also required administration for a problem with his legs. He had kept the faith remarkably well throughout his trials and isolation. I pitied those people because of their tough existence. I felt God's power in administration—before I left, the baby's condition was much improved; and the boy was able to bend his arm almost at right angles, where before he could not bend it at all. Mr. Johnstone gave me a fine souvenir, a walking stick covered with Maori carvings.

We had been almost nine months in New Zealand trying to get permission to go to Tahiti. A letter from President F. M. Smith said he was going to Washington and would take up our case with the French representatives while there. We received a cable from Brother Butterworth on October 1 saying that the Mays had gone. Expecting to receive a visa that month, I relinquished the office of pastor to Jack Gunning, who had arrived in September from Australia.

Big news at last! I was reading on the verandah when the phone rang. Mitta Gunning answered it and said the post office had a cablegram for Vivian Sorensen. I guessed that it was from Eddie Butterworth, since he always used my first name rather than only the initial *V* on a cable. What joy! The message *was* from Eddie, and it stated that permission had been granted for us to enter Tahiti. Just imagine the antics that went on in the house of the Gunnings and Sorensens!

I had prayed in tears the night before about the matter, saying to the Lord that if it was not His will for us to go to Tahiti, could we please return to Australia. I then beheld the General Conference, not exactly in vision, but in my mind's eye. I saw the twelve apostles in my mind, and these words impressed themselves upon me: "What they bind on earth shall be bound in heaven." Then I felt content. I realized that those men had bound on earth by their recommendation that we be sent to Tahiti. This fact therefore was bound in heaven also, and it must be the will of God. I had no doubt that this was a wonderful church and would eventually triumph in the earth. I cabled President Smith the good news.

The shipping company then informed me that the British Phosphate Company had a boat unloading in Auckland that would be going to Makatea, which is near Tahiti. But it did not carry passengers. They said I could interview the ship's master and see if he might be willing to take us, which I did. I offered up some prayers on the way. The master was Captain Jones of the Liberty ship, *Samokla*. The "Sam" stood for Uncle Sam and the "okla" for Oklahoma.

After he listened to my story, the captain's heart was softened. He said that he thought he could do something for us, but he warned me that the ship was only a "slum" ship with no passenger conveniences. Upon my assurance that we did not mind, Captain Jones agreed to take us. He said we could go free, except for the cost of food. Total cost for the trip was thus only five pounds instead of the 55 pounds charged by the shipping company. Although the *Samokla* was not scheduled to call at Tahiti, Captain Jones said he would alter course to come near to Tahiti, where the pilot boat could pick us up. The captain also said he would ask the first and second mates to vacate their cabin so that we would have privacy.

Before the ship departed, we had to get visas in our passports allowing admittance to Tahiti. Apparently the governor had not been in a hurry to send notice of our permission to the consul in Wellington, and the consul could not give us the visas until he had received official word. We had only two days left until Thursday morning, when the ship was due to sail. Then a miracle occurred! The wharf laborers decided that they were going to have a "go-slow strike," so they cut their speed of unloading. That meant the ship could not leave port until Saturday, instead of Thursday.

I was certain that the Lord was providing us with the necessary time to accomplish what was needed to get to Tahiti. God moves in mysterious ways, His wonders to perform! I remembered the case of missionaries Charles Wandell and Glaud Rodger. In 1873 their boat had sprung a leak in calm waters, and they had to put in at Tahiti—the nearest practicable place—to effect repairs. As a result, they were able to resurrect the work of the Lord among the natives.

However, my faith was tested when someone from the British Phosphate Company called the next day and said there was no possible hope for us to go on the *Samokla*. They were taking Mr. Mudge, the harbor master for Makatea, with them. We would have to stand aside to make room for him, his wife, and his daughter. This refusal by the phosphate company was a terrible blow to us. Mr. Mudge and his family were to arrive from Australia by the next flying boat.

I went to see the captain and asked if he could help us. He said to wait and see if our visas came and then to come back and see him.

On Friday, the day before the ship was due to sail, I phoned the French consul. He said, "If you bring Mrs. Sorensen and your daughter to our agent in Auckland, we can get your fingerprints and give you your visas." The governor of Tahiti had finally sent a cable granting permission. I found out later that Brother John Mervin, one of our fine elders in Tahiti, had seen a vision of a ship sailing from the west toward Tahiti with a man, his wife, and little daughter aboard. After seeing this, he appealed again to the governor for our visas. Brother Mervin was an important and wealthy man. The governor, in a fit of anger, called the Chef du Cabinet and told him to send the permit immediately to the consul in New Zealand.

The phosphate company official told the French consul's agent that we had no chance of getting on board the ship since the other family was going. He evidently did this to try to thwart our promised passage. I soon put the consul right about that and then went to see the captain. He was very kind and said he was determined to take us as well as the Mudge family. He told us to come on board that evening. Two other ship's officers offered to vacate their cabin so that we could sail with them. The captain also said that Gwen and Beth could use his bath facilities.

Gwen, Beth, and I went to the consul's agent and finally got our visas. By the time we got back and finished our packing, it was time to go on board the ship. We bade farewell to the little band of loyal Saints and friends in New Zealand, including the count.

The way that God worked was miraculous. All this difficulty in getting to Tahiti showed us just what the evil force tried to do. But God gave us the victory and through His power brought Satan's efforts to naught.

☼ ☼ ☼

The ship departed at 7:30 Saturday morning, Tahiti bound. Sailing out through Auckland harbor was engrossing. For hours we wended our way through the islands of the Hauraki Gulf, including the unique island with a hole through it. We arrived at the open sea about 4 p.m.

With a heavy swell running, the ship rolled badly all night. A ship in ballast or empty always rolls more than a full one. The chairs slid all over the place, and our soup slopped out of the bowls. The little Mudge girl was very sick. Gwen was feeling a bit ill, but little Beth was not affected. She was simply wonderful on her sea legs. Since some of the crew were also sick, we must have been fairly good sailors. The food was plain, but wholesome. Beth really enjoyed it.

On Monday we were invited up on the bridge to watch the crew jettison rockets and shells, which the government instructed them to get rid of since the war was over. The crew threw overboard tons of ammunition, machine guns, antiaircraft guns, and shells. It was a terrible waste. But as I said to the men, "Better to throw them into the ocean than to fire them at other men." It looked as though the whole ocean was on fire when those shells burst. The crew also threw a lot of smoke screen chemicals overboard, which gave off dense clouds of gray smoke as if a volcano had sprung up in mid-ocean.

The next day we were a thousand miles from New Zealand on the *Samokla*. After much negotiation, prayer, and faith in God's power—plus a kindly captain—we were on the bosom of the Pacific. Gwen and I were watching the course of the ship marked on the chart. We were making about 280 miles every day. Our total trip of 2,200 miles was expected to take eight days.

A beautiful full moon on the ocean truly made a

magnificent sight. We looked through the ship's telescope and could see craters and mountains on the moon. I was privileged to explore the ship—the engine room, the radio room, the cook's domain, and other places.

The weather was absolutely perfect, the sea smooth. Next day the temperature was 80°. It was gradually getting warmer. We did 276 miles that day—only 800 to go! Then we crossed the Tropic of Capricorn, our first time in the tropics. It was 86° the previous night. The sea was a marvelous deep blue, the densest blue we had seen so far. The next day we passed through the Cook Islands but did not see them. By then all the albatross had left us; they didn't like hot weather.

One evening the captain said to Gwen, "You take her—the big wheel." The mate relinquished the ship's wheel, and Gwen took over the steering of the ship. She steered for quite awhile. When she had enough, the captain called the sailor, pointed to the wake, and told him he could not steer a ship as straight as that if he tried. Of course, Gwen had been hanging on like grim death to that wheel and keeping it dead straight on the compass.

Friday noon we were 280 miles from Tahiti, and Gwen packed our suitcases. Saturday at 7 a.m. we sighted the island of Moorea, and by 11:30 Tahiti was plainly visible. Looking through the ship's field glasses at Moorea, we saw coconut palms and smoke curling up from cooking fires. We could not see much of Tahiti, however, because it was covered with clouds.

As the *Samokla* neared the city of Papeete, she hoisted flags to signal the pilot boat. Soon we could see a small boat bobbing about on the waves as it came out from the reef. A French pilot came aboard and tried to get Captain Jones to come into port for Sunday, but he refused because the harbor dues were too high.

All the crew of the ship were lined along the rail ready

to wave good-bye to us. Mail and our goods were loaded on the small boat, and we wondered just where we would fit in. The third mate picked up Beth and took her down the gangway, which was lower on the side of the ship. The sea was fairly rough, and the pilot boat went down in a trough of a wave and then up to the gangway. This is when we had to jump onto the pilot boat. It was really scary. Beth was handed by the third mate to someone else at the appropriate moment. We said good-bye to Captain Jones and crew and thanked them for their kind help. The total cost of the whole trip was eight pounds ten shillings, which was a gift.

After we were aboard the crazy little craft, she shoved off. The boat had a small cabin, but the Frenchman left Gwen and me standing precariously on its tiny deck. I said to take madame inside if he pleased, which he did. We could easily have lost our balance and fallen into 6,000 feet of the Pacific Ocean. I will never forget the sight of the good ship *Samokla* as she disappeared in the distance—seeming, as it were, to leave us stranded on a foreign shore.

▼ Missionary Training School class of 1944, Drummoyne, Sydney, with Apostle George Mesley (front center), Blanche Mesley and Gwen beside him, and Vivian behind Gwen

▲ At Tiona Reunion, 1944—front row from left: Gwen, Silvia, Marge Seaberg, and Allan Roles; back row from left: Ruby Sorensen, Vivian holding Beth; Mavis in the center back

▼ Floyd and Gertrude Potter with Bronwyn, Gwen and Vivian with Beth, Morningside church, Auckland, N.Z., 1945

CHAPTER 3

Tahiti, Pearl of the Pacific

A number of people had gathered at the wharf at Papeete, Tahiti—Tahitians, Chinese, and Caucasians. We rightly guessed that the two people coming toward us on bicycles were Eddie and Lilly Raye Butterworth. Quite a number of the church natives had come with them, and we were welcomed with the native greeting *Ia ora na*—literally "life to you."

After some little delay with customs, we were taken to our home in the church compound about a mile from the wharf. The compound was surrounded by a white concrete wall about 30 inches high. We were greatly impressed with what we saw within the walls of the compound. The grounds looked really beautiful with well-kept green lawns and a number of large tropical trees, flowering shrubs, and vines. In that beautiful setting were the white painted buildings—the church, two missionary homes (one on each side of the church), five homes which were rented to native members, and a large *fareputuputuraa* or meeting house.

We arose bright and early the next morning, Sunday, November 4, 1945. I spoke in English at the 11 a.m. service, and Eddie interpreted. That pleased the natives greatly. The Saints from the entire island of Tahiti gathered that night to give us a traditional native welcome. Each group, including children, took turns singing one or two native songs—usually dealing with events from church history—to the accompaniment of guitars. Eddie and Lilly Raye told us what the songs meant.

The Saints then came, put shell *heis* (necklaces) around our necks, and showered us with gifts—including money. By the amount of paper money we received, we thought we were becoming quite rich. However, we found out later that it was not worth much! The atmosphere was quite exciting as each group tried to outdo the others with their singing and generosity.

Following the service, the women's department provided refreshments, consisting of cake and *ciro* (a fruit-flavored drink known as "cordial" in Australia). It was a thrilling evening, which made us feel very welcome. That was our first experience of the sincerity and love of the Tahitian Saints, which we came to know so well in the years that followed.

Tired but happy, the three of us retired, taking our gifts to our new little home a few yards from the church. In the middle of the night, we were awakened from a deep sleep by someone banging on the outside wall of our bedroom. Our first thoughts were that someone might be trying to steal the money that we had been given. Being in a foreign country and having little knowledge of the language or culture, we were quite frightened. I cried out, "*Haere!*" (Go!) It was one of the few Tahitian words I knew. The banging stopped.

The next day we discovered that the banging was caused by the son of the native missionary, Horahitu, who had previously lived in the house. The son had just arrived on a native schooner. Not knowing that his father had moved, he was trying to wake him up. By the way, we learned that Horahitu had been born at 7 o'clock (many years earlier, of course). Therefore, everyone called him *Horahitu*, literally meaning "hour seven"!

☼ ☼ ☼

Let me digress from my story and give some facts about French Polynesia, which was called French Oceania or the Society Islands at that time. French Oceania consisted of the Society Islands (which included Tahiti), the Tuamotu Islands, Tubuai, and the Marquesas. When one looks at these islands on a map, they are mere specks in the mighty Pacific Ocean.

Some islands are quite mountainous (Orahena in Tahiti is more than 7,000 feet high, and Aorai is over 6,000 feet). Hilly or mountainous islands include Tahiti, Moorea, Bora Bora, Raiatea, Tubuai, Rurutu, Rimatara, and Huahine. Most of the islands are atolls, which consist of a ring of coral enclosing a lagoon. Rangiroa is the largest, being 30 miles long. The smallest barely covers a few acres.

The population was largely Polynesian and Caucasian (mainly French). Some Chinese were brought to work on the sugar plantations. The total population during our sojourn was about 40,000, most of whom were French citizens. Although French was the official language, Tahitian was mostly spoken. Some Chinese and English were also spoken.

The religion was mainly Christian. The major denominations in order of membership were: French Protestants (originally from the London Missionary Society), Roman Catholic, Saints (RLDS), Mormons (Utah), and Seventh-Day Adventists.

Tahiti was lush with tropical fruits. Fine mangos of various flavors and varieties abounded. Some of the trees grew to a height of about 60 feet. Bananas, grapefruit, oranges, plantains, pineapples, papayas, guavas, breadfruit, and avocados also thrived. They were delicious.

First impressions of a place can be very important, but they are often modified as one becomes more familiar with the surroundings. It was interesting to look back at the letters I wrote to my parents after we first arrived in Tahiti.

I wrote that Papeete was a bit of a disappointment for us since it was rather dirty, at least by Australian standards. The French authorities insisted that things be kept reasonably clean though, and the whole place seemed rather well run. I had to go to the police station to have my fingerprints taken and to receive a local passport for use when visiting the other islands. The policemen were very courteous, and everything went well.

We found that the RLDS Church was definitely in need of additional missionary support. The opportunities were limitless, if we had the manpower. We had only one active group on Tahiti besides the main branch at Tarona, whereas there used to be quite a few. It was our job to build these up again. Tarona had about 400 to 500 members, which were to keep me busy, especially with the church school needs. We also had branches or groups on 18 other islands in French Polynesia.

As soon as I had sufficient command of the language, I was to be installed as pastor of Tarona. Then the Butterworths would be free to spend a year traveling around the other islands. We then intended to change tasks, with Eddie taking the branch pastorate. There were many possibilities for expansion in Tahiti with about 25 priesthood members at Tarona. By training them, we expected to do much good missionary work. Eddie was itching to give the branch over to me so that he could supervise the missionary work. We hoped to establish the Zion's League on a proper basis and form a group for the many young girls. There was also a great need for visual education.

Our church was highly respected in Tahiti, and the governor told Eddie to call on him for any help we needed. The Mormons and the Seventh-Day Adventists were not as strong there at the time.

☼ ☼ ☼

All the waiting and suspense of getting to Tahiti took its toll on us, especially Gwen. She was exhausted from the upheaval of the trip and moving into a foreign country and culture while caring for a two year old. She had also lost a lot of weight. Eddie Butterworth suggested that we leave Tarona, where we were living, and go into the country for awhile. So in mid-November we went to the holiday residence of Brother Tihoni (John) Mervin, a wealthy Tahitian who had bought the home that Zane Grey occupied while he was in Tahiti writing his book entitled *Tales of Tahitian Waters*. The home was about 25 miles from Papeete.

We left Tarona about 8:30 on a Monday morning in Brother Mervin's car, accompanied by his daughter Dede, her fiancé, and the Butterworths. We also carried some provisions and clothes. Passing through Papeete was a task of its own, as one had to dodge Chinese carts, bicycles, and pedestrians by the score. At the market place we stopped to buy some food, but only procured some bananas since they were sold out of almost everything else. The market, where nearly all the fresh produce and meat were sold, opened about 4:30 a.m. By 7 o'clock very little was left. Leaving the market, we passed the jail and the hospital, both of which seemed spacious.

A paved road led us through countless banana, breadfruit, and papaya trees, not to mention the huge mango trees. Native houses were spaced among the greenery. All those Tahitians had to do for food was to reach for the bananas or mangos at will. The inevitable coconut palm added much romance to the scenery. Skirting the shore, we saw some very pretty coconut-clad islands, dotted here and there along the reef. Some 12 miles away, majestic Moorea pointed its fascinating peaks to the sky—trying, it seemed, to pierce the almost ever-present clouds which hovered above it. It was uncanny how those mountains, poking out of the vast expanse of ocean, attracted the clouds.

Chinese stores on the side of the road sold provisions of a European nature. Eddie did not eat the long loaves of French bread; he said there were too many weevils in them due to the infrequent delivery of flour to the islands at the end of the war.

The road skirted the sea most of the way. The mountains only a few miles away rose steeply to a great height, leaving a narrow, flat shelf between them and the sea. We stopped and looked in a cave hewn out of solid rock by the sea countless eons ago. It did not seem to be a deep cave. Eddie said he had tried to throw a stone to the end, but it landed only partway there. Because of the strange contour of the roof and the perfectly clear water beneath, the actual depth of the cave was visibly deceptive.

The next point of interest was the sugar mill nestled amid fields of sugar cane and controlled by the industrious Chinese. It reminded me of the Maroochy River where I grew up. The sugar fields faded out of sight, and we entered more coconut groves. These merged into dense jungle with nearby towering mountains lifting up their heads. The tiny village of Taravao came into view with its two Chinese shops, a cinema, and a public telephone. Not far away were remains of heathen temples with carved stones.

Brother Mervin's house was situated in an ideal restful setting overlooking a branch of the main lagoon and also the Pacific Ocean. It was rather elevated, affording an excellent view of the great breakers dashing out their accumulated energy on the coral reef. The lagoon immediately below the house was surrounded by coconut palms and other tropical verdure, forming an enchanting sight. Away from the sea on two sides rose mountain ranges of a deep blue, over which clouds almost invariably hovered.

The house in which we stayed was palm-thatched and

very picturesque. It is remarkable how waterproof those palm-thatched roofs were. The palm leaves were woven and wound in such a way that they formed an attractive appearance inside the house, perfectly neat and smooth, while outside they looked rough and unfinished.

A little island in the lagoon immediately in front of the house was covered with palm trees and looked idyllic. Natives in canoes plied to and from their homes in search of fish, which abounded in the lagoons. Tropical fruit was in abundance, with a large number of papayas (pawpaws), pineapples, and bananas. Mangos were not so plentiful as they were near Papeete. Goats and some cows roamed the hillsides.

While there, I studied the language and also recuperated a bit myself; the happenings of the previous few months had also taken their toll on me. A native woman came to do the housework, and she did her best to make things comfortable for Gwen by taking care of her household needs. The Tahitians were very amiable, kindly people. It is no wonder that the Lord gave them the opportunity to hear His gospel.

Beth had great fun chasing chickens around the yard and also the "mows," as she called the cats. It was interesting to note that the animals did not know English—but when they were called in Tahitian, they responded immediately.

One thing that was quite a culture shock to this 29-year-old man (and took a bit of getting used to) was seeing the native women breastfeeding their young in public. I went to the home of the woman who cared for us in order to borrow an *ana*. It is used to scrape the white kernel of the coconut, from which is extracted a white juice like milk—but with a flavor equal to cream. I saw the native woman seated on the grass with a bit of rag wrapped around her and two infants of about 18 months, each trying to get nourishment. It was perfectly natural, but it was just not done in the land of the *popaa* (white man). I felt a bit embarrassed and retired without the *ana*.

We went for a trip in a native outrigger canoe into the main lagoon, where Beth and I had a swim. Beth really enjoyed it—she swam like a fish and did not want to get out. The water inside the lagoon was as calm as a mill pond, while the great waves a mile out pounded incessantly on the reef with a thunder that was awe inspiring. Myriads of small fish and some big ones abounded in these lagoons. We went out to the coral reef and had a good look at the different colored corals: pink, yellow, white, and purplish hues. I dived down and collected some for Gwen and Beth.

That night the natives brought us some excellent fish to eat, which they had speared underwater. After our evening meals we often watched glorious sunsets. Paths of lurid gold filtering through the palm trees reflected on the lagoon, while a native paddling a canoe across the still waters of the placid pond made it a sight to behold. The sun setting over the palm trees was a spectacular sight. Only God could paint such a gorgeous picture.

I had my bicycle sent out so that I could go to the little Chinese store to buy provisions—mostly canned food from Australia, America, and New Zealand. I also rode on sightseeing excursions around the island, which is about 30 miles long and 18 miles wide at the widest point. I traveled almost completely around Tahiti and saw some beautiful scenery, including mountains, swiftly running rivers, and beautiful glades of ferns and tropical verdure.

After I got soaked once, my white pants, shoes, and shirt presented a sorry spectacle. On my return, the native lady who did our washing exclaimed, "Clothes bad! No clean!" However, I relieved her of the trouble. With a bit of boiling and rubbing, they soon became white again. The natives did not boil clothes. They took them to a running stream when they could, beat them with a stick, and rubbed them with soap. They relied on the cold water and their expended energy to bring results, and it was remarkable how clean they got them. The native men looked especially fine in their white suits.

After spending nearly a month recuperating at Brother Mervin's house, Gwen was feeling much better, and I was refreshed. We returned to Tarona, where I had a little study made on the front verandah of our mission house. At the house of a native cabinetmaker, I made a desk. Gwen made the curtains for the study.

A native named Rehi made some much-needed furniture for the missionaries from locally grown silky oak. The Tahitians had not known of the wood's value for furniture-making, and they had been using it for firewood for years.

One evening Eddie and I had a unique experience. We were called to administer to the proprietor of a hotel, a man named Stuart, who had suffered several strokes. While we had our hands on his head, he passed away. I had told Eddie on the way there that I believed he would not be raised up, but the good Lord would call him home. It seemed that he was just waiting for the servants of God to arrive before passing away. Eddie and I conducted the funeral, and many of our native Saints sang for the occasion. That brought comments of appreciation from the bereaved, especially since the natives sang so softly (which was not typical of their singing).

In December, 1945, the governor left for France. Many guns were fired to "blow him away," and a new governor was installed shortly thereafter. That same month heavy rains set in and flooded the mission grounds. We almost needed a canoe to get to the bathroom and toilet, which were behind Eddie's house.

At Christmas we had a pageant at the church. The natives sang the same Christmas carols that we were familiar with, except they sang them in Tahitian. They had a Christmas tree covered with presents for the children. The gifts were supplied by relatives, and some of the children were disappointed when they missed out. Eddie made sure at every Christmas from then on that each of the children received at least a small bag of candy.

January 18, 1946, was the big occasion of the annual business meeting. I heard that normally the Saints had some rather rough times at those events, but Eddie and I foresaw it. He let them exercise their rights, but he did not allow any funny business. Some of those who came to cause trouble were perplexed and did not know what to do.

One very funny incident occurred at the meeting. Eddie read the rules of decorum to the natives, one of which was that no one must leave the room without asking permission of the president. That was too much for one old native brother. He stood up and asked, "What about if I need to go to the toilet?" Poor Eddie certainly turned red, and you should have heard the titters that went up from the congregation! They were certainly characters, those people.

I was elected to be the pastor, church school director, and treasurer of the Tarona Branch. The missionary was always elected treasurer because the natives did not handle money very well. I was glad for the church school director's position since it gave me a free hand to introduce a new system of classes, which was so badly needed.

Gwen was the music director and had complete charge of the branch's singing, which involved a lot of work since the Saints were such a music-loving people. Very soon after our arrival, she stood in front of the people and conducted the choir, much to their satisfaction. Gwen also started to give piano lessons. The students had wonderful ears for music and were quick to learn.

The adult class took my attention. The Saints were studying an old quarterly that someone had translated into their language 15 years before. It was the only quarterly for study they had, and they used it over and over and over again. I was determined that the problem would come to an end, and it did.

It was our belief that many of the island people were descendants of Book of Mormon people who had sailed westward across the Pacific from America. We were certainly learning to love those "sons of Laman," and we felt that our love was returned. They had a certain reserve about them, which characterized our image of the American Indian.

Horahitu, the native missionary, was the epitome of a silent Indian. He gave the impression of being very wise, like the old owl in the oak tree. When he wished to give consent to something, he grunted the way we read that the Indians did. But when he preached, he surely laid down the law and seemed to have excellent liberty. The natives respected his word very much.

The young girls were very interesting—a really fine group who loved the church and were loyal to it. They were happy and carefree and loved to sing. Unfortunately, there were but few young men. I jokingly wrote to my mother that Gwen would have to teach the girls the old maids' chorus—"God Send Us Men"!

Some of the things that happened right at the beginning of our mission were very interesting. I spent a week of great activity in preparing my church school aids, which included making a sand tray and a flannel board. We chose teachers for the various classes, and I got them together for some instructions on new methods of church school work. They were very interested in the flannel board. We also showed them many beautiful pictures that we brought from New Zealand. You should have heard their comments of appreciation. I divided the church school into four groups initially—a men's class, a women's class, a young people's class, and a children's class—with the view of adding another class for children soon. The classwork was going along well, and the natives were accepting the new ideas. Three precious souls were baptized one Sunday. Eddie did the baptizing since I had not yet learned to say the necessary words in the native tongue.

It was the rainy season, and could it rain! It reminded me of the weather in Australia where we lived on the north coast. One night a warning was issued that a hurricane was coming our way, but thanks to God it passed well out to sea. A small river flowed nearby; and when the tide was in, it backed up and flooded the compound. The rain was so heavy that the water rose 18 inches in our yard. Because the house was only two feet above the ground, we were afraid of being flooded out.

It was difficult to get to the common bathroom, which was located behind Eddie's place. It often involved walking through knee-deep water. The natives laughed at us for taking off our shoes and plodding through the water. But they appreciated the fact that we were not above roughing it a bit. They said that we were doing so in the spirit of the old missionaries.

When Charles Wandell and Glaud Rodger had visited Tahiti in 1873, they went out of town some distance to a place called Tiona, the Tahitian word for Zion. The first church of the mission had been there, but it had long since been abandoned. The RLDS Church still owned the land after those many years. We hoped in the future to clean it and make it into a reunion campground especially for the young people of the church. It was all overgrown with lantana and brush, although some fine mango trees still grew there, relics of the past prosperity.

Tiona was elevated, overlooking the beautiful setting of the coral reef on the strait between Tahiti and Moorea. It afforded a lovely view of Moorea, a beautiful island with very rugged mountains and gorgeous scenery. When we stood on the shore of Tahiti and looked westward of an evening, sometimes we saw the most glorious sunsets. The whole ocean seemed to be on fire.

Although Tahiti was a paradise for living in many ways, it had quite a lot of disease. Much of it had been inherited from the white man, who brought venereal disease and other illnesses, such as tuberculosis. I saw some terrible sights among the Tahitians as a result of disease. Eddie and I administered to a man in the last stages of facial cancer. It was a terrible sight, and the odor was nauseating. All that we could do was to pray that the good Lord would relieve him of his suffering as quickly as possible.

The disease of elephantiasis was rampant in 1946. It was caused by filaria, a parasitic worm, and resulted in a thickening and hardening of the skin along with an enormous enlargement of the parts affected, usually the lower extremities. I saw some frightful sights, including a man with a leg about two feet in diameter. Strangely enough he could still walk. Tremendous advancements have been made since then in the treatment of elephantiasis. Some of our young church men and women were engaged in research by the Americans. Very little of the disease exists now because doctors found that they could kill the germ. It reminded me of a snake when I saw it under a powerful microscope.

☼ ☼ ☼

The following situation shows what we had to face even in our first few months in Tahiti. In February of 1946, we had to attend a large funeral of one of our church members, who was the chief troublemaker of the branch. He had once been a leader in the church, but in recent years he started to decline because he allowed an evil spirit to take control of his life. He was only 45 and a very capable speaker, having power to sway many people.

About two months earlier, Eddie and I had warned him concerning many evil things he had done. While I talked to him, the Holy Spirit came to me in power. I gave him a solemn warning in English, which Eddie translated. He was warned that the Lord was displeased with him and unless he repented, he would be removed. I did not say how he would be removed, but that he would be.

Despite those warnings, he did not repent. Horahitu said that God could not raise him up when he was breathing out threats against His servants. It was a reassuring experience to me that God was still directing His work.

The natives hated for a man or woman to die in the hospital. Because this man was close to death, he was taken home to die. His breathing was labored, and he was not conscious. A crowd gathered inside and outside his house to wait for the end.

The natives had great faith in the "quack doctor," who stuck pins under the fingernails and in the feet. If the patient improved, they thought it was because of the pins; then the "doctor" expected to be paid. After sticking needles in this man's feet and hands, the "doctor" said that he had a good chance of recovering. Gwen was there and told me at 10 p.m. that he would surely die that night unless the Lord worked a miracle.

We prayed and administered to him; but his breathing became more and more labored. I shall never forget the terrible look in his eyes as he struggled toward the last. If ever there was a devil in a man, it was in this poor unfortunate. His sightless eyes bored into mine, and I fought the power of the evil one with all my might. About a quarter of an hour before his death, we administered to him again. He instantly became quieter; evidently the evil spirit was rebuked by the power of God. He finally passed away about 3 a.m. Thus the Lord had removed one of the main causes of trouble in the mission.

We had only a few hours' sleep because we had to be at the house at 7 a.m. for a service. The procedure for the *hunaraas* or funerals was interesting. A native elder and I went from the house to the church, walking in front of the horse-drawn hearse. It was the old-fashioned type—like an old cab—with black plumes waving on the top and black nets over the horses. A large crowd followed the hearse.

After leaving the church, Eddie, the elder, and I walked in front of the procession, hats off in the blazing sun. The shopkeepers closed their doors out of respect. When the funeral procession was past, they opened them again. We followed the main street of the town to the cemetery—and were about boiled by the time we got there! The cemetery was situated in a valley, so the sun was especially hot. After a short service, almost everyone threw flowers on the coffin. The widow and many others waited until the grave was filled in and the flower wreaths were placed on it before they reluctantly left.

After the funeral Eddie, Lilly Raye, Gwen, Beth, and I went for a swim and a picnic. Eddie said it was "to wash away our sins." The night after the funeral, the natives had a *tamahanahanaraa* (comforting service); but we were conspicuous by our absence. We had had enough of *hunaraas* (funerals). The natives drank hot black coffee to keep themselves awake at the *tamahanahanaraa* and often stayed awake all night. They took texts from the Bible and talked about them. It was certainly quite an experience.

The natives had another unusual custom associated with funerals. Elaborate "mourning shelters" were built over graves, and relatives lived in the shelters during long periods of mourning. This pagan custom was more prevalent in the Tuamotus than on Tahiti.

About that same time Eddie and I, along with some natives, walked over the church's huge plantation, about three miles from Papeete. An Australian, Brother Stan Ballard, had previously farmed the land. We discussed the possibilities of placing some more people on the property as market gardeners. We were hoping that in the near future the mission could reap more financial benefit from the land than hitherto. Under proper supervision it could be used to support at least three native missionaries.

I made an electric sewing machine for Gwen, which worked well. We ran the motor off a six-volt car battery, since the house current was not suitable for the electric motor I had. I repaired an old electric iron, so she did not have to borrow Lilly Raye's iron. I also made an electric stove so Gwen could cook something quickly if she needed to. That was particularly useful later when our new baby, Marvia, arrived.

Our family doctor, a Frenchman named Dr. Wurfel, was interested in electricity and was fascinated by my gadgets. He introduced me to a friend who had his own electrician's business. I was thus able to obtain many electrical components that would normally have been unavailable.

Beth was two years old and growing into a lovely little girl. She was adored by all the natives, and she amused them to no end by speaking to them in a jargon of French, English, and Tahitian. She learned English very fast and really amazed us at times with the extent of her vocabulary.

Studying the Tahitian language was quite a problem at first because its construction was so vastly different from English. By early 1946 we were beginning to understand the natives better, especially when they spoke slowly—sometimes we could answer them. It was very trying on the nerves to be in a strange country where we could not understand nor be understood. If we had not had some knowledge of French, things would have been much harder for us. Gwen was doing a good job with the choir and was beginning to use Tahitian to instruct the natives.

While we were in Tahiti, it was hard to get the foods we were accustomed to; little things really made us happy. I wrote in a letter home:

"We just received from our Chinese grocer several packets of Arnott's cookies (biscuits), Arrowroot, and Wheatmeal—a real treat; also two tins of Aussie cheese like the kind you sent to us. That was all he could spare us. It came on the boat which brought our mail from Australia."

In 1946 some tidal waves occurred in the Pacific; but the good Lord was with us, and no harm occurred where we were. One day when Eddie and I visited the farm lands, we were up in the hills above the ocean in the early afternoon. I told him that I thought the sea was making a strange noise, and he agreed; but we dismissed the thought and went on with our work.

After I arrived home, Gwen told me a strange experience had occurred. She was sewing at the machine when she heard a crackling noise. Upon hurrying outside to find the cause, she noticed a huge wall of water coming toward the land. Fortunately it was not very high at Tahiti, and it did not do much damage except at one place, where it washed away several houses. She said the waves continued to come for some minutes, about eight waves altogether. Afterward the native boys had a great time catching fish and eels which were washed ashore. We later learned of the damage done by a disastrous tidal wave near Hawaii.

In preparation for the expected arrival of a troopship bringing back Tahitian soldiers from North Africa, many men began to practice native dances. They beat drums to a savage rhythm and performed vigorous motions upon and around wooden trestles, keeping time with the drums. As the time for the celebration drew near, they increased the length and frequency of their practices. Finally it became a nuisance to Wednesday night prayer meetings. The men were not very near to the church, but the sound of the drums carried a long way.

About 200 years previously, when the people celebrated victories over other tribes, the drumming occasions were the rule and not the exception. It made me realize what the Word of God has done for these people in bringing them from barbarism to the light of divine knowledge. We celebrated the organization of the Church of Jesus Christ on April 6 with a special service, and the natives thoroughly enjoyed it.

In the spring of 1946, Eddie and Lilly Raye left to go to the Tuamotu Islands for a couple of months, spending a short time on each of the six islands where we had quite a large membership. While they were gone, my portfolio was increased. I was branch president, church school director, treasurer, bishop's agent (which was a big job there), landlord of the farming lands, landlord of Tarona, and the general policeman of all. I did not mind; however, I wished that I was able to speak the language a little better. Of course, it provided greater motivation for Gwen and me to learn the language faster.

We had a one-day visit from the New Zealand victory parade troops, who were on their way to London to celebrate victory in a large parade with other Dominion troops. We met quite a few of them and had a chat about New Zealand. A number of them were interested in our church grounds, which comprised one of the prettiest spots on the island of Tahiti. All the armed forces were represented, and it was good to hear so many English-speaking voices in the town at one time. The natives always liked the arrival of British ships since the British people and sailors generally behaved themselves very well.

One day we visited the leper colony. Gwen had trained the girls in our choir to sing very beautifully, and they delivered a series of hymns to the people in the colony. Horahitu preached in the following service. The inhabitants seemed very thrilled. Those poor people were pitiful to behold. By 1946, however, the disease was gradually losing its hold on the islands.

I visited the Papeete hospital quite regularly and tried in my poor Tahitian to comfort the patients. They appreciated my coming, which seemed to do some good.

Sunday, May 5, 1946, was a big day in Tahiti, with the arrival of a troopship bringing back soldiers from France. All the island turned out to welcome them. Along with other ministers, we were given a reserved place on the wharf near the governor to see the arrival of the vessel. We rang the church bell for half an hour in honor of the returning troops. Guns fired, and many girls on the wharf sang songs in Tahitian.

About that time, I prayed my first prayer in the Tahitian language, much to the delight of the native Saints. Since Eddie's departure, I quickly became more proficient in the use of the language. It let me know that God was really in charge—for He had given it to me. Two-and-a-half-year-old Beth was singing hymns in four languages: one Maori song we brought over with us from New Zealand, plus Tahitian, French, and English. When she met someone who could speak English, she seemed surprised.

My mother had written and asked me to tell her about myself. I was 30 years old at the time, and it is interesting to look back at my description in a letter dated May 25, 1946:

"Well, really I am a very uninteresting person. But if you would like to learn of me, here is an effort to acquaint you with the facts. First of all, I am very happy in my work here, which is a big factor in any man's success. As a father, I guess I have a lot to learn. At least my little girl loves me, although at times I do get a bit cross with her. She is an inquiring little soul, and all her mischief is caused only by a desire to learn and find out things for herself. She is the most excellent company in the world. If her little trotting around the house were to cease, I would be entirely lost. So you see, I have a few of the instincts of a father.

"I still like to fiddle with electrical things and have just made a foot control for Gwen's electric sewing machine. I am going to make an amplifier for an electric guitar, which I have almost completed. Also I plan to make a portable radio to take when I go among the other islands. Such is almost essential—if Edward had a receiver now, we would be able to transmit a message to him through the Tahitian radio service. This work, while helping the Kingdom, is a bit of a break for me from studying languages. I am not able to serve the church in a musical way, but I can be of use in other areas."

In the islands, the procedure for repenting is of interest. When church members fell into sins, such as drinking, smoking, dancing, gambling, fornication, and so on, they had to come before the branch and confess their sins publicly. Many came as a result of the priests and teachers showing them the error of their ways. However, some were hardened sinners who would not repent. They were cut off.

I had a unique experience in trying to straighten out an errant church member who was in the hospital at the time. She was the mother of six children, although she had never been married. She had also been guilty of other sins, such as drinking and smoking. I talked with her about many things of evil and good, pointing out the difference between them. She was rather sick, and I told her that she should repent because she was ill and desired a blessing from God. I suggested that since she had been content to serve the devil for so long, perhaps she should pray to him—asking that *he* help her in her distress. She said she could not do that. Then I told her that the work of the devil is to lead people into a pit and leave them there. He seems to be a friend for a time but abandons them when great trouble comes. I also explained the love of God and Christ. She gave me a written statement of repentance; I presented it to the Saints for acceptance, which they gave.

☼ ☼ ☼

Apostle George Mesley, his wife Blanche, and their son Gordon arrived safely on June 3. As soon as I heard that their ship was close, I sent a wire to Brother Mesley asking him to prepare his films for public showing. When the natives learned that he had movies, they really wanted to see them. A large number of Saints gathered to meet their apostle and his family, placing flower and shell *heis* around their necks.

Gwen, Sister Mesley, Gordon, and Beth went in a car to the mission home. Brother Mesley and I had to go through customs and obtain authorization to show his films. After wading through the red tape, we succeeded. Then we hurried to the house. Gwen had prepared an excellent meal for them, including roast chicken, tropical fruit salad with coconut cream, and coconut milk to drink.

I had learned earlier about my call to the office of seventy, one of the missionary arms of the RLDS Church. The call had been approved by the Joint Council in Independence, Missouri; and Apostle Mesley was to ordain me that evening.

The church was crowded beyond capacity for the ordination service and the welcome to follow. A huge crowd, including many Mormons, had gathered outside. Brother Mesley's imposing stature made a great impression on the Tahitians, and his excellent deportment completely won their respect. He gave me a charge in simple, direct language. Although the natives could not understand it, by the Holy Spirit they sensed the power that was displayed. When Apostle Mesley finished ordaining me to the office of seventy, he gave a charge to the congregation. With the help of God, I translated. The native Saints were very pleased because I (and the Lord) did not let them down.

During the welcoming, the Mesleys were showered with gifts of all kinds. Sister Mesley completely won the hearts of the women by kissing them on their cheeks as they brought their gifts to her. The Mesleys were so laden with shell necklaces they could hardly walk! Brother Mesley made a little speech of thanks, which I translated for him. I also told him what the Saints were saying to him.

When we started to prepare for the movie, we found to our dismay that the projector would not work—or more precisely, the bulb would not light. That was an opportunity to use my talents. While Gordon and I worked with the machine, Brother Mesley was in his glory—conducting singing with Gwen's assistance. He won over everyone completely by his friendly style, and did they sing! He did not worry about language, and the natives seemed to understand by some supernatural force what he said to them. After much perseverance and tinkering, we managed to get the projector working. The delight of the natives knew no bounds. They were interested in all the scenes, but particularly loved the colors of the flowers.

After that we retired to the back lawn for ice cream and

cake. The Mesleys, Gwen, and I sang songs in English for the Saints; they in turn sang native and French songs for us. They did not want to take their eyes off the Mesleys, and it was midnight before they reluctantly dispersed.

Thinking we would have only that one time together, we talked all night without a wink of sleep. When the morning came, we took the Mesleys to see a particularly beautiful spot and then hastened to the ship. We found that the ship's engine had a cracked piston and would not be able to depart until that night. Emere Mervin, the wife of Elder John Mervin, suggested a picnic at their country home at the other end of the island, to which we readily assented. We boarded their huge Dodge truck with a number of the native Saints, and off we went. The natives sang constantly all the way there and all the way home. Apostle Mesley directed them, standing in the back of the truck, and enjoyed himself immensely. The Mesleys were very enchanted with the beautiful scenery, and Brother Mesley made good use of his camera.

We returned at 4:30 p.m., only to find that the ship would not be sailing until the next morning. The Mesleys then came to our home, and we talked until 9 p.m. But we were all so tired that we finally had to give in and bid each other good night. They returned to their cabins aboard ship.

Early in the morning I went to the wharf just in time to wave good-bye to them. Several Saints had gathered there to see them off, and many tears were shed. Brother Mesley then defied the custom of the sea by descending the gangway to shake hands with latecomers. The captain and the pilot standing on the bridge frowned at him, but he only gave them a cheery wave and finished his farewells. The natives gave them enough fruit and coconuts to last until they reached New York! Some of them told me that the Mesleys made a greater impression on the mission than any other people who had come, as could be expected from an apostle for the Lord Jesus Christ.

☼ ☼ ☼

When the Mesleys had gone, we settled into our regular work. I braved my timidity and stood up in a prayer meeting to tell the natives the nature of a revelation received by Elbert A. Smith. They were all immensely pleased, and I heard comments on the "good speech" of Vivian.

Working with the natives was a little frustrating at times, as many of them were content to just listen to the instruction of the missionary and not think for themselves. Sometimes when I asked them what they thought about a certain subject, they would simply say, "You tell me."

About that time, I fixed up an old engine and circular saw for one of our men to take to the islands where he was building two churches. The work of cutting all the timber by hand was exhausting. With the aid of the saw, he was able to save much time and money for the church. I converted the engine to run on kerosene instead of gasoline, which was difficult to obtain on the other islands. Using kerosene also saved money.

I also made two wind generators for charging batteries when we went to the other islands. One was for Eddie and one for me. They were used for powering the radio and showing lantern slides. Visual education became a big help in our teaching and ministry there.

The week of July 14 was a time of great celebration in Papeete—the commemoration of the fall of the Bastille during the French Revolution. Many of the natives took advantage of it to run wild. Except for the inevitable few, our people did not take part in a lot of the evil. If the Saints were asked what they thought about the celebration, they would say it was *maa maa* (crazy). However, some of the folk songs were really lovely. For several days the natives roamed through the town banging tins, beating drums, dancing, and drinking to excess. The men, although fine-looking specimens in some cases, were often given to drinking and smoking. At one time we could not have blamed them for that. But by the time we were there, they had all heard the message of Christ to some degree.

The next incident is a rather humorous one and was very embarrassing to me. I went on a picnic with Gwen and the girls' chorus. First we played games on the bank of a river; then we went for a swim. Going some distance away, I changed into my swimming trunks and left my clothes by the water's edge, since very few people ever came near that place. I had a great time teaching the girls water games. But that was the end of the fun. When I went to get my clothes, they were gone! You can imagine the trouble I would be in—being the missionary—if I had to ride through town in an open utility truck wearing only my swimming trunks. Fortunately, my coat and shoes were not taken, since I had left them in a different place.

I prepared for the worst and waited for the truck. When cars went by, I ducked behind trees. Just before we were due to go home, a Tahitian woman started talking to the girls. When they told her the trouble, she kindly offered to lend me a pair of her husband's trousers and a shirt to wear. That somewhat saved my embarrassment. I do not think my clothes ever turned up. I hope whoever stole them was a little fellow like me; otherwise he would have a job getting into them.

Occasionally Doctor Wurfel and his wife and their little daughter Danielle visited us. Beth and Danielle enjoyed playing together. Although Danielle spoke mostly French, she could speak a bit of English. Since Beth could speak a bit of French, they got along very well together.

The Butterworths arrived home early one Sunday morning after a trip to one of the islands, where they had been stranded for seven weeks. Lilly Raye told Gwen that the native women of those islands sat up to have their babies; giving birth sometimes took them days.

Radio was still a novelty in the islands in 1946. The natives loved to listen to our wireless. Several of them visited us almost every night since very few of them could afford radios for their own homes. Unfortunately, they did not seem to know when to go home. I hated to tell them to leave, but they could not stay forever.

Two men, a Chinese and a native Saint, were dwelling on our church farm lands at Heberona until one day when an argument developed between them. Apparently the Chinese man was coming at the other man with a large knife. A relative of the native, a 13-year-old boy, threw a stone at the Chinese man and smashed his face. Our native church member attended to his wounds and took him to the hospital. The Chinese man lay there for about three or four days, seemingly recovering. Then quite unexpectedly, we received news of his death.

That complicated matters considerably because the boy—a member of our church—had thrown the stone. Eddie and I, accompanied by the chief judge and the native policeman, visited the scene of the tragedy while they reconstructed the event. We had to go to the court to give evidence. I never dreamed that one day I would be involved in a manslaughter case. The boy was acquitted because of his age. However, one of our older members, whose name was Avivi, was faced with the charge. Avivi was sentenced to several years in prison. But instead, he was used as a gardener by some official in the city. They knew that Avivi would not run away. Sometimes he was even able to attend church services.

One time Gwen and I took care of a little native baby, whose mother had brought her from the Tuamotu Islands. Because the girl was half starved, she was nearly dead. The mother had given her to the old grandmother and never had fed her any breast milk. The poor little girl had had nothing but coconut milk and a bit of condensed milk to grow on. Gwen and I prepared food and instructed the mother how to feed her.

Many of the native women did that abominable thing—they gave away their children when they were born, usually to a relative. I certainly gave them stern lectures against it. There was a lot of work in the islands for Gwen and anyone of her abilities and nature. It was no wonder the Lord wanted her to serve among colored people.

To ask one of the natives to break from an age-old custom was "like asking the sun to stop shining" as I put it in a letter to my mother. Superstition and ignorance had dulled the intelligence and willingness of some of the natives to think independently. However, for the most part they were an intelligent people.

Here is an excerpt from a letter dated August 24, 1946:

"We are busy preparing things for Father's Day, which we are celebrating tomorrow. I realize that I must do some of the holy work of the branch, so I will be baptizing again since I cannot yet preach. I am baptizing three precious souls into the Kingdom. One is an elderly lady, whom I personally have had a hand in converting. She is extremely happy to become one of us. Only last night she told me that she has lived in darkness for all these years, and now she has seen the marvelous light of God. I had baptized her son and daughter recently.

"Although a lot of these people are bad in many ways, yet I'm learning to love them dearly. I would do anything to help them out of their fallen state. They do not seem to have much resistance to sin, yet many of them are fine Saints.

"Sometimes we get disheartened and ask what is the use in trying to work with people such as these. But then we realize that they are all God's children and have just as much right as the whites to the ministry of the servants of God. As Brother Clyde Ellis (an earlier apostle to the Society Islands Mission) had said, when one considers that less than 200 years ago they were idol worshipers—and even practiced cannibalism—then one takes heart at the progress evidenced among them."

About that time the Union Steamship Company started to run regular vessels between Australia and New Zealand and the west coast of the U.S.A. via Tahiti. That gave us mail deliveries much more frequently. Previously we had to wait up to four months to receive our mail.

☼ ☼ ☼

In September Eddie Butterworth and I traveled to the island of Makatea, some 125 miles northeast of Tahiti. It had no harbor, and its sheer cliffs went down 6,000 feet to the bottom of the ocean. Those great cliffs had caves in them, where the native nobles were interred in canoes, most of which had rotted away. I wondered how anyone ever got in there to bury their dead. Jokingly I said to Eddie, "Those poor guys are going to be up against it on resurrection day. They will rise from the dead and find themselves halfway up a steep cliff with no way out!"

We had a large branch of the church on the phosphate-producing island of Makatea. The phosphate company gave all its employees rations of wine, beer, and cigarettes.

Although our men did not drink and smoke, they were selling their rations for large sums of money or exchanging them for food. Eddie preached strongly against that, and we persuaded the offenders to remove their names from the ration lists for alcohol and tobacco and come before the branch to confess and repent.

Eddie and I sang some songs in English to the natives, much to their delight. Quite a number of them knew some English because they came from Rarotonga in the British Cook Islands.

There were no beaches on Makatea. On my first trip there, I baptized a native woman in a pool of crystal-clear cool water in a cave. The water hole was very deep—too deep for baptizing. We had to tread water, while I called her by name and said, "Having been commissioned of Jesus Christ, I baptize you in the name of the Father, and of the Son, and of the Holy Ghost. Amen." I then put my hand on her head and pushed her down to immerse her. That was quite an experience. I was glad that Eddie did not try it—after all, he could not swim!

Our harvest festival was a great success in 1946. We raised the equivalent of 80 U.S. dollars to assist in the general work of the mission. The food was sold by auction, as was the custom of the native Saints—and fantastic prices were realized. One watermelon, the only one there, sold for over a pound (the equivalent of two U.S. dollars). It was good to see all the natives so busily engaged in their work.

Beth, who had just turned three, was a real pal to me. At times I took her on the bike to the church farm lands about three miles out of town. We both enjoyed it very much, and the fresh air did her so much good.

We have reached a place of great importance in our family history—the birth of our second daughter, Marvia, on Thursday morning, December 12, 1946. Although I had tried to persuade the hospital authorities to allow the doctor who had attended Gwen through her pregnancy to deliver the baby, she was delivered by a native nurse. The first meal they presented to Gwen after childbirth was a piece of greasy pork and a bottle of wine. Needless to say, she went without.

Gwen and Marvia did not stay long in the maternity hospital because of the primitive treatments and the noise of a jackhammer outside their window, which did not allow the mother or baby to get any rest. So we took our precious little daughter home.

Heavy rains set in—the monsoon rains which usually occur after Christmas—and the mission grounds were again flooded. A proper toilet was being built in our house; but since it was not finished, we had to suffer through our trips to the outhouse during this rainy season just as we had the year before.

Thus ended the year 1946. The Sorensen family had grown to four, and we were very grateful to the Lord for the blessing Gwen received while having a baby under such primitive circumstances.

After Marvia's birth we went to the holiday home of the Mervins at Taravao near the other end of the island, where we stayed for a few weeks so Gwen could recuperate. Jeanne Mervin went with us. I translated some written materials while Gwen was resting.

The Tarona Branch again elected me pastor. Eddie Butterworth was very pleased with the progress of the previous year, and he wanted to maintain the good work. One Sunday he and John Mervin blessed Marvia at Tarona.

Because of strikes in America and only a few ships from Australia, food became very scarce in early 1947.

However, there was an abundance of rum, wine, and beer from France!

I made a real "rip snorter" electric guitar, far superior to one I had made for my cousin in Brisbane. Teriki, a native church member, was a wizard on the electric and Spanish guitars. One evening he came over to the house with three young men. He played the electric guitar while another native played the Spanish guitar and the two others sang. It certainly sounded sweet. That guitar turned out to be a great asset in our services for many years.

In February, 1947, we were in the height of the cyclone season. We had had much wind and rain the previous week, and the cyclone was a culmination of those effects. On Saturday, February 15, the wind steadily increased. Suddenly it stopped completely for about half an hour, and there was an eerie silence. Then it returned, blowing at gale force. By 12:30 the wind had increased to hurricane force (more than 75 mph), blowing straight in from the sea. The wind was bending the palms at incredible angles. One large tree fell across one of the mission houses, which was near the seashore, and the natives came running to the church. The tree, however, did keep the house from being blown away.

I knelt down in our house and poured out my soul to the Lord that He would stay the wind. Then I nailed up the front door. Marvia slept through it all, even though the noise was terrific. I then went into the church to try and calm the Saints gathered there, and I prayed again to the Lord.

Eddie had gone to the seashore to view the rising sea and to help the people in the houses. The wind kept increasing, knocking down trees and stripping the coconut palms of their branches and nuts. Suddenly the wind changed direction, blowing from the side with even more fury, doing quite a lot of damage to the town—uprooting many houses and trees and scattering rubbish everywhere.

The cyclone lasted for about half an hour; then it stopped as suddenly as it had begun. We then noticed a huge waterspout and whirlwind about a mile out to sea, moving parallel to the shore. Thousands of tons of water are lifted up by those whirlwinds. Eddie remarked to me that had it not been turned away from the mission, all the houses in the compound would have been destroyed—along with buildings in much of the surrounding area.

We heard the next day that a small town at the other end of the island was directly in the path of the whirlwind and was almost destroyed. Two churches were unroofed, and 40 houses were damaged. We could see how merciful the good Lord was to us. If the wind had not turned at the time of our prayers, things would have gone badly since we were so near the seashore. We had to live by faith.

It appeared that cyclones were gradually increasing in strength. I wrote to my parents that I believed before many years a terrible one would come and blot out a lot of the wickedness in the islands. In 1988, I believe, a cyclone did smite the islands with winds of about 180 mph, bringing devastation to many places.

Shortly after that, I preached my first full sermon in the Tahitian language, choosing the theme of "God is Love." I trusted in the Lord, and He blessed me. I had baptized four people the previous Sunday, including one Chinese woman. That was the first time I had baptized a Chinese, but it was not the last. I had taught her the gospel in Tahitian. She brought some of her friends along, and we started a little Chinese group. Since we could not get any follow-up from America, it gradually disorganized. The field among the Chinese people was white and ready to harvest; but we needed literature and other help and could not seem to get it.

My sister Mavis wrote a play about the Restoration. I translated it into Tahitian, and we performed it in April to commemorate the founding of the church. An American named LeTague painted a backdrop of that era, doing a magnificent job with ordinary house paint. He also painted the head of Christ, which I put up in the church.

On the sixth of April, the natives performed the play. The church was packed, and nonmembers outside were looking through the windows. We depicted the first baptism, where Joseph Smith and Oliver Cowdery were commanded by the angel to baptize each other. We did not actually show the baptism, but instead had the words read from behind the curtain. The reader thought he knew it all by heart. But instead of saying, "Joseph Smith, I baptize you in the name of the Father...," he said, "Jesus Christ, I baptize you in the name of the Father." It sounded so funny that I nearly burst out laughing! But most of the natives did not seem to notice. It was the first major play they had ever done, and it was excellent.

Lilly Raye was expecting their first child, and Eddie wanted her to go back to America for the blessed event. She was delayed, however, because someone had conned a lot of money from the Tahitians and was going to France with it. The Tahitians got up in arms to keep him from leaving. French soldiers were posted on guard at all vulnerable spots, including the ship that Lilly Raye was taking to America. They kept the man from leaving, but we thought bullets would be flying at any time. The ship eventually departed with Lilly Raye in May of 1947.

Despite the risk of occasional danger, one thing reconciled us—the natives had a great deal of respect for their missionaries and would not be likely to harm them. I do not think our Saints engaged in the affair. I told them to avoid the trouble and respect the government as is taught in the Doctrine and Covenants.

Eddie Butterworth was desperate to get to America for the birth of their baby, but it did not look as though a ship would be coming for months. As it was, he left on the same plane that carried the "Lady of Fatima." The Catholics believed that Mary had appeared to some shepherd children at the town of Fatima in Portugal, and they were transporting a statue called "Our Lady of Fatima" around the world. Finally Eddie plucked up enough courage to ask the priests if they had a vacancy on board the airplane.

Amid all the flowers, balloons, and everything that the Catholics had for Fatima, the RLDS missionary got into the plane as the native Saints waved and cheered. I told Eddie, "Well, you should be pretty safe on this trip with the Lady of Fatima to care for you." He later confided that his curiosity got the better of him, and he pulled aside the curtain to have a look at the statue. He was quite disappointed. But he said they even had a seat for her to sit on, so she could journey like an ordinary lady!

☼ ☼ ☼

I had an abundance of work once Eddie had gone, taking care of the whole mission as well as the Tarona Branch—which was a job in itself. We had to postpone an island trip because heavy gales had lashed the coast for over two weeks, and no island schooners dared to make a journey.

During that time, I translated the *Commentary on the Doctrine and Covenants* for the priesthood. I found that it revolutionized their concept and appreciation of the revelations because they had known very little about them previously. Although the Doctrine and Covenants was written in modern terminology and under divine inspiration by the latter-day prophets, it had been translated into Tahitian by a nonmember. He did not know the background of the revelations. Thus he lost all or most of the Spirit in his translation.

The Book of Mormon really described the Tahitians—up one day and down the next, quick to anger and often quick to forgive, especially if the white missionary entered into the conflict. I had to act as policeman, trying to keep drunks away from the compound—alcohol was the growing evil in the islands—and sinners from living in the houses of the yard. The natives thought up all sorts of ruses for thwarting that governing of the yard, and I had to be on the lookout continually. I tried to minister to them in love, and I think they respected me for it.

In August, 1947, the *Kon-Tiki* expedition, led by the Norwegian, Thor Heyerdahl, arrived in French Polynesia. The primitive raft landed on the island of Raroia after crossing the Pacific from the west coast of South America. One of the native Saints was among the first to sight the *Kon-Tiki.* My wife and daughters saw the raft arrive in Papeete aboard a schooner. They also saw the entire *Kon-Tiki* crew, who looked very emaciated. The raft was kept in Tahiti for awhile. I later saw it myself and spoke with the expedition scientist and the cook. That expedition substantiated our understanding that the Jaredites and Nephites crossed the oceans with only the winds and currents to propel them.

I will now relate something about the important pearl industry located in the hundreds of low atolls which make up the Tuamotu Archipelago. The natives went out at a certain season of the year to dive for pearl shells, which grew on rocks at the bottom of the lagoons. It was a very dangerous occupation. Sometimes the natives had to dive over 100 feet to get the shells. Their only equipment was a rope with a lead weight on it, a basket, gloves, and small goggles over their eyes. They took a number of deep breaths in preparation; then with a huge breath, they let the lead weight take them swiftly to the bottom.

Some of the divers could stay down a minute and a half or more. When they had their baskets full or could not hold their breath any longer, they gave the rope a tug. Those in the canoe above hauled them up. While they sat and rested, they sometimes opened the pearl shells to see if any valuable pearls were inside. The shells were valuable, but the pearls were more valuable. A true pearl is formed in the body or meat of the oyster, not attached to the shell. We were given a couple of fairly nice ones by the natives.

The terrific pressure at those depths had a gradual detrimental effect on the divers. The natives called it *taravana*, and those affected were really to be pitied. We could generally identify them by their slurred speech and irrational actions.

☼ ☼ ☼

Gwen, Beth, and Marvia—along with Jeanne Mervin, a lovely young Tahitian woman—left in September, 1947, on the Union Steamship Company's *Wairata* to Australia via New Zealand. We had learned that Gwen's mother in Australia was very sick, so the General Church offered to pay Gwen's fare while we had to pay the children's. They planned to be gone for only three months, but the lack of return transportation stretched their visit an extra month.

I think those were the loneliest four months I have ever spent in my life. I had to do some of my own cooking. But

Sister Emere Mervin often sent me my lunch, so I was always sure of getting a decent meal! I was very thankful for that.

The letters I wrote to Australia during that time tell of my loneliness and how I hoped it would not be too long before my loved ones returned. Almost daily I haunted the offices of the Union Steamship Company to inquire about boats coming from Australia. Communication and travel between Australia and Tahiti were very limited. However, God was good to me over the trying months of separation. He sent His Spirit to help and comfort me when I was so lonely that sometimes I even wept.

When I was almost at the point of desperation, something always happened to cheer me—such as the telegram from Gwen telling me that she and the girls were going to fly home instead of waiting even longer for a ship. I sold some of our cherished china to obtain the extra funds to pay the air fare. I also received a letter of commendation for my loyalty from President F. M. Smith. That was very heartening; it was a great encouragement to know that my work was appreciated.

To me the most important event of 1948 was the safe return of my family on January 17. Despite Gwen's apprehension about flying, she and the girls traveled by plane the 4,000 miles from Australia to Tahiti. They flew on Pan American Airways to Noumea and then to Tahiti by the French line Trapas, which used Catalina flying boats. They arrived in Papeete during the morning; of course, you can believe I was there to meet them!

Gwen, Beth, and Marvia were in good health after their trip. Beth had completely forgotten the Tahitian language, but she picked it up again quickly and was soon fluent once more. Marvia had grown from a baby to a delightful little toddler. I was very hurt at first because she did not remember me—but it was not long before she again was a real "Daddy's girl."

In February I performed my first wedding in the native language. After the ceremony, we retired to the meeting house to sing and eat cake and ice cream. It was a real reception, Tahitian style.

In April I went to the island of Moorea for two days with many of our young lads. We had a good time, but the voyage in the small boat was rough. One native boy was seasick. Fortunately the voyage was only two hours long, or others (including myself) would have also become sick. Moorea was intensely mountainous, with sharp peaks of a peculiar shape. The island's two beautiful bays and the sunsets were awe inspiring. Surely God lavishly paints the beautiful scenery of those islands.

Being the only RLDS missionary there for so long was starting to take its toll on me. That was graphically shown in a letter dated April 1, 1948, which I wrote to my parents:

"We shall be baptizing three Chinese on Sunday, and I almost weep when I think of the greatness of the work here and the scarcity of the laborers. I have so much work to do I don't know where to start. But I am, with the help of my good wife, doing my best to keep the flag flying here until additional help arrives. They have selected another missionary to come here in July—if there is a boat. I trust that there will be—the burden is a bit too heavy if one would keep the mission from deteriorating."

The burden had resulted in my health being somewhat run down. But one blessing was John Mervin's country home at Taravao, which he made available to the missionaries whenever we wanted it. Beth and I had a whale of a time crabbing, fishing, and swimming in the lagoon. One time our canoe capsized. Beth, who was just learning to swim, came up like a cork on the other side and grabbed hold of the canoe like a veteran. I was not worried about her very much after that. I was sure that she was going to become a good swimmer.[1]

The short time spent at Taravao helped revive me, and I was ready to return to my work. Really, I was enjoying my ministry. I was minister, bishop's agent, translator, electrician, mechanic, doctor, drama director, and so on—and gaining a wealth of experience.

By that time, I was speaking Tahitian fairly fluently. One Sunday night I preached to a full church about Zion and communism, warning the Saints not to be caught in the net that the devil so cunningly lays to entrap the unwary. I had wonderful liberty, and the natives were really amazed. The sermon lasted 45 minutes, and the people still wanted more. I was so grateful that God had given me command of the language. The natives said it was the most *maramarama* (enlightened, easy to understand) sermon that they had heard.

☼ ☼ ☼

Shortly afterward I made a trip to a coral atoll a long way from Tahiti. The island had only a narrow opening from the lagoon to the ocean; a small boat rowed by four or five men could go through, but that was about all. The ocean waves breaking against the very sharp coral around that pass made it really dangerous. I had traveled on a native schooner to the island. We disembarked into a whale boat, which was propelled by oars. I had my suitcase, containing a change of clothing and some money which I

---

[1] That belief proved true: In 1958 at Boone High School in Boone, Iowa, Beth was in the Dolphins, an underwater ballet group.

had collected from several of the branches on different islands—*ahururaa* they called it (a tenth or tithing).

Everything seemed to be going well until the man who held the steering oar looked back to the schooner, where his girlfriend was waving to him. At that point a big ocean wave caught us and tipped our boat over directly at the entrance to the lagoon. Fortunately I could swim. But it was rather hard since I was wearing a white suit, white shoes, and a pith helmet. I held my suitcase, which was fairly watertight and helped buoy me up. There was the danger of getting smashed on the reef, which could have done quite serious bodily harm—the waves were extremely powerful, and the coral was sharp. But the Lord looked down and saw my plight. I somehow managed to ease through that coral maze, still hanging onto my suitcase, although everything inside was wet. After I reached the main island and was assigned a little house, I put the money and my clothes out to dry.

That is only part of the story. The little hut was one of the nicest on the island. A man and his wife had lived there ever since they married. Although the couple had no children, they wanted them very much. They gave up their home for the missionary, and I had it entirely to myself. They brought me food—their precious canned goods from overseas, breadfruit, lobster (a particular favorite of mine), fish, and other seafood—whatever I wanted. A royal fuss was made over me. I did not encourage it, but that was the type of people they were.

As I finished my ministry on the island and was about to leave, I called the man and his wife into their house. I thanked them very much from the depth of my heart for vacating their home to provide for the servant of God. I then prayed, saying, "Lord, according to Thy wisdom and Thy will, wilt Thou grant unto this couple a child—for they have not turned away Thy servant, but they have blessed him. Wilt Thou please bless them?"

Many years passed, during which time I went back home to Australia before returning again to the islands for another period of service. I was visiting that particular atoll again, and the same lady pointed to a boy paddling a canoe. She said, "That's your boy!"

I thought to myself, "Goodness me! What could she be talking about? She must have me confused with someone else!"

She then said, "Don't you remember years ago when you were leaving our island? You asked the Lord to give my husband and me a child. Well, there he is! That's the only one He's given us, but he is our own flesh and blood!"

How wonderful are the works of God!

On another occasion Gwen, the two girls, and I had gone ashore on the island of Rimatara from the ship which lay outside the reef. That was a mountainous island, but it had a reef around it. We were put in the whale boat for the return trip to the ship, and we arrived safely. But during the second trip out, the steering rope broke; and the whale boat capsized. Fortunately, all the natives who were on it could swim. But just imagine if we and our little girls had been on that same boat when the rope broke. With the ocean waves breaking over the reef, we would not have had a chance. So again I stop and thank God for protecting my family in those outlying islands of the Pacific.

We came across some strange things in the islands. Gwen, our girls, and I went to the island of Tubuai in 1948 on a very fast former American patrol boat. It had been bought and converted to a refrigeration ship to transport beef from some of the outlying mountainous islands south of Tahiti. After we disembarked, the boat went on to the island of Raivavae. We had to wait for quite some time for its return.

I had with me an old engine that I had found in Tony's junkyard in Papeete and subsequently fixed up. It had a generator on it, and I was amazed that it generated AC current. We also had a phonograph/recorder that used paper (cardboard) records. I put the generator and phonograph outside the house where we were staying. The natives came from all over the island to hear the phonograph and see the wonderful thing called electric light. That was in 1948, but many of the natives had never seen electric lights. I recorded their voices, and they were fascinated to no end when I played the sound back for them. Their interest in those things opened the door for me to preach and teach them the gospel.

Tubuai was where Addison Pratt had landed and started the first mission of the church in the Society Islands in 1844. It is a very historical island as far as the church is concerned. Three branches were functioning when we were there. It was also the place where one of the most pathetic situations in my whole ministry confronted me.

One of the priesthood members there came to me and accused a girl in his branch of being a murderess, saying that she had killed her baby. Her father had previously threatened his daughters that if he ever found any of them pregnant out of wedlock, he would kill her. I went to the native missionary, Seventy Horahitu, who knew the people of Tubuai especially well. We agreed to interview the young woman. She told us that she had gone into the forest at night and given birth to her baby, but the baby had died at birth as she was separating it from the umbilical cord. Then she explained how she had clutched her baby to her, kissed it, and then dug a hole and buried it.

That was a most touching story, if true, which I thought it was. While we were on Tubuai, I asked the pastor of her branch to put her case before the people. The young woman stood up, said she had committed sin (but she did not admit to murder), and asked forgiveness. However, the Saints did not forgive her.

Finally the boat came and picked us up. I had decided that we would take the young native woman with us to Tahiti because she was being ostracized by some of the people pointing the finger of scorn at her.

We had a rough trip on the way back. Beth was a wonderful little sailor, however, and she won the hearts of the crew. One night about midnight we noticed that the engines had stopped. The large waves were causing the boat to pitch and roll, and we wondered what was wrong. We knew we could be in trouble because the boat had no sails as did the native schooners. In the morning the captain appeared; he was drunk and did not know where we were. Someone had stopped the engines because they were running short of fuel. Finally Horahitu recognized the contour of the clouds ahead as being over the island of Tahiti, although it was about 70 or 80 miles away. The crew trusted him, so off we went. Sure enough, it was Tahiti; we were never so happy to be at home on *terra firma*!

I felt that the woman's case was too involved for me, so I wrote a report and sent it to the RLDS Church headquarters in Independence. Later I was told that when it was read before the apostles, there was not a dry eye among them. They wrote that they felt I was competent to handle it, so they were leaving the matter in my hands.

The Doctrine and Covenants states that anyone who

commits murder shall be tried by the laws of the land. Therefore, I went to the appropriate French officers in the judicial system and inquired about the situation. They asked if I were laying a charge against her. When I said I was not, they told me that she had not been accused before the governor of her island. They said, "Unless you want to resurrect it all, we are quite satisfied that it was not premeditated. If you're not laying any charges, you can count her blameless before us."

The law of the land had been consulted, and the authorities agreed that they had no charge against her. But she was not yet clear by the church. I wrote to the district president of Tubuai, told him what had transpired, and asked him to put the case of the girl's repentance before the whole district. He did so at the district conference, and the Saints accepted it. That was the end of the matter; but it shows what can happen when such a tragedy occurs. After some time the young lady married a young widower.

In 1948 a huge four-engine Australian flying boat arrived from Trans Oceanic Airways, one of several new airlines. The flying boat brought a lot of mail for us, which was really appreciated. Eventually it became a regular service, and we were able to receive our mail more often than previously.

One poor lad, who had broken his back while Gwen and Jeanne were in Australia, had not improved; he had been so shockingly neglected at the hospital that he had deep-seated bed sores. His parents took him to our church farm lands to treat him with native medicines. First they immersed him in cold water in the mountain springs until the patient was shivering—fit to fall to pieces. Then they removed him from the cold water until he warmed up, repeating the procedure quite often.

They prepared a dugout canoe in which they placed the boy for more extended treatment. After procuring all kinds of herbs from local trees and native shrubs, they pounded the herbs in wooden vessels called *umete* and added them to the canoe. The natives told me that the patient underwent excruciating pain for a considerable time before he was taken out of the mess of pottage. That treatment may have been excellent for bad bruises—it produces a quick healing process—but it is not very useful to set broken bones.

Witch doctors still existed in the islands, but on a diminishing scale. I had forbidden our native Saints to consult them, although one or two still did from time to time. They had a little success through autosuggestion, but none of their cures were of a lasting nature—or none that I was able to ascertain.

Many years ago, in the islands of the Pacific, a group of our priesthood was trying to express the gifts of the Spirit based on statements found in the Scriptures, such as "and if they drink any deadly thing, it shall not hurt them" (Mark 16:18). RLDS Church authorities adamantly discouraged them. Their words must have been very severe, because the practice died out—but so did the outpouring of the spiritual gifts. For many years following that, there was no manifestation of prophesy or tongues or the other gifts, as far as I could ascertain. I felt that the gifts should be used as God intended, but they should not be abused.

One Sunday morning after hurrying back from another branch, I arrived on my bicycle at Tarona and went inside. I noticed a number of young men seated on the front row, and I thought that was unusual. Then the Spirit came over me and told me that the men were there for a purpose and that I was to tell them of their future in the priesthood. Brother John Mervin was in charge, and I prayed that he would of his own accord invite me to speak. He did, which helped confirm to me that what I had received was truly from God. I spoke under the inspiration of the Holy Spirit and told the men that they were to be called to the priesthood—but when, how, and to what office would depend on their lives. A really beautiful spirit was present through the whole meeting. I knew then that the withholding of the spiritual gifts was over, and they could again be used—with discrimination. Subsequently, all of those young men were ordained except one, who was killed when he fell out of a breadfruit tree.

One day while I was working in the yard at Tarona, a young lad ran up and handed me a crumpled piece of paper. In the Tahitian language was written "*Haere mai, haavitiviti, Tu*" ("Come quickly, Tu"). Tu Bellais was a priesthood member whose wife fought bitterly against his attending church. There was no other white missionary there, so I changed clothes and hurried to his place by myself.

As I was going up the stairs, the Spirit of the Lord came over me; I knew that Tu's wife was possessed of an evil spirit. She was lying in the middle of the floor, thrashing around and frothing at the mouth. I laid my hands upon her and in the name of Jesus Christ bade the evil spirit come out of her and trouble her no more. Immediately all of her gyrations ceased, and she became calm. After that experience, she could not get to church quickly enough. Praise be to the Lord, from Whom all blessings flow!

☼ ☼ ☼

Another very interesting event in my life occurred in two parts, separated by decades. In 1948, during the Arab-Israeli war, Gwen and I were in Tahiti listening to Radio Australia via short wave. Then an announcer interrupted the broadcast and said, "We have an odd report that an apparition appeared in the sky over the Israeli forces. The Arabs, who were poised with a great tank army, were stricken with fear; many of them turned and ran. It appears the Israelis are winning the conflict." It was only a brief statement, but both of us heard it.

We heard no word of it from Tahitian sources, and Mother said it was not in the Aussie newspapers. That word *apparition* likely frightened the authorities, so they hushed it up—people are not inclined to believe in apparitions. But the Israelis did win that particular battle and eventually secured liberty for the state of Israel.[1]

The missionary life was an interesting one. We had spent three years and almost six months in the islands by that time and had witnessed many marvelous experiences—

---

[1] Many years later, when I was in South Carolina holding a cottage meeting, I recounted this incident to an Israeli who was present. When I finished, he said, "Mr. Sorensen, that is true. I was an Israeli soldier there." Goosebumps came over me—here was something I had heard back in 1948 with no confirmation, now being confirmed by an eyewitness. He said, "Not many of the Israelis saw it, but the Arabs did." It was in the form of a man in the sky, with a flaming fire around him, certainly an apparition. It was about 4 o'clock in the morning. The Egyptians, who were a superstitious people, were putting on their boots and getting ready for their big daylight battle. Many of them just dropped their boots and ran.

I thought of the statement in Doctrine and Covenants 7:2, where the Lord tells that John the Beloved would stay on the earth and do "a greater work yet among men." He said, "I will make him as flaming fire,...he shall minister for those who shall be heirs of salvation." The Jews are the heirs of salvation. The gospel was sent to them, and the whole of the history of the world has been modified and brought about by the Jews. I believe that the apparition with flaming fire was an actual fulfillment of the Lord's prophecy.

and some trying ones, such as the following:

Two men from an outlying island came into my office one day. They were both elders in the church, but they would not talk to each other. I let them sit in my office and took no notice of them for awhile, letting them glare at each other. Then I spoke to the men, giving them a real lecture before I listened to what they had to say. Their argument was over the fruit of a coconut palm. One claimed that because the root was in his ground, the nuts belonged to him. The other claimed that because the nuts fell on his ground, they belonged to him. Evidently the boundary line went right past the tree.

I felt like some great judge. I asked them, "Have you brethren ever thought of the Christ-like thing to do? Why doesn't one man take the coconuts for one year, and the other man for the other year? Then your problem is solved." That had not occurred to them before. Looking at each other, they burst into tears, hugged, and asked for forgiveness.

On December 23, Eddie, Lilly Raye, and Gary Butterworth finally arrived in Tahiti by airplane. We had tried for months to persuade the French government to grant them visas. Although by the end of 1948, we succeeded in getting theirs, we were still trying to obtain visas for the family waiting in the U.S.A. to replace us.

Eddie managed to get a number of things for the mission from the bishop, including a station wagon, a washing machine, a tape recorder, two refrigerators, and some band instruments. Some other items had been refused; we were fortunate to get what we did.

In early 1949, our family and about 50 members of our congregation left on the schooner *Denise* for the dedication of our church on the island of Tubuai. As was the custom, after we left the wharf at Papeete, Horahitu began praying for the Lord to guide and protect us on the voyage. When

Brother Horahitu (who was known for his lengthy prayers) finished and we all opened our eyes, we were surprised to find that we were back at the wharf! The schooner had returned because someone had forgotten something. Horahitu did not have to pray again when we finally departed, but the natives did sing their customary plaintive song of voyaging on the sea.

After a voyage of a few days, we arrived at Tubuai. Our church building was dedicated in a special service, following which we had a typical Tahitian feast and fellowship. As part of the activities, the natives reenacted the arrival of Addison Pratt in 1844 and the first baptism in Tahiti. It was a wonderful spiritual experience for all, especially for those isolated church members.

Allen and Jane Breckenridge arrived as our replacements in January, 1949. For a couple of months three missionary families were working side by side in Tahiti.

We finally received our instructions to go to Australia. But our church leaders fully expected us to return to Tahiti within a few years for another missionary assignment.

▾ Vivian and Beth in 1946

▾ At Tarona church, 1948

▲ Church compound at Tarona, near Papeete, Tahiti, with mission house at the right of the church

▼ Gwen and Beth in the doorway of the mission house

▲ Typical native hut

► Native climbing for coconuts

▼ Black sand beaches of Tahiti

▲ On the set of the church history play (left to right): John Mervin, Eddie and Lilly Raye Butterworth, Gwen, Emere Mervin, two other Tahitian women, and Vivian

▼ Native schooners used for traveling between the islands

▲ Vivian with Beth and Marvia in 1947

▲ Chinese Saints outside the Tarona church

▼ The raft *Kon-Tiki* in French Polynesia, August, 1947

▲ Mourning shelter built over a grave

▼ Mountains of Tahiti

▼ Missionaries to Tahiti in the 1940s: Allen Breckenridge, J. Charles May, and Eddie Butterworth

CHAPTER 4

Missionary Furlough to Australia

The Tahitian Saints really know how to say good-bye! Just before we left the islands in March, 1949, they had a big send-off for us. Various groups and classes of the church school sang songs to the accompaniment of guitars, and they showered us with souvenirs and gifts. Those who saw us off at the wharf presented the traditional flower and shell *heis* and a kiss on each cheek.

Our family set off from Tahiti to Fiji in a Catalina flying boat. A very heavy wind the previous night had blown the waves of the ocean. They were breaking over the reef, causing quite a swell in the harbor. The plane was loaded with 12 passengers and quite a bit of freight. Each time we taxied forward to get up speed, we hit a swell and slowed down. The reef was precariously close, and our prayers went up with a vengeance. Just at the last minute the plane gained enough speed to lift off and clear the reef—I do not know how much clearance we had, but it seemed to be by a hair's breadth! Thanks be to God, we had made it!

Our first landing was at Rarotonga, which is one of the Cook Islands. It is a mountainous island like Tahiti. As we were coming toward Rarotonga, I noticed a green wet spot on the wing that was getting bigger and bigger. I said to

Gwen, "It looks as though they've got a petrol leak." After I said it, I realized that it might have been the wrong thing to say while we were up in that contraption with our children!

The first thing I noticed after we landed was that the ground crew brought out a tall stepladder. A crewman told us to disembark and wait in the small terminal building, as there would be a delay. I watched the crewmen pull the cowling cover off, get some wrenches, and go to work.

When they had finished, I asked the pilot, "Did you have a petrol leak there?"

The pilot looked at me and said, "You know too much to be flying in these things!"

However, all was well. We made it to Fiji, landing in Suva Bay. Then we took a bus to Nandi International Airport at the other end of the island. We saw an unusually large number of dry creek beds for an island with high rainfall. The bus driver explained, "Those dry-looking beds are very, very treacherous. You might be driving along, and all of sudden a wall of water will come down the creek from a heavy rainfall in the mountains. Many vehicles have been caught in that and washed away."

We boarded the four-engine DC-6 and set off for Sydney, Australia. Along the way we struck some very bad turbulence and were a bit concerned. But some Fijians, flying for the first time, were scared stiff we could see only the whites of their eyes!

They did not have airport radar systems in those days, and the Sydney airport was completely clouded in. That was great news to us because we were diverted to Brisbane, which was where we really wanted to go. We arrived in Brisbane about 2 o'clock in the morning, got a taxi, and headed to the home of my parents. It gave them the surprise of their lives to see us arriving from Tahiti when they expected us from Sydney a couple of days later. But it shows how we were again blessed.

It was a real thrill to be back among English-speaking people, as well as reuniting with our families and church friends from the branch. Our parents were especially happy to see their two granddaughters again.

One thing that really struck us about Brisbane was the change from wartime to peacetime. Gone were the Americans and the thousands of men and women in uniform that had been so common when we had left in 1944. Rationing was also a thing of the past—even gasoline for private vehicles was readily available.

The church had assigned me to Queensland, so we were able to live in Brisbane. My parents shared their big home with us. We had ample room there, and it helped us financially, for which we were very grateful.

Gwen had been teaching Beth some basics in education while we were in Tahiti, but that was not nearly the same as attending school with other children her age. Beth started her first formal education while we were in Australia. She really enjoyed the experience and did very well there.

With our own money, we bought an old four-cylinder Chevrolet in good running order. I believe I was the first RLDS missionary in Australia with a car to help me with my work. That enabled me to cover much more territory in the area, which encompassed several towns. There was only one branch at that time—our home branch, Buranda—but there were many scattered groups of Saints, some 100 miles away. Public transportation was not only costly but slow, so we felt having the car really was justified.

Quite a number of interesting things happened in our two-and-a-half-year "working furlough" in Australia before we went back to the islands. I traveled as far afield as Kingaroy, Dalby, Windsor, Lota, Toowoomba, and even Murwillumbah in New South Wales to minister to the

Saints. I preached, performed administrations, and held many cottage meetings. I also shared slides of Tahiti with the Saints, which was something out of the ordinary for them and was of great interest.

A man named John Heiner had an inspiring story. He had belonged to another church, which had pulled him out of the gutter. He had accepted Christ and cast his sins aside. When he heard the greater gospel—the wonderful gospel of the Restoration—he believed it to be true and was baptized. He was so thrilled with the fullness of the everlasting gospel, the Book of Mormon, and latter-day revelation that he was determined to share it with as many people as he possibly could. He did not care where he met them or who they were. If there was the slightest chance, he "gave them the gospel," as he used to say.

When Brother Heiner traveled to work on a streetcar, he would look for a vacant seat beside another person. He then sat down and started up a conversation. He often asked those he met if they knew about the two houses of Israel. They usually look puzzled, and some would try to brush him off. But undaunted, he kept asking them quietly and nicely. If they showed any interest, he then told them about the house of Judah and the house of Joseph and the two books: the Bible (the stick of Judah) and the Book of Mormon (the stick of Joseph).

Brother Heiner was the supervisor of a very large powerhouse extension in the city, and his boss was a Roman Catholic. One day John made an appointment with him on his lunch hour. He later told me, "I gave him the gospel." He made many friends and interested so many of them in the church that he kept me busy with cottage meetings while I was in Brisbane. Several people were baptized as a result of his sharing the gospel.

I have mentioned the beautiful Tiona Reunion Grounds in Australia, situated about 150 miles north of Sydney on the shore of the Pacific Ocean. The RLDS Church bought the land many years ago. Tiona is on a stretch of land only a few hundred yards long, with the ocean on one side and lovely Lake Wallis on the other. At one end of the beach close to Tiona was a large headland called Booti Booti, hundreds of feet high.

The rich land at Tiona supported groves of cabbage tree palms. Some of them must have been 80 or 90 feet high. The early Saints saw the beautiful place, thought how perfect it was, and named it Tiona (the Tahitian word for Zion), expecting that there the people would be taught to live in love and harmony and serve the Lord Almighty. It has been and always will be a sacred spot to me.

When one climbed up Booti Booti and looked out for miles over the lovely panorama, it was really breathtaking. The beach extended for about nine miles from Booti Booti. I have baptized many people in Lake Wallis, which was very shallow near the shore. We had to walk out about 50 yards to have water deep enough for baptisms.

At Tiona was located the Green Cathedral, the "brainchild" of Apostle George Mesley. It was a lovely open-air cathedral among the palms. Trees formed a natural arch at the front of it so we could look out through the arch and see beautiful Lake Wallis and the low hills across the lake. We saw some gorgeous colors in the sky during reunions when we had "Sunset Reflections"—services of hymns and worship, with the sun setting behind the far hills and reflecting on the lake. The view filled us with awe for God in all His majesty.

In the days when we first went to Tiona, we met in a large tent, the "Mission Tent." The people lived in tents, and most of them did their own cooking. Things changed over the years; the tents generally gave way to cabins and a large dining hall. One upsetting change was that the dirt road through the property was converted into a paved road during the 1960s. Then we had to be extremely careful when going to and from the beach and camping area, since traffic was sometimes heavy on the road.

Part of my assignment while we were in Australia was to preach and teach at two reunions held at Tiona. I shared some of our experiences from Tahiti, which were of great interest to the Saints. Gwen taught some Tahitian songs to the children, which they enjoyed very much.

☼ ☼ ☼

Apostle Roscoe Davey asked me to visit the Saints in Western Australia, so I arranged for a 3,000-mile train trip to Perth. The first day from Brisbane to Sydney (600 miles) was uneventful. The next evening I boarded the *Spirit of Progress*, Australia's "posh" new train, for Melbourne. That was the first view I had of that fair city. I left the following evening for Adelaide, another first for me. After leaving Adelaide, the train moved west to Port Pirie and Port Augusta, two modern industrial cities. We later had to change trains because of the different rail gauges in South Australia and Western Australia (the distance between rails drops from 5' 2" to 4' 8½").

That portion of the journey was very interesting. For 1,000 miles we crossed the treeless Nullabor Plain. The desert was inhabited only by nomadic aborigines, many of whom lived in holes scooped in the sand to protect them from the winds, which could be severe at times. With temperatures of 100° F or higher, it must have been difficult to exist. They needed no roofs because it rained only about once every five years. The rain was probably the only bath they had, since water was at a premium. Their drinking water and food were provided by the trains, which ran about three times per week.

Whenever the train stopped to replenish the boiler water, which was fairly often, the aborigines swarmed around and begged from the passengers. One American said to me, "You Australians should be ashamed of yourselves for not taking better care of these poor people." (Of course, he failed to mention how the American Indians were being treated by his people.) The truth of it was that the aborigines were satisfied with their lives and would not accept any long-term help. They made many boomerangs and a few other artifacts, which they sold to the passengers, and were expert at throwing the boomerangs for plugs of tobacco.

We duly arrived at Kalgoolie, "city of the golden mile," where famous gold mines were dotted all around. I was spellbound at one, where I looked at hundreds of gold bars, worth millions of dollars. We stayed for a few hours and then headed for Perth, arriving there the next morning.

The pastor met me; and we went to his home, where I stayed for three weeks. To announce my preaching series, I had brought a lot of circulars to distribute in the district surrounding the church. We invited many people to attend the special services. Unfortunately, not many nonmembers responded.

A very beautiful experience was associated with my ministry in Perth. A charming young lady was enamored with a married man and was determined to marry him as soon as his divorce would allow it. Her parents, who were strong church members, were naturally distressed. They sought my help, and I made it a matter of prayer.

One morning about 4 o'clock, I was awakened by the Spirit and told to write a message for that young lady. I immediately did so but realized that she would not receive a direct approach without the Spirit's help. I asked the Lord to open the way and soften her heart so I could inform her of the message, and He helped me. Each Saturday morning she walked across the park to catch a train. One day I followed her until we reached the center of the park, which was deserted. I asked her to give me a minute, and she hesitantly did.

She said, "I want no sermon from you." I reached into my pocket, produced the document, and read it to her. The message was very explicit and yet very kind. After I read it, she said, "Show me that." I refused, telling her that she now knew God's will for her. I returned home to Brisbane soon after that.[1]

☼ ☼ ☼

Our long-awaited son, Trevor Charles, was born in Brisbane on June 6, 1951. My father was so proud and happy that he walked around with a big smile on his face all that day—not even speaking a word. Trevor was the only male of his generation to whom we could pass on the Sorensen name in the branch of our family which had arrived from Denmark during the last century.

Thus Beth and Trevor were both born in Brisbane, but

---

[1] Many years later I attended a mission conference in Sydney and was pleased to see the lady's parents. I asked them how she was faring. They replied with great joy that she had come to the conference and had a lot to tell me.

The lady greeted me with, "Brother Sorensen, thank you for saving my life!" What joy filled my soul! She said that when I had left her in the park, she was extremely angry. However, the good Spirit later rested upon her, and she knew that God would be victorious. She was later happily married to someone else. Praise be to God!

Marvia was our precious souvenir from Tahiti. The girls were thrilled to have a baby brother, and they both adored him. Trevor was blessed in the Buranda Branch in Brisbane by his maternal grandfather, Elder N. W. Peisker, and Elder Joseph Edgeworth.

☼ ☼ ☼

The time came for us to go back to the islands. The end of October a freighter called the *Chung King* was leaving for France via Tahiti. We packed our goods and chattels, including a case of powdered milk.

On Beth's last day of school before we left Australia, she took her little sister Marvia with her. Thus Marvia had the experience of a formal school setting, even if it was for only one day. We arranged with the Queensland Correspondence School to provide lessons for Gwen to use in homeschooling our girls when we returned to Tahiti. The girls would do the lessons provided, and we were to mail them back to Australia to be graded.

We said our fond farewells to family members and friends in Brisbane. It was hard to say good-bye to loved ones, and it was especially hard for them to say good-bye to the grandchildren. We did not realize at the time that it would be nine years before we would see each other again.

Arriving by train in Sydney, we stayed with Saints for a few days to await the sailing of our ship. I preached at the old Balmain church on Sunday night, after which the Saints gave us a farewell.

The next night we boarded the *Chung King*, traveling third class to save the church some money. We occupied a six-berth cabin, which was very plain but adequate. At least the whole family could be together. It was not too bad a ship to travel on; but it had French cuisine, to which we were not accustomed at all. In fact, in one letter to my parents, I wrote that a "high-smelling cheese just about drove us out of the dining room." We survived somehow until we finally arrived in Tahiti. The deck of the ship was quite spacious; since there were very few passengers, our children had a lovely playing area.

A few days out of Sydney, we arrived at Noumea in New Caledonia. The ship spent several days there loading nickel and copra. We went ashore, where we found the streets were a mass of red blooms from the beautiful poinciana trees. Beth celebrated her eighth birthday there.

At that time we did not have a church in Noumea, but one was established a few years later, mainly by Tahitians who migrated there to work in the nickel mines. On a hill we saw a church building, which had been built especially for the American armed forces. It showed how much the Americans appreciated their freedom to worship God during the war days. After the ship was loaded, we departed for Port Villa in the New Hebrides.

Sister Nettie Frater had lived in the New Hebrides, where her father had been a missionary of the Presbyterian Church. She later joined our church and was living in Sydney. Before we left Australia, she gave me a letter of introduction to the Presbyterian doctor in charge of the main hospital on the island. After we cast anchor at Port Villa and I was about to go ashore, a man approached and asked if my name was Sorensen. He was the doctor. Nettie had also written to him, and he saw my name on the ship's manifest—along with my profession as a missionary. He asked me which church I represented. As soon as I told him, his face froze. He never said another word to me—he just turned around and walked away. Sometimes the moment the name "Latter Day Saints" was mentioned, that was the death knell. It is incredible the amount of religious bigotry that I have encountered.

On that island we had to be very careful because of malaria. In the evening and nighttime we stayed aboard the ship because the mosquito that carried malaria came out at night. During the daytime we got in the ship's boat or sometimes in big native canoes to go to the island and various places in the big lagoon. We really enjoyed it.

Finally the ship was loaded with copra and headed for Tahiti, arriving there at the end of November, 1951. The native Saints were overjoyed to see us returning to live and work with them. They were apparently very happy with the spiritual ministry we had given them. I imagine they were also glad to see me because I could repair their radios and machines!

▾ View of Tiona—the narrow land between Lake Wallis (left) and the Pacific Ocean (right)—as seen from Booti Booti

▲ Beautiful Green Cathedral at Tiona, looking at Lake Wallis

▼ Buranda congregation, Brisbane—Sorensens' home branch

▲ Beth and Marvia on the Sorensen car in Brisbane, 1950

▼ Beth and Marvia on Marvia's first day of formal school, 1951

▼ Vivian in Perth during 1950 missionary trip to Western Australia

▲ Vivian and Gwen with Beth, Marvia, and Trevor in Brisbane, 1951

▼ Gwen and children aboard the *Chung King*, late 1951

CHAPTER 5

Our Return to Tahiti

After arriving in Tahiti in November, 1951, I was again elected branch president of Tarona. Allen Breckenridge also put me in charge of all missionary work in Tahiti and Moorea, which really kept me busy. One of my first jobs was to translate study material for the church school, since Eddie and Allen had been too busy to do that while I was gone. Before leaving for Australia, I had done a lot of preaching of the gospel; and I was determined to continue that practice. I believe that the simple, basic gospel of Jesus Christ is the very key to the salvation of mankind.

Living conditions in Tahiti had improved greatly while we were gone. It was possible to buy almost everything that we could buy in Australia, even frozen lamb. Apples, grapes, and pears came in fresh on ships. However, white sugar was still being rationed when we first arrived.

The children loved the hot, tropical climate. Trevor was about five months old at the time. Marvia was almost five years old, and Beth had just turned eight. The girls soon remembered quite a bit of the Tahitian language.

I baptized Beth at 3 p.m. on Saturday, March 1, 1952, so that it would coincide exactly with the commencement of the 11 a.m. sacrament service in Brisbane on Sunday (the International Date Line separated us). As my mother and sisters were renewing their covenants, a member of another generation was making her covenant with God. The entire service was in English, and a very fine spirit prevailed throughout. It was a great pleasure indeed for me to baptize her. She was confirmed in English by Allen Breckenridge and John Mervin at the sacrament service on Sunday morning.

With a Tahitian guide, Allen and I made a couple of exploring trips into the mountains, following a winding river which we crossed many times. After a gentle climb toward the center of the island of Tahiti, we came to a lake which is called Vaiheria—the only lake in the world, I was told, which has eels with ears. The eels did not worry me, so I had a swim in the lake.

We went to another place with burial caves high on a cliff. Our guide was a descendant of the ancient people entombed there. He still lived on that property, which had been owned by his family for generations. He was not too keen about taking us up where the *tuputupua* (bad spirits) were, since the natives were quite superstitious about spirits; however, I persuaded him.

The three of us entered a cave, where I picked up a skull and gave it to Allen to hold. I also offered a skull to the native. At first he refused; but when he saw that Allen and I had suffered no ill effects from the skulls, he put out his hand. You should have seen the strange look on his face; but I explained to him that he was holding only the bones of a house (an "earthly tabernacle") where someone had once lived.

Another time one of the natives and I drove to the last village on the far end of Tahiti. There we rented an outboard canoe and made a seven-mile journey to that end of the island to view some inscribed stones. We finally came to a place where we could disembark. Two huge rocks had engravings which depicted the sun with its beams. Probably the ancestors of those people knew a form of writing, but no one seemed to know much about them. I have often wondered if the early natives worshiped the sun as did the Incas of Peru and the early Egyptians. The Tahitian word for sun is *ra*, which is the same as the Egyptian word.

At the end of May, 1952, Jane Breckenridge returned by plane to America with their children and Jeanne Mervin. Poor Allen was left alone. He went through some of the pain and loneliness that I had felt a few years earlier, except that at least he had our company. When I was alone for four months in 1947-1948, no other white missionaries from our church were there.

In August Allen and I took a two-hour trip by schooner to the neighboring island of Moorea to commence missionary work. A fine young church couple lived there. The young man had built a meeting house and a little cottage for the missionaries. We had good attendance at our meetings. We also completely encircled the island on our bicycles, doing the 37 miles in one day.

A native guide led us to an ancient drum stone, which had a small hole on the outside leading to a much larger cavity inside. When struck with a palm frond, it made quite a boom, resembling a large drum. It had undoubtedly been used by the native priests of old to assemble their people. Looking around, I discovered a huge stone, to which the natives did not pay much heed. But I immediately recognized it as a large stone altar, evidently used for sacrifices. It was almost perfectly flat on top and had a neat round hole in the center, which I imagine was used to catch the blood of the victim.

Some 200 years ago the Tahitians had practiced some human sacrifice, such as offering a chief taken captive in battle. They built structures called *marae*, which were sacred and taboo, except for the priests and others who had the right to go there. We saw the remains of quite a few of them around Tahiti and Moorea. At one *marae* on Moorea there was an interesting stone called *ofai taio* or "counting stone." It lay flat on the ground and had numerous small holes in its surface. From legend, it seems that captured enemy warriors were forced to count all the holes in one breath or they were put to death. I can believe that not many survived!

Some of the ancient customs of the Tahitians were quite barbaric; others were much more gentle. All the barbaric customs have been stopped; and the gentle ones have been fostered as much as they were in harmony with the laws of God. The Tahitians were very religious people. When converted to Christ, they attended church regularly and worshiped genuinely.

The story of the *Mutiny on the Bounty* came alive for us in Tahiti. One day in a bank in Papeete, a Miss Adams, who spoke very good English, attended to my needs. She was from Pitcairn Island and a direct descendant of the mutineer Adams and his native wife. On Tubuai we saw the remains of the deep ditches that the mutineers had dug when defending themselves from the natives. The Englishmen had sailed there to steal some of the Tahitian women for wives.

I met an old Tahitian lady who had been present around 1900, when Sister Emma Burton spoke in perfect Tahitian to a women's class. Many of the native women at the turn of the century had been practicing an early custom of forcing their girls to know a man—in the Biblical sense—at the time of puberty. Sister Burton felt the responsibility to explain to the natives why the practice was wrong, but she had never learned the language properly because she was deaf. In faith, she asked the Lord to give her the gift of tongues for that one occasion.

The old Tahitian lady, who had been only a young girl at the time, wept with emotion when she told me that Sister Burton spoke in perfect Tahitian—better than the natives did themselves. Sister Burton explained that God was not pleased with the custom. Because of the power of the Spirit in the gift of tongues from a woman they knew could not speak their language, the women believed the admonition and stopped the practice. The power of God again worked for the salvation of those people.

Not long after we returned to Tahiti, I taught Gwen to drive. When she felt confident enough to take the test, we went to the French gendarme office and made application. The officer took us for a driving test, letting me sit in the back seat. He had Gwen drive through the narrow streets of the town. It started to rain. Suddenly a little native girl pulled a raincoat over her head and dashed across the street, right in front of us. Gwen gave those brakes everything they had! She almost put the French officer through the windshield and me under the front seat! He lowered the window and really bawled that girl out in French. He told Gwen, "Well, madame, you've satisfied me." Then he gave her a license.[1]

When we traveled from one island to another, the native schooners carried plenty of tropical fruits and fresh meat.

---

[1] In 1982 Gwen and I were in Tahiti and were offered the use of a car. We went to the police station to get a copy of my driver's license. They could not find mine, but they located Gwen's license, issued in 1952. We decided that neither of us needed the stress of driving in Tahiti because the traffic was absolutely crazy. The natives drive on their brakes and their horns!

The meat had to be consumed by the time the ice melted, or it would go bad. The next several days' menus included "bully beef," which was salted with saltpeter and preserved in cans. Most of it was imported from Australia. It was quite salty but good to eat. Into a big pot the cook dumped cans of the beef and a lot of rice and onions. The first few times I ate it, I enjoyed it very much. But when we got it day after day after day on a long trip to some of the far-away islands, it became quite monotonous.

The crews were always looking for fresh fish. Sometimes we saw large flocks of sea birds circling around and knew that they had located a school of little fish. The big bonito and tuna fed on the little fish also. We then headed for the flock of birds, trailing a lure or two behind the boat. Sure enough, we nearly always caught a couple of the big tuna, bonito, or other kinds of fish. That was a very welcome change from the bully beef and onion hash.

When the native members of our church went from one island to another, especially if quite a few went, they traveled on schooners. They offered a prayer when they left the wharf, asking the Lord to protect them on their journey. They sang and attended to their various duties on the schooner until sunset; then they had supper and a period of singing and a prayer, thanking God for the safe voyage. They also prayed for protection during the night because they said, "The night doesn't have eyes of its own, and the darkness is often much harder to cope with than the sunlight."

The Saints sang beautiful hymns in the morning and asked God's protection for that day. One of the special hymns was about the trackless ocean and the boat that did not have eyes of its own; so when they set sail, they asked the Great Pilot to guide them. Some of those beautiful old customs have died out because of the innovation of modern means of travel. Members of other churches did not practice such lovely customs, but they often joined the Saints in prayers and singing when they traveled with them.

Tahitians were absolutely wonderful singers and harmonizers, and they were very quick to learn tunes. When a song pleased them a lot at special services and events, they brought money forward as an offering that the song might be sung again. When we went to another island for a district conference, mission conference, or the dedication of a church building, we often had all our regular services during the first couple of days. On the last evening some of the native Saints often came to me and said, "*Faaao*," which means, "Can we sing till morning?"

We generally gave them the privilege because they loved to sing and strum their guitars. They drank black coffee to keep themselves awake and sang all the night through. I generally gave up by about 1:30 or 2 in the morning and went to bed. Once I went through the entire night with them—but never again!

There is little doubt in my mind but that the Hawaiians and the Tahitians, Samoans, Rarotongans, and Maoris are all Polynesians. Their languages are very similar—as are many of their customs. The missionaries have tried to teach the natives right from wrong; and the Lord has surely helped us produce some good-living, kind-hearted, God-fearing Saints.

Allen Breckenridge and I were led to what the natives called *ofai faanauraa* or "birth stone." Before the white man came to the islands, the native women went to the stone at the head of a beautiful valley to bear their children. It must have been quite difficult for pregnant women to climb there. After a baby was born and the mother's strength returned somewhat, she climbed farther and finally arrived at the *anapahu* or "drum cave." That small cave in the hill was somehow linked by a natural tunnel to the foothills. The mother shouted into the cave, and her voice could be heard in the village below. Then friends and relatives wended their way up to see if she had a man-child or female child and to assist them home.

Many Tahitian women still gave birth in a sitting position. It seems that a similar situation existed in Hawaii on the island of Oahu. Right in the center of Oahu are a lot of stones shaped like big chairs, which the Hawaiians call "birthing stones."

On one occasion, a native and I were sitting in my office in Tahiti. All of a sudden, we saw an apparition coming toward us—but his face, his hands, and practically all of him were as black as ink! It was Trevor, who had taken the black ink for the mimeograph machine and plastered it all over his head and hair. We burst out laughing—we couldn't help it! His poor mother had to clean it all up, but eventually she saw the humorous side of it and started laughing. Trevor, realizing something was funny, started to laugh, too.

Another time, Marvia had been told to put the syrup and Vegemite in the refrigerator; and she had not done it. As I was sitting in the office, I noticed that our son was very quiet. I went to the kitchen and found that he had syrup and Vegemite all over himself and everywhere else. We tried to point out to Trevor that you do not smear the stuff all over you, but he was still a bit young to understand.

On New Year's Day of 1953 I was reelected the branch pastor and treasurer of Tarona until the new missionary arrived from the United States. I hoped to be able to turn those positions over to him so that I could concentrate on the missionary work.

In January we experienced a very strong gale, which almost demolished our meeting house. If some of our Saints had not tied the building down with ropes, it would have "wafted into space" (as I wrote in a letter to my mother). The rafters were broken in many places, and we had to demolish a part of the building. However, that destruction was really a godsend. We had planned to construct a new *fareputuputuraa* (meeting house) almost immediately; and we would have had trouble with the natives if we had razed the old one, because it was still usable.

Our entire family was involved with the mission. Our daughter Beth, who at that time was nine years old, often went to a native's place near the local movie theater. There she sold nuts that grew in our yard to the gathering children for five francs a bunch. She put any money she collected into the mission funds.

Gwen and I had a rather unique experience after a native schooner, the *Rosita*, had been caught in some bad gales. It had been missing for more than a month, and we prayed regularly for the crew's safety. One evening we were with the Mervins in the country. As dusk was deepening, Gwen and I observed a schooner with two masts and full sail on a beautiful calm sea. We told Brother Mervin, but neither he nor his wife could see it. I said to Gwen, "You wait and see. That is the *Rosita*—not in reality but in vision—and it will be found soon." She agreed. Two days later we all heard the glad news that the *Rosita* had been found and all aboard were safe!

I completed a second series of lectures in Tahiti with excellent attendance and interest. Old Horahitu said that the very trees under which I preached will bear witness at the day of judgment that the gospel of Jesus Christ was preached to the people in that district. It was a wonderful experience to be preaching in the open in the soft Tahitian night with the beautiful stars and full moon above—something not easily forgotten.

☼ ☼ ☼

Patriarchal blessings can be a tremendous help to a person, especially a missionary. Because I was told in my blessing that I would live long to serve God, I have had faith that I would be spared through whatever conditions of life I might meet. Even when I had to travel from island to island in little motorboats, I never really feared but that I would arrive at my destination safely.

Because I wanted to visit the island of Hereheretue, where the Saints had not seen a white missionary for many years, I sought passage on a small boat. Before we left Papeete, I had heard rumors that the owner was going to set fire to his boat to get the insurance money. I knew he would not destroy himself, and I had faith that he would not harm me—so I set sail with him. When we reached the island of Anaa, the crew put me ashore and said that was as far as they would take me. Out of sight of land, they really did set the boat on fire. Then they rowed back to the island in a lifeboat. I eventually reached Hereheretue. The owner's scheme was made known to the authorities, and he and the crew were later imprisoned.

In March I set off for my missionary journey to the islands. My final destination was the pearl-diving island of Hikueru in the Tuamotu Islands. It took six days to get there. We lived on a diet of bully beef, rice, and fish while on the schooner. First we visited the island of Niau, a small atoll inhabited by many Saints and a few Catholics. I spent a few hours with the natives, who had constructed a two-story church building.

Next we landed on the island of Anaa. I went ashore and met with the one RLDS family living there. Many years ago all the people on that island were church members, but they gradually left Anaa until only the one family remained. Because most of the other inhabitants indulged in alcohol, they were poor and their houses anything but inviting. Our church family had the one nice house besides that of the chief.

We then sailed to Motutunga, which was an uninhabited island except during pearl-diving seasons. Maru, the native elder accompanying me, and I went ashore to fish. The Tuamotu Islands abounded with fish of all colors and description, and they were very easy to catch. In no time we had all the fish we could eat. Maru roasted the fish on the beach, and we ate them with our fingers.

Finally we arrived at Hikueru, the main pearl-diving island of the group. Each evening, on a vacant lot right in the center of the village, I preached to almost all the inhabitants of the island. They were thrilled; they said that was how Jesus preached to the multitudes—out in the open. Some of the natives requested baptism. One of the Mormons was so pleased with my preaching that he gave me several small pearls for our children.

I went diving twice and managed to get some pearl shells in the shallower parts of the lagoon. Through a glass-bottomed box, I took color movies of the process, which turned out very well. The colored corals and fish were simply magnificent and could hold my attention for hours.

While at Hikueru, I helped one of our carpenters build a new church. I made a circular saw machine, which also cut mortises. It was a great help on many of the church buildings.

What I am about to relate is not from personal experience, except for the interview with a man who was present. He was an old man when I was in Tahiti. In 1903 he had been on the island of Hikueru. One of the elders of our church had prophesied that a terrible hurricane was coming and that the people should stay at the little village, where the ground was higher. But many of the natives who were not of our church—and a few who were—took no notice of him. They went down to the low ground as usual. The frightful hurricane struck as predicted, and the waves became higher and higher. They came over the reef, leveled the coconut palms, and swept people away.

The man and his twin children reached the trunk of a big, strong coconut palm. He tried to tie himself and the twins to it, but a big wave crashed over them and pulled the twins out of his grasp. He saw them being swept away in the terrible waves and current. Since his coconut trunk remained firm, he was one of the few survivors.

I understood that one of our missionaries—Brother J. W. Gilbert—was on the island at the time; and he helped the natives by improvising a still out of some old bed iron and things they found. They collected dry coconut palms, made a fire, boiled seawater, and condensed the steam. In that way they made drinking water for quite some time until a French schooner arrived. Through his ingenuity, the missionary helped save the lives of many people.

For the trip back to Tahiti, I traveled on a different ship —one owned by the Mormons. It took only two days to sail back. I was grateful for the shortness of the trip and the excellent food provided. God certainly used the Mormons at that time for the welfare of His servant.

It was good to get home to my family. Leaving them was the only part I did not like about going on those missionary trips. However, the Lord said that he who is not willing to forsake others for His sake is not worthy to be called His servant.

In May, 1953, the new missionary and his family arrived from the U.S. Alan Tyree was a tall, slim ginger-haired young man. His wife Gladys, a recent convert to the church, was a petite, fair-haired woman. They had a three-month-old baby named Larry. Alan was full of knowledge and new ideas, but it hand not been gained through experience. They had some difficulty adjusting to life in Tahiti after what they were used to in America, even though living conditions were much better than when we had first arrived in 1945.

It was a relief to me for Alan to become pastor and take the load of the Tarona Branch off my hands. Gladys took over the music work for the mission. She and Gwen got along well together.

Shortly thereafter, Alan and I held a missionary series on the far side of Tahiti. He played his saxophone to teach the hymns. We had good attendance at the series. The gospel had never been preached at that place before, and it was a revelation to those people. I was thankful that I had the opportunity to take the everlasting gospel before those native Tahitians. They were a very kind people, and I enjoyed teaching them the wonderful words of life. Whoever would have thought that shy little Vivian would have hundreds of natives on the islands listening to him?

We also asked some converted Protestants to bear their testimonies each night. Two native Protestant ministers kept their members from attending. I "took the bull by the horns" and paid them a visit, asking why they prevented their people from attending. They could not answer my questions or charges, especially when I said they were taking away the liberty of their people.

An electronic reed organ that the bishop sent us arrived from the U.S. It was rather badly damaged, but Alan and I repaired it. It played well and really thrilled the natives. I requested that the bishopric use some of the money that was allotted for our new house to buy more portable organs for our branches on the outlying islands. The poor members there were very good about paying their tithing, but they received only a minimum of help from the RLDS Church because of their isolation. The bishop ordered more organs, and the natives were thrilled when they arrived.

In June we started building the new mission home, which was really a one-story duplex that would house the Tyrees and us. The men who built it were church members. Since they worked for reduced wages, I hoped that we would not spend all of the $25,000 that the General Conference had allotted for the construction. I directed the work, which increased my burden; but Alan was learning the language quickly and was able to take increasingly more responsibility. Besides supervising the workers, I also drove the truck to get the sand, gravel, and stones used in the construction. Our two-year-old Trevor often accompanied us in the truck.

The construction progressed quite well. I made a compressed air gun to fill the gaps between the bricks with cement plaster. The first time I used it, I had too much pressure—it blew cement all over me, to the amusement of the natives! They were amazed at all the gadgets I made—especially when they worked properly!

For recreation I sometimes went fishing on Saturday afternoon with the workmen and became quite an expert at catching the fish with a speargun. I made the gun and also a respirator, which enabled me to stay in the shallow water of the lagoons for long periods without coming up for air. It was a fine form of recreation, and the men really loved it. It also provided nice meals of fresh fish. One of our natives speared a huge 130-pound fish. He gave us some of it to eat, and it was delicious—not at all coarse or tough.

Trevor soon became very excited about fish and loved to collect little ones he called "teetee fish." It was quite a nuisance for the men to catch and keep those little fish for him, but they were happy to do so. Trevor carried them around on a string, showing them off until they started to stink. Then we had to dispose of them.

At the end of October, I took the family with me to the mission conference on the island of Apataki. We traveled from Papeete on a nice, clean schooner. After about a 32-hour voyage we arrived at Apataki.

I had a tremendous responsibility at the conference with organizing, teaching, and preaching each night. It pleased me to baptize three people into the church. One young married lady was converted as a result of an earlier missionary series in Tahiti. The deacons constructed a sheepfold at the water's edge; and I had a "shepherd" lead the candidates through the gate while someone read Chapter 10 of John. After I baptized them, they left the water on "a straight and narrow path" that we had constructed. Thus they were led into the assembly of the Saints, who were standing on a slight rise near the edge of the water. The Catholics present were greatly impressed with the significance of the ordinance; therefore much good was done for the church.

Gwen lectured the women very capably and also played a portable organ for the services. When amplified, the instrument sounded like a large electric organ—much to the delight of the natives. I had a fine degree of the Spirit and was used to admonish the people on more than one occasion. Unfortunately we could not stay longer because I had an appointment for a preaching series at Tarona. The Lord provided a ship, which called at another island for a short time and then journeyed homeward.

After we arrived back in Tahiti, I learned that Beth had mastered the art of riding my bicycle. She did so well that she was able to take Trevor and Marvia for rides around the compound. I was very surprised when I saw all three Sorensen children on the same bicycle—Beth was steering and pedaling, Trevor rode on the front, and Marvia was on the back.

☼ ☼ ☼

At the end of April, 1954, we moved into our new house. It had been a tremendous job for me to supervise and work on its construction. But at last we saw that the fruits of our labors were sweet.

About that time I also performed four marriages—all at the same time. Talk about mass production! The fruit of my labor in the missionary field was also sweet, but not to the extent I had really wished. During the previous ten months we had 105 baptisms. Our official membership in the islands was 2,333.

In May I left for a five-week journey to several of the outlying islands, some of which were the homes of church members who had not seen a missionary in 20 years. During the trip, I visited 11 islands (Niau, Fakarava, Kaukura, Manihi, Takaroa, Katiu, Makemo, Hikueru, Hao, Amanu, and Anaa), preached 20 nights in succession, baptized five people, and helped to straighten out many others who were living in sin.

July 14 is a big day for France and the Tahitians—the celebration of the fall of the Bastille in France. For two or three weeks before the event, the natives practiced beating their drums, performing native dances, and competing in all sorts of activities. For the celebration, the natives wore traditional costumes, including very beautiful grass skirts for the women and the men, too. Many came from Bora Bora and other surrounding islands. Men and women did native dances, including the hula, while the men furiously beat their drums. Many of the dances portrayed phases of their culture, such as sowing seed and reaping the harvest.

The men also placed a coconut upon a high pole and

threw spears to see how many "bull's-eyes" they could get. Other events included swimming races in the harbor and canoe races for both men and women. The canoe races—especially those with great double outrigger canoes—were really exciting to watch.

Generally the people of Tahiti were well behaved, with not much intoxication to be seen. But even for a while after the big celebration was over, the natives could still be heard banging their drums in the streets.

The church building on the island of Rangiroa had been started back in the days of Apostle Clyde Ellis, but it had never been finished. When I saw that, I thought to myself, "This is almost disgraceful!" So I rallied the natives, brought them some machinery that I had made, and started to work. I had bolted an electric motor on a 2×12 plank about 12 or 14 feet long. Where the pulley attached, I put a piece of iron out of balance, which made the plank vibrate furiously. When we used that as a vibrator on the concrete floor, the natives were spellbound. The floor finished beautifully. I felt happy about it, too, because it would have been a lot of hard work for us otherwise.

One night with a full moon, Gwen and I decided to go for a little walk in the moonlight by the seashore. It was very romantic. When we were returning, what should we see but the whole family coming to meet us. Little Trevor was in his pajamas and piped up, "Where is Daddy, and where is Mummy?" I told Gwen I guessed we would have to give up romantic moonlight walks for awhile.

Children can be so amusing with some of the things they say. One time while I was typing a letter at Rangiroa, my three-year-old son was sitting on the chair beside me. Looking at me with his big blue eyes, Trevor asked if

Jesus used a ladder to get up in the sky.

Sometimes Beth and I went spearfishing. For a 10-year-old, she did very well at handling a canoe. One day I jumped overboard and speared a large fish. Although it had the spear in it, the fish was not yet dead. Evidently it saw a shark that I did not see and swam beneath me to get away from its natural enemy. Of course, the shark smelled the blood—and he came under me, too! I thought, "Boy, it's time I got out of here!"

I broke the water and yelled to Beth. By then four or five shark fins were cutting the water all around me. The Lord must have still wanted me for a lot of work, stupid fellow that I was. I got into that canoe as quickly as I possibly could, still hanging onto my speargun with the fish on the end of the spear. It was a very tasty fish, which we all really enjoyed.

Gwen and I made a good team. I was able to minister to the spiritual needs of the native Saints, and Gwen ministered to their physical needs. Since there was no doctor on the island of Rangiroa, a woman having trouble with childbirth requested Gwen's help. Gwen was able to go and deliver the baby—one of the wonderful talents that she demonstrated to the people.

We went from Rangiroa to the neighboring island of Tikehau for a district conference. After a rough voyage, we arrived in mid-afternoon and were met by a crowd of excited natives. About an hour later, I remembered that I had left my slide projector in the captain's cabin—and his schooner was by then an hour out at sea. The natives got a speedboat, and we raced after the schooner. We finally caught up with it and retrieved the projector. I was badly burned from the sun and sea spray; Gwen said my face was like a lobster! Despite being very tired from the chase, we went straight to the church. I showed the slides and gave my talk. As usual, Gwen operated the projector for me and played the organ.

Sunday about 3 a.m. we were awakened by the natives, who were slaughtering pigs right under our window. That went on until daylight, as the natives prepared for a midday feast. Somehow we struggled through all the activities of that day—church, business meeting, slides, and lecture. That night after the lecture, the natives started on their all-night singsong, keeping themselves revived with plenty of coffee. We did not stay up for their singsong, but we still did not get much sleep because they were too close to our window.

Monday morning we packed and started off in a small outboard motorboat. About an hour into our journey over the open ocean, we discovered that the boat was leaking, so we turned back. We caught a bigger boat that left late Monday and arrived at Rangiroa on Tuesday morning.

At Rangiroa I administered to a girl who had been suffering from a concussion after a coconut fell on her head. Within about a week she had fully recovered, although she had been suffering acutely for months before. We thus saw that the Lord still works to bless those in suffering and distress when they trust Him sufficiently.

☼ ☼ ☼

Shortly after we returned to Papeete, Apostles Maurice Draper and Charles Hield arrived by airplane. They were really overwhelmed by the Tahitian welcome with *heis* around their necks and a kiss on each cheek. They brought unofficial news from the Joint Council of the RLDS Church that the Sorensens were to go to America next rather than return to Australia. We were disappointed by not going home to see our loved ones, but we were thrilled at the prospect of ministering with the Saints in the land of Zion.

Brother F. Henry Edwards, a member of the First Presidency of the church, arrived two weeks later by seaplane. We also greeted him at the wharf with *heis* and with a kiss on each cheek, according to the French custom. Initially he was quite embarrassed by it. The night of his arrival, the Tahitians had a feast in honor of our visitors. About 500 people wearing colorful *pareus* (sarongs) and *heis* participated in the festivities. All the food was cooked in a native oven—placed on hot stones and covered with banana leaves and dirt. Food cooked that way is really delicious.

We were fortunate to have a 145-pound fish to add to the menu. The two apostles, some natives, and I had gone fishing on the previous Saturday. We had a wonderful time and caught a lot of fish, including the huge one. The only drawback was that the three of us white men ended up becoming red men, due to bad sunburn!

Since some fish were poisonous, the natives fed pieces of the large fish to our cat to see if it would get sick. The cat had no ill effects, so the natives declared that the fish was fit for human consumption.

At last the great day for the dedication of the church at Rangiroa arrived. Brother Mervin's schooner took Brother Edwards, Apostle Hield, Apostle Draper, the Tyree family, and our family to the island. Everyone dressed in white for the service except Brother Edwards, who choose to wear a dark suit. The group looked very impressive, and I shot beautiful color photographs of the people present.

The church was quite packed for the dedication service. Practically everyone on the island turned out—including the Protestants and some of the Roman Catholics. We then had a *tamaraa* (native feast). The women had gone to great lengths to prepare all the pork, beef, fish, *poi*, *urus* (breadfruit), and other dishes to make a real feast, Tahitian style. It was truly a memorable experience.

Gwen, our children, and I were planning to stay on the

island a little longer because there were a few more things to be done. However, the three visiting Americans had to hurry back to Tahiti to catch a plane. The Tyrees were to accompany them to assist in their departure. However, when the time came for them to go, the Mervin schooner had not returned. The only other possible way of getting to Tahiti—nearly 200 miles distant—was on a small copra schooner owned by a native named Huri a Huri. He put Brother Edwards in a little cabin, which was so small that his feet stuck out. Brother Draper and Brother Hield had to lie on the deck. They struck some rough weather on the way back to Tahiti, and at times the waves washed over all the men on the deck! Nevertheless, they arrived safely. Later they often laughed about the experience and how they were well washed with the Pacific Ocean! The Sorensen family waited for the Mervin schooner and had a much better trip back to Tahiti.

◂ The Sorensen family back in Tahiti in 1952

▸ Building a new church in the Tuamotus

▾ The congregation outside the new church at Rangiroa in the Tuamotus

▲ The missionary family in Tahiti

▼ New missionary duplex in Tahiti, first used by Tyree and Sorensen families

▲ Apostles Charles Hield and Maurice Draper bedecked with flower and shell *heis* after a native welcome in Papeete

▼ New station wagon that Eddie Butterworth brought from America for the mission

▲ Typical atoll island in the Tuamotus, with highest land about five feet above high tide

▼ View of beautiful Cook's Bay, Moorea

▸ Giant 145-pound fish speared for a native feast with a speargun that Vivian made

▾ Stone corrals built to catch fish

CHAPTER 6

An International Kidnapping

In August, 1953, our family increased by two. No—Gwen did not have twins! But we took care of the two children of an American couple, Kim and Peggy Powell, who were in Tahiti and in the process of a messy divorce. Both parents wanted the children, but they did not want each other. The girl, "Froggie," was two—the same age as Trevor; and Robin, the boy, was five. The children, who were very well-behaved, were placed in our care by the French court until their custody could be determined.

The following January our act of kindness took a drastic turn. We were still responsible for the Powell children. Around New Year's Day, their mother took them for ice cream as she had done before; but this time she did not return them. Although it was unusual, we did not worry unduly about it. We thought they may have just fallen asleep on the boat where their mother had been staying.

The next morning Gwen walked the short distance from our home to the Papeete harbor to check on them, but there was no one aboard the boat. When Gwen arrived home, a gendarme was waiting for her. "Where are the Powell children?" he asked. After Gwen replied that she didn't know, he said, "I do! They're probably 50 miles out to sea by now!"

We then learned that Peggy Powell and a friend, Jack

Rockefeller (of the famous Rockefeller family), took the children aboard his yacht, *Venturer*, and sailed from Tahiti without the knowledge of the French authorities. When it was discovered that the children had been "kidnapped" by their mother, we were under suspicion as accomplices—even though we had not been aware of what was going to happen. The authorities questioned us quite thoroughly on more than one occasion.

For more than a month we did not know what had happened to the children and their mother. We just had to trust that the Lord would protect them—and us. In early February, however, a letter postmarked Honolulu arrived from Peggy Powell, which exonerated us of any wrongdoing in the matter and described their dramatic voyage to Hawaii. We took the letter to the authorities and waited a few days for it to be translated into French. Apparently the officials accepted her statements because we were finally informed that we were no longer considered suspects in the kidnapping.

This was a fascinating episode in our lives and would have made a good plot for a television drama. It was headline news in the Honolulu newspaper. I would like to present excerpts from the correspondence which told of the escapade and cleared us of blame with the authorities:

"Sorry to have run out on you the way I did. I have hoped and prayed a million times you didn't have any trouble with the authorities over the deal. When I look back on it now, I don't know where I got the courage to do what I did. I really didn't know I'd go through with it until two days before we left. I wanted so much to take you into my confidence, to let you know what I was about to do. But Jack's reasoning was much more from the head than from the heart—as mine was. He warned me that I would only be causing you more trouble by shifting some of the responsibility to someone else. Then, too, I wasn't sure,

even after we'd cleared the pass, that we'd get away with it, knowing Old Scratch as I did."

"Old Scratch" was her name for her estranged husband, Kim Powell. The next paragraph describes her feelings during her last conversation with Gwen. I had not been home at the time she picked up the children. Looking back, perhaps we should have become suspicious that she might try to take her children. A month or two earlier she had suggested that it would be nice if they could spend a night with her. Of course, we felt responsible for them and hadn't allowed that to happen.

"I wish I could express, too, how I felt that last afternoon when I came to get the kids. If I had been held up at your house for another five minutes, I'm sure my knees would have given way. My heart was beating like thunder, and the lump in my throat was about to choke me. I wanted so much to hug you and cry on your shoulder. You had been so good to me and my kids and so very understanding. But I just wouldn't let myself give way at the last minute.

"So it was nip and tuck up to the time we hauled up the anchor on Venturer. *None of us were in the least seasick. The kids really enjoyed the whole business. Robin did his share of dishes, cleaning, and caring for Froggie when Jack and I had our hands full of boat and rope coiling.*

"So many times since leaving Tahiti I have wished I could have let you know what I was about to do. You might even have enjoyed the excitement—and exciting it was—of that sunset takeoff of Venturer *down the channel. We had calms and light airs, then hard black squalls smack out of the north where we wanted to go for the first 13 days. For five heartbreaking days we lay in sight of Tahiti (the engine broke down). I expected any time to see the French gunboat steaming out after us. We worked our way up through the Tuamotus, passing Mata-Hiva one evening—a beautiful sight with the setting sun turning the coco palms golden—*

and my first bitter taste of homesickness for Tahiti.

"But with that uncertain weather, we had to hoist and lower those huge gaffs as many as five or six times a day to catch every little breeze. We had to lower them when it died to keep them from slatting [flapping] to pieces. I got a lot of practice, and after the first few days could do it with my eyes closed in the dark.

"We were ready when, at the latitude of the Marquese, we were struck by a hard easterly gale out of a clear blue sky, which sent Venturer *flying. From that time until we picked up the Hilo [Hawaii] light 16 days later, we had the lee rail under with mountainous seas aboard continually. It was some of the finest sailing I have ever done. What a wonderful feeling to be at the wheel of a boat like* Venturer*! She positively lived and breathed. She seemed to know which way to go even before I touched the helm. But there were times when she became a little rambunctious, and it took all I had to hold her. So I gained a little weight through the shoulders, and there were times my stern felt as hard and flat as that of* Venturer.

"One of the joys of the cruise was that even though he didn't say much, I knew Jack was enjoying the sailing as much as I was. He, too, could 'feel' his ship, and he knew just how much she would take before he had to ease her.

"We blew out one mainsail, tore it to shreds and had to bend on a heavy sea with Venturer *leaping clear out of the water. The jib halyard parted, and Jack had to go aloft to make repairs. The foresail began to give way along the foot under the continual strain, so we reefed [folded] her rather than take the time to make repairs. Then the heavy main parted the bolt rope at the dew. We reefed her, too, rather than waste time heaving-to in the heavy seas. Even under this shortened rig we made 190 miles a day several times. Despite these few difficulties, we all enjoyed the cruise so much. I, for one, hated to see it come to an end.*

"Richecoeur [Peggy Powell's lawyer in Tahiti] had sent a wire to [Peggy's sister aboard the boat] Calypso *in Hawaii telling them of my departure, so my sister was on hand to greet us when we arrived. I, of course, immediately learned that Old Scratch was in Honolulu, gunning for me. I was immediately surrounded by cops, bless them, when we tied up. I thought I could get to the mainland before Old Scratch started any trouble; but the day after we arrived, the deputy high sheriff of Honolulu arrived on the stern of* Venturer *with a writ of habeas corpus. The kids and I were whisked by plane over to Honolulu that same evening.*

"So this afternoon I go to court to face the judge on charges of kidnapping and endangering the lives of the children on a 'dangerously undermanned vessel on the high and perilous seas.' But I shall refresh Old Scratch's memory for the benefit of the judge when the time comes as to how we [the Powell family] sailed out to Tahiti and on down through the Cooks in a 75-year-old British schooner that was not half the vessel Venturer *is—*Venturer, *who was built to take twice the beating she took. I shall also remind him that I'm a pretty good sailor myself and that I was in capable hands.*

"Now that I'm surrounded by cops, I feel very safe and secure and confident that things will come out in my favor. Now that the fireworks have started, I'm glad they are underway and that some sort of a decision will be made soon."

For nearly a year the Powells continued to battle for the children, who had been placed in a foster home by the court. We received a letter from Peggy Powell in December, 1954, in which she told us that the Hawaii Supreme Court had just awarded her permanent custody of the children. Their father retained the right of periodic visitation. We were glad that the messy affair was finally resolved.

This episode just goes to show that missionaries in exotic lands can experience some real adventures, even becoming involved in international incidents through no wrongdoing of their own. It was certainly an uncomfortable feeling to be under suspicion by the authorities for being accomplices in a serious crime. But we knew we were innocent and trusted in the Lord that we would be exonerated, as we were.

▾ Robin, Peggy, and "Froggie" Powell

CHAPTER 7

To the Land of Promise

I completed my ministry to the natives with visits to the islands of Makatea and Tubuai. At Makatea about 300 people came to hear me preach on the lawn of our church. Only two people were baptized, but tremendous interest was aroused.

After our second term of three and a half years in French Polynesia, we started making preparations to leave for the United States. That was nearly as complicated as when we were trying to leave New Zealand. The American Consulate had closed in Tahiti and had moved all their equipment and files to Noumea, New Caledonia. Our applications for visas were forwarded to the American Consulate in Jamaica. We finally got new British passports since ours had expired, but we did not receive our U.S. visas until we arrived in Jamaica.

We arranged for passage on the French ship *Eridan*, which was bound for France on its last voyage. It had plenty of accommodations for passengers. Wanting to save the church money, we again booked third class passage.

I was sorry to be leaving the islands, never to come back as a full-time missionary. But over the seven years we were there, I really felt that we made a contribution to the Lord's work. The mission had grown numerically, and some new churches and a new mission duplex home had been built. Whatever good we did was done in the name of the Lord Jesus Christ. Our family had also learned a lot from our experience in a different culture.

The native Saints sometimes needed discipline—and I was strict, I suppose from being of British stock. However, the discipline was administered in kindness—in real love and concern for them. When they felt that they were being disciplined for their own good, they generally responded positively.

When the time came to say good-bye, the Saints showed their sincere and heartfelt love for us. They smothered us with flower and shell *heis*, as well as kisses on both cheeks. Finally our family was standing on the deck of the *Eridan*. The natives had a tradition that when the ship moves out from the wharf, each passenger is to throw a flower *hei* into the water. If it drifts toward land, he will return someday; but if it drifts out to sea, he will not be coming back. On that occasion Gwen and I each threw a *hei*. They drifted toward the land, so we felt that we would be coming back some day—which we did many years later.

When we left Papeete in March, 1955, and headed due north, I wondered if the sailors knew where they were going. I watched their progress chart; and after a couple of days, we were still sailing north. I asked one of the officers, "Why is it you're taking on a northerly course?"

He answered, "Well, this old ship is very slow. When we get farther north, we catch the equatorial current that will add another three knots to our sailing speed."

I thought of the Nephites, Jaredites, and others who crossed the oceans so long ago. They had only the wind, the currents, and their faith in the Lord to help them.

At last we began to turn toward the northeast; and finally, when we were almost at the tropic of Cancer, we headed due east. We had a good time on board. The food on the *Eridan* was a bit better than on the *Chung King*. On the two Sundays we spent on board the ship, I preached to the Protestant Tahitians in their native tongue. They told me that they would be sorry to lose me at Panama when we left the ship.

When we crossed the equator, the French sailors had their ceremony of the "Baptism of the Line." That was a tradition among seafaring peoples, in which those who were crossing the equator for the first time were initiated by "Father Neptune" and his helpers. The crew built a wooden and canvas structure on the deck, pumped sea water into it until it was about three feet deep, and then started their antics. I had a movie camera; and although I was dodging around to keep the camera dry, some of the scenes I took were surprisingly steady. As they had done with the other uninitiated passengers, the crew grabbed our 11-year-old daughter Beth, whitewashed her with some sort of foam, shaved that off with a big wooden "razor," and dumped her into the pool. She was thus "baptized"!

I had locked Gwen, Marvia, and Trevor in their cabin because the younger children might be upset with the antics; and Gwen certainly did not want to be dumped into seawater. The crew even grabbed a Catholic priest in his black robes, whitewashed him, and shaved him; then in he went! I thought, "Well, it will not hurt him to be baptized by immersion anyway." When they had thus "baptized" all of the uninitiated, they caught hold of the chief officer who was standing by and threw him in. He took it in good humor. They gave Beth a very nice certificate in French saying that she had been baptized crossing the equator. That was some of the fun we had traversing the Pacific.

We kept on chugging toward the Promised Land, and finally we saw the mountains and hills of Panama. The mountains were not very high, but they were visible from quite a distance. As we got closer, we saw a large swing bridge at the entrance of the Panama Canal. When ships needed to enter or exit the canal, the bridge pivoted open to allow them the right of way.

Passing through the locks of the Panama Canal was very interesting. We started at sea level on the Pacific side and floated into the lock. The gates behind us were shut, and big pumps poured water into that lock. As the water level rose, so did the ship, until we came to the level of the second lock. We were then about 30 feet or so above the Pacific Ocean, looking like a ship on dry land. Electric vehicles called "mules," which were very slow and very powerful, pulled the ships through the locks until they could move under their own power. The procedure was repeated through the third lock, when the ship sailed into Gatun Lake, which is a very large man-made lake. We waved to the various passenger and cargo ships that we passed as we headed to the locks on the Atlantic side.

It was a lovely trip through beautiful, lush tropical country. Some passes in the lake were just wide enough and deep enough for the big ships to go through. At the far side of the lake, where the ship was well above the Atlantic Ocean, we entered a series of descending locks. When the water in the last lock was on the same level as the Atlantic Ocean, our ship sailed on to the Port of Cristobal on the Caribbean Sea. We were all fascinated by the whole procedure of passing through the Panama Canal.

That was the end of our voyage on the *Eridan*. We hired a taxi to take us to the airport, where we were to catch a plane to Barranquilla, Colombia, on our way to Jamaica. We were running rather late, so we told the woman taxi driver, "Step on it!" Did she ever step on it—I felt my heart was in my mouth the whole time!

We arrived at the airport in time to board the plane. We flew over the incredibly dense tropical jungle, which grew right to the edge of the Caribbean. Through small breaks in the jungle canopy, we could see a few huts where

Indians must have been living. After we landed in Barranquilla, we refueled and set off for Kingston, Jamaica.

Kingston was also a beautiful place. The airport was on a long arm of land stretching out into the Caribbean. We learned that because it was Easter and the American consul would not be back in his office until Tuesday, we had to wait four days before we could go to get our visas. We hoped that everything would go smoothly.

As we walked around the town, we met a lot of beggars, who asked for money in Jamaican English. As much as we wanted to be charitable, we did not have extra money of our own. We knew that if we gave to one, we would have to give to all. It got so bad, that I said to my wife and children, "We'll have to use some strategy here. Let's speak to each other in Tahitian." After that, when the beggars came and asked us for money, we all spoke in Tahitian. It worked perfectly. The beggars looked bewildered and left us alone, thinking we could not understand them. Although it was a rather cruel thing to do, we really had no choice.

We spent the next day in Spanish Town, an old seat of government in the days of the Spanish Main. We wanted to catch a bus back to Kingston, but between our Australian English and their Jamaican English we had quite a job making anyone understand us. They said something like *booos*. We finally found out which *booos* was going to Kingston, got aboard, and rode to the city.

On Tuesday morning we arose early so we would be at the American consul's office when it opened. After I introduced myself, the consul looked at me as though I were something out of Noah's ark. He said, "We haven't got any visa or information on you here." My heart just about stopped beating when I thought of all the waiting and red tape that we went through in New Zealand. Was it going to be repeated here?

Then someone working in the office overheard him and said, "Oh, there is another file over here." It was ours—and it was up to date. All we had to do was have our fingerprints taken, answer some questions, and sign our names to obtain our visitor visas for the United States.

When we arrived at the airport, the plane was already loading passengers. I was detained to fill out five forms, one for each member of the family; and each form included many questions. Gwen and the children went on through the gate and started boarding. The crew was about to close the door when Gwen yelled, "My husband's still out there filling out the forms! We can't leave without him! He has our passports and visas!" By that time I just about had the forms all filled out—although my writing was barely legible. I did not know if they would be able to read them. At Gwen's insistence, the plane waited. Scarcely were we all buckled into our seats, when the plane set off for Montego Bay.

We had a pleasant flight across the island of Jamaica from Kingston to Montego Bay, seeing the rugged mountains, beautiful blue hills, sugar cane farms, and the crystal clear blue-tinted water of the great Caribbean. Then we headed for Camaguey, Cuba. At that time a fellow named Juan Batista was in charge of Cuba; Fidel Castro was up in the hills in those days before he came into power. The plane landed there for only a short time to refuel and pick up mail. We were allowed to get out and stretch our legs, so now we can say we have been on the island of Cuba.

Passing over the Florida Keys, we approached Miami and saw all of its buildings, canals, beautiful palms, and lush vegetation.

In Miami we were thrilled to enjoy the company of Eddie and Lillie Raye Butterworth and Allen and Jane Breckenridge. What a joyous reunion for us, and what a happy time for our children to play with their children! The

Butterworths were on their way back to Tahiti to replace us. We then went to Orlando and stayed a week with the Breckenridges. I preached at their church on Sunday. The next day Allen and Jane took us to Tampa to catch the plane to Kansas City. We had a night flight for the first time. Almost four-year-old Trevor sat transfixed to the window nearly the whole way, watching the flames come from the exhaust ports of the big engines. The airliners were all propeller-driven in those days.

Bishop Walter Johnson, an Australian, met us at the Kansas City Municipal Airport and took us to Independence. We stayed with the Roscoe Daveys for a few weeks while we looked for a place to live. We then moved into the Maurice Draper home while the Drapers were in Australia. Finally in July, 1955, we moved into a church-owned home on South Crysler Street in Independence. Beth and Marvia were soon able to attend school, but Trevor stayed home since he was only four years old.

My assignment was to do missionary work in the central part of the United States under the direction of Apostle Roscoe E. Davey. My first task in the land of Zion was working in Kansas City Stake with a fellow seventy, Al Scherer, who had just spent a couple of years in Holland. I preached each Sunday morning and evening at various churches in the stake. The people really loved my Australian accent, and it helped make them listen to me.

My next assignment took me to Chariton, Iowa, for six weeks, where I worked with Seventy Virgil Billings, held a preaching series, and conducted cottage meetings. My family joined me for my last week there. On the last Sunday we had seven baptisms, including our daughter Marvia. She was eight years old, and I was thrilled to baptize her.

We then drove to Wisconsin, where we stayed with Brother and Sister George Mesley at their home on the shores of lovely Lake Pewaukee. Brother Mesley, also a fellow Aussie, had ordained me to the office of seventy when he stopped in Tahiti on his way to America in 1946.

After our short vacation there, Gwen and the children caught a train from Chicago back to Independence. I went to Savanna, Illinois, for a two-week preaching series and cottage meetings. That was followed by more preaching series at our churches in Des Moines and Clinton, Iowa; Verdun, Nebraska; Atchison and Fanning, Kansas; and Lexington, Lee's Summit, and Marshall, Missouri. In Marshall I spoke on the radio a couple of days about Tahiti and my missionary work there.

In some places I spoke to students or to other groups about Australia and Tahiti, showing them slides I had taken. The people were fascinated with exotic places so far away, and the lectures also provided good opportunities to introduce the RLDS Church to them. I met several Australian and New Zealand war brides and was often invited into their homes for meals, to talk about their homelands, and to help soothe their homesickness—and mine!

My family became involved with church work in the Center Place. Gwen taught a Sunday school class of young boys at the Stone Church and was an Oriole leader. Beth was president of an Oriole group and her Sunday school class, and Marvia was treasurer of her Sunday school class. Both of our girls sang in the junior choir.

We soon came to love America because the land was beautiful, the people were so kind and friendly, and everything was available in abundance. However, while many of the Saints were living good lives, we had a long way to go to build Zion. I felt that it would take a strong prophet, such as a Moses or an Enoch, to get the people moving to build the city described in the Scriptures.

In October, at the age of nearly 40, I was excited to see falling snow for the first time. It was a very mild affair, but sufficient to mantle the houses and streets with a thin film of glorious white. I had seen snow before on the mountaintops of New Zealand, but I had never seen it falling or close at hand. The next month I got more than my fill of snow and cold when the area experienced the coldest November on record. I had to drive through a blizzard from Independence to Verdun, Nebraska, where I was to hold a week-long preaching series. I stayed in a farmhouse which was not heated on the top floor where my room was located. I nearly froze to death with the outside temperature being only eight degrees above zero. The toilet was outside, like I had been used to on farms; but one's anatomy did not receive the buffeting of such frigid winds in Australia as it did in Nebraska.

Our first Christmas in America was like a traditional Australian one. Our good friend and fellow appointee, Brother Floyd Potter, had arrived from Australia in mid-December and stayed with us for a few weeks. We also invited Brother Hudson Grundy and his family to join us for our Christmas dinner of poultry, ham, and the usual plum pudding. Thus three appointee families from Australia celebrated on the 24th, which was really Christmas Day in our homeland across the International Date Line.

My first trip to Mexico was in February, 1956. Brother Archie Gatrost, one of the American servicemen I had met in Brisbane during World War II, had promised me a trip to Mexico if ever we came to the United States. Knowing my great interest in the Book of Mormon and the Lamanites, he contacted me and renewed the invitation when he learned that we were in Missouri.

When Floyd Potter heard that we were preparing to go to Mexico, he almost knelt before us—begging that we take him with us. The bishop arranged for his financing by making the trip a part of Floyd's itinerary.

Two weeks before we were scheduled to leave, I came down with the mumps and wondered whether I would be well enough to make the trip. Although still a bit weak, I recovered enough so that I was able to go. After we left for Mexico, Gwen, Trevor, and Marvia also came down with the mumps. Beth was the only one who escaped the illness since she had it before in Australia.

Floyd and I drove to Houston, where we were met by Archie, his brother Lyle, his friend Chester Metcalf, and Brother James Renfroe, who was also an RLDS Church appointee. We set off in two vehicles, a brand new van and a big car. We had no trouble with the border authorities since American citizens did not need visas to visit Mexico and Floyd and I already had ours.

A large portion of the journey from the U.S. border south to Mexico City was quite mountainous. We noticed a scarcity of arable land. We drove past terraced hillsides, which may have been farmed by the ancient Americans many, many centuries ago; they were very skilled at that type of farming. The mountains were majestic and clothed in blue. I remember trying to take pictures as we were driving along, but they were a bit blurred by the movement of the car.

We arrived safely in Mexico City. Because only Lyle and I spoke Spanish—and that was very limited—it was difficult to get around. We tried driving to look at the various sites. However, the traffic was so dense and so hideously controlled—if you could call it controlled at all—that the men said, "We've had enough of this." Although they were Americans and had practically been born with steering wheels in their hands, they gave up and put their cars in a storage garage.

We then hired a big taxi to take the six of us wherever we wanted to go. Talk about a wild nightmare and wild drivers! I remember asking one of the taxi drivers, "How on earth do you survive in this place?"

"Oh," he said, "all you need are good brakes and a horn." He certainly demonstrated that philosophy as he frequently hit the horn, jammed on his brakes, and almost put us through the windshield. Although we were terrified, the Mexicans actually seemed to enjoy themselves!

In my opinion, two of the outstanding sites of Mexico are the beautiful snow-capped twin volcanoes of Ixtacihuatl at 17,343 feet and Popocatepetl at 17,888 feet. On that first trip to Mexico, there was not very much smog; and we had some glorious views of the peaks![1] Ixtacihuatl is called "The Sleeping Lady." The top of the mountain is shaped like a lady reclining, her long hair tossed back over her head. She is covered with a blanket of eternal snow. It is absolutely beautiful. Next to her is Popocatepetl, which, according to legend, represents a warrior watching over his lady.

In Mexico City we visited the beautiful floating gardens of Xochimilco and the national museum. I was fascinated by the enormous Aztec calendar stone, which was about 12 feet in diameter and weighed 23 tons. It was carved out of hard volcanic stone—an example of exquisite workmanship. The stone was on the floor of the museum; I could walk around it, examine it closely, and photograph it.[2]

One thing that cast a pall over an otherwise excellent trip was a bullfight we attended in Mexico City. I did not want to see it; but since Archie had bought me a ticket, I

---

[1] The next time I was there, in 1973, we could not see the mountaintops because of the smog.

[2] In 1973 it was suspended on a wall, and we could not see it nearly so well. I was sorry the museum did that.

felt obligated to go. We were all sitting in elevated seats like our sports arenas have. The bullfighter held out his red cape, and the bull charged at it. That was repeated many times until the poor bull was completely exhausted. Then the bullfighter slid a long steel saber down through the front portion of the bull, starting at the back of the neck. As the bull slowly fell to the ground, hats filled the air and shouts of "¡Olé! ¡Olé!" pounded our ears. After the second kill, we were all quite sickened by the cruelty to those poor animals and the accompanying frenzy of the crowd. Even though there were four more fights to go, we all got up and walked out.

Next we drove to the mountain fortress of Monte Albán. The stronghold would have been almost impregnable; it was probably similar to the way the Nephites barricaded themselves against the Lamanites. About halfway up the mountain are quite a few tombs. We were told that from one of them, gold ornaments worth seven million dollars were taken. Very little treasure is left now, much the pity.

Then we went to Oaxaca, down the valley not far from Monte Albán. I have pictures of absolutely exquisite gold ornaments at the Oaxaca museum. We also saw some thin golden plates or leaves which had been found in a tomb. They could quite easily have been of the same texture and thickness as the Book of Mormon gold plates. While there were no inscriptions on them, they show that the early Americans did beat gold into thin sheets. We then drove a short distance to Mitla, which was also quite interesting.

We visited the ruins of Yucatán, where we saw the famous sites of Uxmal and Chichén Itzá. In my opinion, the Uxmal ruins are by far the most ornate and beautiful.

Then we returned to Mexico City. It was a wonderful experience for us to stand on top of the Pyramid of the Sun at Teotihuacán. It is terraced, and we could not see the top while climbing the steep stairs. It is larger in volume than the Great Pyramid of Egypt, although it is not quite so high. All around Teotihuacán is evidence of a thriving city, and many temples to the bearded white god can be seen. There are twelve pyramids in the great court of Quetzelcoatl (perhaps representing the twelve disciples or the tribes of Israel). It was certainly a thrill to climb the pyramids and reflect on the ancient civilizations.

Most of the big pyramids are not just one, but many. A smaller pyramid was built by the early inhabitants; then, as succeeding peoples came, they built over the existing pyramid. At Cholula seven pyramids are superimposed, one upon the other. Of course, so much of the history of those people is shrouded in mystery—the archaeologists have made theories, expounded them, and then blown them to pieces 20 or 50 years later.

I do not say that archaeology proves the Book of Mormon, but I do say it is supporting evidence. The Book of Mormon spoke about the great works of the people, how they built towers, palaces, and other structures. When we see the ruins and the wonderfully fertile valleys of Mexico today, we realize that the Book of Mormon is true in its account of a mighty people, who must have swarmed in millions on the face of the land years ago. Those scattered ruins still remain to testify of the rise and fall of the ancient civilizations in the Land of Promise.

When Floyd and I returned from the heat of Mexico to the cold of the Midwest, we were greeted by a blanket of snow. I immediately resumed my missionary work, with a two-week series of sermons and cottage meetings in Kansas City Stake, followed by a month of ministering in northwest Iowa.

In the town of Moorhead, Iowa, I stayed in the home of

Brother and Sister Davis. Descendants of many of the early Saints lived in the area. Brother Davis told me that his great-grandfather had gone with Lyman Wight to Texas.[1] While there, he heard of the Reorganization and walked all the way from Texas to Moorhead to find out about it. When he discovered the truth, he returned to Texas and thereby helped to break up the Lyman Wight group, many of whom returned to the Reorganization.

I had been at Moorhead for one week when I was called home by Gwen because Marvia was seriously ill. She had a temperature of 105° and was taken to the hospital. Since the doctors did not know what was wrong, I left Moorhead at 11 p.m. after a cottage meeting and drove 265 miles to Independence, arriving at 6:30 a.m. I had a very trying journey, as the roads were ice covered for about 100 miles. At one point along that stretch, the car skidded on the ice, turned right around, and faced the opposite direction. That certainly gave me a strange feeling because once I began to skid, there was really not much I could do except pray and trust in the Lord. I felt that He was with me, and I arrived at the hospital safely. I administered to Marvia, then went home for some sleep. The doctors had been afraid that she had a rare virus; but we were all relieved to learn that it was a very aggressive strain of measles instead.

My work in Iowa on that month-long trip consisted mainly of cottage meetings, visiting inactive Saints, and a week-long preaching series. On one night of the series, 82 people over the age of eight attended, which was very good for a town of 400. Included were the people with whom I was having cottage meetings and several inactive Saints.

---

[1] Lyman Wight had been a Latter Day Saint apostle in the 1840s. After the death of Joseph Smith, Jr., in 1844, Wight led a group of Saints to Texas.

People are interested in foreign missions and experiences that are out of the ordinary. When Brother Glaude Smith was the pastor of the Stone Church, he tried to get me to preach there some Sunday. I avoided him every time I was in town, saying to Gwen, "Why they've got prophets, priests, and presidents to speak to the Saints here in Independence. What on earth would I be doing, trying to speak to them?"

She tried to persuade me that I could tell them something they needed, but I resisted. Finally she plotted with Brother Smith to get me to preach there. She knew my schedule and that I would be home on a certain weekend, which fact she passed along to Brother Smith.

One Saturday in March, 1956, I came home and happened to see the newspaper. Vivian Sorensen was listed for two sermons at the Stone Church the next day. I thought, "Oh, my goodness me!" But there was nothing I could do, since it had already been published. While I was stewing about it and wondering what on earth I would talk about, the voice of the Spirit spoke to me and said, "Bear your testimony."

In the first service, which was rather short because of the blessing of children, I bore my testimony. At the 11 o'clock service the church was packed—there were even people in the aisles. Perhaps it was because it was getting near conference time or perhaps the Saints were curious to hear what a missionary from overseas had to say. Brother Elbert A. Smith was in the congregation, as were J. F. Curtis and Myron McConley, former apostles.

As I had been directed by the Spirit, I again bore my testimony, which included experiences as a missionary in Tahiti. The good Lord was with me and helped me deliver heartfelt praise to Him. When I had finished, I was absolutely amazed at the reaction. As I walked down the aisle to the front door to meet the people, they stepped out of their places and shook my hand. Brother Harold Velt had tears in his eyes when he said, "Vivian, that's just what these people needed—something vibrant, something alive!" Some called it "the sermon that rocked Independence" because the Saints, accustomed to many theological sermons, had heard very little of the rich spiritual experiences of the Lord's working among the natives of the islands.

Brother Chris Hartshorn, editor of *The Saints' Herald*, asked me if he could print the text in the magazine. The sermon, entitled "The Lord's Hand Is Not Shortened," was published in the July 25, 1956, issue of *The Saints' Herald* and was later put into braille for the blind. Many people expressed their appreciation for the wonderful spirit and power that accompanied that simple testimony of what the Lord had done for my family and myself. Praise be to His holy name forever and ever! In May another article that I had written, "The Cause of Zion," appeared in the RLDS Church publication *Guidelines to Leadership*.

In April, 1956, Gwen and I attended our first General Conference. It was a deeply moving experience for us. Over 17,000 Saints partook of the sacrament in three services on the opening Sunday. It was certainly strengthening to meet with so many of like faith. I preached to several hundred people in the Stone Church's new educational building and was once again blessed by the Lord. The text of the sermon, entitled "Spiritual Treasures Available Through Faith in the Restoration," was published in the January 7, 1957, issue of *The Saints' Herald*.

At that conference I was assigned to the Des Moines District, which included north central Iowa. I felt we were off to a good start, having already met many of the Saints from that district. Brother Maurice Draper was the apostle in charge of the area, which included 20 branches.

When we had arrived in Independence a year earlier, we were somewhat disappointed because we expected Zionic conditions to be more evident. But after living there for a year, we were loathe to leave it. We had felt the heartthrob of the Center Place and had shared some of the spirit of Zion with many wonderful Saints.

In May I spent three weeks visiting several branches of the Des Moines District, preaching, and searching for a suitable place for our family to live. We eventually decided on a house in the town of Boone, which had a population of 13,000. It was about 40 miles northwest of Des Moines.

▾ The Sorensen children shortly before leaving Tahiti

▲ Beth, Vivian, Trevor, Marvia, and Gwen preparing to depart on the *Eridan*, March, 1955

CHAPTER 8

The Field Is White

On June 9, 1956, we moved to Monona Street in Boone, Iowa. Our family had just unpacked and settled in when we were given notice that we had to be out of the house within 30 days. Our landlord apologized and explained that his recently widowed sister needed to live there. We found another house in Boone, but it would not be vacant until July 21, at which time we were supposed to be at the Kirtland reunion. The Boone Saints graciously offered to move our belongings while we were gone.

The new house was on First Street, just half a block from the Boone County Hospital and about one block from the school Trevor would be attending. We were actually better off in the new house—the rent was cheaper, and it had gas instead of coal heating. I did not think that Gwen should have to practice shoveling coal—as she was hardly due for "hell fire"!

In my initial travels I found that the people in the district needed much in the way of spiritual ministry. I tried to emphasize the need of personal evangelism and infuse a desire in them to witness. So much interest was stimulated that soon I had more cottage meetings than I could handle. I started making hundreds of slides to aid the men within the district in conducting cottage meetings. My sister Mavis provided some of the artwork used in the slides. Soon I was very busy—preaching nearly every Sunday, making the slide sets during the days, and conducting cottage meetings in the evenings.

One of my major challenges was to tackle the divorce problem and to instruct our people in the sanctity of the marriage covenant. In my opinion, that was a serious failing of our American Saints. We as a church had to make some changes if we wanted to build Zion and not be part of the destruction prophesied by Jesus when He said, "As in the days of Noah..." (see Matthew 24).

In July our family had a wonderful trip east to the Kirtland reunion and then on to Hill Cumorah and the sacred grove. We traveled over 2,000 miles in all and saw a lot of the fascinating country in Iowa, Illinois, Indiana, Ohio, Pennsylvania, and New York. We camped in our car to avoid the cost of motels. I had cut a sheet of plywood to fit on top of the backs of the car seats. Gwen and I slept on air mattresses on the plywood, while the children slept beneath it—Beth on the back seat, Trevor on cushions placed on the floor between the seats, and Marvia on the front seat.

The children were well behaved on the entire trip and were especially liked by the Saints at Kirtland. The Lord spoke to us through Apostle Arthur Oakman, giving a message of commendation. He said that our home would be the abode of angels in the future. Beth and Marvia were only twelve and nine years old at the time; but they worked every day in the Herald book tent with Sister Florence Parker, whom they had met in Independence. They did not tire of the job, but helped faithfully all week. I preached twice, taught the men's class every day, and assisted in the prayer meetings. Brother Oakman preached—and oh, how deep it was! I just sat at his feet and drank it in. He was considered to be the most powerful preacher in the RLDS Church at that time, and I agreed.

The Kirtland Temple is a most sacred structure, which can not be fully appreciated in one brief visit. We were very fortunate to be able to spend a week there and feel the same wonderful Spirit that permeated the temple in the early days of the Restoration. I spent some time alone in prayer on the second floor, the place designated for the School of the Prophets, where I felt the blessed presence of the Master. It was truly a "House of the Lord." I marveled at the sacrifice of the people who built it. But I also feel that dedicated Saints today, given the leadership and the spiritual guidance, would also be willing to sacrifice their all for the building of the Lord's temple.

We left Kirtland after lunch on Sunday and headed for Hill Cumorah, arriving there after a pleasant drive through the states of Pennsylvania and New York. That night we slept at the foot of the hill. I noticed many flat stones scattered around the base of the hill, all quite suitable for making a stone box just as Joseph Smith described that he saw. We drove through the village of Manchester and visited Joseph's home and the nearby sacred grove—a beautiful place in which to meet God. We had a prayer there, dedicating our lives to the great work which had been inaugurated in that sacred place.

Leaving those historic sites, we drove west through Rochester to the Niagara River. When we saw the majestic Niagara Falls for the first time, we marveled at the power exhibited in that natural wonder.

☼ ☼ ☼

After arriving home, we prepared to attend the Des Moines District reunion, held at the Des Moines Central

Church that year since the reunion grounds were not yet ready. Under the direction of Apostle Draper, the reunion was a rewarding experience. I preached twice and was pleased to conduct a baptismal service. The prayer meetings were spiritually uplifting.

In September our three children started school for the first time in Boone. It was Trevor's first time for school anywhere, as he started attending kindergarten for half days. That month the city of Boone was full of excitement because President Dwight Eisenhower and his wife Mamie came to spend the night. Boone was her birthplace, and a big marker stood outside her old house.

Beginning in late August, I started traveling to the various branches around the district, such as Mason City, Nevada, and Fort Dodge (where I also attended the groundbreaking for their new church). At each place we held a week-long series of preaching and teaching, in which I instructed the Saints how to tell the gospel story and explained some of the arguments they would encounter when talking to others. In the afternoons I visited nonmembers and the "Latter Day Aints," as I called the inactive church members. I also set up the local priesthood with slide sets and taught them how to conduct cottage meetings. In that trip I preached every night of the week for twelve weeks in succession, took a week off for Thanksgiving, and then spent one more week preaching. Many cottage meetings and several baptisms resulted directly from that tour.

About that time I wrote to my mother, telling her that in my preaching I rarely had need to refer to my notes. I was training myself to do that as I believed the Bible statement: "For out of the abundance of the heart the mouth speaketh. A good man, out of the good treasure of the heart, bringeth forth good things" (Matthew 12:29-30). We have been instructed to treasure up in our minds the words of life continually, and the Spirit will give that which is necessary in the very hour we have need of it (see Doctrine and Covenants 83:14d).

Gwen was also kept busy with church work. She spoke about missionary work in Tahiti to about 100 women of the Methodist Church in Boone. That was the first of many invitations to tell about the islands and Australia. Later in the year she spoke to a women's club about Christmas in Australia. She also was invited to speak about nursing in Australia before the Future Nurses Club at Boone High School (of which Beth was a member).

A couple of weeks later on World Missionary Day, I spoke to the Women's Alliance Missionary Society. The meeting was held for the first time at our church in Boone. In my talk on missionary work in Tahiti, I gave the women something to think about. I brought in a bit of our doctrine, and it was well received. Gwen had some Tahitian souvenirs on display, which greatly interested them.

From the various speaking engagements, it was obvious that the people of our community in the middle of Iowa were thirsting for tales of exotic locations. If only they thirsted as much for the gospel! As I sat one day at my desk, I looked at a map of the world which I had pinned on the wall in front of me. I was overwhelmed as I contemplated the immensity of the work ahead of us as a church and the slowness of the progress we were making. The results of all my missionary efforts in Tahiti and America were but a drop in the bucket. I knew that we required greater faith to receive the spiritual endowment needed to proclaim His Word throughout the world.

In December we spent some time visiting our friends in Independence, and Gwen and I attended the appointee's Christmas party. We had finished making an 8mm documentary film on the Center Place by recording a sound track with narration and background music. Its first public showing was at Resthaven while we were in Independence.

Early in 1957 I was, as usual, very busy with missionary work. The several weeks of preaching in late 1956 had resulted in many cottage meetings for me and for the local priesthood. Here is a description of my typical week at that time:

I left home on Monday morning and drove 110 miles to Mason City in the north, where I visited some Saints in the afternoon, had a cottage meeting, and slept that night. On Tuesday morning I drove 90 miles southeast to Marshalltown for one cottage meeting at 1:30 and another that night at the home of an Australian war bride and her husband. I slept there Tuesday night, then drove 40 miles to Newton, where we had a "dead" branch. After visiting Saints and holding a cottage meeting at night, I slept there and then drove 35 miles to Des Moines on Thursday morning. I held a cottage meeting there on Thursday afternoon, drove 40 miles home to eat dinner, drove 50 miles to Fort Dodge that night for a cottage meeting, and returned home that same night. Friday I worked around home doing such things as binding slides for my helpers. On Saturday I helped Gwen with the shopping and had a cottage meeting that night, driving a 100-mile round trip. Sunday morning I preached at a nearby church and later went to Iowa State College (now University) at Ames to give lectures on evangelism.

I particularly enjoyed providing ministry to the group of church-member students at Ames, which was only about 15 miles from Boone. The students and I got along very well together, and they soon became active in telling their friends about the church and the group.

One cold night in January, 1957, with over a foot of snow on the ground, Beth accompanied me to my meeting with the student group. As we drove to Ames, the countryside looked like a magic fairyland. The pale full moon and starry sky were mirrored by a million glittering reflections from the snow. It brought to me the reality of the pictures on the old Christmas cards I remembered from my boyhood days. Having Beth along helped build that father-daughter relationship which was necessary for both of us. It also enabled her to mix with a fine class of young people.

I was blessed exceedingly in my work, and I was grateful to God for His blessing. I had personally conducted 11 cottage meetings, which by mid-March had resulted in 20 baptisms. Nine other people also expressed their desire for baptism. We baptized 18 in one service at the dedication of the new Coalville church in February. Apostle Draper was there for the dedication. I was supposed to preach the first sermon in the building after its consecration, but the heavy work schedule and severe winter weather had finally caught up with me—I was at home sick in bed with a bad case of tonsillitis and flu. I wrote my mother that I did not mind being sick, because it was necessary to help me be thoughtful and charitable to others who were ill.

I soon was back on the trail with my missionary work, although sometimes it was hard to stay literally on the trail. One day I was traveling home slowly in my car on a road that was glazed with ice. It was most treacherous driving, and all of a sudden I found myself in a ditch. There was nothing I could do in such a case except pray. The good Lord looked after me—before long, some farmers hauled me out of the deep snowdrift. Fortunately, neither the car nor I was hurt.

In March I spent a week conducting a preaching series at a small branch in Illinois. It appeared that I was getting the reputation of a hypodermic needle wielder—a fellow who can give a good shot in the arm to some dwindling branches. Maybe I should have been a doctor after all! It was only a small town, but the church was filled with Saints and several nonmembers each evening.

Newton, Iowa, was a small and dying branch when we arrived in the district. I spent quite a bit of time ministering there during our first year in Iowa. In May I showed my documentary film on the Center Place and a film of Tahiti. My ministry was rewarded with eight baptisms in one service that June.

Gwen and I continued to receive invitations to talk to various groups about Tahiti and Australia. After we had exhausted those subjects with repeat invitations to the same groups, I had a chance to move into topics of religion which I really wanted to share with them. If they asked me to show slides, I showed them some on the Book of Mormon. In April I talked to a class at a Methodist church in Boone, telling them about the Book of Mormon, sharing all the scientific findings to support it, and showing them slides of my trip to Mexico. The people were amazed by the tremendous civilization left by the inhabitants of ancient America. At the conclusion, they fired dozens of questions at me; the following day I sent some literature to some of the inquirers. It also gave me an opportunity to explain the difference between us and the Mormons, which in itself was worthwhile.

Brother Henry Castings, an aged patriarch, and I were having cottage meetings with a very interested family. After I started to give the lecture on life after death, I felt an odd power, a taunting sort of power, and knew from whence it came. While I was speaking, I was also praying that the Lord would rebuke that evil power.

Later that evening, when we were talking about glories and rewards as outlined in 1 Corinthians 15, I felt the evil spirit begin to weaken and eventually leave altogether. I saw a change in the demeanor of the man and his wife, and I knew that the victory was the Lord's. Even though it was not the last lecture in the series, I invited the family to come into Christ's Church through baptism. The parents and their three children all accepted.

Brother Castings later told me that he prayed all through the meeting. I have always thought the adversary had an inkling of what was going to happen and tried to frustrate the work of God, Who said, "The works, and the designs, and the purposes of God, cannot be frustrated, neither can they come to naught" (Doctrine and Covenants 2:1a).

At that time I was holding seven cottage meetings a week, as well as preaching once or twice each Sunday. But I managed to find a little time to relax by tinkering in my workshop. With a lot of junk which had been thrown away (but to me was very valuable), I built a cabinet that contained a phonograph, a radio, and a television for the family's enjoyment. When we pressed a button, the doors opened and the record player came out ready for use. I also made some necessary furniture for our home.

Many Americans during the 1950s did not seem to appreciate the importance of thrift and the "repression of unnecessary wants." They were enjoying life in a land of abundance and wealth following the Great Depression and World War II. Even among the Saints there was a great indifference to the financial law and especially to the consecration of surplus, which could have been used to assist the gathering and Kingdom-building program. On the other hand, a few Saints sacrificed much to make their dream of the Kingdom come true. Were it not for them, the church might have had no missionary program at all.

In late June of 1957, we set out on a trip to Nauvoo and Carthage, Illinois. The first day we were deluged with rain as we were driving through the end of Hurricane Audrey. We visited Carthage Jail on June 27, the 113th anniversary of the murder of Joseph and Hyrum Smith. Bullet holes in the jail cell could still be seen, and the Mormon guides claimed that the original bloodstains were still visible on the floor. I had my doubts about the veracity of that.

We had our evening meal on the banks of the Mississippi River and slept that night on the former William Marks property at Nauvoo. The next morning Seventy Robert Fishburn gave us an extensive tour of the historical places of interest, including a visit to the old quarry which had supplied the stones for the Nauvoo Temple.

In July our family had our first real vacation since I had gone under appointment. We packed up and drove to Des Moines on Sunday, where I preached the evening service to the combined branches. After driving west for 100 miles, we stopped for the night and slept in the car as on previous trips.

Then we drove to the Rocky Mountain National Park and to Silver Crags, a dude ranch owned by a church member. With the Bob Fishburn family, we made the fascinating journey to Mesa Verde and saw the cliff dwellings. They were very interesting and showed a type of defense used by possible descendants of the Book of Mormon people. That trip went through the Rockies and over the "Million Dollar Highway," which had cost a million dollars per mile to build. Breathtaking curves and deep valleys with towering snow-capped mountains on each side really made it a beautiful trip.

We parted with the Fishburns and headed west toward Salt Lake City. During the trip across Utah, we traveled through desert and semi-desert for hundreds of miles. The colored rock formations and ever-changing contour of the land broke the monotony of the desert. The Salt Lake Valley was better irrigated and fruitful, but it still had the appearance of barrenness—being surrounded on all sides by desert or mountains. The children swam in the Great Salt Lake and enjoyed the novelty of not being able to sink. Salt Lake City was well designed; but I was not impressed with some of the Mormon structures, especially knowing what they represented. The secretive temple rituals especially bothered me. Jesus had said, "In secret have I said nothing" (John 18:20).

Leaving Utah, we traveled through Idaho to northwestern Wyoming and Yellowstone National Park, where we saw the famous geyser Old Faithful, areas of boiling mud, and thermal springs. Seeing the many wild animals in their natural habitat fascinated all of us. Bears posed beautifully for me, as did buffalo, Rocky Mountain sheep, deer, and an elk with his big antlers. We reluctantly began our journey home, passing through the Black Hills—including a visit to Mount Rushmore—the Badlands, and a large Indian reservation on our way. In all, we had a wonderfully instructive trip.

In August we attended the Des Moines District reunion, which was held at the new Guthrie Grove Reunion Grounds on the beautiful Raccoon River. Even though the grounds were still under construction, the Lord more than compensated for any inconveniences by the outpouring of His Spirit. I preached one sermon, helped teach a men's class, and gave the address at the communion service. During a prayer service, we had three expressions of the gift of prophecy. Apostle Draper spoke under inspiration to several individuals, including myself, giving a commendation for my work in the islands and in Joseph's Land. It was almost identical to the message expressed through Apostle Oakman the previous year. I felt that the Lord must have been pleased with my work in His service thus far. He had really blessed our work in the district, with nearly 70 people baptized during the first 10 months of my assignment there.

After the reunion, I resumed my missionary work and soon had a full schedule of cottage meetings. I was especially pleased that Beth and sometimes Marvia accompanied me on some of the cottage meetings to run the slide projector and provide company on the drive. They enjoyed helping me, and at the same time they were learning the truths of the everlasting gospel.

One Sunday night when Beth and I were returning from a cottage meeting, we were caught in a bad thunderstorm. As we were getting out of the car at home, my slides fell into a gutter filled with swift-flowing water. Beth and I dived for them and retrieved all but two slides. It was really a miracle because I was easily able to replace those two with duplicates. I needed the slides again the next Friday night and would not have had time to make replacements.

Marvia wanted to begin music lessons, but she did not have an instrument. In October she was given an old violin made of maple and pine. It produced a lovely mellow tone. It had been made in 1919 by an RLDS missionary named Marcus Cook. Marvia really appreciated it, and she did quite well with her lessons. The Lord has been so good to us. We tried to live on the smallest budget possible and be good stewards with the Saints' money. There was never a thing we needed but what He provided.

At that time I was holding cottage meetings with a Japanese lady in Ames. She was a Buddhist, and I had the big job of convincing her that Christ is the Son of God. She had all sorts of little idols around her house, and each god represented something. I told her that those gods were inanimate and could not influence anyone. At one meeting she asked me to explain the trinity, so I drew her a sketch. She seemed so interested that I went on and drew a diagram of the atonement, which interested her further. I felt the Spirit as I was telling her and was thrilled when she accepted Christ and gave her decision to be baptized.

In November, 1957, I went to Far West, Missouri, for a week's preaching series. The church building was just 50 yards from the site of the ill-fated Far West Temple. Again I was right in the midst of an area that was rich in church history. Not many evidences of past grandeur remained; the once thriving community of Far West was no longer there, and only one house of the original settlement—the home of one of the Whitmers—could be seen. Many of the property owners could show the names of noted Latter Day Saints on their abstracts; some even show the name of Hyrum or Joseph Smith.

With all my travels during the last two years, I had put approximately 63,000 miles on the 1954 Chevrolet. Bishop Kenneth Fowler arranged for us to travel to Missouri to trade in our church car on a new 1958 Ford.

In January, 1958, Trevor showed all the symptoms of appendicitis—he could not sleep; and when he drew his legs up, he cried from pain. I administered to him before leaving for a preaching assignment 40 miles away. I was gone when the worst attack occurred. Gwen telephoned to ask my advice, and I told her to take him to a doctor at once. Then I fell on my knees and asked God to have mercy on our boy. I asked if it were His will, to heal Trevor so the doctor would find nothing wrong when he examined him. Gwen took Trevor to the hospital that morning. The doctor gave our son a thorough checkup and found no evidence whatever of appendicitis or any other complaint. He almost accused Gwen of lying about his condition. The Lord must have blessed Trevor while I was praying 40 miles away. He had no further symptoms, and we were very thankful for the blessing he received.

In February the Sorensen family drove to Canada so we could reenter the United States with permanent residence visas, which would preclude our having to renew visitor visas every six months. On our way to Toronto, we went across the St. Clair River at Port Huron, getting a fine view of Lake Huron. We visited Gwen's Aunt Florrie in London, Ontario, and then went to Guelph, Ontario, and stayed with Hudson Grundy, an Australian who was the bishop to Canada. We had met him and his wife years before at the Tiona reunion in Australia.

In Toronto we received our new visas at the American Consulate. On our return home, we viewed Niagara Falls from the Canadian side and were really amazed at the ice-encrusted falls and huge chunks of ice in the river below. We drove through Buffalo and along the shores of Lake Erie to the Kirtland Temple, and we stayed the night in the old Sidney Rigdon home. The next morning in preparation for leaving Kirtland, we went to the temple and prayed.

After arriving home, I made a large reflector telescope with a four-and-one-half-inch mirror. It was 45 inches long and had two interchangeable eyepieces of different powers, one 60× and the other 120×. It was a huge success—we could gaze with fascination at the moon and planets, the red spot on Jupiter, the rings around Saturn, and the various moons of those bodies. Trevor was very curious, and I had to get him a chair to stand on so that he could see in the eyepiece. Beth was the next most interested in stargazing. I was thrilled that the children had an opportunity to see things that I had just dreamed about when I was a boy. (Marvia was more interested at that time in playing house with the children next door.)

It had always been my ambition to look at the heavenly bodies, and the telescope fulfilled that wish. During the short periods of time I was home between preaching assignments, I was able to indulge briefly in that hobby. It gave me a greater appreciation of God's handiwork and thus enhanced my witness for Him. As I viewed the majesty of the heavens, I was led to exclaim, "Any man who hath seen any or the least of these, hath seen God moving in his majesty and power" (Doctrine and Covenants 85:12c).

I also made a "Sputnik telescope," which was a real gem. It was only of five power in magnification, but it reflected the sky into a mirror so that we did not have to crane our necks—we could sit at ease and look down into it. My big telescope was making friends for me with the neighbors. When they saw me out stargazing, they came over to find out what I was doing. I did not fail to get a word in for the Creator while we were looking. Trevor also had a small telescope that I made. He was showing an interest in hobbies—a boy after his father's heart.

A few months later, I sold my large telescope to a man I had just baptized; and I made a new, more powerful six-inch reflector telescope, grinding the mirror myself. It was a painstaking, exacting job—but the results were worth it. It brought the old moon right down to our backyard so we could shake hands with the man in the moon!

Although that mirror was very good, it was not perfect; so later in the year I started to grind another one. Dave Blair, a chemist at Iowa State College who belonged to the church, helped me silver it. Later I made and sold a telescope to a doctor in Des Moines, an elder in the church. The following year I added a motor drive to improve my telescope so it would automatically follow the movement of a star or planet or the moon across the sky.

My attempt to revitalize the Newton branch the previous year had been successful, so I turned my attention to the Rhodes branch. It had once been a flourishing congregation in a farming area, producing such stalwarts as Roy Cheville and Don Lents. But it had dwindled until only a handful of people attended. I tried to rebuild it, starting with a preaching series. The results were positive, with several cottage meetings and decisions for baptism.

That series was followed by another week's preaching series in Perry. First I showed a travelogue of Australian and Tahitian slides, then preached about the fall of man and the great plan of salvation right down to the Restoration. The people were very interested, and some cottage meetings resulted.

My work was increasing at an amazing rate, so much so that I could not get it all done. With prospective cottage meetings and series lining up in almost every branch, I could not stretch myself to do it all. For a time I was conducting eight cottage meetings and had to drive almost 1,000 miles a week to do them. And that was during midwinter in Iowa!

In May Gwen offered to help at the Boone County Hospital as a volunteer; but when the business manager learned that she was a trained nurse, he practically got down on his knees to ask her to work at least part-time at full nurse's pay. Gwen was thrilled at the opportunity of bringing herself up to date with new developments in obstetrics, and she began working three or four days a week on the maternity floor. The hospital was only a couple of hundred yards from our home. Because of Gwen's major surgery only a year before, I was concerned for her health. I told her that if the job became too much of a strain for her, "I will put my foot down with a firm hand!"

In June, 1958, we learned of the death of Prophet Israel A. Smith in an automobile accident about 60 miles north of Kansas City. Alone and on his way to a stake conference at Lamoni, he was involved in a head-on collision and died about two hours after the crash. It was not a surprise to me; I had felt positive that he would not be presiding over the next General Conference, but that his brother Wallace would. Brother Israel was a good man, who had made a fine contribution to the RLDS Church.

That summer Marvia had a wonderful time attending Oriole camp, as did Beth at youth camp the following week. Trevor was still too young for camps.

☼ ☼ ☼

Our family took a 12-day vacation in July to photograph places of interest that I wanted to use for a documentary film on church history. We had a wonderful time with excellent weather. Our first stop was Nauvoo on the Mississippi, where I filmed many of the historical sites. Our next stop was Carthage Jail.

The Mormons were very cooperative when I introduced myself as "Elder Sorensen from Australia." I had not said that I was a Mormon, but I told the truth—I *was* Elder Sorensen from Australia (just not a Mormon elder). It pays to speak another's language when wanting favors—if you can do it within the truth. The caretakers gave us a VIP tour, allowed us the freedom to photograph all we wanted inside the jail, and even asked us to have lunch with them in their home. We declined that invitation.

In Springfield, Illinois, we stopped to visit Abraham Lincoln's grave. We then drove to Mammoth Cave, Kentucky, which was stupendous—but not as magnificent, in our opinion, as the Jenolan Caves in New South Wales. From West Virginia we traversed the Skyline Drive along the top of the Blue Ridge Mountains into the state of Virginia. We passed into Washington, D.C., where we toured the Capitol, the White House, the various monuments, and Arlington Cemetery. We felt that a visit to the nation's capital was especially beneficial to the children's education.

We then headed to Baltimore and drove through the new auto tunnel underneath Chesapeake Bay. Finally arriving at the Susquehanna River in Pennsylvania, we filmed the area where Joseph Smith and Oliver Cowdery were baptized and ordained in 1829. It felt like a hallowed spot to us. Joseph and Emma's infant son lay buried nearby in an old cemetery, which we also filmed.

We drove to Fayette, New York, and saw the location of the Peter Whitmer home, where the church was organized. Moving on to Palmyra, we visited the sacred grove, the home where Joseph Smith's family had lived, and the building in which the Book of Mormon was printed in 1830. Hill Cumorah, the repository of the Book of Mormon plates, was our next stop. From there we headed to Niagara Falls.

The falls at night were truly magnificent with the colorful searchlights playing on them. In the morning we entered Canada and walked down into the tunnels under the Horseshoe Falls. We were dressed in waterproof clothing and coats because of the large amount of spray in the tunnels. It was stupendous to walk under the cliffs over which the mighty waters cascaded. The thunder of the falls and the majesty of the waters smashing out their energy on the rocks below was something we would never forget. Truly Niagara was a wonderful place.

We drove to Kirtland, where once again we slept in the old Sidney Rigdon home. The next morning we attended church in the temple and left at noon for Wisconsin. We had a good visit with George and Blanche Mesley, and I was able to repair a few mechanical things for them. We then returned home, extremely pleased with the seven reels of film we took during the trip. I had especially asked the Lord to make a success of that venture so we could share those sights with our countrymen in Australia someday.

☼ ☼ ☼

The weather was ideal at the 1958 Des Moines reunion at Guthrie Grove. The Lord blessed me abundantly to give what was perhaps my best ministry yet to a large number of people. He also used me for the first time in a reunion to exercise the gift of prophecy. A wonderful spirit of unity prevailed in my classes among both youth and aged. It was amazing how they would bring out points in perfect harmony with what had just been taught—which became stepping stones to the next thought. I had never seen a more constructive working of the good Spirit.

I was still "on the mountaintop" when we returned home on Saturday evening and received a telephone call from a young lady at Iowa State College, asking me to baptize her. I joyfully agreed. The Iowa fields were surely white and ready to harvest.

On August 24 I addressed the members of the combined Protestant churches at a sunrise service in Ames. It was held at a drive-in theater, and there was a fairly large audience of nonmembers. I spoke on revelation—one can not beat around the bush speaking "pretty nothings" when the world is rushing toward a terrible calamity.

In September I left for Kewanee, Illinois, for a preaching series every night for two weeks. During the day, I visited the Saints in the town. Kewanee was one of those old, run-down, "dead in the wood" branches, which would either revive or die out. It was in a town of 16,000 people; and I did not want to see it die.

I worked there with Dale Bethel, a young man who had just entered the mission field. We had a fine time together. Dale's wife was Suzie, a petite Japanese church member. He had met her in Japan during the Korean War. They would later be assigned by the RLDS Church to Japan, where they helped build our mission there.

During the two-week series, the attendance continued to grow; and interest was good. We seemed to be successful in putting some life back into the branch. I showed slides of Australia and movies and slides of Tahiti. The people felt the inspiration of the Holy Spirit during the presentation of the everlasting gospel.

While in Illinois, I took movies of the historical places in Amboy and Plano. The grave of Zenos H. Gurley had recently been located in an overgrown cemetery near Sandwich, Illinois. I also saw the birthplace of Israel A. Smith and the first church built by the Reorganization. Over the next couple of months, I edited the film and recorded the sound track to complete my church history documentary.

After returning from Illinois, I was home in Iowa for one day; then I drove to Independence to attend the pre-conference seventies' quorum sessions. The 1958 conference was held in October instead of April to allow time to complete the Auditorium. Gwen and I had an enjoyable time at conference while a young couple from Ames stayed at our house to watch the children.

Brother W. Wallace Smith had been ordained as the new prophet and president of the RLDS Church. Brother Maurice Draper, who had been our apostle, was moved into the First Presidency; and a newly ordained apostle, Brother Charles Neff, was put in charge of our region. It was confirmed at that conference that Gwen and I would not be returning yet to Australia as we had hoped; but we were to continue on in Iowa at least until the next conference in April, 1960. I felt that God still intended to use me in the Des Moines District to bring many souls into His Kingdom.

With a renewed spirit, I started a series of "crusades" at several of the branches in the district, beginning at Fort Dodge. We had six baptisms at the end of the first series, with others to follow. My soul thrilled with that outpouring of spiritual power, but I prayed that I might remain humble and always remember where the power came from and why.

Other series followed at Marshalltown, Runnells, and then Knoxville. On the opening night in Knoxville, 186 people (nearly half of them nonmembers) were in a church that seated 140. I finished the series there with some decisions for baptism; and I asked the local priesthood members to hold cottage meetings with the converts, who did not yet know very much about Christ's Church.

The year of 1958 ended on a positive note, with over 20 people in the district making their covenants with the Lord during the month of December. Altogether there were 77 baptisms in the district during the year.

The year 1959 started with an ambitious new program for me that included lecturing to young marrieds and priesthood members and holding several cottage meetings, all within the same week. In January I received a letter from President Smith asking me to be responsible for the new Northwest Iowa District that was forming (which actually extended into Minnesota), as well as my current Des Moines District. I agreed to be the district president, but only until the new district was in motion and functioning on a basis where a local man could be elected to the position. I was not able to do as much personal cottage-meeting work, but instead trained more men to do it locally.

I started working on a new invention or "brainchild" of mine—a small projector using 16mm slides. If successful, it would revolutionize our cottage-meeting work on a local level. I designed a special projector which could be reproduced by volunteer labor and made available to the local men for about $20 each. That was $100 less than other slide projectors cost. Some men of the district donated money to buy a new metal lathe to make parts, and other men worked to mass produce them. I photographed hundreds of 16mm slides to be used with the new equipment.

On Good Friday morning our family was interviewed by the press. The previous Tuesday, the main newspaper in Des Moines had sent a reporter and a photographer to our home to investigate my work. They found me home alone and covered in grease, working on my project. That took their fancy; so they arranged to come back on Friday, photograph the family and the invention, and write up the Sorensens for a special Saturday night page of the paper. Because of the publicity it would give the church, I consented—obtaining a promise from the lady reporter to explain our cottage-meeting program and other things of value. A full page about us with five large photographs was printed in the *Des Moines Tribune* of April 4, 1959—which was also Gwen's birthday.

At the Newton branch, I preached the Easter sermon to 71 people. Only two years earlier, before I commenced working there, only four or five had been attending. The Lord truly blessed us. The branch was still growing, and soon 75 to 80 people were attending regularly. The newspaper publicity had helped to no end, and it continued to do so for quite some time.

In June we held a youth camp for the Des Moines District. My classes on the missionary use of the Scriptures went very well. I took my big telescope along. When the nights were beautiful and clear, the young people were able to admire the heavens. They lined up each night, waiting to look through the telescope. The camp cooks were fascinated and wanted me to bring the telescope to reunion.

We were saddened in June to hear about the loss of three fine church men—Evan Fry, Elbert A. Smith, and Albert Scherer. Al, the seventy with whom I worked when I first arrived in America, was a victim of leukemia, which was diagnosed while he was an appointee in Holland. The church brought him home, and he asked the Lord for ten years so he could be with his children as they grew up. The doctors had given him only a short time to live; but through administration, the Lord extended his life almost exactly ten years.

In July the Sorensens set out on our annual vacation, going to Mexico via Independence. We traveled through the Ozarks and Oklahoma to Texas, rode on a ferry to Galveston, and enjoyed a swim in the Gulf of Mexico—the first time we had been in seawater since arriving in America. One night in southern Texas we had a most difficult time finding a suitable place to stop. When we finally did find a spot, the heat was unbearable in the car; and the mosquitos were just as intolerable outside. We left at 5 a.m. and let the children continue sleeping in the car.

By noon we had arrived at Weslaco, Texas, where the headquarters of our Latin American mission was located. There we stayed at the home of Brother Clair Weldon. That afternoon he and Bob Fishburn took us to a beach in Mexico for a swim. Trevor requested that I baptize him at that place; so about a week later on our way home, I performed the ordinance at Matamoras Beach as the sun was setting. What a lovely, peaceful scene and experience it was! He was confirmed a couple of weeks later in Iowa.

To the best of our knowledge (after checking the RLDS Church records), Trevor was the first Reorganized Latter Day Saint to be baptized in Mexico. I prayed the Father that he might be the first of thousands of baptisms to become a reality in that land of the "remnant of Israel."

On our way home we stopped at Independence again, where I showed President F. Henry Edwards and the Presiding Bishopric my new invention for cottage meetings. By that time, I had made seven of the new projectors. The men were all very impressed. A patent search in Washington revealed that no similar device had been registered, so the patent application process was started.

After returning from our vacation, we headed to the Des Moines District reunion at Guthrie Grove. I preached the sermon on the first Sunday morning. During the week, our son was hit on the nose by a baseball bat. It seemed that his nose was broken—it was bleeding profusely and all bent out of shape. We administered to him and felt a power present which spoke well for his recovery. After Gwen and I took him home, 55 miles from the camp, his nose was no longer crooked but straight. Our family doctor examined him carefully, expecting the swelling to be much worse. If it was no worse in the morning, he said we could all go back to the reunion. That we did. All Trevor had to show for his experience was a beautiful black eye. God be praised! He has truly been good to us and our children.

On the last Sunday of the reunion, the Lord spoke to me through Patriarch Henry Castings, saying that both He and His people loved me and that I was not brought to this land to be ministered to but because of the ministry I was able to give. Brother Castings also said that my work in this land was not finished. In the same message Brother Charles Neff was told that he would accomplish much good in Korea and that the Lord would bring him safely home. Apostle Neff later bore his testimony that I was brought to this land for what I was able to give and not for any other reason. With both men bearing testimony, I felt assured that the message was from the Lord.

About that time I started to experiment with sleep learning, using a tape recorder which was connected to a flat speaker under my pillow. It was set to turn on and off by a timer once or twice during the night while I was asleep. I thought sleep learning would be useful to help the missionaries learn new languages quickly. I had some success with it because it helped me learn Spanish faster. Beth also used it to learn material before examinations. Once when she used it before a history test, she remembered all of the things she had on the tape and received 100% on them; but she did not do as well and received only a *B* on the things she did not sleep learn.

I gave a sleep-learning set to Dale Bethel to see if it would help him learn Japanese. He agreed to give it a month's trial. His Japanese wife spoke first on the tape, and he followed it with the English translation. He reported that he learned more Japanese in that month than he had in the previous two years. I fixed up another machine to help an appointee learn German.

In September we held the conference for the Northwest Iowa District. I was able to shed the task of district president, which went to a local man whom I had recommended for the position. However, I continued to serve as missionary there and in the Des Moines District.

Marvia was the only member of our family who saw Premier Nikita Khrushchev of the Soviet Union when he passed within three miles of our house during his visit to the United States. She went with a girlfriend and had a good view of Khrushchev when his motorcade had to slow down to turn at the intersection where she was standing.

In October I preached the first sermon in the "new secondhand church" at Marshalltown. The Saints had purchased the building from a faction of the Christian Church that did not believe in using musical instruments in their services. There was even a clause in the deed saying that if the building were sold, it would revert to the original owners if the purchaser brought musical instruments of any kind into the building. So on that Sunday we did not use an organ or piano. But subsequently we had that clause deleted from the deed.

☼ ☼ ☼

My patriarchal blessing, given in 1937, said that I was blessed with a degree of patience but that I would need more. That has proven quite true! I could not give cottage meetings and then just leave the people if they did not accept immediately. My love for them encouraged me to return many times until they either accepted or completely rejected the great message. Sometimes I waited six or nine months before going back, and then got their decisions.

One experience showed me how God's Spirit works in people, even when we think they might not be interested in the gospel. I had two series of cottage meetings in the Marshalltown area. One was in the home of a farmer named Mr. Ward. He, his wife, and two teenage children had listened very intently; but at the conclusion of the series, they did not appear to show any interest in becoming members of Christ's Church.

I was also holding cottage meetings with Vic Richardson, his wife, and teenage daughter. He was rated as the second best insurance salesman for his company in North America. When I presented certain propositions to him, he answered in insurance jargon: "I'll buy that, Sorensen; yes, I'll buy that" or "No, that won't pay a dividend." I had to rack my brains and pray that I could speak to him in language that he would understand. When I finished the meetings with no positive result, I told the good Lord and myself, "I'll leave these people alone. I'm not going to plague them."

About six months later, as I was driving on Highway 30, I felt an impulse come into my body and mind to go into Marshalltown. I had just finished a series of preaching services every night that week. I was dead tired, and I still had a long drive home to my family in Boone.

I thought, "Oh, that must be my imagination." I put my

foot down a little harder on the accelerator and passed one road which led into the city. Just before I came to the next road leading there, I heard a voice say, "Go back to Marshalltown." Again I disobeyed and went straight ahead. As I approached the third and last road into town, the words came with very strong emphasis, "Go back to Marshalltown!"

That time I said, "You win, Lord." Then I turned the car toward town.

First I went to the home of Pastor "Slim" Sawtel and told him we had work to do. He wanted to have supper first; but I said, "Slim, I think this is the time to act because I feel that the Lord has directed me here." He conceded, and we drove to Mr. Ward's farm.

Mr. Ward was in the barn doing chores and was very surprised to see us. I greeted him and said, "I've come to get your acceptance of the message that I gave you six months ago. You've had plenty of time to think about it."

He replied, "Yes, and I'm ready." I asked about his wife, and he told me to go inside and speak to her.

When I told Mrs. Ward that her husband just gave his name for baptism, she burst into tears and exclaimed, "I've been waiting for him to say that ever since you were here for those meetings." Their family of four ended up making covenants with the Lord.

Brother Sawtel then suggested, "Now let's go home and have some supper."

I said, "No, there's still a job unfinished. We have to go and see Vic Richardson, the insurance agent." After we arrived at the Richardson house and talked for a few minutes, I said, "I've come to get your name on the dotted line."

He recognized that insurance term and replied, "Well, why not?" Then he turned to his wife and said, "I'm ready if you are, Helen."

She burst into tears. She had also treasured up in her heart the desire to give full allegiance to the pure gospel of the Lord Jesus, as did their teenage daughter.

Because I listened to the voice that told me to go to Marshalltown, seven precious souls were added to the Church of Jesus Christ. If I had gone on home, maybe the right moment for those decisions would have passed. The Lord knows all things, and I was very repentant that I had hesitated at all.

☼ ☼ ☼

When I held a preaching series at Galesburg, Illinois, we had to put folding chairs down the aisles because the building could not hold the crowds after the first two nights. The main benefit was to the Saints of that dying branch, some of whom rededicated their lives with tears in their eyes. Afterward we had three decisions for baptism and some cottage meetings lined up for the local men.

I also held a preaching series at our branch in Winterset, Iowa, which likewise needed help. We were continuing to get decisions for baptism in both districts. Several men were working on cottage meetings, including one who was using my new projector system. In November we opened a new mission at Jefferson, Iowa.

In December I had the wonderful experience of baptizing Ririfatu Mariteragi, a Tahitian who was attending Graceland College. His mother was a member, but his father was a Mormon. Gwen and our two girls sang in his native tongue, and I conducted the service in Tahitian at our big Des Moines Central church. Because a priesthood meeting was to begin at the same time as the baptism, about 40 local men were in the church. They were thrilled to witness the service in another language, and it helped bring to them the realization of the world-wide nature of our work.

During December I gave a series of devotional talks over the radio of Iowa State College at Ames. My topic was the six principles of the gospel.

Sometimes one faces difficult situations in performing the ordinance of baptism. One man who was confined to a wheelchair was converted. He asked, "How am I going to be baptized?" I replied that we could quite easily arrange it. We strapped him to an ordinary straight-back chair so he couldn't fall forward. Two men went into the font first; and two others lowered the man, chair and all. When we tipped the chair backward, the man went right under the water—he was baptized just as much as anyone else, since he was completely immersed in water.

Although we did not know it at the time, we were suffering through what was to be our last Iowa winter. I loved the land of Zion during the other seasons, but I never got used to the bitterly cold, icy winters. The barrenness and desolation were depressing, but even worse was the amount of driving I had to do on icy roads. The Lord blessed me through all the driving—about 150,000 miles during the four years I was assigned to Iowa. I had only one minor accident—when the car slid off the icy road into a ditch; but then no harm was done.

I was meeting with some success, but things were progressing too slowly for my liking. It seemed that the Americans were slacking from their religious fervor which followed World War II, and it was hard to overcome the apathy and indifference that was afoot. They had had it too easy for too long, and I thought that only a calamity would bring them to their senses. (Unfortunately, that is even truer now as I write this than it was in 1960.)

At the next conference, we were anticipating a move from Iowa—probably back to Australia. With that in mind, my main goal for 1960 was to train the local priesthood to carry on the work. Many people in the two districts were showing interest in the gospel. It would be a pity to lay a foundation with those people and not to have a follow-up. I had produced about 10 of my little projectors, and the men in the field were reporting them to be a success.

The prophecy Patriarch Henry Castings had given during reunion the previous year—that my work in this land was not yet finished—was troubling me. We had been away from our homeland for nearly nine years; and as the church never kept Americans away from their homeland for more than four years at a time, I did not see why it should be so with us. With that concern, I visited with the Council of Twelve the month before General Conference.

We talked about my future and the possibility of our return to Australia. Brother Reed Holmes, the new apostle to Australia, had asked for my return. However, the apostles were concerned about Beth, who had only one year of high school left before graduation. It was not very often that they consulted a missionary about his appointment; generally his assignment was first revealed at the General Conference—for better or for worse. They told of their confidence in me and of my ability to work anywhere, giving me the choice of remaining in Iowa or returning to Australia. I said that I preferred to go to my homeland and minister to my own people for a time.

In April, 1960, we attended the General Conference. Since it was also the 100th anniversary of the Reorganization, we decided it was important to take the children with us. At the conference my fears and concerns were dispelled. At last we were going home! I was appointed to the Hunter-Manning District in New South Wales, and we were to live in Newcastle. Of course, our families in Australia were thrilled with the news.

We had a lot of work to do—arranging for shipping and transportation, selling our furniture and other things, then packing what was left. My work in the districts had to be brought to a close to ensure a smooth continuity during the transition to the new missionary.

Marvia was just finishing her first year of junior high school, where she played the violin and was on the honor roll for her good grades.

In May I conducted my last preaching series at Dennison, Iowa, and preached farewell sermons at most of the other branches in the districts. It was very heartwarming and rewarding that the Saints did not want us to leave, but they were happy for our sakes that we were to be reunited with our loved ones after nine years. We had grown to love these people and were sorry to be leaving them.

In early June I went to youth camp with Beth on a Saturday, but only 24 campers showed up. We had 13 on the staff, including myself and Syd Jacka from Australia; therefore, I was free to return home to continue packing. Beth stayed at the camp and made a number of friends. Bill McGuire, a lad from Mason City, and Beth were selected king and queen of the camp. They were destined to meet again several years later.

On Saturday, July 2, we cleaned our house with the help of some of the Saints and left Boone in the afternoon. We journeyed about 80 miles and stayed the night at the farm of the Harkraiders. The next day we continued on to the Center Place, where we stayed with our former neighbors, the Kelseys. That night at the campus we heard a sermon by President W. Wallace Smith.

About ten days later we left from Union Station in Kansas City on a Santa Fe train headed west. Our family was fortunate to have our own sleeper suite on the train. It was a fascinating trip across the western United States as we crossed the Painted Desert and continued on to the Grand Canyon. Gwen's earnings as a nurse enabled us to enjoy the few extras of our journey, like the side trip to the

Grand Canyon. It was certainly an impressive sight. There we watched the Hopi Indians perform some native dancing.

When we arrived in California, we spent a few days in Montebello with Cecil Johnson, a church member who was one of the American servicemen we had met in Australia. I preached three times and conducted prayer services in the Los Angeles area. The Johnsons and their two girls took us to Disneyland and Knott's Berry Farm, where the children especially enjoyed themselves. We also visited Forest Lawn Cemetery, Marineland, the old mission of San Juan Capistrano (where we did see the swallows), Farmers Market, and the Art Linkletter Show (although Trevor was too young to be allowed entrance). After leaving the Johnsons, we stayed at the Ballantynes' house in Long Beach. They had moved into Los Angeles, so we had the whole house to ourselves. While we were there, the Los Angeles area was having its worst heat wave in half a century. The smog was terrible, making our eyes smart and water all the time we were outside.

On the night of July 29, 1960, we boarded the British ocean liner, *S.S. Orcades*, at Long Beach. Several of the Saints from Los Angeles came to see us off. We were very excited as our voyage home was about to begin.

▾ The Sorensens on First Street in Boone, Iowa, 1959

▲ Trevor and Vivian displaying some of Vivian's creations—slide maker, 16mm slide projector, refractor telescope, Sputnik telescope, 6" reflector telescope, and hi-fi cabinet

▼ Maurice Draper, Vivian, and others at Des Moines reunion

CHAPTER 9

Assignment to Australia

As the lights of the harbor at Long Beach faded into the distance, we said farewell to the Promised Land. It caused us quite a pang to leave the Land of Zion, but I thought that perhaps we would return some day—as many people seemed to think and as it had been prophesied by Patriarch Henry Castings. However, it was wonderful to be returning to Australia!

We soon settled into life aboard the *S.S. Orcades*. She was a 23,000-ton British ship of the P&O Orient Line. On board were several other Saints, mostly Australians returning from the General Conference. The accommodations and food were better than we had on the *Eridan* or the *Chung King*. Gwen, Trevor, and I had one cabin, while Beth and Marvia shared a cabin with two other young women. One day someone stole Beth's wallet from her cabin but left some flowers and fruit in its place on her bunk—a thief with a conscience? She was most upset because the wallet contained pictures of her friends in Boone. She never did get it back.

Our voyage from California to Hawaii was on smooth seas. We arrived at Honolulu early on the morning of August 3 and were met at the dock by Rosemary Clark, a young woman we knew from Iowa. Her husband Neil was in the navy and stationed in Hawaii. Since our ship was departing at midnight, they had a busy day planned for us to take in as many of the sights of Oahu as possible. Neil took us to the U.S. Naval Air Station where he worked. There he made Trevor probably the happiest nine-year-old boy in the world by letting him sit in the cockpit of a Crusader jet fighter.

At midnight we headed for our next port of call, Suva, Fiji. Near the equator the captain diverted our ship to sail through the narrow pass between Hull Island and Willis Island. After several days of seeing only ocean, it was a welcome change to view those lush tropical islands. The natives waved to us from the golden beaches, and we waved back. My attempt to film this portion of the trip was not entirely successful because my movie camera lens fogged up when I brought it from the air-conditioned cabin into the hot, humid air.

On August 10 we docked at Suva. We spent the day enjoying the sights of Fiji, which included a performance of native dancing. The natives of Fiji are Melanesian, with dark skins and fuzzy black hair. In contrast to the vigorous dancing of the Tahitians, their dancing is very slow and deliberate, possibly because of the hotter climate in Fiji.

The next day, we set sail for Auckland, New Zealand. There we were met by the missionary, Brother Floyd Burdekin, and his family. His wife Lorna and Gwen are first cousins. We toured Auckland together, including a climb up to the top of Mt. Eden, one of several dormant volcanoes in the Auckland area. The children climbed to the bottom of the crater. Not far from Auckland we visited the church reunion grounds. Late that day we left for Australia, and many of the New Zealand Saints saw us off.

Since we were in the southern hemisphere, it was the middle of winter. A gale hit us with full force as we plowed across the Tasman Sea between New Zealand and Australia. The driving wind and rain as well as the mountainous waves caused the crew to close off all the outside decks. Despite its anti-roll stabilizers, the ship was pitching and rolling in the heavy seas. Most passengers were seasick, and the few who ventured from their cabins soon regretted it. Our family, being rather good sailors, fared better than most.

At last we emerged from the gale into calmer waters as we approached the coast of Australia. The ship arrived in Sydney Harbor on August 20. We were greeted at the wharf by Ruth and Frank Flood and Gwen's father, who had come from Brisbane to meet us. For a few days we stayed with Frank, Ruth, and Carynne at their home in Ryde while we took care of business with the bishop and the mission president.

After taking delivery of our new car, a 1960 Holden, we drove to our new home in Newcastle at the mouth of the Hunter River on the Pacific Ocean, about 100 miles north of Sydney. Like its namesake in England, Newcastle-on-Tyne, it is basically an industrial city with steel works, shipbuilding, coal mining, and other heavy industry. In contrast to its industrial base, the Newcastle area also boasted some beautiful lakes and beaches with excellent waves for surfing. At the time we lived there, the greater Newcastle area had a population of about 300,000.

As we approached the city, we were amazed at the forest of television antennas that stretched before us. In 1960 Newcastle did not have its own television station. To receive broadcasts from Sydney, people had to install 10- to 20-foot antennas on the roofs of their houses.

We stopped briefly at the mission home on Blackall Street in the suburb of Hamilton. It was to be our residence for the next four years. Since we were very anxious to see our relatives, we drove the remaining 500 miles north to Brisbane. The Pacific Highway was a two-lane road in those days, with ferries that took traffic across the large rivers in northern New South Wales. One danger along the Pacific Highway was the possibility of hitting large kangaroos (not deer as in America). Nearer to Queensland the vegetation and crops became more tropical. Banana and sugar cane plantations replaced the dairy farms and temperate zone crops common farther south.

In Australia, as in England, cars are driven on the left side of the road. At times it took concentration to keep from making a mistake. While we were driving north one time, I instinctively went to the right-hand lane after making a turn. Fortunately there were no cars nearby, and my family soon pointed out my mistake—nearly deafening me in the process!

We finally arrived in Brisbane, where we had a joyous reunion with our families. After nine years our parents looked much older but were still in good health. Although Beth and Marvia remembered their grandparents, it was really the first meeting for Trevor, who had been only five months old when they last saw him. It also was wonderful to fellowship again with our church family in Brisbane, where I preached on Sunday.

After we returned to Newcastle, Marvia and Trevor had to start school in mid-year—Marvia in second year at Hamilton Junior Girls' High School and Trevor in third class (boys) at Hamilton Primary School. They adjusted to the new school system very quickly. Beth was waiting until after the Christmas holidays and reunion before entering nurses' training. In the meantime, she worked in Raymond Terrace in a clothing store owned by Jack Jones, a church member.

At the October district conference, I was elected the president of the Hunter-Manning District and soon started improving the facilities in that area. I toured the whole district. That same month I took a group of young men to the Tiona Reunion Grounds for a weekend working bee.

One of the first things I did after returning to our mission home was to plant a vegetable garden, including tomatoes, beans, choko, onions, beets (beetroots), and carrots. I found it relaxing to work in my garden, nurturing the bountiful fruits of the Lord as a break in my main work of nurturing and reaping the spiritual fruits of the Lord. Our family really enjoyed the fresh vegetables.

Beth, Marvia, Trevor, and I donned miner's lamps when one of my prospects invited us to tour a coal mine. We enjoyed the experience very much. It gave us a much better idea of what miners have to endure as they wrestle the "black diamonds" from the earth.

In December, 1960, President W. Wallace Smith and his wife Rosamond stayed with us for a few days before they attended the Tiona reunion. While in Newcastle, Brother Smith spoke to the combined branches of the area at the Hamilton church. Then he attended the appointees' institute held at the Tuncurry church. The Smiths were greatly impressed with the beauty of Tiona where they gave ministry. One morning after they had talked in the children's tent, a boy asked, "Brother Smith, how tall are you?"

He replied, "Five feet, 18 inches!" One could almost see the wheels turning in the children's heads.

Directly after reunion, we sent our three children to visit relatives in Brisbane. They really enjoyed the train ride there and back. A lot of the trains in Australia at that time (and even 10 years later) still used steam locomotives.

☼ ☼ ☼

The year 1961 started off well. The district kept me very busy, and several people with whom I had held cottage meetings were baptized. Besides ministerial work, I felt a need to make our churches look respectable. Most of them were very old and much in need of paint and repair.

Believing that the outside of the houses of the Lord should reflect the Spirit that we enjoy inside, I always liked to see our buildings look good.

About that time, I completed a small tape recorder I had started making in America. I used it to study Spanish with a sleep-learning apparatus; I wanted to be prepared if I were someday called to minister to the descendants of the Lamanites. Later I made a transistor radio. Those hobbies helped keep me sane—acting as a blowoff valve (to use a mechanical engineer's phrase).

Beth passed her entrance examination and commenced nurses' training at the Royal Newcastle Hospital in March. Our first bird had flown the nest! At times I really missed her at Tiona. Although her help was appreciated, what I missed most was the time we spent together.

I started spending quite a bit of time improving our reunion grounds at Tiona. Joe and Rita Smith, the caretakers, had their hands full with maintaining the grounds; they needed help for the big jobs. We needed a hot-shower system, so we bought an old donkey boiler and tanks. With the help of my father, some of the local church men, and some of the boys from Newcastle, we installed the equipment. My father, who was 71 at the time, made a wooden stand for the water tank. During winter that year the tank burst its seams; to effect repairs, it was necessary to dive into the freezing cold water. Our efforts were successful, and the system provided hot showers for many years.

One of my duties was to publish the *Evangel*, the official RLDS Church publication for the Hunter-Manning District. I typed the articles on stencils, ran them off on our Gestetner duplicating machine in my office, and mailed the copies. It was a major task each month on top of all my other duties. Fortunately I was often able to get my family or some of the other Saints to help staple, fold, and address the newsletters.

In May we held our first youth camp at Tiona since we returned to Australia. The camp went smoothly with about 50 youth attending, including Marvia and Trevor. Gwen helped in the kitchen. Using the telescope I had made in Iowa, the campers really enjoyed viewing the moon, Saturn, and Jupiter.

The Lord blessed the missionary work in the district. I traveled frequently throughout the large area, which extended from Port Macquarie in the north, to Tamworth in the west and Gosford to the south. Through the School of the Restoration, I also taught priesthood training classes, which were well received by the men. I held cottage meetings almost every night of the week. Sometimes one of my girls operated the slide projector for me. Nearly 40 precious souls were baptized in the district that year.

I found that the women were much more receptive than the men; many of the Aussie men were indifferent to religion and the things of God. Maybe they had been fooled too many times in the name of Christianity.

In one place in Australia, a religious group called the Gospel Fishermen used to meet near the river. On one particular occasion their leader was going to demonstrate that he could walk on water just as Christ had done. Quite a crowd gathered one Sunday afternoon to watch. The man walked to the end of a long jetty and jumped into the river. Just as he went into the water, a huge fish, probably a mullet, jumped out of the water—it coincided beautifully. Of course, the man sank. But when he came back to the crowd, he was not a bit abashed. He said, "I fell into the hole that the fish left when he jumped out. There was no water there to support me!" It was amazing that people could be hoodwinked by that sort of thing, but some of them believed him!

Since Gwen had experience with girls' work in the U.S., she was asked to start up the Skylark and Oriole girls' programs in Australia. The lecture material was provided through the RLDS Church's Department of Religious Education, which was headed in Australia by Brother Geoff Spencer. Thanks to his enthusiastic support, Gwen taught a course in Newcastle to a very interested and devoted group of potential Oriole and Skylark leaders. The girls' work proved very successful over the years.[1]

Sister Emere Mervin arrived in mid-year from Tahiti. She intended to stay with us for six weeks but ended up staying six months, with occasional trips to visit other friends. Emere was a gracious lady and a good ambassador for Tahiti; we enjoyed her company very much. She came with us to the children's camp at Tiona in September, where she taught native handcrafts.

Marvia had a somewhat difficult time adjusting to her school; she discovered that the Australian girls had already learned such subjects as geometry. But Brother Jim Imrie, a mathematics teacher, kindly tutored her. As a result of his help and a lot of hard work, Marvia was able to pass the state-wide Intermediate Examination at the end of 1961. The next year she moved on to Hunter Girls' High School. Trevor, however, being in a lower grade, was able to adjust quickly; and soon he was top in his class.

In early 1962 I received a letter of commendation from the Joint Council of the church. It was nice to know that they were pleased with my work. But, of course, I was mainly concerned as to whether God was pleased with me. My main desire was to bring souls to Him.

We had the assistance of some very dedicated priesthood members. One was Brother Mervin Richards, who lived in

---

[1] In 1986 the Saints celebrated the 25th anniversary of the girls' program. Marvia represented Gwen and read a history of the beginning of Orioles and Skylarks in Australia.

the small town of Buladelah, which had about 1,000 people. Brother Richards had been the pastor of our church; he was the local undertaker, agent for the bank, chief of the fire brigade (department), and executive board member of the school and hospital. Merv had a service station and was by far the best mechanic in town. He did all that while still being a good husband and a good father to six daughters. Merv was highly respected and made a good name for our church. I held a number of preaching series in Buladelah; but while the people realized that Mervin Richards had something wonderful, they mostly did not want to change their lives.

Another priesthood member in the district, Brother Aubrey Ivers (we all called him Aub), and his wife Kath stood out as bastions of faith. They persistently and regularly went to Laurieton, a fishing village on the coast north of Tuncurry, where they conducted church school. They diligently carried on Sunday after Sunday, teaching the children. In some of those fishing villages, the people were rather rough, alcohol flowed freely, and the young people did not have a good opportunity to learn the proper way of life. But through the love and persistence of Aub and Kath, quite a number of them responded. When I went there and did missionary work among them, several gave their names for baptism.

One cold September morning, we went to the Hastings River, where Aub baptized two young men and I baptized eight. The water was very cold. By the time I finished, I was just about frozen; but the candidates did not seem to notice the cold. As each came out from under the water, he said he glowed with warmth. So the mission of Laurieton was brought into being through the initial efforts of Aub and Kath.

In October at our district conference I was able to shed the burden of district president when Dave Johnson of

Newcastle agreed to take that responsibility. Leaving the administrative details in Dave's capable hands, I devoted my time to the work I loved—telling the gospel to my fellowmen, making slides for cottage-meeting work, and training other men to conduct the cottage meetings. During 1963 I spent two-thirds of my time away from home doing missionary work around the district.

In 1963 Marvia had her final year at Hunter Girls' High School and successfully gained her Leaving Certificate after passing the state examinations. It was also Trevor's last year in primary school. He was elected captain of the school by popular vote and continued to be top of his class. Beth was doing well and enjoying nurses' training.

☼ ☼ ☼

One amusing thing happened about that time. Sister Eileen Ahrens of the Wallsend branch raised budgerigars (parakeets). She gave a young bird to Trevor, who adored it. He named it Timmy and worked hard to get it to talk. After we followed the recommended procedure a couple of months, Timmy still did not talk. As the bird grew older, we suddenly realized what the problem was—Timmy was really a Tammy! And unlike the human species, female budgies don't talk as well or as much as males.

We returned Tammy to Sister Ahrens, who gave us a new budgie—which really turned out to be a Timmy. Boy, could he talk! For the six years we remained in Australia, Trevor and Timmy were "best mates." Timmy entertained us with phrases like, "Twinkle, twinkle little star, I am Trevor's budgerigar." Once he learned to talk, he chattered up a storm.

When Gwen was away for a couple of weeks one time, I taught Timmy to say, "Gwen, you're my sweetheart. Kiss me, please." Boy, was she surprised when she returned.

We also taught Timmy his name and address in case he ever got lost. Right after he mastered the address, however, we moved! We tried to teach him the new address, but he was forever getting them mixed up. Fortunately, he never became lost.

Gwen relieved a desperate nursing shortage at the small Buladelah Hospital. At one point she was the only registered nurse there. The money she earned gave us a few extra pleasures, such as a television set. It was lonely while Gwen was away, but Beth came home when she could and cooked meals for us. After Buladelah, Gwen did some nursing at a geriatric hospital close to our home.

☼ ☼ ☼

One Sunday when I was preaching at Port Macquarie, where the Saints met in a house, a Brother and Sister Hobden walked in and introduced themselves. They were vacationing on the coast and had heard that I was holding meetings. After the service was over, they expressed a very keen desire to have me come to their home at Dubbo, about 300 miles inland.

Brother Hobden was a farmer in a big way. He raised sheep and grew wheat. He lived inland, a long way from the coast and a long way from the nearest church. Forty years earlier he had been going to a chiropractor, where he met and struck up a friendship with Walter Haworth, who was the president of the Australian Mission in those days. The outcome of it was that Hobden and his wife were baptized. For four decades they never had access to the church, but they read the Word of God every evening. Before they went to sleep, they read from one of the Three Books and prayed. Thus they kept their spirits fed while teaching their children and grandchildren the gospel.

Brother Hobden believed that with the extra instruction

of a good missionary series, there would be several decisions made. Our family spent a wonderful week at Dubbo with the sheep and wheat farmers and taught them the gospel. The Hobdens had done a good job—11 people decided to commit themselves to the Lord and become members of His church.

There was no suitable water for baptism on the Hobden property, but a beautiful river flowed through a nearby ranch (station). The owners of that station thought highly of Brother Hobden, and they readily agreed when he asked if we could use a big water hole in the river for the baptisms. Those precious souls added to the church at that time were all through the persistence, love, respect, study, and faith of Brother and Sister Hobden.

In August we experienced a sad loss in our family. Gwen's sister Ruth Flood had given birth to a second daughter, Frances Lynne, in late 1962. She was a sweet and cheerful baby; but when she was about eleven months old, doctors discovered that she had a brain tumor. Marvia went to be with Ruth and Frank and was there when little Lynne passed on to paradise. It was a sad funeral that Brother Walter Swain and I conducted at the Ryde church in Sydney.

As time permitted I continued to help at Tiona. Some brethren (and sometimes sisters) from the district joined me there on "working bees." In 1963 we painted the service hall, made two new shents (permanent shelters with canvas sides), and fixed the drains for the showers. My father came again and helped us put in concrete paths to some new rest rooms. Bishop Hudson Grundy spent a week helping us while my father was there.

Brother James Kemp, the mission president, assigned me

to the Tallebudgerra reunion, which was located on the beautiful beach between Murwillumbah and Coolongatta. That reunion served the Saints of the Queensland and northern New South Wales areas. Gwen, Marvia, and Trevor were able to accompany me. It was especially enjoyable because many of our relatives and old friends from Brisbane were in attendance. Brother Jack Gunning, who was the seventy assigned to the area, was in charge of the reunion; and I assisted him.

☼ ☼ ☼

In 1964 Marvia started attending Newcastle University; and Trevor was admitted to Newcastle Boys' High School in Waratah, the top high school in the area. Only six boys out of more than 40 in his class were accepted at that school, so it was quite an honor.

Trevor took piano lessons from Brethren Ken Thornton and Harry Ley, Jr. He was also active in the Pathfinders—the boys' equivalent of the Orioles. They met weekly at the Wallsend church and learned scouting skills—including knots, first aid, cliff rescue, camping, making rafts, following trails in the bush, etc. This group was led by some fine young men, including Ken Archer and Brian Roberts.

That year we moved into a home on Turner Street in the Newcastle suburb of Lambton. It did not belong to the church. We bought that house with the money saved from Gwen's nursing work. It was the first house we had owned since our little home in Brisbane when we were first married.

The house on Turner Street was 25 years old and built of weatherboard, with a brick front and corrugated iron roof. It sat on a hill; and from the front verandah, we could see the Pacific Ocean about six miles away. At night the lights of Newcastle were visible. We had a large fenced backyard in which I soon planted a vegetable garden and some lady finger banana trees that my father had sent me from Queensland. The house was on stilts at the back (due to the slope of the land), and there were a couple of enclosed rooms underneath, which contained the laundry, Trevor's chemistry set, my books, and the workshop. We had fun outfitting the house with secondhand furniture.

Tiona still needed attention. We had new caretakers there, Harold and Ivy Pollard. In September Brother Alec Ahrens and I went to Tiona and built a new 2,000-gallon water tank with the help of Harold Pollard. I pulled apart the electric motor that ran the tank's pump and replaced the condenser. It then ran as good as new.

In November we held a large party in our backyard to celebrate Beth's 21st birthday. Australians make much more fuss about the 21st birthday than people normally do in America. Such parties were usually very elaborate affairs with formal invitations, a lot of food, gifts, and entertainment—usually only exceeded in significance and size by a wedding reception.

Beth passed her final nurses' examination in December, and we attended her graduation ceremony at the nurses' quarters of the Royal Newcastle Hospital. It was not a grand affair, but it was quite nice. Beth looked lovely in her R.N. (sister's) veil, and she was so gracious. Although she had passed her exams and graduated, she did not finish her required four years of training until the following March.

About that time, Marvia started working at the same hospital. She was an assistant social worker and did a lot of driving to visit patients.

Our son did well at school, but he was not top of his class since the competition was much keener (the students were the "cream of the crop" of Newcastle). He became extremely interested in rockets. He studied library books about them and soon became quite knowledgeable about the technicalities of rocketry.

Trevor and some friends formed a club, and I helped them make several rockets. Sometimes they bought rocket motors which were ready to insert and ignite in cardboard and balsa rockets; but they got more fun, I think, out of the larger steel rockets that used propellant they made themselves. Some of their rockets were almost three feet long and about one and a half inches in diameter. The metal nozzles, nose cones, and other parts were made in my workshop.

About a half dozen of Trevor's schoolmates launched their first large rocket at an abandoned World War II emergency airstrip north of Raymond Terrace. On their first attempt, instead of shooting up into the air, the rocket fell over and shot along the ground. It stopped about 50 feet away and started a grass fire, which fortunately we were able to stamp out quickly.

After the rocket cooled off, the boys refueled it and set it back on the pad. Just as one of the lads pressed the ignition switch, two fighter aircraft of the Royal Australian Air Force flew directly overhead at an altitude of no more than a couple hundred feet. Fortunately, the rocket did not ignite. If it had been one of the later, more successful rockets, it could easily have hit a plane. One of those bright young lads quipped to me, "Mr. Sorensen, it's a good thing we didn't shoot down one of the planes; or the newspaper headlines would have read, 'Schoolboys Shoot Down a Quarter of Australia's Air Force!'"

Making and launching those rockets was truly an adventure! Some of them had parachutes, which deployed at a certain altitude to lower the rockets gently to the ground. Sometimes there were payload cabins on the rockets. One time we got some very ferocious "jumper ants," put quite a few of them in the cabin, and shot them up in the air.

The payload section came down by parachute. We checked the ants, found they were just as ferocious as ever, and called them "astroants."

The club continued launching rockets until Trevor finished high school in 1969. Little did we suspect that his making rockets would eventually lead him into aerospace engineering in the university and that he would become a real "rocket scientist" working on the American space program. But that is a story for another chapter.

☼ ☼ ☼

In 1964 I was able to put to good use a new tool that had just come on the market—an electric spray gun. I was soon using it extensively. It greatly increased the speed and ease of painting our church buildings.

That December Beth and Marvia attended the Tiona reunion in New South Wales as their work permitted. During the same week, Gwen, Trevor, and I attended the Mountain Hut reunion in Victoria. Brethren Floyd Burdekin, Hudson Grundy, and Jack Imrie were the other appointees there. The James Kemps were also in attendance, but for only part of the week. After Sister Kemp left, Gwen taught two classes for the women. That year Victoria had the coldest summer on record; the weather was windy most of the time. Of course, we really felt it since the reunion grounds were nearly 2,000 feet above sea level.

Gwen started working at Western Suburbs Maternity Hospital in Waratah in 1965. Since the hospital was located a few miles from our house, she bought her first car—a 1951 Austin A40 with a manual floor shift. Gwen really enjoyed her maternity work. I used to joke that at the hospital she was busy "hatching"; while I, with weddings and funerals, was busy "matching and dispatching."

Marvia continued her social work for the hospital. As

part of her duties at a geriatric hospital, she had to sing solos. In 1965 she was also elected Zion's League leader for the Hamilton branch, evidently following in her father's footsteps. She did a good job since she was very outgoing and enthusiastic, got along well with people, and had a lot of good ideas for the League.

My manual and spiritual labors continued. I helped install a freezing room at Tiona, painted the roof of the Teralba church, built a gem-polishing machine for children's camps, painted cabins and the caretaker's cottage at Tiona, and made the public address system for the new Buladelah church. Right after it opened in March, we held a preaching series for five nights to a near capacity crowd.

☼ ☼ ☼

The first Saints meeting at Tiona had built a long pier or jetty out into the lake so that people coming to reunion in boats could get ashore. There were no roads then. By the 1930s, when we attended reunion, there was a road to Tiona; but we had to cross the entrance of Lake Wallis by ferry from Tuncurry to Forster. By the 1960s a beautiful bridge spanned that entrance, making it even more convenient when I was a missionary there.

Later in the year, I did electrical work at Tiona with Brother Kevin Wall, who worked for the electric company in Newcastle. We were able to connect to the newly installed main power system and thus able to do away with the war-surplus electric generators that had been supplying power at Tiona. For my family I also made a transistorized stereo radio, tape recorder, and record player. It was something new in those days.

Besides the cottage meetings, preaching, and other Church work, I taught a scripture class at Bouragal High School, where several of our young people attended. Australia did not have the same "separation of church and state" as is held so dear in America. Each of the public schools had one period a week for scripture classes, which were taught by outside ministers. Students were allowed to choose which denomination's scripture class to attend; or if their religion was not represented, they could use the time to study.

A dreadful drought hit New South Wales the summer of 1965. Long droughts always led to frequent bush (forest) fires. The main highways in my district all had two lanes. At times I had to drive along with a wall of flame on one or both sides of the roadway. Other summers were just the opposite, with too much rain and the resulting floods. I then had to drive through water covering the highway; or if the water was too deep, sometimes a farmer's tractor towed the cars through.

Beth accompanied me in May on another trip to Dubbo and helped run the projector for all the cottage meetings. Because the drought was so bad, each morning she went with Brother Hobden in his jalopy to hand-feed his sheep. After she returned from that trip, Beth moved to Sydney and worked at Ryde District Soldiers' Memorial Hospital for a year to obtain her obstetric nurse's certification.

In May I was acting caretaker at Tiona for a few days while the Pollards went north for a holiday. I managed to get all the heavy work. People were vacating their cabins after the school holidays, and I had to scrub all the floors to make them ready for the new arrivals.

The work of the church in that area had begun in Tuncurry, a small fishing village on the coast of New South Wales close to Tiona. Some of the stalwart missionaries of the Restoration preached there, with some conversions, especially in a big family named Wright.

Sister Ella Wright of Tuncurry was a very courageous and diligent lady. In the years when the little group was neglected and the menfolk had died, she carried on with a church school. She brought up quite a number of children with the knowledge of the everlasting gospel. I used to preach to them whenever I could. It was amazing to see the response of those children, some of them teenagers. Quite a number of baptisms occurred because of the faith and the tenacity of that good woman.

One cold winter Sunday I was to perform a baptism for a gentleman at Wallsend church in Newcastle. The deacon had placed a big immersion heater in the font all night and forgot to remove it in the morning. Generally during baptisms I preceded the candidate into the font, but that time the man stepped ahead of me. He touched the first step, let out a yell, and jumped back! While I wondered what was wrong, the deacon realized that the heater may have been the problem. He quickly removed it, and we proceeded with the baptism.

Afterward, one man jokingly said to me, "There was a pretty good spirit in that baptism!" There could have been a very tragic result instead because Australia uses a 240-volt electrical system. But the protecting power of almighty God did not allow that to happen.

With the help of my sister Mavis, we put together a very attractive color brochure that described the Restoration Movement and the upcoming events of the latter days. It was printed by Standard Publishing in Sydney, which was owned by Brother Vic Alberts. That brochure received many compliments and was used extensively in introducing a great number of people to the restored gospel.

☼ ☼ ☼

Our children's camps had been growing in popularity and size, so in 1965 I decided to have two camps at Tiona —one during the first week of the school holidays and the other during the second week. The camps were highly successful, and much good resulted from them. Four of the young people asked for baptism while there, three from Tuncurry and one from Tamworth. After the camp, I baptized five others from Tuncurry in Lake Wallis.

The camps that we conducted—first in Australia and later in America—included worship and prayer services, scripture classes, campfires with songs and skits, the usual choices for recreational activities, and craft classes. One unique craft class that we started in the mid-60s was model rocketry, taught by Trevor. The boys and girls made their own model rockets of cardboard and balsa wood, and we bought engines for them. We always ended up with quite an assortment of colors and shapes. On Friday afternoons, instead of having the usual recreation period, the whole camp participated in the launching of those lovingly crafted rockets. Most flew remarkably well, and the young people caught them as they floated down by parachute. Those events were always big hits.

Another very popular activity was the Scripto game, which I introduced at the camps. It was based on a television version of tic-tac-toe, except that all the categories and questions were based on the Scriptures or church history. I made a board that was about three feet square with three rows of square blackboard panels to record the *X* or *O* in chalk for the team that answered the question correctly. Beneath each of the panels was the name of a category. By rotating rods behind the board, we changed the categories. We split the campers into two teams, and they had many hours of fun playing the game. Of course, they were also learning the Scriptures and church history in the process.

The culminating event of the week was a concert and banquet on Friday night with the crowning of the king and queen of the camp, who were elected by popular vote.

Camps were a lot of fun for the young people, but even more important were the spiritual benefits they gained. The closing prayer service on Saturday morning was always a moving experience.

☼ ☼ ☼

Dave Johnson, who worked as secretary for the Klosters Ford car dealership, had resigned as district president so he could use his long service leave to travel with his wife Agnes and attend the World Conference in 1966. However, there was no long service leave in the army of the Lord, so it was necessary for me to fill his place and again serve as the district president. During the year of 1965 we had more than 40 baptisms in the district.

We started 1966 with more baptisms. One Sunday in early February I went to Tamworth for a business meeting, confirmation, ordination, and sacrament service.

In response to consideration of some upcoming calls of men to the priesthood, I once had a wonderful experience. I was asleep, and in my dream I was praying about the men I had in mind for ordination—one in particular. I had asked the question, "Lord, is he called to the office of teacher?" I saw the word *NO* in black letters on a dark background. It was easily read, but it gave no light. I then asked, "Is it perhaps to the office of priest?" Then I saw the word *YES* stand out in front of me, beautifully written in shining silver. Of course, I had my answer. It was the only time I had that type of experience.

Gwen began a six-week vacation in February, but she was not idle during that time. She participated in the Orioles' institute and did a good job of organizing the women's institute. She was also a speaker at the World Day of Prayer for Women held in our Tuncurry church.

In February we received some much-needed help when

my brother-in-law Frank Flood entered appointment and was assigned to our district. He and Ruth and their daughter Carynne moved to Newcastle; Frank concentrated on the Newcastle area, while I ministered to the rest of the district. The Hamilton branch had just bought a large tract of land with a house at Charlestown, so the Floods stayed there initially. During 1968 and 1969, we worked hard to have homes for the aged built on that property.

Gwen and I escaped for eight days in March to spend our honeymoon at Bombah Point, which was on a lake about 10 miles from Buladelah. That was not our "second honeymoon," because we never had a first. Since we were married during World War II, there was no time to take a honeymoon. A church member in Buladelah loaned us her caravan (trailer), and we had the use of a small motorboat. We had a wonderful and relaxing time together.

In June Marvia became engaged to Terry Thompson, a young man who was a deacon in the church. I had baptized him at John's River when he was a youth. The wedding was set for March, 1968.

Beth completed her year's obstetrics training in Sydney and returned to be an operating room nurse (known in Australia as an operating theatre sister) at the Royal Newcastle Hospital. That was what she most wanted to do. It was certainly good to have her back. Before she returned, our son caught the train to Sydney to spend a couple of days with his big sister.

We replaced Gwen's old car with a 1959 Vauxhall Victor, which Trevor often borrowed when he was 17 and old enough to get a license. In exchange for his driving privileges, he later helped me overhaul the engine and paint and reupholster the car. Since my Holden was referred to as the "Church Car," Trevor's friends started calling the Vauxhall the "Church Mother's Car."

With the arrival of Frank Flood to the area, the church

headquarters decided to divide the region, starting in November. Frank's assignment was to the recently formed Newcastle District, while mine was to the Northern New South Wales District and all of unorganized New South Wales. The people elected me district president, which certainly did not afford much time for missionary work. My new area covered nearly all of the former Hunter-Manning District, minus the Newcastle area, plus all of New South Wales nearly to the Queensland border and most of the inland area to Canberra and to the west.

Since Gwen, Beth, and Marvia were all working in Newcastle and we especially did not want to take Trevor away from the good high school he was attending, we decided not to move. Instead, Gwen bought a small trailer (caravan) that I towed behind my car to the areas where I was working. I parked it behind a church or on some property of the Saints to be my home there for a few weeks. The trailer provided me with independence and some privacy to study undisturbed. It also meant I was not a burden to the good Saints, who were always willing to open their homes to me. Of course, I was very lonely during those trips away from home; but that was a small sacrifice to pay for the opportunity to serve the Lord.

My new area included some groups of Saints who had been fairly isolated from the church. Often the work was kept alive only due to the faith and convictions of certain strong individuals. One such case was at Bowraville in northern New South Wales. It was a small town, which had considerable temptations and evil influences to cause people to stray. However, Brother Ernie Kelsey kept the faith and enabled our church there to stay open. His family, along with the Ballards, was the nucleus of that branch. They welcomed me, the new seventy, with open arms; and I did what I could to help those good Saints and revitalize the work in that area.

☼ ☼ ☼

At Willow Bend on the north arm of the upper Nambucca River, Max Ballard allowed us to use a portion of his farm for youth camps. We renovated an old house to use as a dormitory. We sometimes had difficulty with nonmember girls from around the area—some of whom were daughters of tavern owners and friends of our church members. We wanted to help and encourage the girls, so we welcomed them at our camps.

Two or three places had been pulled away between the wall and the ceiling of the old house, and the girls used to climb over the wall. Max had placed some heavy wire grates over the holes, so everything seemed safe. But during my first youth camp there, I learned that some of the girls had a hacksaw and were trying to cut a hole in the grates so they could sneak out at night to meet the boys.

I walked over very carefully and quietly entered the room to see what they were doing. Two or three girls were so busy concentrating on their work that they didn't see me. After a short while, I asked, "Would you like me to give you some help?" With a look of alarm they handed me the hacksaw—they knew their little escapade was over.

We also had to combat the bringing of fireworks to the camp. On one occasion I arranged for an inspection of suitcases. Sister Kath Ivers, the head cook, looked through the girls' suitcases, and I checked the boys' luggage. We thus uncovered and confiscated a large cache of rockets and fireworks. We didn't know where to put them, so I said, "Kath, there's only one safe place, and that's under your bed! Just don't light any matches in the night, or you might go up through the roof!"

At the end of the camp, we tied bunches of fireworks to some old arrows, lit them, and shot them way up in the hills. They went off with some tremendous explosions that reverberated through the hills. The campers had their fun—yet it was disciplined fun. No one was hurt, and everyone heard all the noise of the fireworks.

Three or four of the nonmember girls came to me and said, "Brother Sorensen, we want to thank you for such a marvelous camp. Thanks to your discipline, we enjoyed ourselves. If we had been left to do what we wanted to, like we were in some camps, we would have done things that would have caused trouble." That was one of the best compliments ever paid to me. Young people need discipline; they want discipline; and they respect discipline.

A remarkable couple by the name of Dunn had been converted at the Hamilton branch in early 1966; and after baptism, they moved to Condobolin. They started a youth club as an alternative to the pubs and illicit liquor that enticed the children and young people of the town. Their endeavor grew rapidly until more than 100 youth were attending. Some of them started taking an interest in the church, saying it must be a good church because of the care the Dunns showed. There are many ways to win the hearts and souls of people to the army of the Lord.

One letter I wrote in 1967 describes what my life was like as the missionary to the Northern New South Wales District:

"Here I am way out in the woolly west—the hot west, I should say. The temperature has been over 100 whilst I have been here. I have towed my trailer from Newcastle to Sydney, Goulburn, Canberra, Cowra, and now Condobolin. I will be visiting Parkes and Dubbo later this week. We are trying to start up some work at Canberra and possibly at Cowra, where rather promising situations exist. I hope we are successful. Last Sunday, February 5, we had our bap-

tismal service at Tiona. I performed the baptisms, five being ushered into the Kingdom at that time with more to follow.

"Returning on Sunday evening, I spent one day at home and set off for Sydney and Goulburn on the next. I found five members in Canberra and some good prospects. Spent two full days there. Next stop was Cowra. We have five members here, too, and some apparent prospects. I hope to return there in September and conduct some cottage meetings. I am now at Condobolin. The Dunn family here are the only members, and they are finding their witnessing quite difficult. The townspeople like "grog" too much, it seems. I will be leaving here on Wednesday for Parkes, where we have a few members, and then for Dubbo. I think it is true about the crows flying backwards to fan themselves out here. I am fortunate though—the Dunns have an air conditioner, and we had our communion service in reasonable comfort."

After that trip, Gwen and I had another short vacation at Bombah Point. Then I was busy with a different aspect of my work. The evening after we returned, I had a wedding rehearsal, followed by the wedding on Friday evening. Then I jumped into my car and raced to Taree (within the speed limit, of course) for a wedding rehearsal that same evening and another wedding on Saturday afternoon.

Another letter reveals some of my feelings about the progress of my work at this time. Some of what I said has even more relevance today. I am glad that I could not see then where the RLDS Church was heading—as it is today—or I would really have been depressed.

"My work drags on with very little progress, and sometimes I wonder if the Lord has rejected us because of our lack of interest and diligence in His work. At the mission conference, many discussions about the new look in the church took place amongst members of the priesthood.

Some of the beliefs and opinions put forward would leave you bewildered."

Although Beth was enjoying work in surgery at the Royal Newcastle Hospital, she wanted to return to America for a while to practice nursing there. Brother Maurice Draper was very helpful in providing information and assistance in that regard. Since Beth needed psychiatric nursing experience and training, she transferred to the Shortland Clinic in Newcastle. Upon completion of her training there, she had the necessary qualifications to sit for the state board examination later to receive a Missouri nursing license.

☼ ☼ ☼

Our son continued to do well at school. More importantly, he was taking his religion seriously. On one particular occasion he and some friends who had attended Zion's League at our church sat in on a Methodist scripture class at the high school. The minister was telling the boys that they should be good missionaries and spread the Word of God throughout the world so that the heathen natives could learn of Christ and be saved—otherwise they would be condemned to hell and eternal damnation.

Trevor asked the minister, "What about the primitive natives of past ages who never had the opportunity to learn of Christ? Are they condemned, too?"

When the minister said, "Yes," Trevor told him that it did not seem like a fair and just God to condemn people without even a chance of salvation. (Of course, we believe that all people are given an opportunity to hear and accept the gospel—if not in this life, then in the hereafter.)

Then the minister got hot under the collar, especially when the boys started to chant, "What about the natives? What about the natives?"

The minister then yelled, "Forget about the natives. Just worry about yourselves!" He demanded to know what religion Trevor belonged to. When my son told him, the minister's face turned bright red. He exploded, "You are condemned, young man! The Book of Mormon is evil!"

Trevor asked, "Have you read it?"

The minister replied, "Of course not; it is the work of the devil!"

Trevor then said, "Well, how do you know it's the work of the devil if you have not even read it?"

The minister was so befuddled that he would not allow our son to ask any more questions nor make any statements.

☼ ☼ ☼

In May, 1967, I took Trevor and another lad, Gregor Dickinson, up to Willow Bend with me for a children's camp. Towing Frank Flood's new utility trailer, we left Newcastle after Trevor finished school on Thursday afternoon. We were not far past Raymond Terrace when a wheel parted company with the trailer and went spinning away into the bush. A great trail of sparks followed in our wake as the axle dragged along the road. We were delayed for quite some time because we had to return to Newcastle for another trailer.

There were 50 children at the camp, including 43 nonmembers. Trevor and Gregor were wonderful help. Trevor taught a rocketry class and took charge of the recreation. Although I was very strict with the campers, they evidently enjoyed themselves, and the camp was a success.

The water in the stream running through Willow Bend was very pure. It teemed with aquatic life, including mullet, catfish, bass, turtles, and eels. Before the camp started, Barry Ballard, Gregor, Trevor, and I went spearfishing with great success using snorkling gear. I used the same spear gun I had made in Tahiti years earlier.

We had a unique experience one night when Max Ballard drove his big tractor up and down the shallows of the stream. With the help of a bright spotlight, several of the boys went eel hunting. The eels measured about three to four feet long. When they spotted an eel, the boys would chase it down, kill it with bush hooks, and put it into a gunny sack. After more than a dozen eels had been caught, everyone retired to a campfire, where the eels were roasted and eaten by some, including myself. They tasted a little like greasy chicken—and I did not really care for them.

In one of the deeper holes in the stream, Barry later speared an eight-foot eel that was as thick around as my arm. That monster had razor-sharp teeth, which took its toll on Barry's hand before he, Trevor, and Gregor were finally able to kill it on the bank.

I was spending a lot of time away from home on the Lord's business. For a six-week period in July and August my weekly schedule looked like this: Cottage meetings in Grafton on Monday, Coff's Harbour on Tuesday, Nambucca Heads on Wednesday, Argent's Hill on Thursday, and Bowraville on Friday and Saturday. Then I preached twice on Sunday. I also painted the Bowraville church. The church hall had never been painted, and it looked so unsightly that I just had to do something. It can never be said that I have neglected the appearance of the house of the Lord in any place.

While in Coff's Harbour I stayed with a young couple named Tommy and Nancy Strickland. Tommy was a pilot; and on one occasion he took Gwen, Trevor, and me up in a small plane for a flight around the area. The northern coast of New South Wales is so scenic, with banana plantations and green fertile farmland separated from the azure blue ocean by a strand of golden sandy beaches.

My big project at Tiona in 1967 was to install a water system. We made a drop bore machine using a length of pipe about three inches in diameter suspended over a pulley by a rope. When the pipe hit the ground, it filled half full of sand. We pulled it up, emptied the sand, and dropped it again and again. We drilled down about 25 feet, but failed to find fresh water.

I went to the Newcastle Water Board, told the manager we could not find good water, and asked for help. He sent a huge machine to drill for water. The operator of the drill went down about 28 feet and found an ample supply of water for all our needs except for drinking and cooking. When I asked what we owed him, he said, "Oh, just the money for the men transporting the machinery up here and back." The Lord really blessed us—for a mere pittance we had a constant supply of water.

Because we also had peak periods of use, we needed a reservoir of water. In Buladelah I had noticed two huge discarded boilers, which had once provided steam for a sawmill. The authorities told me we could have them if we could remove them. Tom Gooch, who had a moving business in that town, managed to get them to Tiona—with a lot of difficulty negotiating some bends in the road.

The boilers were terribly rusty inside. With an oxy-acetylene torch I cut a manhole in the end of each horizontal boiler. Once inside, I cut a little hole in the other end so we could flush out the rust. Some of the boys who had fired rockets with us got in the boiler and helped bang the rust off with hammers and wire brushes. We could work only so long; then we had to come out and get some fresh air. Trevor had bought some gas masks at a war surplus store, and they were very effective. When we came out of those tanks, we were covered with red rust from gas mask to foot and looked like aliens from Mars. The boys thought it was great fun, and I was glad they did because it saved me a lot of work. I painted the interiors and closed the holes to make reservoirs.

In October, 1967, we saw Beth off on her journey to the Land of Promise. She was disappointed that she could not be at Marvia's wedding, but everything had already been arranged for her trip. Although we were very sad to see Beth go, we tried to reconcile ourselves because she had gone on the Lord's work—to nurse the sick and suffering of His church in the Center Place. We were fortunate to have such a lovely daughter, who was interested in the church and the welfare of her fellowmen. On her way to America, Beth stopped in Tahiti and had a wonderful time renewing acquaintances there.

Trevor earned advanced levels in the School Certificate state examination, for which he was granted a Commonwealth Scholarship of $500. He used the money to order an electronic organ kit from Heathkit in America. We had fun constructing the organ when it arrived. Trevor then played it in a music group formed by him and a few of his school friends. One boy played drums, two played electric guitars, and one sang. Unfortunately, they conducted their practices in our house. Poor Gwen was nearly driven up the wall with the noise. I was home for only a day or two and heard them practice, and it was about all I could take. However, I was glad that our son was showing an interest in music again.

The boys performed at a concert at the Hamilton church during district conference the next year. What a noise they produced! But they had fun, and the young people in the audience seemed to enjoy it. Actually, that organ ended up being useful in the work of the Lord because we used it to provide music at camps and reunions in Australia and later in the Carolinas.

Marvia's 21st birthday party was held in December in the backyard of our home on Turner Street. The yard was brightly lit and decorated. Marvia wanted to have a dance band; and without telling her family, she hired a group. When they arrived, I exercised a father's prerogative, made a decision, and sent them away. As a minister, I was not comfortable in providing that kind of entertainment. Marvia was upset for a bit, but she soon forgot the band in the excitement of the food, good friends, gifts, and games. Altogether she had a most memorable celebration.

We attended the Tiona reunion in December of 1967. In a class I taught, I had my first major battle defending the truth against the "new thought" men. They were trying to trash the stories of Enoch's Zion, Noah, the virgin birth, and other beliefs. The Lord triumphed, and it was those men who ended up confused—not me. Their theories could not stand up to my personal experiences and the written Word of God. Many of the people present told me that their faith was strengthened as a result.

At that reunion our son received his own personal confirmation of the power of prayer. He was an avid surfer, having bought his own surfboard earlier in the year. One afternoon during reunion, he and a couple of other fellows were out on their boards. Trevor was the farthest one out when a series of very large waves hit him. He lost his board and began swimming for shore. As wave after wave crashed onto him, he started to weaken—only occasionally was he able to come to the surface for a gulp of air. Then he prayed fervently for the Lord's help. The Lord listens to His children. Just when the situation seemed most desperate, Trevor felt a sandbar beneath his foot. Then the waves weakened so he was able to make it to shore. That was the closest he had ever come to dying, and he was convinced that he was saved only by the Lord answering his prayer.

Early in 1968 I traveled out west again. On my return, Gwen and I went to Brisbane for a few days to visit with our parents. Her father, who was not very well at that time, was especially glad to see us. I then attended the business meeting at Grafton, after which my wife and I went for what was becoming our annual vacation to Bombah Point. I returned to Newcastle the first weekend for the elder's institute, at which I had a speaking assignment. The second weekend Gwen and I went to Taree for sacrament, where I gave the address, and to Wingham for the evening preaching. I thoroughly enjoyed taking my wife about with me. Trevor and some of his mates came up to Bombah Point one Saturday and had a good time with us. Jim Richards brought his ski boat from Buladelah and took the boys water skiing. Immediately after our holiday, Gwen went to the Women's World Day of Prayer at Buladelah, where her sister Ruth was the speaker.

Beth had settled in as a nurse at the Independence Sanitarium and Hospital. She enjoyed participating in all the church activities. She wrote, "The Yank guys are crazy!" Within three months of her arrival, she had received a marriage proposal—which she declined.

On March 23, 1968, Marvia married Terry Thompson in the Hamilton church. She looked simply beautiful in her white wedding gown. I escorted her down the aisle and then performed the ceremony. Gwen looked lovely, too; and I told her that she was the best looking lady in the place. Marvia's eight-year-old cousin, Carynne Flood, was the flower girl; and she was as cute as could be.

The attendants and guests enjoyed a wonderful "wedding breakfast" (the first meal of the newlyweds) before Marvia and Terry flew to Norfolk Island off the east coast of Australia for their honeymoon. On their return, we made half of our house available to them as an apartment (flat) by building on an extra bathroom and kitchen.

I continued to be extremely busy performing cottage meetings and improving our church facilities. I built a sander from an American vacuum cleaner motor and an old electric drill. It worked wonderfully to sand the old paint off the John's River church, which I then repainted with the help of one of our local men, Brother Dave Donkin. When we did the final touches on the outside painting, the temperature was 108°.

The John's River church was our only country church in Australia. The striking contrast of the beautiful white church nestled in the lush greenery and surrounded by high hills was lovely to behold. I often used to say as I looked down that valley, "How green was my valley." Several church families farmed along the nearby Stewart River. Before I had my trailer, I always found a very welcome bed and lodging there when I was doing missionary work.

A church member in the town nearby had the contract to put an addition on the John's River church. He did most of it without charge. His wife was quite an artist; and at my request, she painted some aborigine art on the end wall of the fellowship hall. It was really excellent, showing the life of the aborigines, just as they had depicted it in the rock paintings and caves in central and western Australia. People often remarked that it looked authentic.

I continued my trips and ministry out west. The small group that we had started in Canberra was growing, and in Dubbo 30 people came to hear me speak. The word was spreading—but still too slowly.

It pleased my heart to see that Trevor was keenly interested in the church. He was elected leader of the Hamilton Zion's League; and a group of 20 or 30 young people attended, including some of his friends from high school. One of them, John Farrell, was eventually baptized. After we left Australia, he married Cathy Masterson, one of our church girls.

☼ ☼ ☼

One of the unpleasant aspects of my work as a minister was to conduct funerals and deal with human tragedy. While I was in John's River, Brother Elbert Ivers was killed in his car on the John's River Road. His poor young daughter Mara was at home that day studying for an examination the next day. I had the sad task of taking Elbert's wife Merle to the scene of the accident. Then I spent some time with her and Mara in prayer, asking God to give comfort to the family and a special blessing that Mara would be able to do well on her exam.

There is a distinct difference between Australian and American attitudes on the matter of funerals. Most of the Australians, other than the Roman Catholics, are cremated. The Americans are much more sentimental about the body that is left. Most Americans prefer to be buried in cemeteries that are meticulously manicured. I never have understood the American sentimentality. After all, the body is only the shell that houses the person. The real essence of the person—the spirit—has gone back home to our heavenly Father from whence it came. The body has been discarded by the spirit; and it is meant to go back to the earth from whence it came, awaiting the time of the resurrection.

In May we held our district children's camp at the Willow Bend campground. Willow Bend was in a picturesque setting on a creek flowing through the property of Brother Max Ballard. Brother Ray Burdekin of Brisbane and Sisters Carol Kingi and Beverly Wilkerson assisted in running the camp, which had 90 children attending. We also had the help of some young people who were veterans of many such camps.

Beth began attending Graceland College in Lamoni, Iowa, in September. While there, she acted as nurse to the Graceland concert choir when it went on tour. Her decision to attend college was quite fortuitous because there she became well acquainted with Bill McGuire. He had just been discharged from the U.S. Air Force and was completing his degree at Graceland on the G.I. Bill. He was a handsome young man from Mason City, Iowa, who played on the Graceland football team. I knew his family when I was a missionary in Iowa. By one of those interesting coincidences in life, Bill and Beth had been elected king and queen of a youth camp that was held in Iowa in 1960 (as I related earlier). Little did they realize!

We were having an unusually hot and dry spring that year. Bushfires started ravishing the countryside. At the end of November, a huge fire threatened Tiona while I was there; and we had to organize all available resources to combat it. With the help of the good Lord, Who changed the wind in our favor for half an hour, we managed to keep the reunion grounds from being burned. Then the wind veered back to the northeast again and blew with all its fury. The palm trees on the other side of the grounds became blackened stumps, so we could imagine what would have happened to Tiona.

There was a good spirit among the people at the reunion that year. While I preached only one sermon, it was powerful—replying to criticisms that I had heard about our doctrine. I had lain dormant long enough and felt that some of the erroneous teaching had to be stopped. Most people appreciated it very much, but a few were critical. At least the sermon was different, and—as most people said—most timely. They called me "The Striker" after that. The sermon was the talk of the camp for days. One high priest berated me and said that it was the most negative sermon he had ever heard. However, after he slept on the matter, he came the next morning and apologized.

On the last morning of the reunion, we had a most beautiful baptismal service at the Green Cathedral. It was more or less a private service, not part of the reunion; but a general invitation was extended, and more than 100 people came to witness young Oliver Ivers' baptism. The morning was perfect. Although I had to walk a long way into Lake Wallis, my voice carried clearly so that all on the shore could hear every word. It was pleasing to see so many people interested enough in the ordinances of the church to come early in the morning to be part of the service which God blessed with His Spirit.

I spent the first month of 1969 preaching, baptizing, and confirming in the Taree and John's River area.

In February, at the request of Apostle Lents, I went to New Zealand to provide ministry for a month. It was quite an experience to fly over on one of the new big jets. I had never flown by jet before and was most happy with my maiden flight. It was so much smoother and quieter than the propeller-driven planes. We flew at 37,000 feet with the beautiful cloud masses below us. It took only two hours and 20 minutes to make a trip which had taken us four days by boat in 1945.

The Saints in New Zealand seemed happy to see me again. Although some of the older ones had passed away, others remembered when Gwen, Beth, and I were there 24 years previously. Some of their children were very ably shouldering the work of the church.

It was opportune that I was in New Zealand at that time. Two young Tahitian ladies were studying in Auckland and living with Saints. When I spoke to them in their native language, they were thrilled. I was able to straighten out some misunderstandings that had arisen because of language barriers.

While I was in New Zealand, Gwen received an exciting letter from our daughter Beth. In contrast to her previous letters—which often told of her dates and said, "But this is not it"—this letter told of going out with Bill McGuire and said, "I think this is it!" Before long they were engaged.

After I returned to Australia, Gwen and I drove to Brisbane and spent a week with our parents. Brother Duane Couey of the First Presidency was on a tour of the Australian Mission and traveled with us back to Newcastle. He visited a couple of the branches in my area on his way to Sydney for the mission conference.

The conference was a huge success, and an excellent spirit predominated in all the sessions. The two brethren from America, Brother Couey and Apostle Clifford Cole, gave excellent ministry. On Monday we finished with a boat ride to Parsley Bay in Sydney Harbour, where we enjoyed a picnic.

While in New Zealand, I had met some church members from America who were on a world tour. They were Wilmer Andes, with his wife and teenage daughter, and Ammon Andes and his wife. Ammon was a professor of aerospace engineering at the University of Kansas. I suggested that he come to Newcastle, where I knew my rocket-mad son would love to talk with him. In April they visited Newcastle; and Trevor spent the evening talking with Professor Andes about rockets, engineering, and the American university system.

We had another wonderful children's camp at Willow Bend in May, where Trevor helped me once again. While we were at the camp, a letter arrived at our home from President W. Wallace Smith asking if we would consider an assignment to the North and South Carolina and Georgia Missionary Development Area. As Gwen read the letter to me over the telephone, we realized that we were to see the fulfillment of Patriarch Henry Castings' prophecy. Being asked to come back to America to labor in a missionary field after nine years in Australia really pleased me because I loved doing missionary work.

It was a big thing to ask Gwen to uproot her home again and leave Marvia behind, but she has always been willing to put her Lord first. We agreed to go, as long as our departure could be delayed until November to give Trevor a chance to finish his final examinations for high school. The Presidency agreed, and we prepared to say good-bye once again to the good folks in Australia.

Since Trevor now had an opportunity to go with us to America, he decided that he should take it and further his aerospace studies in the land that was about to put men on the moon. His previous contact with Ammon Andes proved to be very valuable because the professor helped him make all the necessary arrangements to attend the University of Kansas the following year.

I continued my traveling throughout New South Wales, visiting Forbes, Cowra, Canberra, and Dubbo in mid-year.

We renovated the old church at Tuncurry, not far from Tiona. Brother Kelsey, two other men, and I burned off the old, blistered paint. After we quit work, I went to a cottage meeting at Wingham. When I returned, the fire brigade (department) was at the church—the building had caught fire! We had taken every precaution to hose the walls with water before going home to eat. Brother Kelsey had checked the church and found no trace of fire or smoke, but an hour later the building was in flames. Apparently the fire started because the walls were full of grass from sparrow nests. Half the church was burned, including the roof.

Since the insurance money was insufficient to pay for a new church, we decided to repair the old one. Frank Flood and Brother Helmer Anderson, a carpenter, came from Newcastle. The three of us worked like Trojans to install a new corrugated iron roof. Plasterers then came and replaced the ceiling. We ended up with a very beautiful building, compared with what had been there before. Later in the year Trevor helped me paint the church.

Beth completed her first year at Graceland College but then decided to work at the hospital in Leon, Iowa. She shared an apartment in Lamoni with Marilyn Roth, a New Zealand girl, whose parents were good friends of ours. Beth and Bill were planning their wedding for December so that we could be there.

In August we held a youth leadership camp at Willow Bend. About 40 youth attended, coming from as far south as Newcastle and as far north as Grafton. We had an excellent camp although the weather was abominable, with 12 inches of rain in five days. That was especially hard on the boys, whose sleeping quarters were in sheds made from old corrugated iron sheets, which were perforated with nail holes. The boys used a lot of chewing gum that week to patch those holes! Still, they were in excellent spirits, and much good was accomplished.

Since the bus could not cross the swollen river, we used a car trailer with a board laid on it as a ferry to get the girls and women across. Some boys and I pulled the makeshift ferry across the river several times to get them all over. This episode did have its humorous moment when Gwen, Sister Kath Ivers, and Sister Rita Jackson had to lie on their tummies and be ferried across. When we reached the other side, we tipped the trailer up and slid them off onto *terra firma*!

I was frantically trying to finish as much of my work as possible before moving to America. At the same time, we were very busily trying to cut through all the red tape to get to America with permanent residence visas. I made another trip out west in September, and Gwen was able to accompany me. While we were in Canberra, we had our first glimpse of snow falling in Australia.

In October we held the district conference at John's River, with an excellent spirit of participation in prayer and testimony and great fellowship in the meetings. Brother Jim Kemp preached Saturday night. He was due to relinquish his position as mission president at the end of the year and return to America. I gave the sacrament address, and Apostle Don Lents preached to a packed house on Sunday evening.

Gwen and I drove to Brisbane for one last visit with our families, leaving Trevor in Newcastle to sit for his state Higher School Certificate examinations. When he completed his last examination, Trevor caught the train to Brisbane and joined us. After an all-too-brief visit, we returned to Newcastle, where I gave my farewell sermon at the Hamilton branch. The Saints there gave us a heart-warming send-off.

Before we left Australia, we received the exciting results of Trevor's examinations. He passed with honors and was awarded a full four-year Commonwealth Scholarship to attend any of the universities in New South Wales or the Australian National University in Canberra. The latter was significant because it meant that he placed among the top 200 in the state in the examinations. Notwithstanding the scholarship, Trevor still planned to attend the University of Kansas.

We departed from Sydney on Friday, November 30, 1969, on our way back to the Land of Promise. Marvia accompanied us to America, where she was to be Beth's matron of honor.

▲ Australian appointees at Tiona reunion, early 1960s—left to right: Geoff Spencer, Peter Taylor, Don Alberts, Syd Jacka, and Vivian

▼ Vivian with Rosamond Smith and President W. Wallace Smith at Hamilton branch, Newcastle, in 1960

▲ Ferrying ladies across the flooded stream at Willow Bend campground, 1968—Gwen lying at left; Vivian in back; Max Ballard, the property owner, at right

▼ Dining hall at Tiona Reunion Grounds (photo from 1964)

▲ Gwen, Marvia, and Vivian, Newcastle, March 23, 1968

CHAPTER 10

Journey Back to Zion's Land

As our jet airliner ascended from the Sydney airport, we looked back at the homeland that we were leaving again for an assignment overseas. The coast disappeared behind the clouds, and we felt sadness at leaving many good friends and relatives behind. It was especially hard for Gwen and me since our parents were getting old; we did not know if we would ever see them again. But at least Marvia and Trevor were with us, and we were headed toward Beth.

It was a good flight from Sydney to Auckland, New Zealand, where we spent a delightful day sightseeing. The weather was perfect—sunny and warm, which was rare for New Zealand in November. At night we went to some swimming pools fed by natural hot springs, where we went swimming. On Sunday Gwen spoke to the women at the Papctoetoe branch at 10 a.m. and at the Auckland branch at 11 a.m. I preached at Papetoetoe at 11 a.m. and at the Auckland branch that night.

We left Auckland at midnight Sunday on Air New Zealand for Papeete, where we arrived about 6:30 a.m. on Sunday, since Tahiti is on the opposite side of the International Date Line. Before landing, the big airplane circled Tahiti and Moorea for several minutes. We had a marvelous view of their rugged mountains and deep valleys of lush green, set into a sapphire-colored ocean. The rising of the sun above the ocean was a sight not to be forgotten.

When we landed and cleared customs, we found a large crowd of our church people waiting to greet us. What a welcome! If ever I had any doubts about the appreciation of our work by the Saints there, they were then dispelled. We were almost smothered by so many *heis* that we had to take some off to breathe. The natives kissed each of us on both cheeks, as is their custom. Trevor was embarrassed —he had never been kissed by so many women before. The other passengers on the plane were wondering who in the world we were, obviously celebrities.

Not having a wink of sleep the night before, I preached to over 400 natives that morning. I managed to get one hour's sleep that afternoon, then preached again on Sunday night to a large crowd. I wondered whether I should ask for overtime pay for four sermons on the same day! There is no doubt that the Lord blessed me with the language, much to the delight of the native Saints. Many members from the outlying islands had been in Papeete for a mission conference. When they heard that we were coming, they waited an extra week to see us again. We stayed with the missionary to Tahiti, Brother Everett Graffeo, and his family.

Ririfatu Mariteragi, the young Tahitian whom I had baptized in Iowa when he was attending Graceland College, was under appointment. He took us sightseeing around the island. For Gwen, Marvia, and myself it was a time of renewal; but for Trevor it was a time of discovery. He had been too young to remember much from our previous stay in Tahiti. The native Saints studied him very carefully, not having seen him since he was three years old. Marvia did her best with the language and was able to understand some of what the natives said. Various families invited us to their homes for meals. They fed us so well that by the time we left, food no longer interested us.

On Monday night I spoke to the priesthood and was asked to preach again on Wednesday night. Though I was still very tired from all the running around and overeating, the Lord blessed me with clarity of thought and fluency in the language.

Before we left, the native Saints gave me a large amount of money—it was worth more than 200 U.S. dollars. I gave half of it to Brother Graffeo to be used toward a project for Tahitian youth; but I asked him not to tell who gave him the money. With the other half we purchased a shortwave radio, which enabled us to listen to the news of our homeland and even broadcasts from Tahiti at times. We were certain that the natives would have been pleased.

We parted ways with Marvia temporarily on Thursday night. She was going to the United States via Mexico City, while Gwen, Trevor, and I were flying to Los Angeles. We later learned that Marvia enjoyed her visit in Mexico, where our missionary, Brother Wayne Simmons, made her very welcome.

Our plane left Friday morning. The Saints came to bid farewell, again smothering us with shell necklaces. The Pan Am plane was delayed a short time while the natives finished their farewells. When we arrived on board, the other passengers were envious because we had so many shell necklaces that we could barely carry them all. We extricated ourselves from the *heis* and put them into plastic bags supplied by a flight attendant. She was thrilled when Gwen gave her a bag of necklaces. The young lady then picked out one of them, put it around her neck, and gave one to each of the other crew members. They wore the necklaces all the way to Los Angeles.

After Tahiti had faded into the distance, the only island we saw was Makatea. I had been there often and recognized it immediately. Our flight was eight hours long; but it was quite comfortable since the plane was nearly empty and we were able to stretch out and nap.

During our weekend stay in Los Angeles, we stayed at the home of Sister Knowlton. Brother and Sister Blaine Bender took us sightseeing. I preached at the Temple City branch, where we enjoyed the fellowship of the Saints.

We flew to Kansas City the next morning and were quite surprised when Beth came running out to meet us at the municipal airport. She had talked the authorities into allowing her out onto the tarmac. Trust our Beth! We were also surprised by the freezing temperatures and the snow on the ground. That was quite a shock after the warmth of Australia, Tahiti, and Los Angeles. Our wardrobe was not adequate for such temperatures, and one of the first orders of business was to buy some winter clothing.

Gwen and I stayed in Independence with Dolph and June Roth, who were long-time friends from Australia and New Zealand. The Roths had gathered to the Center Place a short while earlier. Trevor stayed with the Reed Holmes family, which included a couple of children about his age.

After Trevor went to Lawrence, Kansas, for interviews, he was accepted in the aerospace engineering program at the University of Kansas and was to start his studies for the spring semester at the end of January.

Because Beth was being married in Lamoni, Iowa, we had a good opportunity to visit friends in Boone. On Sunday I preached at the old Boone church and was happy to see so many familiar faces. We were delighted to renew old acquaintances; but the 10 inches of snow on the ground made us glad that our new assignment to the North and South Carolina and Georgia Missionary Development Area meant we did not need to face Iowa winters again.

The next Sunday, December 21, 1969, I proudly escorted our daughter Beth up the aisle to her waiting groom Bill McGuire and then performed the sacrament of marriage. Brother Roy Kopp assisted. Marvia attended her sister as matron of honor. After the beautiful service, we realized that a blizzard had commenced, causing many guests to leave before the reception. That night we drove through the snow back to Independence.

The next morning Marvia was returning to her husband in Australia, and we went to the downtown airport to see her off. After good-byes, Marvia boarded the plane. Just a few minutes before take-off, the newlyweds came running into the terminal. Brother Holmes asked one of the officials if Beth could go aboard to see her sister, and the man very kindly allowed her to do so. Our girls had a big hug and a cry; then Beth hurried back to the terminal. We all watched the plane depart. As prophesied in my patriarchal blessing, there would be many sad partings in my life; this was certainly another one of them.

After spending the holidays in Independence, Gwen, Trevor, and I set out for South Carolina. We had decided to live in Greenville because it was fairly central and there was a good-sized branch there. Trevor really enjoyed our new church car, so I let him drive most of the way. We were quite interested to hear the accents from various regions as we traveled across the country. For example, we heard hillbilly radio announcers who were a real contrast to people we had encountered in the Midwest and others we would hear in the South.

We finally arrived in Greenville, where we stayed with the Carol family while we looked for a house. Sister Carol had such a broad southern accent that it was difficult to understand all she said, but we finally got used to it. Most of the members of the Greenville branch were either northerners or from the midwest, so we understood them easily.

Although we arrived in Greenville during the coldest winter on record, the Saints soon warmed us with their welcome. There were about 50 members in the Greenville branch, and they met in an old white wood church building near downtown. The pastor, Brother Doyle Launius, was especially helpful in finding a home for us and getting us settled. We bought a house at Mauldin, just outside of Greenville. It was a split-level, brick-veneer home with three bedrooms and a large two-room basement on a half acre of land.

Brother Harry Doty, a president of seventy, and Apostle Donald Chesworth came shortly after we arrived to help define my areas of responsibility and expectations for the region. We drove to Atlanta for an area meeting. Atlanta had its own seventy, Brother Tom Morman, which reduced the territory that I had to cover. Tom and I were able to work well together at the reunions, camps, and retreats.

Our baby bird flew from the nest when Trevor left to start his studies at the University of Kansas. We were apprehensive about the negative influence of the university environment, but we trusted the Lord to be with him. Trevor attended the Lawrence branch regularly and also joined Liahona, the church-sponsored campus youth group.

Gwen and I traveled to meet the Saints and become acquainted with our new area. On successive Sundays we drove to Charleston, South Carolina; Charlotte, North Carolina; and Augusta, Georgia. We were really impressed by the friendliness of all the Saints.

Brother Roy Cooper was the pastor of the Charleston branch. He and I had many wonderful experiences in cottage meetings as we labored in the Charleston area, seeking opportunities to tell the gospel story and revive the inactive Saints. Roy and his wife, Dorothy, have a high place in my esteem because of their steadfastness.

Gwen and I drove to Independence in early March so I could attend the quorum meetings that were held before the

1970 World Conference. We visited our son in Lawrence for a few hours; and while I attended the sessions, Gwen went to Lamoni by bus to visit Beth and Bill.

Attending the seventies' quorum sessions that year was most depressing for me. For three difficult days we discussed the problems of the RLDS Church, and my eyes were opened to the condition of the church worldwide. Many of the seventies were very upset to find that the church—which we believed possessed the fullness of the gospel of Jesus Christ—appeared to be declining both spiritually and numerically.

I also learned about the "Position Papers," which were presented by leaders of the church in an attempt to clarify our position on certain doctrines and procedures. They were very different from the true doctrine of Jesus Christ. I felt that if I were told to preach and teach those concepts, I would have to resign from appointment.

After the quorum sessions ended, we drove back to Greenville for a couple of weeks, during which time I presided at a youth retreat and conducted a few cottage meetings. Trevor joined us for his spring vacation, and the three of us then drove back to Missouri for the World Conference.

The 1970 World Conference showed the extent of the struggle between the new liberalism and the unchangeable Restoration doctrines. Many of the delegates were distressed, and they challenged the efforts of some members of the leadership. Most of the attempts to change the fundamental doctrines of the church were defeated. However, it was obvious that the struggle was going to intensify in the future. During that conference some outstanding old soldiers in the army of the Lord retired from active appointment: F. Henry Edwards, G. Leslie DeLapp, Charles Hield, and Roscoe Davey.

At that conference I made up my mind to resign from

missionary appointment—I could not be a purveyor of material such as found in the "Position Papers." Because I needed to talk with Harry Doty about another matter, I went to his office in the Auditorium. He was out of the office, so I sat down to wait for him.

I was really stewing over my decision to resign. The church had been my life; and I had enjoyed the call to be a missionary, to preach the gospel, and to bring salvation to the souls of men. While I was seated there and feeling sorry for myself, a voice spoke to me and said, "Go back to South Carolina and preach My gospel and leave My church in My hands." That was all that was said—but it was with such conviction and power that I almost saluted. I had to take notice.

I believe the emphasis was that as a seventy my work was purely what the first part of the message said, "Go... and preach My gospel." "Leave My church in My hands" meant to me that the Lord will look after the church; He will bless it, punish it, or do whatever He likes—that is His business. My responsibility was to teach the fullness of the gospel and to bring souls unto Christ.

I left that office with a completely different attitude. Not wanting to disobey my Lord, I went back to the North and South Carolina and Georgia Missionary Development Area and preached the gospel of Jesus Christ. Because of that and the willing response of members and nonmembers alike, we achieved a 10% increase in membership—which was nearly unheard of in the RLDS Church! The Lord truly keeps His promises when we do His will.

☼ ☼ ☼

On one occasion in 1968 as I was traveling in Australia, I had set my trailer up in the pasture of some older Saints. Things had happened in the church in Australia that I couldn't approve, and I was really upset. I resolved to go to the top of a nearby mountain to pray, and I told the couple that I would be back before too long. Alone on the mountaintop, I looked out over the beautiful Pacific Ocean and asked the Lord to help me through the problems that were confronting me.

I came back later that day, opened the door of my little trailer (it hadn't been locked because I was way out in the bush), and noticed a small booklet lying on the table inside. It was called *Three Visitations of Christ and His Coming in Glory*. I picked it up and thought, "Oh, the Seventh-Day Adventists must have been here." They often made predictions about the second coming of Christ.

That evening I picked up the little booklet and started to read it. I hadn't read very far before I saw these words: "We, of the Reorganized Church of Jesus Christ of Latter Day Saints." I thought, "How did that get here?" I read the booklet all the way through before I went to sleep.

The next morning I went to the house and thanked the couple for putting that book on my table. They said they never put any book on the table and that they had never heard of that particular booklet. I asked if they had had a visitor, but they didn't know of any. Someone would have had to walk right by the back of the house to get to the trailer. They had a good watchdog and said he didn't bark.

So the mystery deepened. How did the book get there? I still don't know! I inquired of others in that area and no one had ever seen the book, let alone put it there. But it came as a tremendous help to me at that time because of the low condition I was in.

Because I respected him as having a prophetic gift, I wrote to Brother Arthur Oakman and asked him certain questions about the book and what he thought of it. I also wrote to Brother Adolph Lundeen, the author of the booklet. Brother Oakman replied quickly. He said that he was well acquainted with the booklet and had taught it at various reunions and at the Stone Church. Then he made this statement: "If what Brother Lundeen has written in that book is not true, God help the church."

Brother Lundeen finally answered with a letter six pages long. He told me how he came to write the book and that he had the confirmation in a vision from John the Baptist that he had done right. I had told him of the miraculous way in which it came to me, and he wrote that a man in Vancouver had received one in a similar way.

Coming home from that 1970 World Conference, I had an experience which tied both of the previous experiences together and acted as a confirmation to me. We stopped at Odessa, Missouri, and visited with Brother Lundeen. He was quite sure of his predictions about the three visitations of Christ.

He told us about the pastor of a large branch in Canada who had a vision of the church's future. He saw a large amber diamond-shaped sign which depicted a warning just as diamond-shaped road signs do. An ordinary wristwatch was suspended in front of it, and the hands were both pointing to the figure 2. An angel with a large sharp sword came and split the sign in two. The lefthand part became dull and dark in color, and the other part became almost white.

The pastor prayed for the interpretation, but did not receive it until a member of his congregation returned from Independence with a copy of Lundeen's book. When the pastor read the book, the Spirit bore witness to him that the watch in the vision represented Christ's coming in the second watch. The sign represented the church and the existing division. When Christ comes in the second watch, He will cleanse the church. Those who are cut off will wither away, lose their light, and become darkened. Those remaining will develop to greater purity and become whiter than they are now.

After what I have seen happen in the RLDS Church over the last 25 years, I believe that this vision could very well be valid.

▲ Bill and Beth McGuire, Lamoni, Iowa, December 21, 1969

CHAPTER 11

In the Heart of Dixie

Our return trip to Greenville was most enjoyable—it was springtime, and the countryside was dotted with dogwoods in bloom. Soon after we arrived home, I set out on a 1,000-mile journey around the area to preach to the Saints. I visited two congregations in Georgia and arranged to conduct cottage meetings on a regular basis. I also ministered in Charleston, South Carolina, and two branches in North Carolina. After returning home, I really enjoyed planting our spring vegetable garden.

In 1970 America was full of unrest and violence. The rebellion of some young people at the universities was terrible. Even in Kansas, Trevor did not escape the turmoil. A curfew was imposed at his university after the student union was set on fire. The streets of Lawrence were being patrolled by the National Guard, but even that was not so bad as what was happening at other universities.

I also had my own encounter with the turmoil. In May I was staying at the home of Pastor Bill Sarratt in Augusta to commence a cottage-meeting series. On our way to the meeting, we heard the announcer on the car radio advise motorists to avoid certain streets because of congestion. Bill did not pay much attention, thinking the problem must have been caused by a car accident. But I detected something in the man's voice and told Bill that I thought there must be trouble. Fortunately, we decided to use an alternate route. Later we learned that we could have run right into an ugly riot in which six black people were shot to death, 60 people injured, and much damage done.

During our cottage meeting the man of the home, who was in the military, received a phone call ordering him to be on alert. We quickly finished our meeting and returned to the pastor's home by the same route we had come. I could not sleep much that night because of the screaming police sirens, the crackle of gunfire, and the blazing of buildings lighting up the sky.

The next morning Bill and I went to look around; we had often seen riots on TV but never had seen the result of one in reality. The worst-hit areas were cordoned off, but we were able to drive into one section of the Afro-American area. We were appalled to see the damage there. A supermarket had been razed; everything inside had been looted, and the big freezer containers had been smashed to pieces. A service station owned by a white man had been entirely destroyed. A brick building had evidently been bombed, and it was a smoldering heap of rubble. The National Guard was called in, and the city reminded me of pictures I had seen of bombed cities in World War II.

I was horrified, but I also realized that this was but the beginning of sorrows for a people who were turning their backs on God. I was reminded of the Word of the Lord, which says: "It shall come to pass, among the wicked, that every man that will not take his sword against his neighbor, must needs flee unto Zion for safety. And there shall be gathered unto it out of every nation under heaven; and it shall be the only people that shall not be at war one with another" (Doctrine and Covenants 45:13a-b). Early the following year several people, black and white, were killed in Wilmington, North Carolina.

There seemed to be a certain undefinable hardness among many people regarding the value of human life. I believed that it would increase as more and more men were trained to kill and then thrown back into society without negating their training. One of our pastors in North Carolina had been a Marine from World War II until the Vietnam War. He said that after years of being taught to hate and kill, it had been most difficult for him—even with the gospel—to administer peace, forgiveness, and love. Just imagine how those who did not have the gospel must have felt and fared.

The Lord God has uttered an unalterable decree that the people of America shall serve Him, the God of the land, or be destroyed when they are fully ripened in iniquity (see Ether 1:30-35). The destruction will not come from without, but from within. It will really be a more terrible punishment than destruction from without, because it will pit brother against brother and sister against sister. Many people have taken God's rich blessings for granted; and—like the Book of Mormon people of old—they have forgotten God. I feel that the Lord cannot be patient forever with them in their rebellion and sinning. I can see the handwriting on the wall for Joseph's land.

In my missionary work I traveled throughout the three states—preaching, counseling, and conducting cottage meetings. When I first moved into that area, no two branches or groups were closer than 100 miles to each other. In the month of July, 1970, for example, I drove more than 4,000 miles. Gwen was able to accompany me on some of those trips; and she did her part, talking to women's groups and bearing her testimony.

There were many military bases in the area, including Camp Lejeune and Parris Island Marine Bases, Fort Bragg, Charleston Naval Base, Cherry Point Marine Air Station, and Shaw, Pope, and Warner Robins Air Force Bases. My work eventually took me to each one of them. Lieutenant Colonel Fisher and his wife were instrumental in developing our group at the big Shaw Air Force Base, which was just outside Columbia, South Carolina.

Until Gwen could be certified for nursing in South Carolina, she started teaching piano to make some extra money. She also bought a small printing press, which we set up in our basement. We eventually became quite expert with our little press, printing the letterheads for my church correspondence, letterheads for the *Evangel* newsletter (which I started up later that year), and cottage-meeting homework sheets, as well as business cards, wedding invitations, and receipt pads.

There in the "Bible belt" I had cottage meetings with a number of Southern Baptists. Generally they were students of the Bible, but I felt that they had really been blinded by the craftiness of men. Many of them were fine-living people who believed that "once in grace, always in grace," that they were saved and could never fall—no matter what they did. Often they would argue over various points of doctrine, but I could prove the truth to them using their own Bibles. It is hard to save people who believe they are already saved; but I did not budge an inch on the truth, and many of them eventually accepted the greater light of the everlasting gospel.

In Augusta, Georgia, we held cottage meetings with a man and his wife who were Baptists. The man had seen the greater light of the Restoration and had consented to be baptized into the Church of Jesus Christ. Because his wife had not given a definite answer, I asked her on Saturday night if she also planned to be baptized on Sunday.

She answered, "No, not yet." I did not try to push her, but continued to talk with them about the gospel.

As I was preparing to leave, I said, "Well, Dennis, I'll see you tomorrow."

"Will it make any difference to your plans if I'm baptized, too?" his wife asked.

Overjoyed, I replied, "Yes, it will enhance them." She then explained that during our conversation—which was about the three Nephites and John the Beloved—she had a wonderful experience and change in her heart; and she was ready for baptism.

After her baptism the next day, she looked radiant. A Roman Catholic lady, with whom I was also having cottage meetings, shook her hand. Both women hesitated for a moment, and then they fell into each other's arms. What a strange happening—a Roman Catholic congratulating a Baptist for becoming a Latter Day Saint!

At the end of May we were joined by Beth and Bill, who visited for a couple of weeks, and Trevor, who was living with us for the summer. They accompanied us into the beautiful mountains of North Carolina and to Myrtle Beach. After her three years in the Midwest, Beth was simply delighted to see the ocean again; and Trevor really enjoyed going surfing.

That summer Tom Morman and I directed the reunion, which afforded us an opportunity to meet many more Saints in the tri-state area. I got along particularly well with the young people and looked forward to the youth camp that we were planning.

In July I conducted my first ever military funeral for a church member who had been a Marine in World War II. Many nonmembers were present, and they commented that they had never before heard such a funeral sermon. Of course, they had not been taught before about life after death and the fullness of the gospel.

We found so many fine prospects in that area, and the real cry was for more laborers to go into the vineyard. I rejoiced in the opportunities for telling the message and for the willing ears which were being opened to hear the old, old story. To God be the glory!

In August Brother Morman directed our youth camp at Camp Buckhorn in the mountains not far from Greenville. The friendship and fellowship among the 50 campers was as good as I had ever seen. Trevor was in charge of the recreation and taught a rocketry class. On Friday night, a prayer and testimony meeting was the spiritual high point of the week. I was directed by the Spirit to bring words of counsel to the campers.

Gwen was elected music director of the Greenville branch, and I started a monthly newsletter called *Evangel* as I had done in Australia. Although editing and printing *Evangel* each month was quite a task, it helped unite the Saints by providing ministry and news of activities. We continued printing the newsletter every month until we left the area in 1978.

I started making slide and tape sets to help the priesthood conduct cottage meetings. The Lord blessed the work; many people were baptized, including several Roman Catholics and Baptists.

Gwen and I celebrated our 28th wedding anniversary on October 17 in Charleston. Roy and Dorothy Cooper, who knew our weakness for seafood, invited us for a seafood dinner at a restaurant called The Trawlers. Anniversary dinners with the Coopers became almost annual events, which Gwen and I really enjoyed and appreciated.

In November Mel Launius and I flew in a twin-engine Cessna aircraft to Pensacola, Florida, to attend a priesthood institute. Mel even let me take the controls for a short while. We had a very fine experience with the priesthood; the testimonies of the seventies were outstanding. The Lord used me to bring a message to the men. Brother Harry Doty and others assured me that the Spirit of the Lord had directed the ministry which was given. The Master was certainly at work among His faithful priesthood in the Southeast.

The new year of 1971 started with cottage meetings in a home where the father, Charles Mueller, was Jewish and the mother and teenage children were Roman Catholic. It was most interesting talking with a Hebrew. Of course, he was a liberal Jew, or he would not have married outside the Jewish faith. At various times Charles asked questions about things that I had already explained. After I answered them, he said, "I knew what you said, but I wanted to be sure my family understood." They responded very well to the message of the gospel and gave their decision to be baptized.

The year shaped up to be a busy one. As the work expanded, new groups were formed; and many new prospects were found—which meant even more driving and cottage meetings for me, with preaching series in Greenville and Augusta and a youth rally in Charleston. We started a new group at High Point, North Carolina, where four families of church members were very enthusiastic about spreading the gospel in their area.

Some Baptist friends went on a trip to Australia, and we arranged for them to be met by Saints at each stage of their journey. They were amazed by the acceptance and hospitality shown by our people toward them. Traditionally a wonderful worldwide fellowship was found in our church, which was not found in many others. Jesus said, "By this shall all men know that ye are my disciples, if ye have love one to another" (John 13:35).

In January I had a unique experience as a TV star—well, maybe not really a *star*! I drove to Raleigh and went to a television studio with Brother Ed Geiersbach, who was a self-sustaining seventy. I had been invited to be the guest minister on a program entitled "Church of Our Fathers." The host asked Brother Geiersbach to introduce me; then he asked a few questions about our work in Raleigh and about Australia. The experience was interesting, but it was also quite trying because of the dazzling lights—I think they must have been adjusted for taller men because they got me right in the eyes! I watched the show with some Saints on Sunday, and their reaction was quite favorable.

We were saddened in early February to receive news of the death of Gwen's father, Elder Norman Wallace Peisker, who had been ill for some time. Gwen was not able to return to Australia so soon, but she was happy that he had been relieved of his suffering and was in the arms of God. Dad was a good man and remained loyal to his covenant with Christ until the end. I am sure that he is in the paradise of God, awaiting the great day when the trumpet shall sound and the dead in Christ shall rise first.

It was always difficult to be separated from our families in Australia—especially at a time like that. But we knew that although we made some sacrifices for the work of the Lord, they were insignificant compared with the sacrifice He made on Calvary and all through His earthly life.

While ministering to the Saints in Athens, Georgia, I met an inactive elder, a professor from the University of Georgia, who invited Gwen and me to his home. Although our formal education certainly could not compare with his, through the influence of the Holy Spirit we were able to encourage the family to become active again.

The missionary work was proceeding slowly but surely. One outstanding experience occurred at Charleston during a Sunday service. I had been holding cottage meetings with a family in which the mother was a church member and the father was a Roman Catholic. The man came to the service that day because their baby was to be blessed. During the sermon, High Priest Curtis Cunningham told of the conversion of the Jew from Greenville. The Catholic man later said that he was suddenly unaware of the congregation around him. It seemed as if he were sitting alone, feeling that the sermon was wholly for him and that he must also respond by being baptized. Later he was baptized into the church.

At the end of April, we had a beautiful baptismal service at the edge of the lake at Camp Buckhorn. Eleven people were baptized that day, including a former atheist, the Jewish man, his Roman Catholic family, and several others. They said they did not feel the cold of the water.

In May I attended a priesthood institute in Pensacola, with 254 men present. The emphasis was upon witnessing for Christ. Apostle Russell Ralston concluded the meeting with a spiritual message directed to several individuals.

I stayed with Beth and Bill in Lamoni in early June and attended a priesthood institute on the campus of Graceland College. Brother F. Henry Edwards was given a standing ovation by the 550 men in attendance. He then presented an inspirational paper. I had a rich spiritual experience during that presentation in which Brother Edwards made some profound remarks relating to the stewardship of priesthood. He emphasized that we are not to be agents of "bright ideas" brought forth by men of our day, but ministers of the gospel of Christ. I had fasted breakfast that morning, and the Lord filled me with a different kind of bread.

Trevor had received a call to the office of priest, which he accepted. The good Spirit was present in abundance as I ordained him on June 14 at the Greenville branch. That was a big event in our lives. Trevor taught the young people's class at the Greenville branch that summer. During a preaching service at Wilmington the following month, it was a thrill to be assisted by my son—the first such experience since his ordination.

We had a wonderful youth camp that summer, with 37 young people present. Gwen helped with the meals, was camp nurse, and also taught a handicraft class for the girls. Trevor had brought his electric organ and big amplifier and was in charge of the camp band. He also taught the model rocketry and swimming classes and was counselor for one of the boys' cabins. I made another Scripto board and found that the American campers enjoyed playing Scripto as much as the Aussies did.

At that camp we had a Friday night banquet and concert and chose the camp king and queen. The king, a young Baptist fellow named Crawford Roberts, was perfect for the position. He told everyone that they had to laugh at his jokes whether they were funny or not because he was king. He also chose the "volunteers" for cleanup duty after the banquet!

It was probably for the best that Trevor had difficulty finding employment that summer. He was thus able to spend the entire week at the youth camp. The Lord provides for those who put Him first. After the camp Trevor found employment painting fighter aircraft which had been overhauled at the nearby Donnelson Center.

In August our reunion was held at an altitude of 3,500 feet in the Great Smoky Mountains of North Carolina. It was an excellent reunion, with close to 200 in attendance. Apostle Russell Ralston was in charge and preached in the evenings. I conducted the daily prayer meetings. After one service, I was directed by the Lord to bring personal messages to three people, which I delivered privately. One was to David Garrett, a staunch Baptist, who had put off joining the church for some time. Just 10 minutes before the baptismal service was due to commence that week, he gave his decision to be baptized.

During the preaching services in the evenings, I worked with the children under eight and showed them movies. I taught the junior high class and had a very fine response from the students. On the last morning, they became profoundly interested in the temple and Zion. I asked them, "Wouldn't it be wonderful if your generation completed the redemption of Zion?" They agreed. I said that was possible in any generation that kept the commandments of the Lord.

After Bill McGuire graduated from Graceland College, he and Beth came to South Carolina to spend three months. They arrived in late August and were planning to leave for Australia in late November to live there for a couple of years. During their stay with us, they were both able to find temporary employment.

In September Bill and I attended a priesthood and men's retreat held at the same grounds in the mountains where we had the reunion. Gwen, Beth, and two other ladies did the cooking for us. Apostle Ralston, Seventy Harry Doty, and Bishop Joe Baldwin gave good ministry. After the retreat, I drove Bishop Baldwin around the area so he could teach stewardship to the Saints. That year we had an 18% increase in tithing and a 6% baptismal increase.

In September and October we organized new groups at Asheville, North Carolina, with about 26 people, and at Winston-Salem, with about 20 members. There were good opportunities for growth in those areas.

Beth, Bill, Gwen, and I drove to Charleston in October and went on a boat trip to Fort Sumter, where the first shots of the American Civil War were fired. We enjoyed learning about its historical significance.

Gwen passed her state board nurse's examination in October, which meant she was fully qualified to practice nursing in South Carolina. In December she commenced work in obstetrics nursing at the new St. Francis Hospital in Greenville.

☼ ☼ ☼

I have always maintained that we convert people by preaching the gospel of Jesus Christ. When they are smitten by their past lives and want to get right with God, they become true Saints. My missionary program was getting underway for helping the local priesthood present the wonderful truths of the restored gospel to their friends and relatives. Each team of one or more priesthood members had a projector, screen, six sets of slides, and cassettes, with my voice giving the study. I always gave teams a challenge of four or six baptisms a year—whatever I thought was reasonable for them in the districts or towns where they lived.

One rather competent young man said, "Only six baptisms every year? That will be easy!"

I responded, "These are to be people from outside the church—not our own children who have reached eight years of age."

I was elated with the results accruing from the missionary system using the slides and cassettes. I visited all of the prospective members so that they could meet "the man behind the voice" and endeavored to attend the final lecture of each group to answer any questions and invite the people to pray for their personal testimonies of the veracity of the gospel. One particular night I was speaking at three cottage meetings in Charleston at the same time—two on tape and one in person.

The results began to come in, and the man who said it would be easy did baptize six adults in the year. Another man baptized four, another man three, some only two, some one, some maybe more than six. Thus our baptismal rate began to increase, and many souls were brought to Christ. The men all spoke highly of the system, so we continued to expand it.

☼ ☼ ☼

Beth and Bill departed for Australia on November 30. We were very sorry to see them leave us, but we knew Beth would enjoy being with her sister and grandparents again. They stopped in Tahiti to give Bill the opportunity to see where Beth had spent seven years of her childhood. Shortly after arriving in Australia and visiting relatives in Brisbane, Beth was given a nursing position at the Royal Newcastle Hospital, where she had done her nurse's training. Bill obtained a position as sports master at St. Pius X Catholic boys' high school. They made their home in Newcastle with Marvia and Terry in our old house, which had been divided into two flats.

In December we held a service in a military chapel near the Pope Air Force Base in North Carolina. The members there were mainly army and air force personnel. I showed the documentary film of the church's early history and preached on the all-embracing love of God through Christ. I stayed at the home of Brother and Sister Morgan.

At Raleigh I held my first meeting with a black family and showed them the church history movie. About 10 people were present, including children, and we had a very profitable time. They asked many questions about the church. One older gentleman asked why they were just now hearing of something that had happened over 100 years ago. I explained that religious bigotry had prevented the gospel from growing much in the South.

☼ ☼ ☼

We started the year of 1972 with a youth rally at Greenville that drew 50 young people and resulted in four baptisms, including two young marines from Camp Lejeune. They had both been in Vietnam and had seen some horrible atrocities of combat. One of the marines was really sick at heart until he met Claude Krause, a gunnery sergeant and a member of the RLDS Church. Sergeant Krause stood out since he normally wore a smile—something quite unusual among the marines. When asked, "Why are you always smiling?" he had answered, "It's because of my church." After one such occasion, he was able to minister to this young marine and hold cottage meetings with him. The boy was given a new hope in life, and the friendliness of the Saints helped him make his decision to be baptized.

The missionary work was progressing, especially with the advent of the new slide and cassette system. We had 30 baptisms in the area during 1971, and the prospects looked even better for 1972. We established a new group in Swainsborough, Georgia; 10 nonmembers were at the meeting, and they bombarded me with questions. I left a missionary kit with the elder there. In May we also organized a group in Columbia, South Carolina.

Gwen's mother arrived from Australia in mid-February, and we drove to Atlanta to pick her up. Of course, we were thrilled to see her again. She was a petite lady of 76, who had never flown before; yet she flew by herself all the way from Brisbane. She withstood the trip well, probably better than a lot of younger people.

Mother accompanied us on some of our journeys around the area. Near the end of March, she saw her first snowfall, which began just an hour before we left to drive to Wilmington. She had never seen snow before in her life and stayed glued to the window as she watched it falling. It was a rather wet snow, and Mother was like a little girl making her first snowball. We ran out of the snow as we traveled east; so we told her she was very fortunate to have seen it, especially that late in the year. On that trip she also had her first look at the Atlantic Ocean.

We attended the 1972 World Conference in Independence. Gwen's mother was a delegate for Brisbane, and Trevor was a delegate for the Newcastle District. We were delighted that Frank and Ruth Flood were also able to be there, so we had a nice family reunion on the Peisker side.

The conference went better than the previous one, I thought. But there were still some things that troubled me, especially in the document submitted by the prophet. I was quite concerned that the commendation which said God was pleased with the members collectively and individually seemed to include all the church. He could hardly have been pleased with many of us. It likely gave some a sense of smugness so they would say, "All is well in Zion."

That certainly was not consistent with the remarks of the outgoing presiding bishop, Walter Johnson. He told how the RLDS Church was dying and that we desperately needed new members if we were to survive. The church had had a net increase of only 1%—and that rate was falling. Tithing and contributions were also reduced.

After returning from conference, I baptized a Vietnamese woman, with whom I had completed a series of cottage meetings. She was married to a U.S. serviceman, who was a church member; and they were soon to move to Alaska. I then traveled to Charleston, where the congregation was meeting in a remodeled house. Praise to the Lord, they had outgrown it! They had a short business meeting and decided to buy an acre on which to build a new church.

I love to baptize out in nature whenever possible. We had planned a baptismal service for quite a few candidates in a lovely little lake at Camp Buckhorn. The weather had been inclement for some time, and I prayed that the Lord would stop the rain at the time of the baptism. The next morning there were still ominous, black clouds in the sky. The pastor was sure we would have to baptize in the church because the lake would be muddy from the heavy rains.

Early that morning, I drove several miles to check the lake; I found that the water was not muddy at all. It was still raining a little; however, in the west the sky was clear. I returned and told the pastor, "I believe that we can have the baptism up there." The rain did stop, although the dark clouds still looked threatening. Just when the Saints reached the water's edge, a great black cloud came over. If ever my faith was shaken, it was then. But that cloud did not spill its water on us, and we got through the service with just one or two sprinkles. Everyone knew that the Lord had blessed us and kept us from getting soaked. It was a strengthening testimony to those people, who had to meet many tests of their faith in days to come. We gave the Lord the glory for that beautiful experience!

☼ ☼ ☼

In Australia both Beth and Marvia were expecting their first babies. Gwen had been saving her nursing wages so she could accompany her mother back to Australia in early June in time to witness the births of our first grandchildren. The hospital granted Gwen a three-month leave of absence although she had been working there only six months.

Gwen and her mother flew from Kansas City to Sydney, where both of our girls met them. They arrived in Newcastle just a few days before Beth gave birth to John William McGuire on June 21.

My family in Brisbane sent a round-trip ticket so I could visit my children, grandchildren, and aging parents. Some of the Saints in the area gave me money for expenses on the trip. Apostle Ralston readily gave his permission, saying, "Go and enjoy yourself with your loved ones in Australia." I set out for my homeland on August 1 after an absence of almost three years.

I went first to Brisbane to visit my parents. There I talked to my father again about how necessary it is to be baptized in order to enter the Kingdom of God. He was a good man and was always willing to help the church with its building projects. He often attended church with my mother; but despite his knowledge of the gospel, he had refused to enter the waters of baptism. Father explained that he did not plan to be baptized because he wanted to be with his mother in the hereafter, and she had not been baptized. I asked him how he knew that his mother had not accepted the gospel on the other side, since she was such a good woman.

A few days later Father said to me, "Son, about this baptism business—I would like you to baptize me on Friday in the font at the Coorparoo church." My happiness and love for my father were indescribable as I immersed him in the waters of baptism during a private service. He was confirmed at the Coorparoo branch. He walked to the front of the church as straight and proud as a young man, and I laid my hands upon him in confirmation to receive the gift of the Holy Ghost. That was one of the most joyful and fulfilling moments in my life. How I have thanked the Lord for that privilege!

I explained to Father that although he might not be able to attend church every Sunday, he should at least try to attend the sacrament services. He replied, "Son, I intend to —I haven't done this thing by halves."

I believe the Lord preserved his life so he could accept the everlasting gospel. After Father's baptism I asked the Lord to extend his life at least a year so he might have time to live the gospel and prepare for the afterlife. The Lord bountifully answered my prayers; and Father lived three years after his baptism, dying peacefully at the age of 85.

I flew from Brisbane to Sydney and then to Newcastle, being met at the airport by Gwen, Marvia, and Terry. We went directly to the Thompson and McGuire house, where Bill and Beth introduced little John McGuire to his grandfather. What a thrill that was! We enjoyed our stay in Newcastle and our visit with our daughters, their husbands, and our many friends.

When the Saints from the area came to hear me preach at Newcastle and Taree, Brother and Sister Ernie Kelsey traveled all the way from Bowraville to meet us. On my way to Taree, I baptized an eight-year-old girl in Lake Wallis at Tiona. Her mother was delighted because I had given ministry to her family many years earlier.

The time for our departure from Australia was rapidly approaching, and Marvia had not yet had her baby. On August 23—just five days before we were to leave—our second grandson, Michael Andrew Thompson, saw the light of day. I blessed his cousin, young John McGuire, on Sunday morning, and was sorry that Michael could not be blessed at the same service.

Monday morning we went to see Marvia and her baby at the hospital and obtained special permission to hold Michael and take pictures. I took him in my arms and asked God's blessing on him, not in a formal manner, but just as a grandfather holding the Melchisedec priesthood. Leaving Marvia and Michael in the hospital again fulfilled the prophecy in my patriarchal blessing, which said there would be many sad partings in my life.

Beth and Bill drove us to Sydney, where Gwen and I caught the plane back to the States. We both received warm receptions when we returned home. The staff was certainly happy to have Gwen back at the hospital.

☼ ☼ ☼

In October while visiting a family in the mountains of North Carolina, I had another "first" when I held a cottage meeting in the county jail. It was not for the prisoners, but for the sheriff and his deputies. Some others were present, including a woman who said she had been kidnapped and had escaped (but it turned out that she had had a fight with her husband and was there for sympathy from the sheriff).

Another first occurred in November, when I had a series of cottage meetings with a deaf boy. His mother was a church member, and she interpreted my lectures in sign language.

In December we started a group again at Warner Robins Air Force Base in central Georgia. The Saints enjoyed a sacrament service—the first meeting there in more than two years. I left some material and instructions so the 23 people present could carry on until I could visit again.

Sister Bert Schinzing worked as an industrial nurse at the nearby General Electric gas turbine plant, which had recently opened. Gwen interviewed there, was offered a position, and decided to change jobs. Just after Christmas, she started work as an occupational health nurse. Not only did the new position offer better pay, but it was less stressful and much closer to home.

Our area had a record number of baptisms and tithing filers in 1972. When asked what our secret was, I declared that it was to teach the everlasting gospel and to trust in the power of God. Our missionary work was helped greatly by the missionary kits—we had 15 baptisms as a direct result of their use.

In January of 1973 five people from our area, including myself, flew to Mexico to visit the archaeological sites. Gwen was unable to accompany us since she had just started her new job. Our first stop was in Yucatán. There we visited the famous ruins of Chichén Itzá and Uxmal, which are by far the most ornate and beautiful. It was a thrill to climb the tall pyramids and think of the people who built them. Palenque was perhaps the most interesting ruin that we visited. There we saw stone writings which had not yet been deciphered. My limited knowledge of Spanish was of value in the areas where few spoke English.

We rented a car and drove to Mexico City, where we saw President W. Wallace Smith and his wife, who were also tourists. After visiting the museums and seeing the sights for a couple of days, we flew back to Greenville—the end of a wonderful trip. I felt much refreshed and strengthened to continue promoting the Book of Mormon as a sacred book of the ancient Americans.

I drove through the scenic Smoky Mountains to the appointees' retreat in March, which was held at Paris Landing, Tennessee. At first I was quite disappointed with the seminar, which emphasized the secrets of big business success but left out the spiritual aspects of the gospel. However, after a wonderful experience during the worship service the second morning, the whole tone of the retreat became more uplifting.

In April Gwen went with me to Charlotte for the dedication of the new church; 151 people were present, which was marvelous. A very fine spirit prevailed, first in our worship service, then in the actual dedication service, where Bishop Harold Downey was the speaker.

We held an Easter sunrise service at the rehabilitation center in Charleston, where about 45 of the residents and the Charleston Saints were in attendance. It was a simple but beautiful experience, which ministered to many of those people. At the 10 a.m. service at the church, I preached the Easter sermon; and we had two ordinations.

In May I was called to administer to a black man, who lived with his wife in a little house in rural North Carolina. Although the house did not look like much from the outside, it was spotlessly clean and tidy on the inside. Both of them were in tears after the administration, largely because a white man was willing to minister to them in their time of need.

That same night I went with Seventy Ed Geiersbach to a home for a meeting with about 12 black people. One had been to Sydney, where he had been treated well by the Aussies. That may have helped make him more receptive to what I had to say. I felt right at home with them, knowing that they have the same feelings, emotions, and ambitions as we do and that God's love is extended to them just as much as to us. During the next few years, I was able to share the gospel of Jesus Christ with many more black people—although not as many as I would have liked.

Trevor graduated in May of 1973 from the University of Kansas with a Bachelor of Science degree in aerospace engineering. We were naturally very proud of him. Gwen and I went to the university for the graduation ceremony, which was held in the football stadium. A storm had been brewing, and the lightning flashed as we gathered. The crowd began to scatter, and the ceremony was pushed on at great speed. I suspect that few have ever been graduated so quickly. Trevor returned with us to South Carolina, and for a short while he accompanied me on some of my cottage meetings and trips.

☼ ☼ ☼

Brother Tom Morman left in June for his new assignment in California, and Seventy Jack Fears was assigned to take his place in Atlanta. However, there was a gap between their assignments that summer, which meant that I had the responsibility for two youth camps back to back. We had a problem getting helpers since so many parents worked. The senior high camp was the second week, and I was very tired. I think the campers could see that I was being stretched to the utmost, and they were pretty decent through it all.

At the final prayer meeting on Saturday morning, however, only a few prayed; then the meeting went absolutely dead. I felt responsible because I hadn't been able to keep up the spiritual level of the young people through that whole week. I stood and prayed, "Lord, beat me with the stripes of these young people. Don't beat them because they don't know or understand everything. I have failed, so please beat me with their stripes."

No sooner had I sat down than one young man, Greg Parker, arose and said, "Lord, don't beat Brother Sorensen with my stripes. I haven't been as attentive and helpful and careful as I should have. Beat me with my own stripes for the things I deserve." That started a chain reaction. Members and nonmembers alike, their faces bathed in tears, stood up and asked the Lord to beat them with their stripes and not to beat me.

The Lord saw fit for those young people to bear their burdens as they should, and we had a magnificent finale to that prayer meeting and that camp. When we went down the mountain, the campers were different. Their faces were lit up, and they were vibrant and full of life because the Spirit of the Lord had touched them.

In mid-July our son set out on an epic adventure by flying to Europe, where he spent nine weeks backpacking. During his travels he met several of the German Saints and Bruce Nelson, a friend of Beth's from Graceland. Trevor stayed a couple of days with Brother Everett Graffeo, the appointee in Germany, and attended a mission conference in Hannover and our church servicemen's retreat at Berchesgaden in Bavaria. There he was with the family of

Colonel Fisher, whom he had met at Shaw Air Force Base.

Trevor was the first of our Sorensen family to return to Denmark, the homeland of our ancestors. I wished that I could have been with him on his adventure. He wrote that Denmark was a beautiful country. When he looked to see if Sorensens still lived there, he found 21 pages of them in the Copenhagen phone book!

We had the largest reunion ever in August, with well over 200 attending. It was also the finest reunion to date in the area, with an excellent spirit of participation by all. Apostle Russell Ralston brought an inspired message to us on the final morning. He was extremely pleased with the spirit of the people, and he agreed to write an editorial for the *Evangel* newsletter.

About that time Gwen and I purchased our first property in the land of Zion—part of a 160-acre farm just south of Warrensburg, Missouri, about 50 miles from Independence. We bought 40 acres, including the house, barn, and ponds; Mel Launius bought the other 120 acres and some cattle. Beth and Bill were planning to return from Australia in 1974. Since Bill wanted to work on his master's degree, it seemed an ideal situation for them to live on the farm so he could attend the university at Warrensburg.

In October Trevor returned home and spent five days with us, sharing the slides and tales of his trip to Europe. He then drove to Dayton, Ohio, to start a new job with a small aerospace company doing work for the U.S. Air Force near Wright-Patterson Air Force Base. He started attending the Beavercreek branch of the church in Dayton.

The Arab-Israeli war, although lasting only about a month, was having quite an effect on this great nation. It was becoming harder to find gasoline, which resulted in long lines at the gas pumps; and prices had skyrocketed. All of the appointees received notices to minimize driving and to conserve energy as much as possible. I had already switched to a smaller, more fuel-efficient car; but the costs and restrictions had some effect on my missionary efforts because of the large area I had to cover. However, the missionary kits widely use by priesthood in a number of branches saved a lot of driving on my part.

Frank Flood was assigned to the Santa Fe Stake in 1974. He and his family moved from Australia to Independence in January, and Gwen was thrilled to have her sister Ruth at least in the same country again.

In January, 1974, I visited the Cherry Point Marine Corps Air Station in North Carolina to organize a new group. I was given VIP treatment when a colonel—an elder in the church—had me taken all over the base, up into the control tower, and out onto the tarmac with the aircraft. There I watched one of the British-made Harrier jets take off vertically, hover just a few feet above the ground, and land. The Marines received me well, especially so when they learned I was an Australian.

Our area was one of the fastest growing in the church because the Saints were missionary minded and the Lord was blessing their witness. There is no substitute for the true gospel of Jesus Christ in the lives of His people.

The Greenville branch built a new church, which was completed in early February of 1974. I had the honor of preaching the first sermon in the new building, and Gwen played the piano. The service was held in the fellowship hall because the chapel furniture had not yet arrived.

In the sermon, I warned about the devil being overactive toward the end of the latter days. While I was speaking inside, the devil was creating mischief outside the church. Roofing nails had been placed in front of the tires of the Saints' cars, and altogether 12 tires were punctured. A man who lived across the street from the church admitted to laying out the nails—he resented our parking on the side of the road near his place. Because the man was not repentant, Pastor Mel Launius asked the sheriff to take action to avoid a similar incident in the future. I was not fully in favor, but I did not vehemently oppose it because we are told in the Doctrine and Covenants to appeal to the laws of the land for redress.

Several people later remarked about the truth of my sermon because the devil surely had been at work. We knew we could expect that sort of thing when the church was flourishing, as it was there. A positive result came from the incident as other neighbors expressed contempt for such a deed and became more sympathetic toward us.

In early 1974 we instituted a new program that enabled the Saints in the area to serve their communities spiritually and physically. We started day-care centers in our church buildings to care for the children of working mothers. Sister Ferne Launius of the Greenville branch already operated a successful day-care center, and she helped to get our program going. I believe Greenville was the first congregation in that area with such a program. Others followed, and each was a good witness in the community. The profit from the centers helped us pay for our church buildings.

Brother Harry Doty informed me that three of the fastest growing areas in the church were where Houston Hobart, Eddie Butterworth, and I were missionaries. We three preached the gospel of Jesus Christ—the only power which frees men from themselves.

At 2:15 a.m. on March 21, our phone rang. Gwen and I bounded out of bed to hear Bill McGuire's voice. Our third grandson, Richard Carl McGuire—all nine pounds eight ounces of him—had just been born in Newcastle, Australia. Beth and the baby were both doing well. We were thrilled; but it was hard for the grandmother to be so far away from the event, especially since Gwen had been there for the births of the first two grandsons.

☼ ☼ ☼

We attended the 1974 World Conference in April. Gwen was a delegate for the Newcastle district. I drove to Independence prior to conference for the seventies' sessions, stopping to see Trevor in Ohio on the way. We were having a gasoline shortage due to the problems in the Middle East, and at times I had to wait an hour or more in line to get gasoline. As a result of the shortage, many delegates —including Gwen—flew in for the conference.

I felt that the 1974 conference was a good one, ending with a note of reconciliation. I told my mother that it was a "people's conference." There was a tremendous spirit present, which seemed to hover over the assembly and cause the delegates to unite while they discussed business.

A highlight of that conference occurred when Sister Rosamond Smith, wife of the prophet, asked to speak to the assembly. She told the Saints that her son and daughter, Wallace B. and Rosalee, had been taught the Three Standard Books and the gospel contained therein. She also said that she had not discussed her statement with her husband; we could see that he was really surprised.

One outstanding product of the conference was a very timely message through retiring Presiding Patriarch Roy Cheville, which admonished the whole church to be unified. The leaders were cautioned not to try to force their pet programs and ideas upon the people. That direction had a noted effect on them.

The conference made a change in the assignments of the apostles. Brother Russell Ralston, who had been in charge of our area, was replaced by Brother Don Lents. Frank Flood was ordained a bishop at the conference, fulfilling a statement I had made to him years previously in Newcastle. The Floods had settled fairly well into life in Independence, but their daughter, Carynne, really missed Australia.

☼ ☼ ☼

After conference Gwen flew to Greenville; but I went to the farm near Warrensburg and worked like a Trojan for four days, putting a new ceiling in one room and planting potatoes, peas, and some fruit trees for Beth and Bill.

In April Trevor lost his job as an engineer when the Air Force canceled the contract he was working on. He moved to our home, where he worked for the summer.

A major event at that time was the return of Beth and her family from Australia. They flew back in early May, going first to the home of Bill's parents in Marshalltown, Iowa. The flight must have been quite an ordeal for them, traveling with a six-week-old infant and a nearly two-year-old toddler.

Gwen, Trevor, and I were able to meet them in Independence in late May. It was quite a reunion! When Beth and Bill arrived from Iowa, they were towing a trailer full of furniture. The McGuires then moved into the house near Warrensburg. They loved the property. Bill said that even though the house was old, it was a mansion compared to the small apartment they had in Newcastle. Bill was employed by Mel Launius part-time to look after his portion of the farm, including his cattle.

My church work continued to make good progress. The Charleston mission became a branch, and we had regular meetings at Warner Robins Air Force Base. I was not doing quite as much personal missionary work as previously. Rather, we were training many Saints to present the gospel through cottage meetings. They were thus able to experience the joy of witnessing and bringing souls to Christ. That was really better than relying on the missionary in charge to do all the work.

We held our children's camp that year for the first time on the Willimon's farm at the foot of the Smoky Mountains, not far from Greenville. The Friday before camp, I built a shower and bushman's toilet for the boys and a shelter in case of rain. On Saturday we brought chairs, tables, and other things from the church. That afternoon the bombardment of the campers began—about 40, which was plenty for our limited facilities. We had a good camp. The children were as funny as a barrel of monkeys, but I did not let them worry me. Strict discipline was the secret.

In June Gwen and I drove to Warrensburg, taking a used refrigerator and rolls of carpet in a pickup truck. We spent a week working hard with Bill and Beth to make improvements on the house. While there, we bought an old Massey Harris tractor. I believe it was the one Noah used to haul animals to the ark. It burned a lot of oil—but for $275, what could be expected? We also bought a brush hog, a hay rake, and hay baler. My grandson John wanted to help Daddy and Grandpa, but at two years old he was much more of a hindrance than a help. I called him "John the Wrecker"!

Bill enrolled at Central Missouri State University in Warrensburg in the fall to work toward his master's degree in education. His tuition and other expenses were paid by the government G.I. Bill. He continued to work hard on the farm to make additional income to help his family.

Reunion that year was held in the Smoky Mountains; it was cool—a welcome relief from the 100° weather we were having in Greenville. Apostle Don Lents and Brother Jack Fears gave good ministry. I preached one sermon about the unfinished work of the church. I told the Saints that the regathering of Israel had commenced when Moses appeared to Joseph Smith at the Kirtland Temple and gave him the keys of the gathering of Israel and the 10 tribes from the north. Many of our people had not heard of that. It was pitiful what they did not know about God's purpose in us as a chosen people.

I relinquished my other scheduled reunion sermon to Brother Allen Breckenridge, who was there most of the time. He and his wife Jane had been with us in Tahiti, and Gwen and I were very pleased to see them again. Allen, still under appointment as a patriarch-evangelist, bore testimony of God's power in his life.

Early one morning Brother Larry Rife came up the hill and awakened us. He said, "Someone is sick down the hill near my place, and we would like to have Sister Sorensen come."

When Gwen arrived, she found that the man was frothing at the mouth, apparently possessed by an evil spirit. She told Brother Rife to go back and get me, saying, "This man needs administration!"

I looked at the man and could see what the trouble was. Although he seemed perfectly healthy, he was delirious at times. I called on Brother Rife to anoint the man with oil. Then I said, "In the name of Jesus Christ, thou foul and evil spirit, depart." Immediately the man was pacified; his eyes opened then shut, and he went into a normal sleep. Later the same morning that man came to the prayer meeting. During the testimony period he stood and said, "Don't ever let me hear any of you people saying there are no such things as evil spirits. Ask Brother Sorensen and Brother Rife if there are evil spirits. They will tell you we had an incredible experience early this morning." To the glory of God that man was liberated!

It is interesting how word gets around. One day I was called to the phone; and a lady asked, "Are you the Reverend Sorensen?" She had heard that I was an exorcist. I told her I was usually called Elder Sorensen and that the Lord Jesus Christ was the only real exorcist. She expected me to be some charlatan who took money to cast out evil spirits. I soon set her straight and never heard from her again.

That shows how the world misconstrues the things which are written in the scriptures.

Trevor left home in August and headed for the Midwest. He stopped by Warrensburg and helped bring in the 1,100 bales of hay Bill had harvested with our "new" equipment. Trevor then enrolled in graduate school at the University of Kansas, where he obtained a part-time job as a research assistant. That was exactly what he needed for his thesis, and it paid all of his expenses. Brother Ammon Andes, who was one of his professors, and his wife Bernice generously let Trevor live in their furnished basement for only the cost of utilities and some painting.

In October Gwen attended a nurses' convention held in Winston-Salem. I drove her there and took care of some church business in the area. Our branch had a booth at the county fair, and I had supplied Pastor Joe Burkart with a lot of tracts and information about the church. The booth introduced the restored gospel to a number of people, of whom a large portion were black. The Mormons had a booth not far from ours, and the black people soon learned that the Mormons at that time would not accept any of their race into the priesthood. When they came to our booth and saw a picture of a black man being ordained in Haiti, they were favorably impressed.

As far as I know, we were the first in the RLDS Church to commence work among the black people in the South. Our success was largely due to Seventy Ed Geiersbach, who was using our equipment, slides, and tapes. Initially he had been invited to a black church by one of their members. That black man began to visit our church, and he and his wife and children were soon baptized.

Before I left, about 25 black people were in the Raleigh congregation. There was no enmity or bigotry in evidence; both races seemed to mingle very well, proving to me again that salvation is for all men. I do not know what happened to the work among the black people after I left, but I know that we laid a good foundation. Gwen and I have ministered to Australians, Tahitians, Vietnamese, Chinese, Hawaiians, Eurasians, Canadians, Koreans, Japanese, and people of many other nations. All people are blessed of God if they will acknowledge Christ as the Savior of the world and seek forgiveness and a remission of their sins.

☼ ☼ ☼

One unusual incident occurred in October, when a wild turkey flew onto a man's property at Greenville. The man looked in the phone book to find the name of a turkey farmer so he could buy a tom turkey to breed with the wild female. Who should he pick but Mel Launius, the pastor of the Greenville branch. In the course of events, Mel learned that the man's father, also living in Greenville, had been baptized by Brother Hubert Case in 1929. Mel taught the man and his wife and children the everlasting gospel, with the outcome that they became members of the church. That was all because a wild turkey chose to fly onto his property. God moves in mysterious ways, even using a turkey to initiate contacts with nonmembers!

Marvia had written earlier to tell us that she was pregnant again, but we received quite a shock in early November when she called and told us that she was going to have twins! Gwen made plans to return to Australia to be with Marvia after the twins were born.

Early in 1975 Don and Betty Willimon donated 35 acres of land to the church to use as a campground. Betty was seriously ill with cancer, and it was her sincerest wish that the property be signed over to the church before she died. I chaired the reunion grounds building committee.

Beth started the new year by obtaining employment as an obstetric nurse at the Warrensburg Hospital. She worked evenings while Bill was at home to look after the boys. Trevor tried to visit every other weekend to enjoy Beth's home cooking and to play with his young nephews.

I was on a missionary trip when Gwen received the word that our identical twin grandsons were born January 18, 1975, in Newcastle. She phoned and gave me the good news that Marvia and the babies were doing very well. Mathew Charles Thompson was six pounds seven ounces, and Adam John Thompson was five pounds thirteen ounces. My sister Silvia had traveled from Brisbane to be with Marvia and help her for a few days after she and the twins came home from the hospital.

At that time the church's policy was to provide for foreign missionaries to visit their homeland every four years. We had not taken advantage of that policy in the five years since we left Australia. (Our trip in 1972 was personally financed.) Therefore, we requested some financial help from the bishopric so Gwen could visit our children and grandchildren. Bishop Francis Hansen wrote that I should accompany her and that the church would pay the expenses for both of us to visit our homeland. That was a "bolt from the blue."

I still had plenty of work to do in the area before we left on our trip. Gwen, Brother Harry Doty, and I drove 300 miles to Wilmington, rested an hour at the pastor's home, then drove 55 miles to Jacksonville, North Carolina. On Sunday we attended a baptismal service in Wilmington, where three adults were baptized. I baptized one of them, a young expectant mother. (Later I jokingly told someone that Brother Doty would likely silence me for baptizing a baby!) After an ordination service that morning, we drove 170 miles to Charleston for another ordination service that evening.

☼ ☼ ☼

In early February Gwen and I departed for Australia. It was truly a joyous reunion when we arrived in Newcastle, saw our daughter again, enjoyed seeing our grandson Michael, and first laid eyes on those beautiful twin boys. After a few days in Newcastle, I flew to Brisbane, leaving Gwen with Marvia for a while longer. My mother and father, sister Mavis, and Ray and Judy Burdekin were at the airport to meet me. I was agreeably surprised at the appearance of my parents. Although Father had aged and was a bit weaker, he was so independent that he still drove his car and mowed his lawn. Mavis was on vacation and thus was able to drive me around. I had brought my 8mm movies and showed one each evening to the loved ones. A couple of days later, my family went up the coast to Maroochydore, where I had spent much of my boyhood.

On Sunday night I preached at the Coorparoo Branch. The "fair-haired boy had come home," and there was a large crowd present. Ray Burdekin asked, "What is this, a district conference?"

Gwen joined me in Brisbane for a few days to visit her mother and our relatives. We soon returned to Newcastle so we could spend as much time with Marvia as possible before returning to America. I especially enjoyed playing with my two-and-a half-year-old grandson Michael while the others were fussing over the twins. All too soon it was time to depart for home.

The return trip was very tiring but uneventful, except for one marvelous day in Tahiti. We flew from Sydney to Papeete, arriving about 11 p.m. local time. We were met by a small number of native Saints and spent the night in the home of Brother Etienne Vanaa, the mission president. After breakfast, Sister Vanaa took us in their car to look at the new church buildings. We later visited Sister Naomi

Bennett, who was almost blind, and her husband, Manua. I had frequently traveled on his schooner when I served there. Manua kissed me on both cheeks several times, and Naomi clung to Gwen's hand as long as we stayed with them. Later we drove completely around the island. By then, heavy rain had set in; but it did not deter us. We inspected some property that the church had bought at the Isthmus of Taravao. It was a lovely spot on which to build a house of worship.

We called on Ah Sam, the Chinese church member who owned a grocery store. He and his Tahitian wife were delighted to see us. They loaded us down with canned food (which we left with the mission president) and some cookies and Tiare Tahiti perfume. We finished the marvelous day with some of the Saints at the mission president's home; then we caught the plane for Los Angeles.

☼ ☼ ☼

By the time we arrived in Greenville many hours later, we were thoroughly exhausted but thankful for such a wonderful four weeks. I preached the next day at the Greenville church. It was a bit difficult because I was still suffering from jet lag, but the Lord was with me.

While I was gone, my missionary work had backed up—especially many requests for the slide and tape sets. I received a phone call from Chicago and was asked to come and demonstrate my missionary methods to the district officers. Another appointee had shown them my material, and they ordered 16 sets. I was later told that several baptisms resulted from cottage meetings using those materials. Harry Doty also called to say that he needed several more sets. That was followed by phone calls from Detroit and St. Louis requesting more. So the work went on. I was glad the materials were helping to bring souls to Christ, but it certainly kept me busy.

During April I attended a youth retreat, held meetings at Warner Robins Air Force Base and Swainsboro in Georgia; arranged to commence meetings again in Beaufort, South Carolina; preached at Wilmington and Camp Lejeune, North Carolina; spoke to the priesthood and a women's group at Raleigh; attended a young marrieds' retreat; baptized one young man; started a new group at Anderson, South Carolina; and printed and mailed *Evangel*. On one of those trips I was away from home for two weeks. I was still preaching the gospel, and the Lord was still giving the increase.

The baptismal service held during the young marrieds' retreat was a unique experience. It was the first time that I asked the candidates to bear their testimonies just before they were ushered into the water. It was also the first time that I had conducted a baptismal service on a long, wide jetty leading out to deeper water, like Tiona's used to be. The Saints from Wilmington came for the service, and all of us stood on the jetty. I baptized the young husband first and asked him to remain with me and escort his wife out of the water following her baptism. Many people later said that they were deeply touched by the service.

In mid-May Beth called one night and said that she was not just *at the hospital*, but *in the hospital*! The previous day had been so beautiful that she went for a ride on their horse. The horse shied when a bird flew up in front of it, and Beth was thrown to the ground. She was in ice packs when she talked to me, but the doctors said there was nothing seriously wrong with her. We did not know at the time that Beth was expecting; fortunately no harm was done to the baby.

The wonderful thing about our work in the Southeast was that over 80% of our members attended church in most branches and missions, with some regularly as high as

95%! Notwithstanding the recession, our tithing for the first quarter of the year was 20% greater than that of the same period the previous year. The Lord was working with the preaching of the Old Jerusalem and the New Jerusalem gospel in the area. Brother Doty asked an apostle how many converts the liberals were getting. He slowly shook his head and said, "So very few, it does not really amount to anything." People want the message of Christ and the Spirit of God which goes with it.

Unfortunately it was not all growth throughout the area. In early June I had to close out the bank account of one group. After four years of services and administering to the needs of many people, almost all the Saints had moved away or were in the process of doing so. I told the former pastor's daughters not to feel too badly—their father's work had not been in vain because many people had been ministered to and a number were brought into the church during the time of his service.

In late June of 1975, Gwen and I set out on a trip to remake our documentary film on church history, as well as to take some still pictures for the missionary slide sets. My old church history film, made 20 years earlier, had been shown so many times that it was almost worn out. After visiting the various sites of historic interest, such as Kirtland Temple, the sacred grove, Hill Cumorah, and Nauvoo, we drove to our farm in Missouri.

We decided to sell our farm after Bill graduated and he and Beth would be moving to a different area. After a bit of searching, we found an ideal five-acre parcel between Oak Grove and Lone Jack in eastern Jackson County, about 25 miles from Independence. The property had a small stream, seven beautiful hickory trees, and some huge oak trees. It was an excellent place to build our retirement home. We closed on it in August and later in the year sold the Warrensburg property.

In early July we drove back to South Carolina. Trevor came with us, driving his own car. He then went on to Florida, where he had a pass to watch the launch of the Saturn rocket for the Apollo-Soyuz mission. We enjoyed his company for the few weeks he was with us, and he helped us by scraping and repainting the woodwork on our house. It was a good opportunity for the father and son to be together.

One night I was lying in bed reading Arthur Oakman's book, *He Who Is*. I reveled in the account of Enoch and his conversations with the Lord. While I pondered it, I was taken very close to the veil and could almost see through it. The veil was translucent, not transparent. I could see soft and glorious light beyond it, but it was diffused. My sinfulness was making it like that—but the veil was so thin. I was given to know that if I had been more righteous, the veil would have been transparent and I could have seen the Lord. I yearned to go beyond—but it was not yet my time. No one can take that wonderful experience from me. We are in a great work, and its consumation will be glorious.

The missionary work was progressing well, with a good number of converts entering the church. One lady in Raleigh, after praying that the Lord would lead her to His church, opened the phone book and spotted the name of our church. She contacted the local seventy, Brother Ed Geiersbach; and he held cottage meetings with her family. As a result of that experience, I was prompted to urge our pastors to have the church's name in the telephone book.

The Lord was at work in spite of the problems in the church. He had opened the way in many foreign countries without our aid, and He was putting a desire into the hearts of the Saints to gather. Many of them were buying land in Missouri in preparation for the building up of Zion.

☼ ☼ ☼

In July our area suffered a tragic loss when Richard Page, our pastor from Charlotte, and his two younger sons were killed in a private plane crash in Mississippi. He was survived by his wife and oldest son. The funeral service was truly a marvelous experience, with about 300 present. Brother John Midgorden, a bishop from Independence who was an old friend of the family, preached the sermon. He read from the Book of Mormon and Doctrine and Covenants, which really made the nonmembers sit on the edges of their seats. We also sang some favorite Restoration hymns, such as "The Spirit of God like a Fire Is Burning" and "O My People, Saith the Spirit."

Sister Norma Page, the widow, was sharing the gospel with her sister-in-law within an hour after the service. The lady had been so impressed with the message that she asked Sister Page about the other books the minister used, "which sounded like scripture." Dear Sister Page forgot her grief as she began to explain the Scriptures. She also mentioned that Brother Sorensen had made a set of slides which they could see at a later date. The sister-in-law replied that she most certainly was interested. Although suffering such a terrible loss, Sister Page put the Kingdom first and shared it in testimony with her relative. That is what our faith is all about. That is why I am glad to be a Latter Day Saint.

In August, 1975, more than 300 people were registered for our reunion. Bishop Francis Hansen and his wife and daughter were present; and he gave excellent ministry. My one sermon at reunion caused quite a stir. I felt the burden of the Lord upon me to change my sermon topic at the last minute. As soon as I surrendered my will to God's, His

Spirit came in abundance; and I spoke under inspiration about the things that the adversary was using to sap the life of God's people and about how cunningly he was laying his snares. Social drinking was one; adultery and permissiveness, women aspiring to the priesthood, and open communion were others. I had such liberty that I could have gone on and on—but one hour seemed enough. After the sermon, the people stood around in groups for a long time and discussed what had transpired.

In the final prayer meeting on Sunday morning, Seventy Jack Fears turned to me and delivered a message from the Lord. It was powerful in its assurance that my work was accepted by God and that, because of my testimony, many precious souls had been brought into the Kingdom. I was told to continue to uphold His truth, that He would sustain me, and that many more would yet rejoice because of my ministry. I left the reunion feeling refreshed.

A couple of weeks later, Brother Doty called to say that Bishop Hansen had told the Joint Council members they had better investigate what the appointees and elders were teaching and preaching in the South. The Saints there had the best baptismal rate of the whole church and were among the best tithepayers. He said that perhaps a little of their therapy would help in the Center Place. Of course, we were preaching the gospel as the Lord told me to do five years earlier. It is the gospel of Jesus Christ that converts people from their worldly ways to the ways of the Master.

After the 1975 reunion, I went on a grueling two-week trip around the area. I visited Warner Robins Air Force Base, Swainsboro, and Brunswick in Georgia; confirmed a Korean lady we had baptized at reunion; traveled to Fort Stuart and Charleston, where I stayed with the Coopers; visited a Thai girl, who was married to a church member, and asked her to join the church; and submitted the names of four young men for priesthood calls. The possibilities for missionary work were growing and growing, and I trembled as I thought of the exhibition of divine power we could have as a sanctified people.

In late September, 1975, while at my home in South Carolina, I received a phone call from my mother. My father had suffered a heart attack and was in the hospital. A short time later, I learned that he passed away quite peacefully while my sister Mavis was holding his hand. I was not surprised because I had a premonition of his death. When I had said good-bye to Father at the airport earlier that year, I felt that it would be the last time I would see him in the physical body. He knew I loved him dearly and that I was overjoyed at the decision he had made to be baptized. How marvelous was the Lord to us and to him—extending his life so that he could accept the gospel of Christ. At his death he was 85 years old.

The Lord blessed me abundantly during that time of grief. Somehow I could not mourn for Dad. He was a very fine man and a practicing Christian—not just a Christian in name only. He hardly ever worked on the Sabbath. I can remember it on only one or two rare occasions. He used to say that those who worked on Sunday were never any better off—and he was right.

Gwen and I went to a women's retreat in October. The cooks were men, who insisted that they wait on the ladies all the time and not even give them any "KP" to do. The meals were excellent. Gwen gave a fine lesson on the physically healthful Zionic home, which brought forth much discussion. The prayer meeting on the final morning was unique, with a marvelous spirit present. Gwen said she was so full of the Spirit that she wanted some time alone to enjoy it to the fullest. We completed the retreat on a perfect morning with a baptism in the lake.

We suffered another sad loss that month, when Sister

Betty Willimon succumbed to cancer after much suffering. She was a very gracious lady. Shortly after her death, we began work on the property which she and her husband had donated to the church for our reunion grounds. The plans were drawn by a church member, Brother Julian Evans, who was an architect. Then we were able to start building the Betty Willimon Campgrounds out of the wilderness.

We bought a high-loader, which is like a bulldozer but with a bucket instead of a blade, and hired a man to operate it. He worked wonders and soon cleared the roads and smoothed the parking lot. He then excavated the sites for the dining hall and sanctuary, leveled the locations for the cabins, and cleared away the trees for the playing field.

I printed a call for help in *Evangel*, and the Saints responded by giving materials and several thousands of dollars in contributions for the building fund. We utilized a great amount of volunteer labor, including some from nonmembers. The Lord was really blessing us with the work, and I was praising His name daily because of the outpouring of His love.

One day in December while I was working at the reunion grounds, I was called back to Greenville to administer to a little baby boy named Lee Lloyd. He was in intensive care; so I had to scrub up and don a gown, then place my hands through holes in the incubator to administer to him. The little child weighed only one pound 14 ounces. He was really struggling for life, and he was indeed a little fighter. For many months I went nearly every week to administer to him. He gradually won his fight for survival.

About that time, I bought some plans for a little crawler tractor (minidozer) and decided to make one. I went to the nearby engineering firms and asked them for scrap pieces of steel, which they willingly gave me. I was able to fabricate many of the parts, thus saving a lot of money. The minidozer worked remarkably well at the reunion grounds and later at our property near Oak Grove.

Because of the unseasonably warm winter, the work on the reunion grounds progressed well. We built a bridge across the creek, and some men from Raleigh cut down all the trees that would be flooded by the lake. My new mini-dozer dragged the cut trees, and we loaded them on trucks. We took the larger trees to a nearby sawmill to make lumber for the dining hall and bath houses. I was enjoying the hard work on the reunion grounds and felt remarkably well—although I did not have quite as much get up and go as I had 20 years before.

By the end of the year, both Trevor and Bill had received their master's degrees—Trevor's in aerospace engineering and Bill's in education. Bill was able to turn his part-time work at the Hughesville High School into a full-time job, at least until the summer. Trevor decided to continue working toward his doctorate. But before starting the spring semester, he took off for a six-week trip to Australia—his first time back in six years. We were thrilled that he was able to see his sister, three nephews, grandmothers, and his other relatives and friends again. I often thought of him while he was down under, wondering if he were riding the surf at that particular moment.

Seventy Harry Doty and I drove to North Carolina in mid-January of 1976, when we made the Tri-Cities mission into a branch. I had helped organize that mission, which had grown to about 80 members and was flourishing.

In Independence on February 22, Beth gave birth to our sixth grandson, David Michael McGuire. Trevor told his mother, "Mum, I guess that I'll have to produce the granddaughters."[1]

---

[1] And indeed he did, although it was not until 15 years later that our first granddaughter was born.

On March 24 Gwen and I became citizens of the United States. Were it not for our belief and faith in the prophecies of Joseph Smith, we would not have done it. Australia, like the U.S.A., is a democracy and a good nation to live in. However, we believe in Zion and the literal fulfillment of the prophecies. Throughout my ministry I have preached Zion, and we have a desire to be a part of its establishment.

Directly after taking the oath of allegiance, I headed to Independence for the quorum sessions prior to World Conference. Gwen joined me later. The conference was a monumental one in many respects, with the major event being that Wallace B. Smith was designated to replace his father as president at the next conference two years later.

The first Sunday of conference I blessed our new grandson in the Auditorium chapel. His other grandfather, Carl McGuire, assisted; Frank Flood presided; and Trevor offered the benediction. Two-year-old Richard was kissed on both cheeks, in French custom, by several Tahitian ladies. After the first startled look, he really enjoyed it. Later when Bill asked Richard how the Tahitian ladies kissed him, he turned up one cheek and then the other. He was as funny as a circus!

In July Bill obtained employment at the 360-acre Andrew Drumm Institute (Drumm Farm), a boys' home in Independence. He served as a counselor, helped the boys with sports, and performed other tasks around the farm.

Trevor continued to work very hard on his doctorate at the university. In April he phoned with some big news—he had just won first place in the central region of the United States in the graduate level student paper competition of the American Institute of Aeronautics and Astronautics. Neil Armstrong, the first man on the moon, was one of the judges. Trevor was also selected to represent the United States in the international student paper competition to be held later that year. We were proud of his accomplishments and the fact that he still kept faith in the Lord and remained humble.

☼ ☼ ☼

One day in late spring, the Lord intervened in a fire at the reunion grounds. We had cleared a creek bed to make a lake, which we hoped would be good for swimming and other activities. We had pushed all the trees into the middle of the creek bed, and I set fire to them while there was no wind. All of a sudden, a terrific wind sprang up, blowing sparks onto the ground that we had not cleared. Because there was a drought, everything was tinder dry. I thought to myself, "Oh, no! Here's a major forest fire!"

I drove quickly to the Willimons' home and called the forest rangers. They were busy with other fires but said they would come as soon as they could. I knew they would be too late, so I prostrated myself on the earth—lying flat on my face and stomach—and poured out my soul to God that He would stay the fire. It was really a time of emergency. If the fire got away, it could cause tremendous damage to the neighboring properties. After my prayer I drove back to the creek bed and was amazed to see how quickly and completely the fire had stopped!

Don Willimon was beating out the last little remnants of flames just as they were creeping to the property line. Don said that when he first saw the fire, it looked hopeless. He could not understand why it went out when the wind was still blowing. The ranger came later and asked, "Why did you call us? There's no fire here." When we showed him where the fire had been, he was very surprised that it had gone out. But I know how it stopped—it pays to lie on our faces and humble our souls before almighty God.

With the advent of spring weather, our progress on the

reunion grounds was more noticeable. By the beginning of summer, the electricity was hooked up, the septic tanks installed, and the dining hall and bathhouses were nearly completed. By June we had finished the lake, and it was filled with water. In August I began to devote more time to missionary work. There were many prospects—and that, after all, was my first love and calling.

During the first week of August, we held our reunion on the new Betty Willimon Campgrounds. It was a huge success, with about 250 people registered. Most of them camped in tents or campers. Brother and Sister Don Lents and I stayed in the Don Willimon home nearby. In my first sermon I described some of the miraculous ways in which the Lord had blessed us in getting the grounds ready and approved for reunion. For example, we received permission to use our water system at 8 p.m. on Friday, with the reunion starting on Sunday morning. Our final electrical installation was done on Saturday morning, just a few hours before the deadline.

My second sermon was on the subject of Zion. The Saints were overjoyed with the message, and they showed it with applause—only the second time in my preaching experience that had happened. It made me think of the time in the Book of Mormon when the people clapped their hands for joy. Of course, the Lord had ministered to the people, so the glory is entirely His.

☼ ☼ ☼

In September Patriarch Harry Hearn conducted a workshop at Raleigh entitled "Love in Action." While I was preparing for the prayer and testimony service, I was directed by the Spirit. That day we had a marvelous, almost Pentecostal experience. There I ordained a black man to the office of priest. With a very noticeable surge, the power of

God went through my right arm to his head. The young man was so overcome with the Spirit that he was unable to leave his seat after the ordination without help from another brother. There was hardly a dry eye in the place. After that experience, if we had needed any further witness of God's calling members of the Negro race into the priesthood, we would have been hard to please.

After the final service that morning, while still in the Spirit, we administered to Brother Harry Hearn, who had a serious health problem. We felt the Lord's power during that administration. I was also shown that when the Lord chose to take Brother Hearn, there would not be a sudden change but a smooth transition from a mortal state to an immortal state. He was prepared to go, and it was a wonderful experience for me to relate that to his wife. The day after the administration, Brother Hearn went to the doctor, who took a blood sample and said that the problem had been resolved.

Surely the Lord blessed His Saints that day—a people who were united and in a condition for such a blessing. A couple of years previously, they had been fighting and squabbling and sent for my help. Now they were one in the Lord, and He was blessing them. One priest stood up to bear testimony and said that he had to ask the Lord to stay His power, as he could not bear any more. An elder rose and called his pastor "blessed." Such is the power of God at work. I wrote the pastor a note during the preaching part of the service: "We have been sitting in heavenly places." The young black priest felt the presence of the Spirit of God with him all day Sunday and Monday. It reminded me of the experience I had at a street meeting in Australia, when the Spirit was with me for three days afterward as I went about my regular work.

A few weeks later, Gwen and I went to Columbia, South Carolina, for a business meeting. I told the Saints about the pentecostal experience we had at Raleigh and encouraged them to carry on in Columbia. Most of our people had moved away from there—it was the third time we had a good group started, only to have the Saints move.

I continued to work on the reunion grounds, but at a much less hectic pace. The dining hall was the next major project, and it was not completed until the following year. We were able to put the reunion grounds to good use again in October, when we held an older youth retreat. All those attending worked on the grounds on Saturday afternoon.

In our spare time, Gwen and I enjoyed planning our retirement home. While on a trip to Missouri the previous month, we had planned for a lake on the property and decided on the location for the house.

In September on his way back to Australia, my nephew David Wright spent a couple of weeks with us. He had been touring Europe and working in England for several months. Because he and Trevor had some similar experiences, they enjoyed comparing notes about Europe. There must be something in those Sorensen genes—I would have enjoyed traveling the same way when I was young.

In the fall I preached a series in Raleigh. I was actually a bit nervous since it had been quite a while since my last series. Of course, I always felt inadequate standing behind the pulpit. But the good Lord was with me, and the Saints were blessed.

One Sunday in December, Gwen and I went to Augusta, Georgia, where I preached. I was overjoyed when a young married lady, with whom we had been working for five years, told me that she and her husband had decided to be baptized. She asked me to perform the baptisms in early spring because they wanted an outdoor service in natural surroundings. I had often wondered why they had procrastinated their decision for so long. However, I had waited patiently on the Lord; and the harvest finally came.

About 3 a.m. just before Christmas, Trevor arrived home with Laurie Launius and Cheryl Geiersbach, two Graceland College students. He had a frightening drive from Lawrence, Kansas, traveling on icy roads through rain and blinding snow. However, he drove with all the skill he had acquired from seven years in the snow belt. He said that the Lord was his copilot, just as He had been for me on many similar occasions in Iowa.

Trevor had completed the course work for his doctorate, and after Christmas he went to California to do the research project required for his degree. He worked at the NASA Ames Research Center on the Pioneer Venus mission, which was to send four probes into the Venusian atmosphere in late 1978. We missed him that much more, knowing he was so far away in California. But he was not nearly so far as Marvia and her family.

Early in the new year of 1977, I received a phone call from Steve and Marilyn Adkins, who had been students when we lived in Boone. After cottage meetings, they had been baptized and later were married. Steve, a priest, was now the missionary coordinator of his branch and was preparing for some cottage meetings. Remembering the part that my slides had played in their conversions, he asked for a set, which I readily sent. He was thrilled to receive them and wrote a letter of appreciation for my work with him, his wife, and the other college students at Ames, Iowa.

About that time another miracle of healing occurred. I went to administer to a very sick baby at 3 a.m. She was taken to the hospital, where another elder and I administered to her again. A spinal tap had indicated that she had spinal meningitis. That afternoon the mother called to tell me the baby was doing well. She was soon home, but the doctors could not understand how she had improved so quickly. Praise be to God, the great Physician!

All the main roof trusses of the dining hall at the reunion grounds had been put in place, but we had not finished the roof because of bad weather. One day in February Don Willimon called to tell me he was sick and that I would be, too. He said not to go to the reunion grounds unless I was strong enough. Finally I plucked up my courage and drove there, only to discover that all the rafters were flat on the ground. A fierce wind had blown them all down. It was a test of our faith to see if we would rebuild, but we did. Within a couple of months, the men of the district provided some "working bees," and we soon repaired the damage to the roof.

Because of the poor economy, Brother Willimon had to move to Elkhart, Kansas, to take over his Ford dealership. He had been my right-hand man at the reunion grounds. We were able to manage without him, but he had made it so much easier.

Two carpenters from North Carolina helped for several weeks with the construction. The dining hall and kitchen were finally completed one week before reunion. One of the men, Harry Martin, moved to Missouri that summer.

We were saddened to learn in March of the death of Brother Dolph Roth in Independence. He had been a member of our Zion's League in Brisbane so many years ago. Patriarch Henry Schaefer gave the funeral sermon and did a magnificent job. Beth attended and said that she felt as though she had been in a worship service instead of a funeral. That is often said of Latter Day Saint funerals—they are a time to celebrate the passing of a loved one into paradise rather than a time of mourning.

In June, Bill McGuire left his job at the Drumm Institute and started work as the family activities director for Center Stake. He was in charge of the Campus—RLDS Church property near the Auditorium, with an outdoor amphitheater, swimming pool, and volleyball courts. Later Beth and Bill moved into a mobile home located on the Campus.

A significant milestone in our lives occurred in June, 1977, when Gwen officially retired from her job as an industrial nurse at General Electric. She continued to work there part-time until we moved. We had much to do in preparing for building our retirement home and arranging the move to Missouri early the following year. We had just received the plans for our new house from the architect, and Gwen spent many hours poring over the details.

I was planning to retire early at the age of 62 and move to Jackson County, and already I was receiving requests for ministry in the Center Place.

We headed for Texas in July, where we attended the Bandera reunion. There I preached a sermon every evening. We enjoyed the fellowship of the Saints and received many invitations to return. We then drove to Missouri to see our family and our property.

In August, 1977, we attended our last reunion in South Carolina. The gift of prophecy was much in evidence, and we were commended by the Lord for our work in His vineyard. Two patriarchs spoke to us with great power and promises for our future—both in this world and in the world to come. I also related a vision I saw of the triumph of Zion in the future and spoke by inspiration to the priesthood and to Sister Ardie Launius, who really needed God's reassuring voice at that time. Others were spoken to during the week, and excellent counsel was given. By the end of the reunion, there was a feeling of cleanliness and freedom from the influence of the world.

Seventy Jim Doty, the new missionary assigned to the area, was also in attendance. Jim said that he was concerned because it would be a difficult task to follow in my footsteps. I responded that he was not supposed to replace me, but to be himself and to give his unique ministry. God has endowed each of us with talents, and we must develop and use them to the best of our ability to His glory.

We again drove to Missouri to see the progress on our new house south of Oak Grove. The concrete for the basement was poured, and the main frame of the house went up shortly after. Elder Dave Heath and his construction crew, who were all priesthood members, framed in the house. It was good to see that preview of Zion. Tony and Ian Mackay (originally from Bowraville in Australia) owned an electrical business and did the wiring for the house. Harry Martin and Bill McGuire did some of the finishing.

While in Missouri, I preached at the Gudgell Park church and spoke to the older youth of Center Stake. On our final Sunday there, we went to the Liberty Street church and listened to Brother F. Henry Edwards, who preached a strong sermon on the spiritual gifts.

Back in South Carolina, we visited the more distant branches and groups. That series of trips was especially memorable because Gwen was able to accompany me. The Saints went out of their way to show appreciation for our ministry over the years. Eighteen of them at Charleston took us to Folly Island and treated us to a seafood dinner for our 35th wedding anniversary.

That particular trip in October was my last one to some of the groups. We went to the Marine base at Beaufort, South Carolina, then to Savannah, Georgia. That is where General Sherman ended his march to the sea during the Civil War. Gwen had not been there before, and I had promised her a view of the old part of the city—quaint and very historic with its old shops and cobblestone streets. We then visited Brunswick, Georgia, and Warner Robins Air Force Base, where I preached, participated in an ordination, and conducted a business meeting. The group which

I had started there was thriving, and I was loathe to bid them farewell. The numerical strength of the RLDS Church in the North and South Carolina and Georgia Missionary Development Area had increased from 450 to over 1,000 during the eight years of our assignment there. The increase was really even greater, because many more Saints had moved away than had moved in.

In late October of 1977, we held a priesthood institute at the reunion grounds—the last activity there until after winter. More than 45 members of the priesthood were present, plus three ladies to do the cooking. The focus of the retreat was to encourage the men toward better preaching, public prayers, and missionary work. I spoke to them about things to come. The men were really on the edges of their seats during that time and bombarded me with questions in the discussion period. As men of God they needed to know something of what is going to occur in the future. I told them of the choice seer to be raised up, the work of the building of Mount Zion, and the gift of the Holy Spirit of Promise. Many had not heard of some of those things.

I was also busy making slides and tapes again. My lectures were on a large reel-to-reel tape recorder; with five cassette recorders connected to the output of the large one, I made five cassette tapes at a time. Even then it took quite a lot of time and care. A California firm duplicated the slides in 100-foot rolls. I cut them into proper lengths for each lecture and included instructions to tell the priesthood members how to place them into cardboard mounts.

The construction of our new house was progressing well. Frank Flood called one morning and asked if I believed in fairies. When he had hired a man to install the insulation in our new home, the man said he would start the following Monday. But upon his arrival, he found the job already done! Frank thought that was impossible; but then he learned that some of our good friends who had moved to Missouri from the Carolinas had done the job the previous Saturday!

As the new year dawned, we had to spend much of our time packing. Although I was laid up with the flu for a few days, we managed to make one last trip to North Carolina. When the weather turned unseasonably warm, I was able to use a couple of days to do some final work at the reunion grounds. We also held a retreat in the mountains on some property that was owned by a church family.

☼ ☼ ☼

On Sunday, February 12, I preached my last sermon as an appointee to a full Greenville church, which included about 30 nonmembers. Some of the Saints had driven more than 100 miles to be present. Gwen said that I did not let the Lord down, nor did He let me down. I had excellent liberty and talked about the great latter-day work and the prophecies which are near fulfillment. The people paid rapt attention, and many of the nonmembers expressed their surprise and satisfaction at our beliefs. A potluck dinner and hymn sing were held after the sermon, and the Saints presented us with some lovely gifts to show their appreciation for our eight years of service among them. It was with deep feelings that we bid them adieu.

I officially retired the next day, February 13, 1978, which was my 62nd birthday. The following quote is from the end of the last letter written to my mother while I was still an appointee:

"Well, dear ones, I guess that this is the end of an era—almost 34 years as an appointee and a lot of water under the bridge. I would not exchange my life for any other—only a better one—and am grateful that the Lord could use me to help a little in the preparing of His vineyard."

◂ Launching a rocket at a youth camp in South Carolina; Vivian in left background

▾ Willow Bend camp, 1967, consisting of an old farmhouse —dining hall and quarters for girls—and two metal sheds for boys' cabins

▸ Vivian and Doyle Launius leading a baptismal service at new lake at Betty Willimon Campgrounds

▾ Vivian and Harry Martin in front of the meeting hall they are building at the campgrounds at Pickens, South Carolina

▸ The McGuire grandsons—John (1972), Richard (1974), and David (1976)

◂ The Thompson grandsons—Michael (1972), Mathew (1975) and Adam (1975)

▲ First Quorum of Seventy at the 1974 World Conference—Vivian, Harry Doty, and Houston Hobart at center front

CHAPTER 12

Not Retired but Retreaded!

After 34 years under church appointment, we ended one era of our life. But a new period of opportunities to serve the Lord and preach the gospel was beginning.

Just before leaving Greenville, we bought a new Ford pickup. It was the policy of the RLDS Church to give a vehicle to each retiring appointee, and we were later supplied with a Pontiac station wagon.

After saying farewell to our friends in Greenville, Gwen and I started out in the pickup truck for the land of Zion. Although we traveled on slippery and icy roads in Indiana, where many cars and trucks had skidded off the roads, the Lord was with us. We finally arrived safely at Beth and Bill's house in Independence. Since our house was only partially completed, we stayed with the McGuires until after World Conference. The wintery weather impeded our efforts; but finally in late March we had a few days of balmy spring weather, during which we were able to work on the house and plant our garden.

We were thrilled that Trevor was able to come from California and spend about 10 days, and together we attended the 1978 World Conference. On the first Sunday morning, the usual three sacrament services were held in the Auditorium, with approximately 18,000 Saints attending. Trevor served the communion with other priests and elders for all three services. It took only ten minutes to serve the 6,000 people at each service. During the conference, we met Saints from many places, including Australia and Tahiti. Some delegates to that conference had been little children in Tahiti when we were there under appointment.

President W. Wallace Smith tendered his resignation, not without some emotion, and recommended his son as the next president of the RLDS Church, according to the document presented at the previous conference. The delegates approved Wallace B. Smith overwhelmingly. For my feelings of the time, I would like to quote from a letter I wrote during conference:

"Wallace B. is making a tremendous impression for good. I hope that he inherits some of the prophetic genius of his great-grandfather, for surely the church needs it for such a day."

The Auditorium was packed to capacity for the ordination of the new prophet. Beth and Bill sang with the Stone Church choir during the service.

At the end of the conference, Gwen and I had to go up on the rostrum with other retirees for recognition of our service to the church. I would have preferred to skip the ceremony because I hate fuss of any kind. All they seemed to have done at that conference was to make speeches and applaud people. It wasted so much time when so many important things needed to be done for the Kingdom.

Shortly after the World Conference was over, Gwen and I moved into our new home at Oak Grove. We literally had to camp in the house since it was unfinished and there was no running water. Beth and Bill often came. Bill's strength and height were particularly useful. Several others also helped us at various times. Aub and Kath Ivers (from John's River in Australia) had attended the World Conference, and they stayed for a few days afterward so Aub could help with the plumbing before they continued on their world tour.

We had a small garden close to the house, and a larger garden on the other side of the stream which ran through our property. We grew a large variety of vegetables and some fruits, which we thoroughly enjoyed for the many years we lived there. As I wrote to my mother, "The Land of Zion is surely smiling and beautiful, and the Lord is blessing us abundantly." I could hardly wait for the end of each winter so that I could plant the seeds for the coming year's harvest.

Because of our location out in the country, we were not able to hook up to city water or sewers. When we first moved into the house, we pumped water out of the stream for cleaning; and we carried drinking water from a neighbor's house. That summer our water situation improved significantly when we had an underground cistern installed. To replenish the cistern, I mounted a large water tank in the back of our old pickup truck. We then hauled water from the water tower at the nearby town of Lone Jack.

During that first summer, we hired Curtis Clemens, a local brother in the church, to bulldoze a pond next to the stream. I calculated that when full, the pond would hold about a million gallons of water, which came partly from the stream but was mostly from runoff rain water. Before the pond was full, I made a jetty out from the bank. We used water from the pond to irrigate our gardens and pumped pond water to the house, where we used it initially for washing and to flush toilets.

Our goal was to become as self-sufficient as we could. I made a wood-burning stove from an old electric water heater. It produced plenty of heat for the house, especially when I added a fan and ventilation system to distribute the heat. Bill gave me an old riding lawn mower, which I repaired and soon had running well.

Even though I was putting a lot of time and hard work into building the house and tending the garden, I was not neglecting church work, despite my retired status. As I used to tell the Saints, "I am not retired but retreaded—and I have a few good miles in me yet!"

Our new home congregation was Oak Grove. We found it to be large but very friendly. We were not exactly regulars, since I so often had to preach elsewhere. Brother Lyle Smith was the pastor for most of our time there. He and his wife Sherrie always made sure that we felt right at home in their midst. Seeing them together often reminded Gwen and me of our parents. Lyle was a very big man, well over six feet tall; and Sherrie was petite. Both Dad and Gwen's father were about six feet tall, while our mothers were not quite five feet tall.

I had a preaching series at Gudgell Park congregation in Independence and ordained an elder at the Slover Park church. I was making and distributing many sets of slides for cottage meetings and preaching nearly every Sunday, often twice, at various congregations.

We traveled to Iowa in July of 1978 to attend the Des Moines Stake reunion. The 265-mile drive was tiring but enjoyable. Iowa had received plenty of rain; and the countryside looked pretty as a picture, with fields of soybeans and waving corn.

Gwen and I had demanding schedules at the reunion. I taught two classes each day on missionary methods, preached twice about Zion, assisted at all prayer meetings, and by request bore testimony many times at special services. Gwen was the assistant nurse. About 400 people were on the grounds, and the Lord blessed them with His Spirit. One young man came to me at the end of the reunion and said that he had avoided me all week. But my testimony the night before had caused him to have a dream. In that dream, I was a lighthouse giving off the light of

Christ and the gospel; and the man was told to heed the guidance.

In early October we held a preaching series at Seneca, Missouri, for the Saints in the southern Missouri and northern Oklahoma region. We had a wonderful time, and the Lord richly blessed my ministry. The attendance grew toward the end of the series, and we had a packed house on Friday evening. After the sermon, we retired to the banks of a clear creek for the baptism of three precious souls.

Many members of the Seneca branch had just returned from an Indian powwow held at the RLDS Auditorium. One evening we were invited to the Henry Williston home. Brother Williston was a full-blooded Choctaw Indian. As we entered the car, his wife said, "Well, you have been captured by Indians." When we approached their house, a conventional home, I asked Brother Williston if that was his wigwam or tepee. He explained the difference between the two Indian structures. He had an ingenious rope and pulley system to open his gate from inside his car. After seeing his operation, I told him that I had just learned the Indian rope trick.

Later, while we were at Perry, Iowa, for a preaching series, I visited a man I had helped to convert 18 years previously. He had bought the first telescope I ever made. It was still in excellent condition, and his grandchildren were using it. We were in Boone on that same trip, and Brother Gene Crandell gave me one of the 16mm slide projectors I had invented. He said he had used it for years before buying a big carousel projector. I was pleased to accept it to add to my "museum" of treasured possessions.

At Thanksgiving we were happy to have a real family reunion with the McGuires, the Floods, and our son, who flew back from California. After Thanksgiving, Trevor, Gwen, and I drove to his home in Sunnyvale, California. Trevor took us for a tour of San Francisco—a very striking city, which reminded me of Sydney with its headlands, harbor, and bridge. We also went to the NASA Ames Research Center, where Trevor was working on his doctorate. The Pioneer Venus spacecraft had just started orbiting Venus, and we saw mission controllers scanning monitors which showed spacecraft signals beamed back to Earth.

☼ ☼ ☼

Gwen and I then flew to Los Angeles, where we caught a non-stop flight to Auckland. We stayed there four days before flying to Sydney, arriving there on December 12—Marvia's birthday. The Thompsons met us at the airport and drove us to their home in Newcastle. It was certainly good to see them again. Our young grandsons had really grown since we last saw them. We stayed a few days in the Newcastle area renewing friendships and spent a week relaxing at Tiona as a Christmas gift from Marvia and Terry. The next week was the Tiona reunion. At Brother Jack Gunning's request, I taught a class on evangelism, preached, and assisted in other services.

After reunion, we drove to Brisbane to see our aging mothers and other relatives and friends. We spent an enjoyable month with them. In February we drove back to Newcastle via the New England Highway. We stayed with Sister Bev Wilkinson in Tamworth, where I preached on Wednesday evening to about 25 people. The next day we drove along the Oxley Highway to Wingham. During that drive we stopped at a roadside rest area, where we were highly amused by the rest rooms. The men's room was labeled "Fred," and the women's was labeled "Wilma." Each had a picture of the respective Flintstone's character. Trust the Aussies!

After spending a few more days with Marvia and her family, we caught the Flyer train to Sydney. Sister Joan

Flood met us and drove us around the city. Our trip to Manly on the hydrofoil was almost like flying on water. It was the first time Gwen and I had been on one. While in Sydney, I helped teach a class about evangelism at the Leichardt church and preached at the Drummoyne branch on Sunday morning and at a district service Sunday night.

When we returned to Newcastle, I was kept busy there as well. Our son-in-law Terry took a week's vacation, and we painted their house. I preached twice at Hamilton, participated in discussions at Teralba and Wallsend, and visited the Saints at Anna Bay. It was with great sadness that we finally had to leave our daughter Marvia and her family once again as we headed for home.

Brother Dennis Hansen met us when we flew to Auckland, New Zealand. On Sunday morning I participated in the service at Papatoetoe and preached at the main church at Morningside that evening. That night we went home with Sister Olive Ingham and her husband to their farm about 50 miles north of Auckland.

The next day the Inghams drove us into the Northland. We went to the Bay of Islands and saw the house where the Treaty of Waitougi was signed in 1840—when the Maoris agreed to accept the rule of Queen Victoria. We stayed in a new cottage next to a lovely waterfall. Then we drove farther north and saw the oldest stone building in New Zealand, then through orange orchards to the beautiful Hokianga Harbour on the west coast, and down through the magnificent Waipeia Forest with its great Kauri trees. We returned to Auckland by bus and ended our stay in New Zealand by bathing in some hot spring pools.

☼ ☼ ☼

The next day, we boarded a plane for the United States. Trevor met us at the San Francisco airport, and we spent the night at his place. Then the three of us drove to Lawrence, Kansas, where Trevor gave the oral dissertation defense for his doctorate.

A man called shortly after we arrived home and wanted additional sets of cottage-meeting slides and tapes. He said his branch had just confirmed four people as a direct result of using the recorded gospel message, and they expected to add other souls to the Kingdom within a month. So even when not present physically, I was still able to share the gospel.

I spoke to the women of the Oak Grove branch one evening about the drug problem. What I told them then is still true today—that the drug problem is largely the result of our affluent society. Our youth have had it too easy—if they want something, Mom and Dad rush to give it to them. Because they do not have to struggle for the necessities of life or anything else, many young people get bored and resort to drugs and other destructive pastimes.

In early May Trevor moved from California to Oak Grove after he successfully passed his doctoral orals and completed his dissertation. His last Sunday in California he preached at his home congregation in San Jose.

Two young ladies from Australia, Rosanna and Marguerite Bakker, spent a few weeks with us. They accompanied us, as did Beth and Bill, to Lawrence, Kansas, on May 21, 1979, for Trevor's graduation ceremonies at the University of Kansas.

We went first to the doctoral "hooding" ceremony. Trevor looked so distinguished and dignified as the hood robe was draped around his shoulders and he heard the words: "Trevor Charles Sorensen...Doctor of Engineering." Only a very few others graduated with him because the subject was so difficult. He made Sorensen history as the first doctor in the family, although it was not exactly the type of doctor we had expected when he was a young boy showing an interest in medicine.

Trevor helped me build a deck at the back of our house. After that, we dug a toolshed into the ground underneath the deck. One day he said, "Dad, you have given me a few hard jobs in my day; but digging this elephant's grave has been the hardest." We also built a bridge across the stream to provide easier access to the big garden.

On June 4, two days before his 28th birthday, Trevor left with his backpack and a ticket for Europe. He intended to hitchhike until his money ran out or he found a job. We were very sorry to see him go, but we had faith that God would protect and bring him safely home. Trevor eventually returned after nearly six months of traveling in Europe and the Middle East.

The Independence area was hit with severe storms and high winds in early June. A tornado hit the Campus, where the McGuires lived in a mobile home. It twisted off some trees and did a lot of damage. Each side of their home was littered with debris and twisted trees, but their flimsy house did not tremble. Beth said they were completely unaware of the wind's force. It was a clear case of divine intervention if ever there was one.

Two days later, the Lord also miraculously saved me. Gwen and I were buying concrete blocks for our deck support, when the man helping us climbed a stack of blocks to get one for us. I was standing to one side. As he removed one concrete block, another became dislodged. It fell, missing my head by inches. The corner of it made a slight dent on the end of my right shoe. It could easily have killed me or smashed my foot. Immediately I gave thanks to God. That experience confirmed my belief that He still had things for me to do in the building of Zion.

That summer Gwen and I attended the Central Missouri Stake reunion, which was held about 25 miles from our home. The Holy Spirit was in rich attendance for the 200 people there. I taught a class on evangelism and preached.

We had scarcely arrived home from that, when our phone rang and we were invited to another reunion at the Lake of the Ozarks. There I was to preach every night. Although I had a lot of work to do at home, I told Gwen that as long as the Lord lent me breath, I could not say no to requests for ministry.

During the summer of 1979, we continued to work hard on finishing our home and tending to the garden. We had brought many different types of vegetable seeds from Australia, which all seemed to thrive in the Land of Promise. Gwen worked like a Trojan helping me harvest the bounty. She then canned a lot of it in a canning kitchen I had built in the basement of the house.

Our pond had filled up; and we stocked it with catfish, bluegill, and perch. I enjoyed catching fresh fish for our meals, but I think I actually enjoyed feeding the fish each evening even more. The catfish grew into monsters; I caught some weighing more than ten pounds.

I built an air conditioning system for the house, which pumped water from the bottom of the pond where the water was always coldest. The water circulated through some condensers, where air blowing on the cold pipes was cooled and distributed throughout the house. The water was then returned to the pond. The system worked remarkably well.

At various times during the summer, old friends stopped by to see us and our retirement property. Some of them, like Claude and Janet Krause, even helped with the work. We made many improvements to our home, including laying concrete footpaths, painting, adding stone facing on the front of the house, and planting cedar trees along both sides of the driveway. After a day's hot work, I enjoyed going for a swim in the cool water of the pond and consuming delicious Aussie watermelon under the shade of a huge hickory tree. We have many pleasant memories of those times.

I was still very active in church work. I conducted cottage meetings and continued to make and distribute the slide and tape sets. I preached at many different congregations and had preaching series at Slover Park, Oak Grove, Lexington, Central Missouri Stake, and Kansas City Stake. The last congregation I preached at in the Kansas City Stake series was an inner-city church, and about 45 blacks were in attendance. Very few black people attended in the congregations where I usually preached; therefore, it was good to see so many there.

Beth reached a major milestone that summer when she passed her state board examinations and was officially accepted as a registered nurse in Missouri. She was then employed as a surgical nurse at the Independence Sanitarium and Hospital.

In October, 1979, we were saddened to learn of the deaths of two strong men of God. Brother Floyd Burdekin died of cancer in Australia. I had spent many enjoyable times with big Floyd during my assignment over there. An appointee of the church, he was married to Gwen's cousin, Lorna. Seventy Jack Fears, who had been in Atlanta while we had been assigned to the Carolinas and Georgia, died of a brain tumor. I felt that the souls in the prison house must have been in need of some preachers to teach them the gospel, because a couple of good missionaries had just been recruited.

In February Trevor accepted a position with McDonnell Douglas in Houston, Texas, as an engineer on a contract with the NASA Johnson Space Center. Gwen and I drove to Texas later that month to help him move. He gave us a tour of the space center, where we saw some moonrocks and the spacecraft used during the Apollo moon mission. Trevor's first task at NASA was to design ascent-abort targets for the space shuttle's computers. The targets that he computed were on board the first flight of the shuttle in 1981, but fortunately the astronauts did not have to use them. I preached one Sunday at the largest RLDS branch in Houston, where Bill McGuire's brother Les and his family attended.

We attended some of the 1980 World Conference in April, although we did not go as much as we had during previous conferences. We did enjoy the fellowship of the many friends from Australia who were there.

The following Sunday, I preached at the Second Church congregation in Independence. My topic was on priesthood. During the service, Bill McGuire was ordained to the office of elder by his father Carl and myself, with Carl giving the ordination prayer.

During the year, I had preaching series at several congregations in Missouri, Iowa, South Carolina, and North Carolina. The Lord gave me strength and blessed me abundantly. All I had wanted to do for many years was to please Him and be used by Him for the establishment of His Kingdom, and it seemed that He was really using me. We had very good attendance at all the services, and it reminded me of the large attendance when I had preached at the Coorparoo and Drummoyne branches in Australia the previous year. The Saints were hungering and thirsting to hear the gospel. As the Book of Mormon states, "Blessed are they who shall seek to bring forth my Zion at that day, for they shall have the gift and the power of the Holy Ghost" (1 Nephi 3:187).

I warned the Saints not to be led away by the Protestant ministers with their talk of the "rapture" because that is one of the most anti-Zion things that I know. The devil is using many deceitful ideas to try to lull the Saints into believing that there will be no gathering to this land, but that Zion will be wherever they are. The Book of Mormon forecasts that very type of lying in the latter days—anything to get the Saints to disbelieve the prophets.

☼ ☼ ☼

Work continued on the house. I made a dehydrator so Gwen could dry fruits and vegetables. I also bought a hydradrill and searched our property for a sufficient supply of good water. Drilling finally paid off when we found water of excellent quality which was sufficient for our needs. With a steady supply, we were able to stop our regular water hauling.

We had a wonderful time at the Jefferson City reunion. I preached eight sermons on Zion and the gathering. I was really slated for only six, but insistence from those in charge caused me to preach two more. The Lord blessed me as perhaps never before; my mind was clear and my memory excellent. I did not use a note for the whole eight sermons, and the Spirit of the Lord provided the material presented.

I was given to understand that deliverance of the captives includes the casting out of evil spirits by the power of the Lord through His ministry. The Lord has allowed me to do that at times. Many people, possessed by the spirit of adultery, homosexuality, and so on, are captives of evil spirits and need them cast out in the name of Christ. That came out in my sermon without forethought. A number of elders said it was the first time they had ever heard that from our pulpits. They were greatly impressed with the whole presentation.

I also told the people that if they wanted God to be with them in the Saturday morning prayer service, which was the last one of the reunion, they must sanctify themselves the night before and come prepared with an eye single to the glory of God—and not come just seeking signs. They responded marvelously, and the gifts of the Spirit were very much in evidence. I was the last to speak (not directly under the Spirit), and I told the Saints that we had been recipients of much grace that morning.

Gwen played a very important role at that reunion when, about four o'clock one morning, she delivered a lovely baby girl to the wife of the caretaker. Everything went well, and Gwen became quite the heroine of the reunion.

In July, Bill McGuire baptized his son John (our oldest grandson) in Independence. I confirmed him with the assistance of Bill.

We managed to survive the great heat wave and drought of 1980. We had over 100° F for eighteen days in a row (a record), with the temperature at our place reaching as high as 112°. I do not know what we would have done without my air conditioning system that used the cool water from the pond. We had a good harvest earlier in the summer, but our late crops were failures. Even the trees were withering, and some died. The land was simply parched. The drought was finally broken in mid-August when we received over six inches of rain. It was amazing how quickly everything went from brown to green with that watering from heaven.

In August I preached on the Campus in Independence. It was the largest crowd (1,100) so far that summer. The Saints were wanting to hear the gospel, and the Lord again blessed us abundantly. I was given the subject, "What Latter Day Saints Believe about Marriage and the Family." While not an easy sermon topic, it needed bringing to the fore, especially in light of the church's high divorce rate. Following that sermon, I had telephone calls from several people who were wanting help with their marriages.

That same month we attended a camp at Lake Doniphan for disadvantaged children. The children were practically all nonmembers, and many of them were in wheelchairs. I was pastor to the girls and taught three religion classes a day on our spiritual heritage. Gwen was the nurse for the children who were not in wheelchairs.

In September, 1980, Gwen and I had a parting of the ways—she went with Beth to a Center Stake women's institute at Lake Doniphan, and I went to the Jefferson City reunion grounds to conduct an institute for the Melchisedec priesthood of that district. Among many other things, I talked to them about sanctifying themselves as Moses tried to sanctify the children of Israel before they entered the Promised Land and as Joseph Smith tried to sanctify the priesthood prior to the dedication of the Kirtland Temple. We fasted for the weekend and had an outstanding experience.

☼ ☼ ☼

Gwen and I drove to Greenville, South Carolina, in October, where I held a preaching series and was truly blessed by the Lord. It was good to see our old friends again. One of the men I had helped convert, who had been a Southern Baptist, was talking about how Brother Sorensen preached without using notes. All of a sudden he said in his dry southern drawl, "I know his secret! Do you ever notice that when Brother Sorensen preaches, he occasionally closes his eyes? Well, he has his notes written on the inside of his eyelids. That is how he manages!" Needless to say, there was much laughter at my expense.

We stayed with Don and Yvonne Willimon at Pickens, South Carolina, where I preached three successive nights in the basement of the dining hall at the new reunion grounds. I also had preaching series at Charleston and Wilmington. In Charleston the Coopers revived the old tradition and took us to a restaurant for a delicious seafood dinner in celebration of our 38th wedding anniversary.

Gwen and I had always enjoyed driving through the Great Smoky Mountains in North Carolina and Tennessee, having done so during each season. On the trip back to Missouri, we went through the mountain range during the peak of the fall colors. The scenery was truly spectacular. Finally Gwen said that she was growing tired of saying, "Oooh" and "Ahhh" with each new revelation of beauty. Surely the Lord put those colors there for our enjoyment.

The young people of Center Stake had asked me to be the teacher at a retreat. I accepted and spent a marvelous weekend with about 60 young singles. They had originally asked me to give only one lecture on marriage and the family; but I ended up giving four, which occupied the entire Saturday. They were most attentive and apparently enjoyed the presentations and discussions. I talked about prayer, stewardship, marriage, and Zion. On Sunday morning at the prayer and testimony service, the response was excellent and spoke well for those young people.

The following Saturday, Bill McGuire drove me to Lake Doniphan, where I talked to the Zion's League of Center Stake about family life. That night Beth and Ruth sang in the choir for the performance of Handel's *Messiah* at the Auditorium. Gwen, Frank Flood, and I attended.

☼ ☼ ☼

Trevor flew from Houston to spend Thanksgiving with us. Four days later, Gwen and I left Kansas City and flew to Australia to visit Marvia and her family and our elderly mothers. The trip was possible because my life insurance policy had reached maturity, and we were able to take advantage of some inexpensive air fares. Before we left, there was a severe ice storm; it really made us anticipate the warm summer weather in the southern hemisphere.

We spent a couple of weeks with Marvia and Terry and

our three adorable grandsons in their new home in Kotara South, a suburb of Newcastle. The new house had an above-ground swimming pool, which provided welcome relief from the summer heat. Since we had spent our last Christmas in Australia with Marvia's family, this time we went north and spent Christmas with our mothers in Brisbane. They were both in their 80s but in fairly good health and spirits.

We stayed in Brisbane until mid-February. I preached at a couple of branches there, and we enjoyed the fellowship of our old friends. Every day I visited my mother at the nursing home. She was relatively well and mentally sharp, and I enjoyed our chats and sharing together.

Gwen and I caught the bus back to Newcastle, which was much more enjoyable and relaxing than driving ourselves. Because of a good soaking rain, the countryside was a lush green, in direct contrast to the burnt brown of drought that we had seen on the way to Brisbane.

I was again kept quite busy with the work of the Lord, preaching at several churches in the Newcastle area, including Hamilton, Teralba, and John's River. I was not too happy with the overall condition of the RLDS Church in Australia. However, I was encouraged by a report from the Mountain Hut reunion; the apostle had told the Saints that if any of them were inviting nonmembers into open communion, they were violating the basic laws of the church and had better desist.

We took a train to Sydney, where we played tourist, enjoyed fellowship with old friends, and attended the wedding of our niece Carynne Flood to Peter Law. Frank and Ruth had come from the U.S. for the big event.

In mid-March we said our sad farewells again and boarded a plane for home. On the way, we spent five days in Tahiti, where we had a wonderful time. It rained a lot for the first few days, but that gave us some rest. We stayed in a little house made for the visiting missionaries. It overlooked the ocean and the beautiful island of Moorea. The natives nearly killed us with kindness and brought us all sorts of fruit, much more than we could eat. I had the privilege of baptizing a young lad and being the spokesman at his confirmation, all in Tahitian. His mother had been a piano pupil of Gwen's years ago.

On Sunday morning I preached to a combined congregation from all over the island of Tahiti, and the church was packed. I was a bit hesitant for the first two or three minutes. Then the Lord took over, allowing me to preach a 45-minute sermon—a good dose of the gospel for the native Saints—in fluent Tahitian. We all knew that I could not have possibly preached with such liberty had not the Lord brought to my remembrance that language which I had not spoken for 26 years (except in isolated short instances). Gwen was asked to give a testimony at a worship service, and with my help she wrote it out and read it.

Aua (Jean Tapu), who had been a young man when we were first assigned to Tahiti, had become very successful in the pearl business and was a high priest in the church. He and his wife Estelle had a lovely home on the waterfront in Papeete. One day he took Gwen, me, and the native patriarch, who had been delegated to look after us, by plane to beautiful Moorea. He rented a jeep, drove us around the island, and showed us the spectacular scenery.

We arrived back home in Missouri just in time to plant our garden. It was certainly nice to have been away for the four coldest months of the year. Now we could enjoy the spring, certainly a beautiful time of year in America.

☼ ☼ ☼

The space shuttle successfully flew on its maiden voyage in April of 1981. After that flight, Trevor accepted a new position as an assistant to the NASA flight directors. He worked very closely with the astronauts and became good friends with some of them. Whenever anyone visited him, he took them on special tours of the space center. Trevor was involved with developing the flight techniques and rules used on each shuttle flight, and he worked in mission control. As part of his new job, he learned how to operate all the shuttle controls. He even got to fly in simulators with the shuttle crews during simulated launches and landings. He certainly had an exciting job—being part of history-making events.

The summer of 1981 was wet and pleasant compared to the scorcher drought of the previous year. Our garden thrived in the good weather and rewarded us amply for our hard work. We had a great harvest, and I really enjoyed being able to share the abundance of the Promised Land with others.

To help store the additional food that we were harvesting and preparing, Bill and I dug a "hippo grave" next to the "elephant grave" that Trevor had so aptly named previously. The hippo grave was actually a "root cellar" that we dug into the hillside beneath the deck at the back of our house. We poured concrete foundations for the walls and put on a concrete roof, which was then covered with dirt.

Not only did I have an elephant grave and a hippo grave, but I also dug a "snake grave." In order to get the newly-discovered fresh water from the well to the house, I had to dig a 60-foot trench that was at least 30 inches deep to avoid freezing in the winter. What a job! We had some heavy rain, which partly filled the trench; so I had to dig it out again, lay the pipe, and then cover it.

In June we traveled to Versailles, Missouri, in the Ozark country. The church group there had really grown. The Saints had purchased a large tract of land and had commenced a small Zionic type community, building log cabins from the oak trees on the property.

That summer we attended reunion at Lake Doniphan and took our seven-year-old grandson, Richard. There were about 250 people present, with a large number of children. I was blessed in my work teaching classes and preaching two sermons. The classes were on "Growing Spiritually in Discipleship." I used the Three Standard Books at great length and had the people read out of them. Each afternoon I took Richard fishing, and he proved to be quite a good little fisherman.

There were a number of special education campers, who either were retarded or had Down's syndrome. We found them to be especially lovable and receptive. After I had preached a really strong sermon, a lad with Down's syndrome came and embraced me three times. Apparently he did not do that to anyone else. I felt that the Lord was telling me through the boy's pure, simple mind that my sermons were acceptable to Him.

I was once again busy nearly every Sunday—preaching and teaching classes at various congregations. I had preaching series in Iowa and Walnut Park, taught classes at priesthood retreats, and again served as pastor to the girls at a camp for disadvantaged children. Those were supposed to be my retirement years; but, of course, "there can be no furlough granted...in the army of the Lord."

When we were in Tahiti earlier in the year, our friend Jean Tapu suggested that I return and minister to the Tahitian Saints. As one of the young men I had personally trained and helped during our sojourn there, he had not forgotten the gospel which was taught to him then. He had been very impressed with my sermons and told me there was a dearth of gospel preaching in the islands. He was now a very wealthy man, having made his money by growing and selling cultured pearls. He wrote that he was presiding over all the branches in Tahiti and requested that

Gwen and I come for three months so I could do missionary work, mainly on the islands of Tahiti and Moorea. He offered to pay all our expenses.

When we booked our flights to leave on the trip in February, we learned that we could save about $200 per ticket if we traveled to Tahiti via Australia—which is several thousand miles farther—than if we flew to Tahiti directly. It seemed crazy, but it did allow us to stop and see our families before starting the work in Tahiti.

☼ ☼ ☼

The year of 1982 stands out as an exceptional year in my memory. In January I spoke to the Liahona group at Central Missouri State University in Warrensburg about dating, marriage, and the family. A number of questions came up, and some students talked privately to me later. It was wonderful to help fine young people like those.

During that same month, a man and his wife visited us. A year earlier he had brought his teenage daughter to me for help. At that time I prayed to the Lord to deliver her from an evil spirit, which seemed to have taken hold of her life. The parents said that we would not recognize the girl as the same person. It is wonderful and rewarding when people come back especially to share their joys.

On February 2 Gwen and I flew directly to Brisbane, where we spent a few days with our families. I preached there and gave the communion address at the Coorparoo branch. We had another sad parting in Brisbane because our mothers were getting old and frail. Indeed, that was the last time we saw Gwen's mother.

We flew to Canberra, the Australian capital city, where

Marvia and her family were residing. Terry had been transferred there for two years. We spent a week with them. Our grandsons were delightful, and we had a good time together—including playing cricket. They seemed to take a great liking to Grandpa and Grandma. On Sunday we went to church, where I preached to a number of people, including some nonmembers. It was a very rewarding experience to have people ask, "Do you remember having cottage meetings with me?"

Leaving Gwen with the Thompsons, I flew to Tahiti on February 21. My flight took off at 10:15 Sydney time, Sunday evening, and arrived in Papeete at 8 a.m. Sunday morning—earlier than we left, thanks to the International Date Line! Apostle Ken Robinson was also on the plane. I sat by him some of the time, and we had a good discussion. A few Saints met us at the airport. We went to the church, where the apostle preached and Jean Tapu interpreted for him. After church we were invited to a home for a typical Tahitian meal with Jean, his wife Estelle, and others. It certainly brought back fond memories.

It rained incessantly the first week I was there; but after that, we had mostly clear weather. The following Sunday, I preached at the Tiona branch to a large crowd, including an English-speaking tourist. After the sermon, she told me she did not understand a word I said; but she was glued to her seat by a spirit she had not experienced before. She wanted the text of my sermon—in English! Jean was very pleased that I had made some slides in the Tahitian language, since they had a dearth of study material.

Using the slides, I taught a class on Monday nights at Tarona. Before I came with the slides, classes were averaging about 20 people. By the time the classes ended, they were averaging over 100 people.

Meanwhile, Gwen was enjoying her extended visit with Marvia's family. In early March she caught a bus to Sydney, where she met Trevor, who had just arrived from the U.S. They spent the rest of Sunday together. Gwen left Sydney on Sunday night and arrived in Tahiti on Sunday morning, just as I had. Some Saints and I met her and placed the usual *heis* around her neck.

We were thrilled to have Don and Marge Alberts arrive in Tahiti in mid-March for a visit on their way from Australia to America for World Conference. We had an enjoyable time together, including a trip to Moorea.

Gwen and I enjoyed serving the Tahitians, and we were kept very busy. They really appreciated the gospel, and God blessed them with His Spirit. I baptized and confirmed some people at Tarona and Heberona and preached many times. The possibilities for missionary work there were endless, but unfortunately my time was limited.

On April 7, Trevor arrived from Australia on his way home. He had quite a story to tell us. He had been interviewed on an Australian Broadcasting Commission radio program about the space shuttle. He was then hired by an Australian television network to act as a technical consultant during the STS-3 shuttle flight in March. So our son was on television almost every day for a week. He was also interviewed on radio and television in Newcastle and appeared in a couple of Aussie newspapers—quite the celebrity!

Then he traveled north to spend some time with his relatives in Brisbane. He was the last one of our family to see Gwen's mother before she passed away.

Trevor spent two days with us in Tahiti. Although the stay was too short, he enjoyed himself immensely. He was interviewed by a reporter, and a large front-page picture and article about him appeared in the French language newspaper. The Tarona branch held a welcome for him, and he looked handsome decked out in flower and shell *heis*. They also gave him some native gifts.

In April we went to the Tuamotus and spent two weeks on an atoll (a ring of coral islets enclosing a large lagoon). It was about 20 miles in diameter. While other trees grow on them, only the coconut palms reach a great height.

Jean Tapu farmed cultured pearls in the lagoon. He had about 18,000 pearl oysters and expected to harvest about 6,000 black (grey) pearls, plus a few cream ones. Black pearls are the most valuable. He suspended the oysters on trellises made from welded water pipes. I did some welding to help repay him for our plane fare.

We lived on fish and literally dozens of large sea lobsters, which were very delicious. I had opened my big mouth years ago about how I enjoyed lobster—and we were swamped with them, much to my delight!

A week or so later, Gwen and I flew to the little island of Tubuai. It had been 33 years since we had been there, and things had changed in some ways. With a much cooler climate than Tahiti, it was an ideal place to retire; a number of Frenchmen and Americans lived there. One day a man took us in his boat completely around the picturesque island. We enjoyed the trip very much, although the wind was strong and the sea was quite rough. I was busy each night sharing the gospel with the natives of the island, and the meetings were well attended.

In May of 1982 we received the sad news that Gwen's mother had passed away in Brisbane at the age of 86. Gwen was unable to attend the funeral for several reasons, including the fact that her visa for Australia had expired. However, she bore the news well. The natives were so kind to her, it was wonderful. Gwen's mother was a loyal soul, and God had undoubtedly taken her to paradise to await the great resurrection.

We had one unusual incident at Tubuai. As we arrived, the French gendarme (who was a very irritable fellow) took our passports from us and put them in the pocket of his trousers. Unfortunately for him, his wife threw his clothes into the washing machine without inspecting them and gave them a good bath. Gwen had put the passports in a strong plastic pouch, which protected them somewhat. The gendarme panicked when he discovered what had occurred—he knew it was a serious international offense to damage or destroy the property of another government.

He told one of our church girls what had happened and returned the passports via her. But he avoided contact with us until the day of our departure. Just before we were to board the plane, he came and offered me his hand. He was quite embarrassed as he attempted to muster the little English he knew. Because of his emotion, he practically forgot even *that*. I had to help him out in French to make his apology. The natives saw that and were greatly gratified to see the fellow brought down a peg. I told them I was happy to receive his apology because then we could leave Tubuai without one bad thought or memory.

A crowd saw us off; and Gwen and I were given some presents, including colorful quilts and beautifully woven Panama hats. We had a smooth flight back to Tahiti on a Fokker Friendship airplane—it was certainly more comfortable than traveling between the islands on a schooner! After a short stay in Tahiti, we left Papeete for the U.S. A large group of Saints saw us off and gave us a number of shell *heis*. We were sorry we had to go—three months with those warm-hearted people really bonded us to them.

After a pleasant 4,500-mile flight, we arrived in Los Angeles on time and had the smoothest trip through customs that I can remember. However, that was the calm before the storm.

We were scheduled to travel to Kansas City on Braniff Airlines; but while we were overseas, Braniff went out of business. A TWA ticket agent wanted to charge us $600 for a flight to Kansas City. However, the Lord smiled upon us; and United Airlines accepted our Braniff tickets. We had a fine flight back and were met at the airport by the McGuires and the Floods.

☼ ☼ ☼

It was good to be back at our own home. I enjoyed laboring in my garden, which was starting to blossom as summer approached. While we were gone, our neighbor had done the early planting for me.

Beth, Bill, and the children often came to visit us. Our grandsons paddled around in a small rubber boat and caught fish from our pond. The Tahitians had said that they supposed I missed the ocean, but I told them I had my own private ocean at my back door—with fish in it, too! They were delighted with that news.

The summer of 1982 I had the privilege of performing two weddings. The first was for the granddaughter of our neighbor, a nonmember. It was held at Unity Village in Lee's Summit, Missouri. The other was in the chapel at the Sanitarium in Independence. The groom was Bruce Edgeworth, the son of our good friends Len and Val Edgeworth from Brisbane. They flew from Australia for the wedding, and we were able to give them a feast from our garden when they visited our home.

I continued to make the missionary slide sets to fill several outstanding orders. Really, the church should have been producing them and not leaving such work up to a man like me. In fact, I was the only one I am aware of who was providing basic slides for the missionary effort at that time.

In September we had a very profitable and lovely experience at the Center Stake Women's retreat at Lake Doniphan. About 300 were present, including many younger women. Sister Barbara Roberson, the women's leader, had asked three conservative seventies to give most of the ministry; and all of us were singularly blessed with the good Spirit. Sister Aleta Runkle Page was the only lady teacher, and she excelled as always. I gave the keynote address on Friday evening. At the final commitment service, the Lord used me to bring a message of counsel and commendation to the ladies; and it was very inspiring to me as well as to them.

About a week later, I escaped what could have been a severe accident. While I was pouring cement, I slipped in the mud and fell into the hole which I had dug for my pump. A bar of reinforcement steel was protruding and could have pierced my jugular vein. But as I fell, it grazed my throat just a half inch from the vein. So I was thus still able to preach and tell the gospel story. I am extremely thankful for that blessing.

Gwen and I drove to Raleigh, North Carolina, in early October, where I held a week-long preaching series. That congregation was where we did so much work with the blacks. They were still loyal and attended very well. The black Saints greeted us with hugs as did the others, and we really felt at home. The branch was racially integrated, and the members worked well together. The congregation had built a new church among the tall pine trees, and I called it "the church in the wildwood."

After the close of the series in Raleigh, Gwen and I drove to Harkers Island and stayed with the Ervins. Carlos Ervin, a geographic surveyor, had been to Australia. His wife Irene was converted from the Moravians, but he was of another faith. Two years earlier he would not allow prayer in the home, let alone scripture readings. But this time, Irene asked me to read from our Three Standard Books and pray; and he did not object. In fact, he asked my opinion on certain verses—which was a big improvement. We were invited back anytime.

They took us out fishing in their launch, both in the inlet and on the Atlantic. We fished with rods; and Gwen was the most successful, landing two fish at a time on two occasions. We also let down nets and caught a number of bluefish and other varieties. We had a most enjoyable day with the Ervins and two neighbors who accompanied us.

Leaving Harkers Island, we drove to Wilmington and spent the night with the pastor and his wife, Harry and Edna Martin. I had ordained him to the office of elder. I often stayed with them when I was a missionary to that area. The next day, we drove to Charleston and saw the Coopers, old friends of ours. I had spent dozens of nights in their home. Roy and I used to go on cottage meetings to nonmembers and also to visit the Saints. Friday night, they and another sister took Gwen and me to a seafood restaurant to celebrate our 40th wedding anniversary.

On Saturday we drove about 200 miles inland to the Betty Willimon Reunion Grounds and saw the unique tabernacle the Saints of that area had completed. But we were disappointed with the lack of care shown to parts of the grounds, especially the lake. On Sunday I preached at the new mission there. Some church members from Greenville attended the service.

Don and Yvonne Willimon surprised us when they, along with Doyle and Ferne Launius, took us as their guests to the World's Fair at Knoxville, Tennessee. We drove in our car because it was on our way home to Missouri, and they went in theirs. We spent a full day there and saw only a small percentage of what was available; however, we did visit the Australian booth. It was a thoroughly enjoyable day provided by the generosity of our South Carolina friends.

Back in Missouri, Gwen and I continued to make good progress on our house. By the end of the year, we had finished the family room in the basement. I laid the carpet squares, which were all samples given to us by a member of the church in the carpet business. That saved us a lot of money. I had always been very careful to be a good steward over the money of the Saints all through my missionary appointment days, and we were also trying to be frugal in our retirement.

The year 1983 started with a tragedy in our family. Our niece, Carynne Flood Law, suffered severe, life-threatening injuries when she fell onto some rocks at Booti Booti near Tiona. Frank and Ruth Flood immediately flew to Australia to be with her as the doctors worked to save her life. I believed that the same God who protected her from instant death could also heal her if He so willed. I was praying very diligently for her welfare. Then the experience of Sister Emma Burton and her daughter Dora (as related in the book *Beatrice Witherspoon*) came to my memory. Dora had been run over by a large heavy roller, and it was evident that the Lord must have sent His angels to bear the roller up so that Dora was not crushed to jelly. Emma dismissed the doctor and relied on administration by the elders for the complete recovery of her daughter.

The Spirit said to me that the Lord is still able to do such things when He can find the faith such as Emma had. That encouraged me in my petitions. Carynne eventually recovered after many months in the hospital and several operations to repair her many broken bones and damaged organs. The doctor told Frank that only by divine power was she alive.

Two elders from Independence, who did not know much about the casting out of demons, brought a nine-year-old girl to see me. The girl was an abused child living with her grandmother, who was not a church member. Doctrine and

Covenants 28:13 says, "Power is not given unto Satan to tempt little children, until they begin to become accountable before me." After the girl's eighth birthday, it seemed that the evil one did enter into her through one of his angels; and she became almost impossible to manage. While I was talking with the grandmother, the girl was most restless. Except for Gwen's mothering, I believe she would have been almost unmanageable.

We administered to the grandmother first, then the girl. Three elders laid our hands on her head, and I offered the confirming prayer. In the name of Christ, I commanded the evil spirit to come out of her and depart. Just after I had said those words, she made an attempt to pull out from under our hands. But the other elders held her firmly to the chair. I had almost finished my prayer when she attempted again to get away. I knew that the evil spirit was trying to take her with him, as he was loathe to leave his house of abode. All at once he left her.

After two weeks, one of the elders called me. He said the girl had changed tremendously and was now obedient and loving. A short time later the other elder called and said the girl had received *A's* in her exams, where before she had received *F's*. God still works with His priesthood who believe that He is unchangeable.

In January Gwen and I had a very interesting experience at Harvest Hills on the east side of Independence. The Saints there were experimenting with Zionic community living. I was invited to speak about "New Beginnings," which I did with exceptional liberty and direction. The sermon was followed by the adult class, which discussed what I had presented. There was a marvelous spirit there, and I had the opportunity to answer questions and expand on the subject. Later in the month I was invited to minister to the older youth of Harvest Hills.

We drove to Houston in February to see Trevor. We visited the NASA Johnson Space Center and especially appreciated being introduced to a number of astronauts such as Bob Crippen, who flew on the first space shuttle flight with John Young. All the astronauts we met seemed to be humble, ordinary folks and very friendly.

I preached two sermons at the Bay Area branch, where Trevor attended, and bore my testimony on Wednesday night. Don Everett and his wife Anne took us to see the big San Jacinto Monument, which honors the Texan victory by Sam Houston over the forces led by the Mexican leader Santa Anna. There Texas gained its independence from Mexico. The monument is over 500 feet high—15 feet higher than the Washington Monument. Of course, that was intended since Texans must have the biggest *everything*! We also saw the battleship *Texas*, which fought in both world wars. Don and Anne took us for a tour through the huge Exxon petro-chemical plant where he worked. All the massive equipment there boggled my mind.

We arrived home safely, found that all was well, and thanked the Lord for having blessed us so abundantly. Before leaving home we always prayed for our safety as we traveled and asked the Lord to protect our property while we were gone.

In March, Frank Flood and I went to the Scottsbluff District conference in Nebraska. As we drove through the great prairies, we thought of the millions of bison that had roamed there years ago and of the red men who had hunted and relied on them for almost all their livelihood.

Scott's Bluff is an enormous outcropping of rock rising about 800 feet above the plain and about a mile long. The Oregon Trail wound its way over the prairie and through a pass in the bluff. Another interesting sight was Chimney

Rock, which looks like a huge tapered chimney—a great landmark for the early wagon trains.

Frank and I evidently provided the Saints with the spiritual ministry they craved. I had a remarkable experience as I arose to teach my first class on "A New Look at Stewardship." My few notes and scriptural references about stewardship were all forgotten when the Spirit prompted me to talk on "The Stewardship of Our Emotions." That was something I had never thought of before. The Lord opened my mind, and one wonderful thought after another flowed into it.

Later that same month, Gwen and I traveled to Sperry, Oklahoma, where I preached eight sermons. Some of my slide sets had been purchased there, and quite a number of baptisms resulted from their use. Praise God from Whom all blessings flow!

We were thrilled to have Marvia, Terry, and their boys visit us in April. We had a wonderful time. Of course, the big thing was to have Beth, Marvia, and Trevor together again for the first time in 13 years. The six grandsons enjoyed fishing in the pond, and they caught a number of fish. We feasted on those and the abundance of vegetables from our garden.

That was Terry's first trip to the U.S., and he seemed to be quite impressed. After a few days, the Thompsons continued on their tour of America. Then they returned to our place for another enjoyable two weeks. It was sad when we had to part company.

During mid-1983 a devastating hurricane or cyclone smashed into French Polynesia. Afterward, our good friend Jean Tapu sent some photos of the island where he had his pearl business. It looked as though an atomic bomb had been dropped on it. He said that all the houses were destroyed, and only our church building remained standing. A total of 283 people crammed into the church during the storm, and the water came over the entire village to a depth of three feet or more. However, the church stood firm, and no one was killed. What really caught my eye was the manner in which Jean started his letter: "Life to you and Gwen in the name of our Lord, Who continually blesses us." Just imagine—a man saying that after the fierce tempest of God had wiped out all of his possessions on that island.

I shared that with the Saints at the Oak Grove Branch at prayer meeting one evening, saying, "We, who have not experienced such a loss, still do not praise and thank God as this man did in his adversity." Almost immediately a young lady stood and with great emotion said that she was going to do something unusual in her testimony if the Lord would help her. She started to sing, "Praise God from Whom All Blessings Flow." Immediately her voice steadied, and with beautiful clarity and power she sang on. The congregation joined in with her. A lovely spirit was present, and we had many fine testimonies.

The summer of 1983 brought another terrible heat wave, reminiscent of the dreadful summer of 1980. On many days the temperature was over 100° F, and my garden suffered somewhat despite my best efforts to keep it watered. I was reminded of a terrible heat wave we had when I was a young man living in East Brisbane. Some evenings we went to the seaside, swam until 10:30, and then tried to go to sleep on the back lawn at home.

In early September, our grandson Richard was baptized at the Enoch Hill church in Independence. It was a private baptism, including only his relatives and the pastor and his family. Richard was a sensitive little guy, just like his grandfather, and did not want to be baptized in front of a crowd. His other grandfather, Carl McGuire, gave the address and admonition. Then Bill baptized his son; and I confirmed him, with Bill assisting. I felt the Spirit very strongly and told Richard of possible work for him in the Kingdom of God if he would allow Jesus to lead him. Beth's face was radiant. We were thankful that Trevor was able to fly from Houston and participate in that service. He gave the benediction and received a spiritual blessing himself during his prayer.

While Trevor was with us, he helped me mix concrete for the project I had underway to channel more water into our pond. He worked hard trying to spare his father the heavy work. It was good to work with him, and I enjoyed it very much. My engineering feat was successful; later in the year when we had about two inches of rain, the additional runoff nearly filled the pond.

In late September we started on another trip to the Carolinas. We drove first to Winston-Salem, where we stayed overnight with Lois and Truman Smythe. The next day Truman took me through the huge tobacco plant there. I did not really want to go; but once there, I found the maze of machinery was fascinating. What a pity that the know-how and money were wasted in making "coffin nails"!

The next day we set out for Raleigh. I preached that evening and the next and gave the sacramental address on Sunday morning. We always enjoyed mingling with the black Saints in Raleigh.

From Raleigh we went to Harkers Island, where we had a relaxing time fishing and digging clams. We went out on the bosom of the Atlantic Ocean with Carlos and Irene Ervin in their 33-foot boat. The fish were not plentiful, but there were enough. Gwen proved to be the champion again, catching a big flounder.

We then drove to Wilmington and to Greenville. At the nearby Anderson mission, I conducted a preaching series, as well as taught a couple of classes at a junior high camp. I also administered to a number of sick folks and visited many others. It was certainly good to fellowship with our old friends in that area.

During the series in Anderson, I used a fundamental approach to the RLDS Church's liberal "Faith to Grow" program. I told the Saints that as a seventy I was not an administrative officer but a preacher of the gospel. I spoke on "Faith to Grow Spiritually," "Faith to Grow in Stewardship Observance" (addressing the stewardship of our emotions), and "Faith to Grow Numerically." On the final day, I spoke of "Faith to Hang On to the Rod of Iron." The Lord blessed us very much, indeed.

At Anderson a black lady who attended my first Sunday sermon had a miniature recorder to tape my message. I was so intrigued that I asked her where she got it. The patriarch for that area, Curtis Cunningham, saw me admiring it and must have made a mental note to get me one. During the week, I went into a store and priced a mini tape recorder. However, the Spirit of the Lord told me not to buy it because the patriarch would be bringing me one. On Sunday, when he presented me an excellent recorder—so small that it fit in my shirt pocket—I was not surprised. I told him of my experience, and he was very happy indeed. I tried to pay him for the recorder, but he wouldn't hear of it.

After we returned from the Carolinas, I attended a retreat for seventies and discovered that nearly all of them were new men—much younger than I—and very few of my old friends were there. It was obvious that the torch was being passed on to the next generation.

In November Frank Flood was asked by Apostle Roy Schaefer to attend and appraise a charismatic service held in our Walnut Gardens church in Independence. Gwen and I had attended a similar service there the previous year, at which I spoke to those Saints on the doctrine of deliverance—warning them of the misuse and abuse of the spiritual gifts. We had been losing some of our people to the charismatic movement, which is a pity because it was through the Restoration that the Lord had reintroduced the spiritual gifts to the world. Remember that the ministers of the 1820s did not believe that Joseph Smith, Jr., had a vision or was visited by an angel. They said all that had been done away.

Brother Charles Neff told us that for the last two months the church had had 0% growth in the domestic field. We needed to do something different about our missionary work in America. I knew we would have to preach the basic gospel again if we wished to grow—a conclusion that seemed to escape leaders of the RLDS Church.

Later in the month, I had a preaching series at Grain Valley, Missouri. The first night I had planned to speak about the history and purpose of Christianity, but my thoughts were directed to topics which seemed unrelated to the subject. After the service, the pastor and some other members said that I had covered material which was most needed by the branch and certain individuals, including one girl who was becoming enamored by other churches.

Because of my experience with evil spirits, I was called to a home to administer to a girl of 18. I knew she had received abundant religious training from her childhood. But when she went to Graceland College, she began doing things which were against her moral principles. The evil one is trying to ruin and destroy our young people through drugs, alcohol, and sex.

The moment I set eyes upon her, I could see the difference in the girl I had known for years—a change from a beautiful flower in the Lord's garden to a wilted imitation of her original beauty. Another seventy and I laid hands on her, and I called upon the Holy Spirit to rebuke the evil force. She was truly blessed after the administration.

One Sunday in December I preached for the first time at Resthaven—where I spoke with many old timers, including

Brother F. Henry Edwards, Brother Roy Cheville, and Sister Mable Davey. It was wonderful speaking to the valiant people who had borne the brunt of the battle and the heat of the days that were past. I saluted them for their steadfastness and courage as they grappled with the problems of the world and the church in their generation.

During the cold winter months when I could no longer work in my garden, I kept myself busy in my workshop. In the winter of 1983-84 I made a new stereo cabinet and started building a windcharger. If I could harness the wind to drive a generator, it would help heat our house in winter and pump water in summer. The purpose, of course, was to reduce our electricity costs (besides being fun to make). Gwen kept quite busy that winter with painting and framing her works of art.

☼ ☼ ☼

The new year of 1984 was a particularly memorable one for us in three respects. The first was the World Conference, which turned out to be a pivotal one in the church's history (apparently for the worse); the second was my mother's 90th birthday; and the third was the marriage of our son—at last! But more of these events later.

In February Gwen and I again drove to Houston to visit with Trevor. He introduced us to his new ladylove, Lori Thatcher, whom he had started dating the month before. She was a tall, thin church girl from Houston. I thought she looked a lot like Lady Diana, so I started calling her "Lady Di."

Trevor took us to his place of work, and we viewed some of the films showing man's landing on the moon. We had a wonderful time visiting with him; and we were so blessed that he was healthy, happy, and active in the church.

☼ ☼ ☼

During the year, I kept very busy with church work. In March I had a successful preaching series at the Kentucky Hills congregation in Independence. I encouraged the Saints to write questions relative to my sermons and submit them after the service each evening. I took the questions home and prepared answers for the next evening. It was really popular, and a lot of good questions were submitted. Obviously the people were listening and thinking about what I said.

Gwen and I attended the World Conference in April as delegates representing areas in Australia. Some of the events that took place at the conference were very troubling to us. We were particularly concerned about the document which opened the door for the ordination of women. We were not able to support the document, but it was accepted by the majority of the delegates after much debate. We knew that great and portentous events were not far distant and that the advice of Jesus is just as strong today as in the days when He said: "Whoso treasureth up my words, shall not be deceived" (Matthew 24:39).

April 12, 1984, was my mother's 90th birthday. I can not improve on what I wrote to her at the time:

"You have been a wonderful mother; and the most precious thing that you have bequeathed to me is the everlasting gospel, which no man can take from me because it is true."

We got some great news in May, when Trevor and Lori announced their engagement. Our fervent prayers that our son would find a Godly companion had been answered. Trevor said he followed my example when he proposed. He and Lori were in Cozumel, Mexico, with the NASA Scuba Club. With a rising, almost full moon, he took her to the seashore and asked her to be his wife.

There had also been a full moon on the night I had taken Gwen to the seashore and proposed. However, Trevor did not eat onions for dinner as I had so my sister would not get suspicious about my plans. Poor Gwen has never quite forgiven me for that, and I don't blame her!

Trevor and Lori came to visit in July so she could meet more of his relatives. We all had an enjoyable time at our house, swimming in our little lake, eating watermelon, and getting better acquainted with our future daughter-in-law. Beth's boys had prayed so hard for Uncle Trevor to get a wife, and they were pleased to see that the Lord was obliging. I asked them, "Well, will she do?"

They all answered, "Yes!"

By summertime I was busy working in the garden and also making a concrete wall across the creek to form a dam from which I could pump water. I mixed the concrete with an electric mixer, but it was still hard work.

Richard and David McGuire (ages 10 and 8 respectively) visited for a few days, and we thoroughly enjoyed them. I made David a go-kart (trolley) with four rubber wheels, and he was so happy. The weather was hot; and Richard asked David, "Don't you think you are overworking Grandpa?"

David came to me and said, "Grandpa, Richard said that I am overworking you. Is that so?" I laughed and assured him that he was not. However, I felt very appreciative of their concern about an aging grandpa. There is an epilogue to this story. David took his go-kart home, and it appears that it started a craze in his neighborhood—other grandpas were pestered to make them for their grandchildren.

In July we helped at Camp Opportunity, run by Sister Ardie Launius, our very good friend from South Carolina, who was living with her family in the Harvest Hills community. The camp was for older abused children. It must have been wonderful for them to know that there is a better world than the one to which they had been accustomed.

Gwen and I drove to Des Moines in October, where we had a unique experience talking to the "Mong" congregation. They were from Laos, and some had been "boat people" who had found their way to America. Through an interpreter, Gwen and I told them about Tahiti. I spoke some Tahitian to them; and Gwen sang in Tahitian, much to their delight. They sang hymns in their language. The little children could speak English very well, and the tiny ones interpreted for their parents. They all seemed to be very nice people and quite sincere. We thoroughly enjoyed our association with them.

They were members of another church and were very upset that we should ask them to be rebaptized into the RLDS Church. They said that they had already been baptized into Jesus Christ—accepting Him as they did through the preaching and teaching of the Missionary Alliance Church. I drew their attention to Acts 19, where Paul rebaptized some disciples who had already been baptized with the baptism of John. They responded that the situation was different and did not apply to them. I then referred them to Hebrews 5 about priesthood and authority; that caused them to think more deeply. We had a good possibility there of a number of baptisms, if the people could be convinced of their need for rebaptism. I told the priesthood in Des Moines to pray earnestly because only God could help them see the light.

In October, 1984, when I was 68 and Gwen was 65, I wrote a letter describing what it was like getting old:

"Gwen and I are trying to grow old gracefully, and we find there are many things we cannot do with the alacrity that we once did—for instance, jumping out of bed. I used to wake up and take a dive out of bed, but now I have to sit on the side of the bed for a bit and then stand up. I guess the arteries are a bit more constricted now than when

I was younger."

We went to Houston for Trevor and Lori's wedding in November. The beautiful service was held in the Bay Area church. I did not stick to a "read service" only, but spoke as I believe I was led. Almost everyone present expressed their appreciation for the service. The reception followed at a nearby country club. While the American custom is not a "wedding breakfast" as was ours in Australia, nevertheless, this one was very near to it—with all kinds of delicacies, including lots of crab claws and shrimp, of which I took due toll. Lori's going-away dress and hat made her look like a cover girl on a fashion magazine. The bridal car was filled with balloons, which our grandsons David and Richard enjoyed bursting.

After staying in downtown Houston that night, Trevor and Lori returned to her house to finish packing for their honeymoon. That afternoon her parents whisked them off to the airport to set out for their five-week honeymoon to Tahiti and Australia. That same day, Gwen and I started in the other direction for our Florida trip.

We passed through extensive sugar cane plantations, reminding me very much of the Maroochy River of Australia. In West Palm Beach we stayed with John and Mickey Pritchard. On Sunday I taught a class on the Book of Mormon, gave the sacrament address, and preached at night to a large crowd, including some Haitian refugees. There was quite a missionary effort among them, with some joining the church.

We then drove to the southernmost point of the U.S.—Key West, which is only 90 miles from Cuba. We toured historical sites, such as the Hemingway and Audubon homes. I climbed to the top of the old lighthouse for a wonderful view of the island. Coconut palms made the place look like Papeete. At one place we drove over a seven-mile-long bridge; and I thought that the Hornibrook

Highway bridge—at one and a half miles—was long!

After our trip to sunny Florida, it took a little while to get used to the ice and snow of the Missouri winter. However, even such wintry weather has its positive side, as shown in this passage which I wrote to my mother in January, 1985:

"I am sitting here looking out on a winter wonderland, with the snow many inches deep—white and beautiful. Our pond is frozen over; and the snow has left all types of strange, fascinating patterns on it. The ice frozen on the trees is still sparkling in the sun like millions of diamonds or beautiful crystal. Surely the Lord is the master Artist and Creator of beauty."

After I preached at Oak Grove one Sunday evening, I visited with a lady who had previously told me about a bad condition which existed at the hospital where she worked. It seems that evil spirits had caused a lot of trouble among the nurses and others. Some time before, I had asked the Lord in a special prayer to rebuke and cast out those evil powers from their midst. The woman told me that things had miraculously returned to normal, and she thanked God for His intervention. The Lord is still at work in casting out demons, although many in the church today disbelieve and laugh at it. Some say there is no devil, thus fulfilling the Book of Mormon prophecy (2 Nephi 12:27). I know what the Lord does, and no man can take that knowledge from me no matter how much he may scoff.

Early in 1985 I was visiting some of the "bruised and brokenhearted" and found it quite a rewarding ministry. I also discovered that my sermons on cassette tapes were being sent far and wide. When I think of a backwoods boy from Australia—cutting cane and milking cows for a living—having his thoughts circle almost the entire earth, I am conscious of what the Spirit of God can do if we allow Him to work within us.

Despite the turmoil in the church, the Lord continued to move in the hearts of the Saints. There was a more pronounced movement toward Zion from His people living in Canada and other outlying parts of America. During the seven years we had lived in Missouri, many hundreds of people had gathered from as far as Hawaii; and many new branches were being formed.

In March, as the weather became warmer, I started working on my garden again. I love to be a husbandman and work with the Lord in making His earth respond. By summer I was starting to harvest the fruit of my labors. We had grown some enormous kohlrabi (one weighing 21 pounds), giant beets (more than one and one-half pounds), and tomatoes (some weighing up to one and three-quarter pounds). It is truly a blessed land.

Gwen and I drove to Lockwood, Missouri, in June, where I gave the communion sermon. We stayed with the pastor and his wife, Hubert and Luanna Coose. Sister Coose gave us some *Saints' Heralds* from 1926 and 1927. One of them had a complete list of all the tithepayers for the entire church for the year 1926. When Gwen was looking through them, she found my mother's name listed: Ruby Sorensen and the sum of one pound, two shillings. Gwen and I were both immensely proud to see that even back then—when I was only ten years old—my mother tried to obey her Lord in that respect. I knew that my dad was against her paying tithing in those days; she had to try and save what she could from the housekeeping money. The thing that struck me was her loyalty to the gospel and her God. Gwen also found her father's name and the amount he paid. It seemed incredible that every tithepayer was listed there—even the Tahitians with their odd names.

In July I preached at Bates City. After the service we invited Seventy Marcus Juby, his wife, and son for dinner. Brother Juby, a doctor of agronomy, was half American

Indian. He had worked with the Indian Ministries Department of the RLDS Church, which subsequently had closed. We soon formed a friendship and went together on cottage meetings and to other priesthood activities.

I flew to Augusta, Georgia, in July to administer to Sister Powell, who was on her deathbed with leukemia. I had baptized her, her husband, and her son when I had been a missionary in that area. She rallied from a coma long enough to tell her family to pay my airfare and ask me to come to administer to her. After the administration, her condition improved somewhat; but she was appointed unto death, and she died about a month later.

Sister Powell had requested that I conduct her funeral service, so I returned to Augusta. There were at least 250 people present, mostly Southern Baptists. Another elder of our church assisted, and I preached the sermon. The Holy Spirit was present in great abundance, and I had no difficulty in recalling the texts I needed from both the Bible and the Book of Mormon. I explained the atonement, baptisms, grace, faith, and the glories. You could have heard a pin drop. The Spirit then directed me to turn to the widower and two children and give them special guidance and comfort. A number of people asked me for the Bible texts supporting the glories, and I referred them to 1 Corinthians 15.

Our daughter Beth had quite a long talk with me in early August because she wanted me to write my autobiography. She said it would be a pity to deprive her boys of our spiritual experiences. I consented to begin research to see what I could gather.

By mid-1985, it was obvious that the RLDS Church was headed for a severe crisis, precipitated by the controversial document accepted by the 1984 World Conference—but that was not the entire cause. Already many hundreds of Saints were meeting in separate fundamental groups in the

Center Place. I also continued to minister to the regular branches and congregations of the church, but I tried to keep off controversial subjects. As a seventy I was called to preach the gospel, and many years previously the Spirit had told me to do just that. I felt singularly blessed by the Lord in taking His message to my fellowmen.

A variety of results occurred when the Saints met in stake and district conferences to consider women in the priesthood. At the Santa Fe Stake conference in September, with about 800 Saints in attendance, the women candidates for ordination were rejected by a large majority. Some areas of the church had already approved and ordained women, however, while others had not submitted names up to that time.

On November 27, 1985, Gwen and I boarded a plane in Kansas City and set out on a journey to see our loved ones in Australia. After a few pleasant days in Hawaii, we flew on to Cairns in northern Queensland; there we enjoyed sightseeing. We went by steam locomotive to Kuranda—a beautiful trip through fields of sugar cane, up a ridge of mountains, and past some waterfalls. At Kuranda we ate our first hot meat pies in many years. Back in Cairns we had a delicious seafood buffet dinner with John and Sandra Morris, friends of Trevor and Lori, with whom they had stayed the previous year while on their honeymoon. They also showed us the lights and sights of Cairns, including indoor cricket.

Our flight to Brisbane followed along the Great Barrier Reef, thus providing a picturesque view of several islands on the way. I never lost my love of flying and fascination for airplanes, which is why we have always tried to get window seats.

In Brisbane we had a joyous reunion. My mother was at her home to greet us. For a 91-year-old woman, her condition was excellent. Although her body was frail, her mind was still remarkably sharp. Of course, she was delighted to see her fair-haired boy again. We enjoyed two weeks with my mother, my sisters Silvia and Mavis, and many other relatives and friends.

All too soon it was time to leave. Just before Christmas we flew to Sydney, where we were met at the airport by the Thompson family and Carynne and Matthew Law. That afternoon we drove to Newcastle and spent Christmas with Marvia and her family.

While in Newcastle we learned that Sister Calcott, a lady who had lived near us in Hamilton, was still alive at the age of 98. She always replied to the parting phrase of "See you later" with "If we're spared." She had obviously been spared quite a long time!

On New Year's Day of 1986, we went with the Thompsons to Tiona. Reunion was over when we arrived, but we enjoyed a relaxing week in a cabin. I went fishing a lot and walked to Flat Rock at Booti Booti three times—a good two-mile walk along the beach and climbing on the rocks.

One Sunday we accompanied Sister Joy Richards to our church in Bulahdelah, where only a very small group of Saints attended. Gwen and I bore our testimonies and I preached. We had a potluck dinner afterwards and visited with the Saints for quite a while. Brother Merv Richards had been the pastor for 38 years; but he was well into his 80s, and his health was poor.

After returning from Tiona, I worked like a Trojan fixing the Thompson's swimming pool deck, digging up their old driveway, and laying concrete for a new one. That was not bad for a 70-year-old man!

Later in January we all drove to Katoomba in the Blue Mountains, where we stayed at the Floods' holiday house at Leura. We enjoyed visiting the picturesque spots in that area, including the famous Jenolan Caves, waterfalls, the scenic railway, and a cable car with a 1000-foot drop.

At the end of January, we visited Jack and Mitta Gunning in Melbourne. They drove us to points of interest in and around the city, including some of our newer churches, and to the Dandenong Ranges, which contain beautiful huge trees and gullies full of tree ferns.

At Phillips Island we joined several hundred spectators to watch the fairy penguins parade at dusk. Hundreds of penguins came out of the ocean and marched up the beach like a parade of sailors in their white suits. It was flood-lit, but the penguins did not appear to be bothered by the onlookers. They marched undisturbed to their burrows, where their chicks were clamoring for food, and fed their young with partially digested fish.

After a brief stop at Sydney, we had an uneventful flight to Christchurch on the South Island of New Zealand. From the plane, we had a marvelously clear view of the Southern Alps. We spent the night in a hotel there and toured the vicinity. The next day we began a bus tour of the South Island. We went to Queenstown, which is on a beautiful, clear lake in the Southern Alps. Then we passed through rough sheep country and arrived at Te Anau on another large, lovely lake. We traveled through beech forests with huge trees, rugged snow-capped mountains, and the one-and-a-half-mile-long Homer Tunnel to Milford Sound. We then transferred to a launch, which took us nine miles through the fiord to the Tasman Sea. Only God could have made such majestic, awe-inspiring scenery.

We retraced our trip to Te Anau and then traveled to Invercargle and visited "The Bluff," the farthest point one can drive on South Island. There we saw the "Southern Ocean" spread out before us. A very strong southwest wind nearly blew us off the lookout landing. We visited Dunedin, which is the Gaelic name for Edinburgh. It was a quaint old Scottish city, and mostly Presbyterian churches were in evidence. We saw one Mormon church on the main road. Dunedin was very hilly; and the main city center was octagonal around a park. Then we set out for Mount Cook, New Zealand's tallest peak—over 12,000 feet high. What a majestic picture it made with its snow-white covering—mostly glaciers because the snow had already melted. The Maoris call it Aorangi or "cloud piercer."

From New Zealand we flew to Tahiti, where we planned to spend two weeks. Our host, Jean Tapu, was away in France; but his wife, Estelle, took good care of us. We decided to cut our stay in Tahiti short by a week as we were very tired and eager to get back to our own house.

It was good to be home after living out of suitcases for three months. Our house and property were in fine shape. We were welcomed back at the Oak Grove church like long-lost friends and were thrilled to see the large attendance at the two preaching services on Sunday and the prayer meeting on Wednesday night. There must have been over 100 at the prayer meeting. It was wonderful to hear the little children praying again. We missed that in Australia and New Zealand, since the Saints there did not have Wednesday prayer meetings very often if at all. Marvia, with good reason, was very worried about her boys and the lack of religious education in her area.

At the beginning of 1986, I told Gwen that we would likely not be asked to do very much church work because of our fundamental stance. But I was 100% wrong—I had to decline many requests. "Old-time preachers" were getting hard to find, as teddy bear and clown worship were taking their toll. During the year, I preached in a number of congregations in Missouri, as well as Plano, Illinois, and a country church in Iowa.

We did not actively participate in the 1986 World Conference. That was the first time in years that neither Gwen nor I were delegates. Seventies were no longer "ex-officio delegates," and I did not even have the right to vote in my quorum unless I was a delegate. That was very different from previous years. Appointees who were not delegates—and there were very few of them—were given reserved seats in the balcony to view the proceedings.

It gave me a great deal of pleasure to work with my sons-in-law with their home-building enterprises. In Australia I had helped Terry with the deck of his swimming pool, and now I helped Bill with his. We laid the floor and installed a door between the deck and the house.

In May I donned my first tuxedo ever to assist in the wedding of Marcus Juby's daughter at the Stone Church. I conducted the first part of the service, and the father of the bride married the couple.

One of the sad events of the year was the illness of our dear friend, Ardie Launius. She had cancer, and it was pitiful to see her suffer. Each Tuesday I administered to her and shared some delicacies from our garden with her. Ardie's mother-in-law, Sister Delcie Launius, came from South Carolina to be with her. The 88-year-old lady was thrilled with her first flight in a plane. Her husband Jeff had died the previous year at 90. He had the best memory of any person I ever met. He could tell the exact date on which he visited his neighbor to borrow or discuss something. I guess when the Lord judges him and says, "Now on September 10, 1936, you committed a certain sin," Jeff will say, "Begging your pardon, Lord, but it was on September 9 at 11:55 p.m.—not on September 10." I wish I had a memory like that for Bible texts.

That summer some raccoons got into my sweet corn and

really made a mess of it—even though I had a three-foot-high chicken wire fence around it. The Lord did not "rebuke the devourer for my sake," but he sent Marcus Juby to me instead. When we told him the sad story, he asked if we would like to get some corn to make up for the loss. He took me to a farmer friend who grew about five acres of sweet corn just to give to anyone who wanted to pick it. As it turned out, the raccoons were happy and well fed, and so were we.

☼ ☼ ☼

At the end of August we went to Oklahoma with Brother Juby. His wife and son had already flown there to have more time with their relatives. Gwen and I stayed with Jack and Jonnie Faye Basse at Sperry. On Friday our host took us to Tulsa, where we toured Oral Roberts University and its hospital. After the tour, we were ushered into a prayer room; and Oral Roberts and his son prayed (on tape) for all of us. While the prayers were playing, the lights were dimmed; one of the women employees came around the circle and placed her hand on the shoulder of each of us for a short time. That was a strange experience!

On Saturday, Marcus and Chris Juby, Karl Guthrie, Gwen, and I drove 75 miles to the Cherokee Indian powwow at Tahlequah. About 2,000 Indians were present, mostly Cherokee, which was the tribe of Marcus and his wife. A woman, the temporary acting chief, delivered a speech about the progress and problems of the Indian people. After lunch at an Indian restaurant, we went through the Cherokee museum, which was very informative. Movies told of the driving of the tribe from the Carolinas to Oklahoma in the 1830s—the notorious "Trail of Tears," when thousands of Indians died en route.

At dinner time they furnished everyone with a free meal

and entertained us with gospel music. The actual powwow consisted of prize presentations and Indian dancing. We thoroughly enjoyed ourselves.

☼ ☼ ☼

After returning home from the powwow, we headed to Illinois, where we showed slides and spoke at meetings near Amboy and Plano. Afterward, we drove 400 miles to Lamoni, where we stayed with the McGuires. The next day I preached at Elk Chapel, close to Lamoni.

It had been an excellent summer for my garden. I dug up a sweet potato that weighed five pounds and was like a small football. I took it to Sister Ardie Launius and told her I was getting mean and could only spare her one sweet potato. Then I produced that monster! She always seemed to enjoy my Australian sense of humor.

Gwen and I attended a retreat for the Buckner congregation in September, 1986, with about 90 in attendance. It was held at Camp Chihowa in Kansas. I taught two of the classes, assisted in the prayer meeting, and preached the Sunday morning sermon. The theme was on the establishment of Zionic homes. The stake president, a very liberal-minded man, made an unannounced visit. I had never met him and was surprised that he was seated next to me during the service. I was not afraid of the liberals, but it was upsetting if they brought a contrary spirit with them. I prayed to the Lord that His Spirit would prevail, and He did not let me down. Most of us—including myself—were in tears by the end of the sermon. The stake president prayed the benediction, referring to many things I had said in my address. Later I sought him out, and we agreed that a wonderful spirit had been present.

In October we had a joyous homecoming when our three chicks were together with us again. Terry Thompson had been selected as the best manager for his entire company in Australia for the past year. He and Marvia had thus won an all-expenses-paid trip to Hawaii plus $1,000 spending money. They were also able to find inexpensive fares from Hawaii to Kansas City for a one-week visit.

Lori and Trevor came from Houston for just the weekend, and Beth and Bill also joined us. On Sunday we all went to the local Oak Grove church, where I preached and Trevor offered the invocation. Then we returned to our place for one of Gwen's famous dinners. Frank Flood was able to join us; Ruth was currently in Australia with Carynne, who was undergoing more surgery related to her fall. Marvia and Terry spent a lot of their time with Beth and Bill since we had been with them just a few months earlier. Terry caught about a dozen big channel catfish in our pond.

In November our dear friend Ardie Launius passed to her reward—a merciful release from the suffering caused by that terrible cancer. Ardie was one of God's choice creations. She was able to hold her newborn granddaughter Jessica Hawley in her arms just a few days before she died, and she was fully conscious at the time. She had requested that I preach at her memorial service, which was held at the Parkview church in Blue Springs. Only a short amount of time was left after others had paid tribute to her memory, but the Holy Spirit helped me to cover effectively many things that needed to be said. We have a wonderful knowledge of the destiny of man and should witness about it to all people. The church was packed, so undoubtedly many nonmembers were present.

We were happy to have Brother Viriamu (William) Bennett and his wife from Tahiti visit us for a couple of days. I had administered to him in Tahiti 10 months previously when he looked like "death warmed over." In fact, Gwen had said that without divine intervention he would probably die in a short time. He testified that after the administration, he began to improve and was given a new lease on life. Praise to God Almighty!

After preaching at Knob Noster one Sunday, I had quite a long talk with Tom and Susan Hairabedian of that branch. They had been instrumental in getting the Book of Mormon translated into Hebrew and had completed the work except for proofreading, which was to be done by a Hebrew professor at the University of Missouri. At the end of the week, they were going to Israel to arrange for the first printing of the book. The translation work had been done through contributions from interested Saints and was to be ready when the gospel should go to the Jews as predicted in the Doctrine and Covenants.

The Hairabedians gave me a page of the translation in the Hebrew language. It was a real thrill to have this in my possession as I have longed for the day when the Book of Mormon would go to the Jews in their own language. The new book was titled *The Record of the Nephites* instead of *Book of Mormon*; the word "Nephi" has a very lovely meaning in Hebrew—something like "light of love."

Beth finished some specialized training to be a nurse for the first heart surgery team at the Independence Sanitarium and Hospital. That was quite an accomplishment, and we were very proud of her.

In early 1987 we started a joyful undertaking. Gwen and I drove to the McGuires each week, where Gwen gave John and David piano lessons and I went through the missionary slide sets with the boys. They took turns operating the slide projector. I could see that the training which Beth and Bill had provided them was paying dividends because the boys asked me the most sensible questions. It was a great feeling to minister to my grandsons in that way. I just wish I could have also done it with our grandsons in Australia.

One Sunday I preached to a large group at Grain Valley in Blue Valley Stake. The people there were hungering and thirsting for the gospel, and the Lord surely gave me wonderful liberty. My subject was "What was Restored by the Restoration?" The people asked me why I finished on time, saying they could have listened for hours. I told them that enough was as good as a feast, and I didn't want to give them "religious indigestion." Do not think that I am boasting, for without the Spirit I cannot preach.

In February Patriarch Henry Schaefer and I spent a day at a women's retreat at the Buckner congregation. The theme was "Bearing a Positive Testimony and Enduring to the End." During the dedication service, Brother Schaefer spoke under inspiration to the approximately 50 ladies present. It was a message of hope, love, and patience—inviting them to overcome the many obstacles which were plaguing the Church. I was very blessed in the presentation of my classes. The next month, Brother Schaefer and I also gave ministry to more than 150 women at a one-day retreat at the Parkview congregation in Blue Valley Stake. That was also a marvelous spiritual experience.

Patriarch Curtis Cunningham, an old friend and brother of ours from South Carolina, passed away in March. He had been suffering from leukemia. When I had administered to him at his wife's request, I asked the Lord to remove his suffering. A few days later, the Lord took him home. Sister Cunningham asked me to conduct the funeral service at Warsaw, Missouri, where they were living, and then travel with them to Illinois for the interment. I was pleased to oblige.

Despite the de-emphasis of the fundamental doctrines by some in the church, there seemed to be a movement by others for more missionary work based on the "everlasting gospel." Five fine young men approached me for specialized training. They came to my home once a week to learn missionary methods and the doctrine of the Church as it was restored in these latter days. I shared some of the study material that Herman Peisker had given us in 1944.

A couple of months later, two additional young men attended my missionary classes. Their families had just gathered from Oklahoma. The young men were immersing themselves in the Holy Scriptures, which will stand them in good stead in the future. It is the Word which converts people, after all, not programs or seminars or seminaries. They really picked my brains during those classes, and it was delightful. I thought of the statement, "Old men for counsel, young men for war." Of course, this was a war of truth against darkness and deception.

Gwen and I visited a fundamental group (which some called a "splinter" or "dissident" group) in Independence one Sunday morning. There I preached to about 100 people. I had informed the apostle of my intention, asking, "*If* these Saints have strayed, is it not our duty to try to bring them back to the fold, as Jesus said?" He did not try to prohibit me from preaching there.

We were thrilled to receive a belated call from Marvia for Gwen's birthday. The call was made even better when she told us about the baptism of her twins, Mathew and Adam. With them, all of our grandsons had made covenant with the Lord in the waters of baptism.

In early April of 1987 Gwen and I took advantage of extremely cheap airfares and went to Texas to spend a few days with Trevor and Lori. He had quit his aerospace engineering job and was working full-time developing software and running his own computer software company.

We then went to McAllen, Texas, on the Mexican border, where we visited a few days with Wayne and Verniel Simmons. They shared some enlightening information with us about archaeological findings supporting the Book of Mormon. Brother Simmons had led a number of expeditions of Saints into Mexico to see the ruins. He and his wife took us over the border, and Gwen had a great time shopping in the market at Reynosa. The articles she bought were quite inexpensive since the peso was very weak—taking about 1,200 to equal a dollar.

On Sunday we had a sacrament service at McAllen, and I preached to a houseful. After our lunch we visited Padre Island, off the Texas coast. It was good to see the briny again. The next day we flew back to Houston, where we spent a couple of hours with Trevor and Lori, before continuing on to Kansas City and home.

Soon after our return, I spent a week at home as a bachelor. Gwen stayed at Beth's place and looked after our grandsons while Beth and Bill went to Padre Island for a week. It was a well-earned holiday for both of them. Beth had been overworked at the hospital since they had started doing open-heart surgery.

The public water line finally went past our property, and in May I had two men come and help me connect to it. We continued to use water from the wells on our property for irrigating the garden. It is marvelous how the Lord programmed the watering of this land of Zion. By placing the great Rocky Mountain chain where it is, He diverted the moisture of the Gulf of Mexico into the interior of this land. The moisture from the Gulf waters the land with about 35 inches of rain a year—ideal for raising all the wonderful crops that are produced in the Midwest.

Our garden was flourishing. The grape arbor was bending under the weight of grapes, and the corn was nearing harvest. However, I had to combat the cunning raccoons, which came out at night to devour the corn. This year I implemented some deterrents which stopped them. I surrounded the garden with an electric fence, which didn't kill the raccoons but surely gave them a jolt they would not forget. I also fixed a radio in the center of the corn patch and turned it on each evening to frighten them. To add to their dismay, I had the radio tuned to a rock music station. If the neighbors heard it, they must have wondered about our taste in music.

I received a letter from Apostle William Higdon informing me that some people in Australia had accused me of distributing subversive literature to the "dissident" Saints. I wrote and told him how completely misinformed he was. Six copies of the Book of Mormon were all I had ever sent to Australia. I was guilty only if the Book of Mormon were classed as subversive literature!

On several occasions, the pastor of the Lexington branch and I had administered to a woman in his congregation who had been starving herself. She was confined to bed in a pitiful condition after an evil spirit had possessed her. I asked the Lord to rebuke it in the name of Christ. Some months later, the pastor told me that I wouldn't recognize her because a marvelous miracle had occurred since those administrations. Praise be to God from Whom all blessings flow! That was the type of experience that gave me the strength to go on.

The next month Gwen and I attended a retreat at Webb City near Joplin, Missouri. There Gwen taught a class on "The Zionic Home," and I taught four classes about "The Holy Spirit." We had an excellent prayer meeting at the conclusion of the retreat, and two spiritual gifts were manifest—one through me and one through a high priest. All present were greatly blessed.

In late September, Gwen and I set out on a trip to the South. We went first to Mobile, Alabama, where we spent four days with the George Givens family and attended their branch on Sunday morning for the sacrament.

After the service, several family members met to witness the administration of Brother Ancel Jernigan. Many of us had fasted since Saturday evening. After a round of prayer in which everyone took part, I asked the Lord to send a messenger to help me because no other elder was available. The Holy Spirit came in great abundance, and I rebuked an evil spirit in the name of Jesus Christ. The brother had been starving himself to death because of the lying of the evil spirit. He was so weak he could hardly walk.

Later that afternoon, he surprised us all by rising out of his chair and walking quickly around inside the house from one room to another. He repeated the circuit three times, and his wife and daughter were truly amazed and delighted. When his son and daughter-in-law returned, he performed again for their benefit. Then he began eating in order to regain his full strength. That was truly a remarkable experience.

We traveled on to South Carolina, where we stayed in the new log home of the Willimons in the foothills of the Blue Ridge Mountains. I spoke at their branch on Sunday.

I think that it would be appropriate to relate here that the reunion grounds we had worked so hard to build in South Carolina had a very ignominious end. We had built a lovely facility with a kitchen and dining hall on the top floor and storage areas, classrooms, and a first aid room underneath. Until the time I left appointment in 1978, the whole reunion grounds had not cost more than $60,000. That included the buildings and the roads, a small lake for swimming, and a ball field. People could not get over the low cost of it all. Many of the businessmen around the area were really pleased with the project, and they assisted us in various ways by giving us cuts on prices of material and services.

However, that beautiful dining hall and everything in it

was later gutted by fire. No one knows the cause for sure, but they blamed the electrical circuits. Anyway, that was the end of the reunion grounds because the church then sold the land. It almost broke my heart. That was some of the sorrow which came with the joys of missionary work.

We then went to Charleston, where we stayed with Dot and Roy Cooper. After a few days of visiting with the Saints, we returned to Greenville and then back home. It was a wonderful three weeks; we saw many old friends and were able to minister to a number of the Saints.

We received a letter from a friend in Tahiti who mentioned a very strange cult that practiced human sacrifice on some distant islands. The French had sent a gunboat and soldiers to arrest some of the participants. The devil was certainly having a wild time there. Surely there was a need for the gospel among those people.

In December we learned of the death of Brother Merv Richards of Bulahdelah. He died after a lot of physical suffering, but rejoiced in the Lord to the last. He was one of the finest men I have ever known. One could write about him like Mormon did of Moroni, the great general: "If all men had been, and were, and ever would be, like unto Moroni, behold, the very powers of hell would have been shaken for ever; yea, the devil would never have power over the hearts of the children of men" (Alma 21:140).

After a break for the Christmas holidays, we continued the missionary classes for the older young people. There were then 14 attending, including one married couple. It was a wonderful experience to see those eager young people yearn for knowledge about the gospel.

My work project for that winter was to make a dough mixer for Gwen after I saw a picture for one in a magazine. She tried it out with some ordinary white flour first. When the loaves came out so well, she tried it with her good whole wheat flour. It saved a lot of hard work, and the home-baked bread that resulted was truly delicious.

Brother Frank Engelbrecht and I started experimenting with reproducing my missionary slides onto video tape. In the past, there had been an enormous demand for the slides and cassette tapes; and many hundreds of people had entered the waters of baptism through their use. However, the presentation needed to be modernized; and videotapes are much more convenient than slide projectors and tape players. Brother Engelbrecht operated the video camera and slide projector as I spoke the message that accompanied the slides. People in America still loved my accent, and that helped.

One Sunday, Gwen and I went to June Roth's for the dedication (consecration) of her home to the work of the Kingdom. We were joined by her family and Brother and Sister Gary Butterworth. Gary offered a prayer and read a scripture, and I spoke about what the Lord required in a Zionic home. I then offered the prayer of consecration.

We attended the seventies' banquet Saturday evening before the 1988 World Conference. That was my last official function as a seventy in the Reorganized Church of Jesus Christ of Latter Day Saints. I had been ordained a seventy in Tahiti by Apostle George Mesley in 1946. Later I learned from Apostle Roscoe Davey that the presidents of seventy had a very pronounced experience at the time my name came up for consideration. He assured me that I need never doubt as to my calling being divine. That has stood me in good stead over the 42 years I served in that office before I was honorably released from the First Quorum of Seventy. Although I was released, I felt the same power as before and knew that the Lord called me to continue preaching the gospel to the children of men.

During the year, I preached at Marshall, Kingsville, Blue Springs, Bates City, Oak Grove, Maple Grove, Grain

Valley, and Odessa in Missouri and ministered at priesthood and women's retreats. I was still getting so many calls to preach and teach that I had to refuse some.

An odd thing happened one Sunday during the sacrament service at the Odessa Branch, where I was to give the communion address. We had all the preliminaries over and the emblems served, and it was time for me to speak. It was 11:40 when I started. The pastor had said, "Never mind the clock." When I bent my head down to read the scripture, I barely noticed the deacon set the clock back 20 minutes. I told the congregation, "You have a sneaky deacon here." As far as I am aware, that was the first time that had ever happened to me. However, I followed *my* watch and finished about 12:05.

The summer of 1988 brought a severe drought to much of the nation. Our temperature was over 100° for days on end. My poor garden was feeling the impact; but I was able to pump most of the water it needed, so the effect was not too bad. The Lord was very kind to us, and we had a good harvest.

The day after Thanksgiving, Gwen and I set out on our last journey together to Australia. We were met by Mel Clark in Hawaii and stayed at his home, which is on the side of Oahu opposite Honolulu. He acted as our native guide and chauffeur as we toured the island.

We then flew to Cairns on the north Queensland coast and spent four days, staying at the Colonial Club, a resort hotel. While there, we caught the train up to Kuranda in the mountain range—having enjoyed the beautiful trip so much previously, we decided to take it again. While on a boat tour to visit a rain forest near Cairns, we saw some aborigines washing their clothes in the river. They were beating them with sticks, which reminded us of the way some of the natives in Tahiti did their laundry. At a stop on the river trip, some aborigines put on a concert featuring their native dances and music. They tried to teach one of the white men in our group how to play the didgeridoo—a long hollow stick—and the results were hilarious since they were also playing a prank on him.

We caught a large catamaran tour boat out to Green Island on the Great Barrier Reef. An underwater observation room provided us a fine view of the tropical fish in their natural habitat. As we were visiting Green Island, Christmas carols were playing, including "Winter Wonderland"—which seemed quite out of place on the tropical island with the temperature close to 100°.

On December 5 we arrived in Brisbane, where we were met by my sister Mavis. We stayed with her in the family home while we were in Brisbane. Our mother was in a nursing home, and we visited her each day. We had an enjoyable couple of weeks with our friends and relatives. Mavis drove us to Maroochydore and along the Maroochy River, where our family had lived for a few years.

We visited Ted and Val Miles. He had served with the police force in New Guinea and had a fascinating collection of native weapons and artifacts. We also visited Harry and May Steadman in Murwillumbah in New South Wales, where I once again saw the spectacular Mount Warning. From Brisbane we took a boat trip along the Brisbane River to the Lone Pine animal sanctuary. Then we visited Len and Val Edgeworth at Tarragindi and Gwen's brother David, whom we saw in Toowoomba.

We enjoyed a family reunion dinner at my Aunt May Sorensen's house in Sherwood. My mother was able to be there with us, along with my two sisters, my brother-in-law, Allan Wright, and my cousin Ettie. We all realized that this would probably be the last time we would see my mother in this life, since she was nearly 95 and very frail. Despite the sad feelings, I was comforted by the reassurance that her reward was secure.

At last we had to bid farewell. We then flew to Sydney, where we were met by Marvia and her family and by our niece Carynne and her young son Matthew. From Marvia's home in Newcastle, we could see beautiful white cockatoos in the trees. Although quite expensive in America, those birds are very common in the wild in Australia, even in a city like Newcastle.

We enjoyed Christmas with Marvia, Terry, and our three teenage grandsons. Trevor and Lori had planned to arrive Christmas morning from America, but their journey was delayed by a fuelers' strike in Sydney. Consequently, we had to eat Christmas dinner without them. We met them later at the Williamtown airport. The following day we had another feast so that Trevor and Lori would not miss out.

Trevor rented a car and drove us to Nelson's Bay for a pleasant day's outing. Soon after, we packed Marvia's minivan, Terry's car, and Trevor and Lori's car and set out for Tiona, where we welcomed the new year of 1989. After spending a couple of days with us at Tiona, Trevor and Lori continued up the coast to visit our relatives in Brisbane. The rest of us spent two wonderful weeks at Tiona. I did a lot of hiking, mainly with Michael; he was amazed at my agility. We went to Flat Rock twice and right over Booti Booti. I wanted videos of the beautiful panorama of Tiona from there—and I got them. One afternoon Gwen and I enjoyed a walk on the beach to Booti and back. I also went fishing with Terry and the twins; we enjoyed eating the fish and some crabs that we caught.

While staying there, we visited Barry and Wendy Ballard, who used to attend our youth camps in the 1960s; and we enjoyed a barbeque with Bob and Bev Wilkinson from Tamworth. It was wonderful renewing old friendships.

A baptismal service was held at Tiona for Alva Robinson's 11-year-old daughter (the granddaughter of Brother and Sister Harold Pollard, the former Tiona caretakers). Just before the service started, a man came forward and asked for baptism. To my utter amazement, it was Ellis Stewart, formerly of Anna Bay, with whom I had labored many years. What joy filled my soul as we baptized both of them and confirmed them in the Green Cathedral! A large number of on-lookers were there, and a wonderful spirit pervaded the whole service. The nonmembers were favorably impressed. I would have loved the opportunity to be the missionary there again, for the field was white and truly ready to harvest.

Upon our return to Newcastle, we celebrated the 14th birthday of our twin grandsons, Mathew and Adam. I also finished some of the work I was doing around the house for Marvia and Terry.

Roy and Daphne Schubert, whom I had baptized years earlier, took Gwen and me to their home at Werris Creek for a weekend. The drive was pleasant; near Tamworth we stopped at a lookout called "Who'd-a-thought-of-it." I wonder who thought of that!

On Sunday we worshiped in the home of our hosts; and there I blessed their grandson, the baby of Helen and Peter Archer. Bev and Bob Wilkinson and quite a few nonmember relatives were present. We caught the train back to Newcastle on Monday. Brother Schubert was an engineer for the New South Wales Railway. Because he furnished us with first class tickets, we had a comfortable ride in an air-conditioned coach.

While in Newcastle we visited with many old friends, including newly baptized Ellis Stewart and his wife Val. Gwen really enjoyed renewing her friendship with Agnes Johnson.

At the end of January, 1989, we went to Sydney, where

we spent a few days with Joan Flood, Frank Flood's sister. While there, we visited Don and Marge Alberts. He had been the bishop of the Australian Mission during my assignment to New South Wales in the 1960s. Gwen and I then rode on the ferry from Circular Quay across beautiful Sydney Harbour to Manly, which was one of the highlights of our sojourn in Sydney.

Finally the time came for me to say farewell to my homeland forever. Although I did not know for certain that it would be my last visit to Australia, I realized that I was getting too old for such a long and demanding trip.

We flew to Tahiti and were met by Jean and Estelle Tapu, who were our hosts for the next two weeks. After spending two days in Papeete, we flew in a little airplane to Apataki, a coral island about 200 miles from Tahiti.

During the sacrament service Sunday morning, Gwen and I caused quite a stir. Because a woman was up front and gave the invocation and the blessing on the bread, we refused to partake of the emblems when the elder serving them came to us. That really bothered the native Saints because it was a sign to them that we were living in a sinful state! After the service they welcomed us with a reception and beautiful flower headdresses and *heis*. I told Gwen that she looked like a queen. When given the opportunity to address the Saints, I explained the reason that we did not partake of the sacrament. I assured them that we were not living in sin, but it was because of things that were happening in the church in the *fenua roa* (big land).

On Tuesday we went on a small outboard motorboat over the ocean to the island of Kaukura. When I preached at our church there on Wednesday night, the Lord again blessed me with the language. We had another welcoming service and a tour of the island. On Thursday we left for the island of Aratua, which was one of the worst hit by the cyclone of 1983. Sunday morning I preached in Tahitian with good liberty to a large crowd—much to their surprise since we had been away so long. Of course, I knew that the fluency with which I spoke came from the Lord.

On our trip back to Apataki, the sea was dead calm so we were able to engage in some deep-sea fishing. I hooked a big bonito; but as I was reeling it in, a shark grabbed it. What a fight ensued! However, the shark was too strong, and it got away with my fish.

Gwen and I had enjoyed serving the Saints in those outlying islands. Evidently we were the only whites to have visited them for some time. Back in Tahiti we stayed at the home of Jean and Estelle. Our good friend Emere Mervin, who was 81 years old, caught a bus from Papeete to visit us. All too soon we boarded a plane for our flight home.

Despite a wonderful trip, it was good to finally get home. I was soon deluged with requests to preach and teach from pastors of RLDS congregations and from some of the numerous "Restoration branches" which had recently formed. Several thousand Saints—including most of those in our home branch of Oak Grove—were meeting in more than 200 fundamental groups. I found a fruitful field of ministry among them. In Wilburton, Oklahoma, I preached two nights at a reunion where 510 fundamental Saints were in attendance.

After Gwen and I returned from Tahiti, some things occurred which caused me to take a rather drastic action. I was being left out of preaching assignments in the congregations of the RLDS Church, so I asked the apostle in charge of the Central Field why that was happening. In all, I visited with five different apostles and four stake presidents who had some authority over areas where I worked.

Each of them said that it was because I was not upholding the present program of the church—"The Faith to Grow Program"—and all its ramifications.

Instead, I was preaching the everlasting gospel as contained in the Scriptures—just as I had been doing for 40 years and as I had been directed to do by the Lord!

I was concerned about changes in basic doctrine and believed the new program had proved to be a dismal failure. The last *World Conference Bulletin* showed no growth in church membership in the U.S. and Canada for the past two years. The Presiding Bishopric's report showed a loss of at least 8,000 tithing filers; and matrimonial statistics—with one divorce in every two marriages among church members—were no better than those of the world.

I told RLDS Church leaders that I liked the slogan "Faith to Grow" but that I treated it differently from them. I taught faith to grow spiritually, economically (stewardship), and numerically (membership and missionary work).

Finally the local stake president said that if I continued to preach to the "dissident groups," he would silence me. I informed him that Christ had called upon me to preach the everlasting gospel and that I was responsible to Him rather than men. I told him that I was not able to minister with men and women who had departed so far from the teachings of the Lord Jesus Christ. If I had the invitation to teach and preach the gospel to the fundamental Saints, I told him that I would not refuse.

Soon I was operating as a seventy exclusively to the hundreds of fundamental Restoration branches. We were again having excellent spiritual experiences. I am sure that the Lord was not angry with me, because my preaching and teaching were more powerful than ever—even though I was aging. However, Gwen and I never removed our membership from the RLDS Church, and I did not resign from my priesthood before the Lord.

☼ ☼ ☼

In April I taught a class on the Book of Mormon at the Stone Church in Independence. It was quite a challenge. The next weekend we went to the Restoration branch at Decatur City, north of Lamoni, Iowa, where I was to preach two sermons, one at 11 a.m. and the other at 2:30 p.m. But when I awoke on Sunday morning, I had a very sore throat—it was nearly swollen closed. I knew that I had no hope of preaching without divine aid. I asked Carl McGuire to administer to me—which he did, assuring me that the Lord would bless me. When I started to preach that morning, all my sore throat symptoms left me. With all the talking I did at the potluck dinner which followed, my throat began to get sore again. But I received another blessing when I stood to preach at 2:30, and I completed my work with no inconvenience.

The following month we traveled to Woodbine, Iowa, where I visited and preached. We stayed with Karen and Lee Killpack, Bill McGuire's sister and brother-in-law,

When we returned home, I continued reproducing video tapes of basic lectures on the faith of Christ's Church as taught by the earlier missionaries. The videos were still being used effectively to convert people to Christ. I charged only a nominal fee to cover the costs of the tapes and wear and tear on my copying machines.

In June, 1989, Marvia called from Australia to tell us that my mother had just departed this life. We appreciated receiving the news so promptly, and we were especially grateful to my sisters Mavis and Silvia for taking such good care of Mother during those last few years.

Mother lived great, and she died great at the age of 95. I am sure that her eternal spirit is now in the paradise of God. What a reward that is to her! She remained faithful to her baptismal covenant and endured to the end, which warrants salvation. I thank God for her resoluteness and courage—often against severe odds—when she upheld the truth of the everlasting gospel, the truth of the Book of Mormon, and the revelations of God to His latter-day people. I had a wonderful mother. The greatest thing she did for her three children, after giving us life, was to share the message of salvation through Jesus Christ our Lord. She was valiant in her testimony of the everlasting gospel, and great shall be her reward in realms of eternal light.

▾ Vivian receiving his retirement plaque from President Wallace B. Smith at the 1978 RLDS World Conference

▲ Sorensen "dream retirement home" near Oak Grove, Missouri, with vegetable gardens beyond the stream

▼ Richard McGuire driving Grandpa's minidozer

▼ Vivian Sorensen—"a man outstanding in his field"

▲ Vivian baptizing in Lake Wallis, Tiona Reunion Grounds

▼ Gwen, Beth, and Vivian posing with Trevor C. Sorensen, doctor of engineering, University of Kansas, 1979

▲ Lori and Trevor Sorensen, Houston, November 24, 1984

▲ Estelle Tapu and Gwen at a native banquet

◂ Vivian and Gwen in Tahiti during retirement years

▾ Jean and Estelle Tapu opening oyster shells and searching for pearls

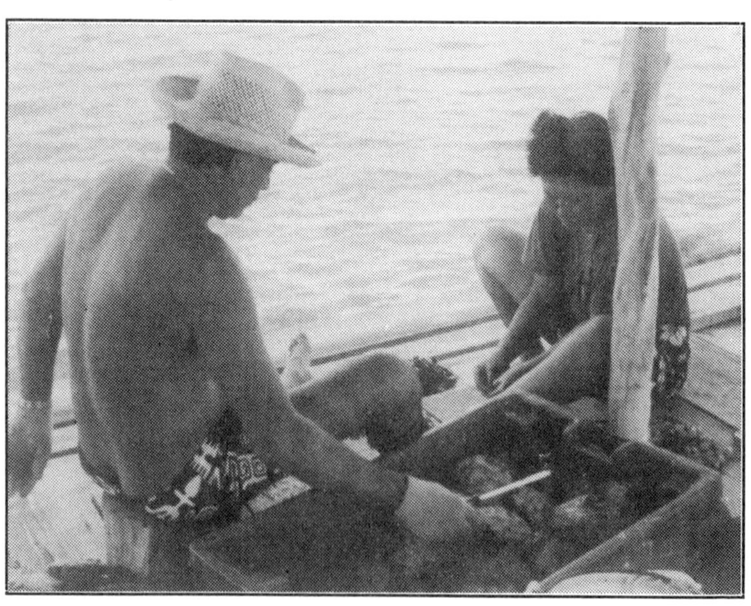

▲ A typical, friendly reception by the young Tahitian Saints

▼ Sorensen home on Beverly Road, Independence, Missouri

▸ Vivian visiting his 94-year-old mother, Ruby Sorensen, in Brisbane, 1988

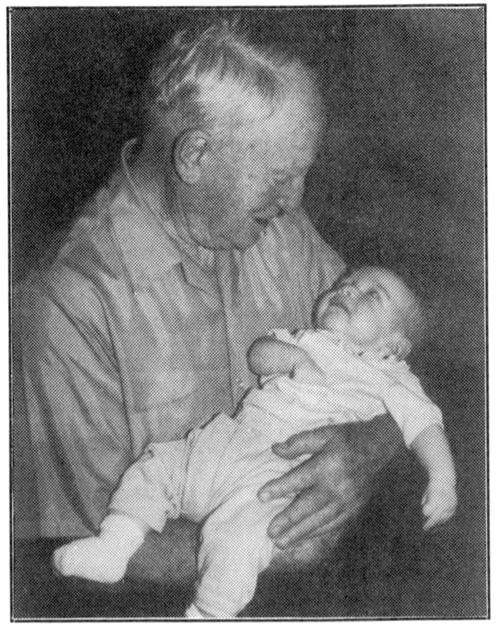

◂ Vivian and his granddaughter, Angela Sorensen, December, 1991

CHAPTER 13

Fulfillment of a Dream

In late August of 1989, an unexpected opportunity allowed Gwen and me to fulfill a lifelong dream to visit Europe. Trevor and Lori had invited us to join them there for a couple of weeks. They left the U.S. about a week earlier than we did and were to meet us in London. Because they had both been to Europe before, they were to be our guides and chauffeurs.

Leaving Kansas City on a Wednesday afternoon, Gwen and I were already seated on the plane and nearly ready for takeoff. Suddenly our names were called, and we were asked to go to the front of the plane. There Beth and Bill, along with Ruth Flood—who had all been delayed on their way to the airport—were waiting to see us off. After about five minutes with them, we had to return to our seats. We were touched that the airline personnel had allowed them to come on board and see us like that.

Strange as it seemed, we had to go to Dallas-Ft. Worth to catch a DC-10 for Europe. Before long we had a beautiful view of the glistening lights of Montreal, Canada.

After arriving at Gatwick Airport, England, we cleared customs and immigration very easily. Since we were a little early, Trevor and Lori had not yet arrived. There was a bit of consternation, and we hoped that everything would be all right. After all, we were in a big airport in one of the biggest cities in the world—and not a soul that we knew. After a short while I felt a tap on the shoulder and heard the words, "Hi, Dad." I was relieved to see our son and daughter-in-law.

Trevor had some bad news for us—my camcorder and his beautiful cameras had been stolen in Brussels a couple of days earlier. Even though the camera cases were locked out of view in a rental car, someone smashed a window of the car and grabbed them. The irony of it all was that the camcorder was American; therefore it would not work with the European system, and it would have been hard for a thief to sell. I made do with the 35mm camera I brought with me and my microcassette audio recorder.

We rented a car and drove to the Clearlake Hotel across from Hyde Park in central London, where Gwen and I rested from our trip. That afternoon we set off on foot and by the Underground (subway) to see London. We decided first to visit St. Paul's Cathedral, which was designed by Sir Christopher Wren in the 17th century. We thought it was absolutely magnificent. There we heard the choir practicing and saw the names and statues of notable people of the British Empire, some of whom are buried in the cathedral. Then we went to Trafalgar Square to see the monument to Admiral Nelson. The square is also famous for its pigeons. We saw hundreds of them being fed by the tourists. Well fed, I might add—they were certainly fat! We then headed toward Westminster Abbey and Big Ben to take some pictures. We saw Number 10 Downing Street and the Queen's Horse Guard in their resplendent uniforms and armor.

Our sightseeing again entailed riding on Underground trains, which roared along at terrific speed. During World War II, it was in the Underground—the "tubes," as they are called in slang—that many of the inhabitants of London, the women and children particularly, took shelter from German bombs. Some of the Underground lines are very deep. We could imagine the platforms covered with people, always wondering whether a bomb would get through somehow or whether their homes would still be standing when they emerged.

The next day we went into Westminster Abbey, where we were fascinated by the Gothic architecture, and then hurried to Buckingham Palace to see the changing of the guard. An enormous crowd of people watched the guards, who were dressed in bright red uniforms and big bearskin busbies (hats).

After lunch we took the Underground to the Tower of London, a dismal-looking place because it had been a prison. We saw the Tower Bridge, which goes across the Thames River. The river was a little wider than I had expected. In fact, a big cruiser, the *H.M.S. Belfast*, was anchored on the far side as a war memorial; yet there was still plenty of room for other boats and ships to go past.

Then we parted ways. Lori and Gwen went to Madame Tussaud's wax museum but found that the line was half a mile long. Their next stop was the famous Harrod's, one of the largest department stores in the world. They said they could have stayed there for a week.

Trevor and I walked from store to store looking for a replacement for his camera. Trevor is taller than I am, and his legs are longer. While I could keep up the same pace, I fell a bit behind every step because he took longer strides. But by panting and puffing I kept up with him fairly well. It started to rain, so we decided to go to the Imperial War Museum, which we found was comparable to the one in Canberra, Australia.

After that we met Gwen and Lori and drove south toward Southampton. The motels were full due to the long weekend. However, we were able to find accommodations at the White Hart Inn in nearby Salisbury, where some king or queen had once stayed centuries earlier.

The next day we looked at the magnificent Salisbury Cathedral and then drove to see the famous Stonehenge monoliths. They were just sitting in a field—but we had no trouble locating them because of all the tour buses parked nearby.

Our plans to see the Roman baths in the city of Bath were thwarted by heavy holiday traffic. We saw houses on the hills in the distance but decided to bypass the city.

Finally we crossed the border into Wales at the Severn River. We could see the city of Bristol in the distance. Due to the large number of chimneys discharging smoke, it appeared to be an industrial city. As we started to drive through the Welsh countryside, we noticed that the walls of the houses were all white. Most were two or three stories high, usually with slate or thatched roofs. In England most houses were a darker red brick color.

We began to see hills and then small mountains. Trevor took us through the Brecon Beacons National Park, where we enjoyed the beautiful mountainous scenery. It was a nice change after the lowlands of England. There was little farmland, but we could see sheep in the distance—tiny white dots against a green and gray background of cleared land on the mountainsides. Trevor said that northern Wales had many castles. We saw one, partly in ruins, which dated back to about A.D. 800, making it nearly 1,200 years old.

Back in England we passed through the Midlands, a region that was not as pretty as the areas farther south; part of the land was quite drab. Late in the day we arrived in Stratford-upon-Avon to view the birthplace of William Shakespeare. I never saw a larger crowd of people at a shrine than I did there; Trevor could not even find a place to park, so he had to let us out to walk. Gwen and I went down the street, took a picture of Shakespeare's birthplace, and looked in the windows. But we didn't have the time to take a tour inside. At a park by the Avon River, we saw a statue of Shakespeare.

After we left Stratford-upon-Avon, we drove through the outskirts of the city of Oxford, one of the great seats of learning in the world. We had a lot of trouble finding accommodations but finally located a new hotel in Rochester, just southeast of London. We enjoyed a fairly good night's sleep and set off toward Dover and the Continent.

The white cliffs of Dover are very imposing. Only the older people may remember the World War II song which says, "There'll be blue birds over the white cliffs of Dover . . .tomorrow—when the world is free." At Dover we visited the Painted House, some Roman ruins which were recently discovered beneath dirt, grass, and sand. Some of the paint was still preserved. The house had a number of rooms with a clever central heating system. The Romans built a fire outside the house, and the heat came through ducts and warmed the whole place. We were told that it was the best Roman relic in all of England.

After Trevor and Lori returned the rental car, we boarded a hydrofoil to cross the English Channel. The white cliffs of Dover made an impressive sight from the English Channel as they gradually faded into the distance. Because it was a very windy day, the channel was rough. We were glad that the hydrofoil skimmed over the waves. While it pitched around quite a bit, the big ships and vehicular ferries we saw were being tossed around even more. The hydrofoil did about 40 mph, and the trip to Belgium took about two hours.

We turned into shore as we approached Oostende, Belgium. All along the waterfront we saw massive concrete bunkers and fortifications from World War II. Once ashore we had to hurry to catch our train to Brussels. That train was as smooth as any I had ridden on. I think the rails were welded as they have done in Australia in certain places; we did not hear the clickety-clack, clickety-clack that occurs when the rails are not welded. The train sped along over the beautiful Belgian countryside, which was mainly farming area. There was a large quantity of corn growing (we did not see much corn in England) and a lot of cattle, mostly Holstein-Friesians. Canals with trees along each side were winding through the fields. The houses we saw in Belgium were of a similar style to those in England and Wales, but they were somewhat narrower.

We disembarked at Brussels North, where we had to change trains for Luxembourg. After about 20 minutes our train, the *Italian Express*, arrived. But we soon discovered that it wasn't much of an express! The train was very long, and we saw that our second-class carriage was at the far end of the platform. With Trevor carrying their heavy luggage, he and the ladies soon got ahead of me as I struggled with our big, heavy suitcase. I was puffing away badly when Trevor came running back to help me after getting his wife and mother aboard. By the time we had reached the car, the doors were closed in preparation for departure. In two or three languages (maybe even including Tahitian!) I said to the conductor, "Open, open, please open!" Reluctantly he finally opened the door, and we climbed into our carriage. After all that, the train did not start moving for several more minutes.

We were supposed to get into Luxembourg that evening. But I noticed the train was not running very fast, and we would be late. Suddenly we came to a halt in the middle of nowhere, somewhere between Brussels and the border with Luxembourg. A conductor told us it might take two hours to fix the engine trouble. It did. As we just sat talking, we started to get quite hot since the air conditioning was off. They even turned off the lights in our car (except for a few emergency lights), I suppose to save the batteries. It was soon dark outside.

Because we were becoming quite thirsty, Trevor asked the conductor if they had any drinks. He must have thought we wanted alocholic drinks, because he said no. I then suggested to Trevor, "Let's go for a walk and see what we can find." We walked through about six or seven carriages. Near the end of the train, we saw some people bargaining with a porter about drinks. When our turn came, we were able to get some ice-cold drinks that he had in a refrigerator. On the way back to our car, many people saw us with cans of soft drinks and asked—mostly in French or German, but a few in English—where we got them. I answered one lady in French, "Oh, about six or seven carriages down." She nearly hugged me and headed off, as had others we told.

Finally the train started moving slowly with a jerky motion. We arrived in Luxembourg about midnight, nearly three hours late. So much for the *Italian Express*! We were fortunate to find accommodations at that hour at the Hotel Empire, just across the street from the station. After checking in, Gwen and I collapsed onto our bed—only to discover that it had a mattress with weak springs (the type I hated) so we rolled right into the middle.

After a short night's sleep, we awoke to the terrific noise of trains, cars, and airplanes taking off. We ate a continental breakfast of rolls, butter, jam, and some cheese. After breakfast Lori and Trevor went to get a rental car. They returned with a nice-looking Ford Scorpio. We piled everything into the car and set off for Germany.

Gwen probably thought of all her ancestors on the Peisker side, who had come from Prussia and Germany. We drove through Germany for a while on two-lane highways and then traveled on the autobahn, which is a mad speedway. Trevor was driving 80 mph, and many cars went by us like lightning.

Then Trevor said he would like to show us a little of

France, which had not been in our plans. After traveling over the lovely rolling hills in Germany, where the farms looked so green and beautiful, we got off the autobahn and cut across the northeast corner of France to the big city of Strasbourg. We stopped briefly for lunch, so Gwen and I got out of the car and actually stood on French soil.

Then we crossed the border into Germany and went into the Black Forest, where we took the more scenic highways. The forest was so dense that not much light came through the trees. We visited the ancient city of Freiburg, which has many old buildings and cobblestone streets. The Freiburg cathedral had particularly large and beautiful stained-glass windows.

Leaving Freiburg, we crossed the Rhine River and entered the city of Basel, Switzerland. We found a youth hostel, where we could spend the night. A little creek ran nearby, gurgling as it made its way to the Rhine. Trevor did not want to risk losing his parking place at the hostel, so we walked nearly a mile around central Basel looking for a place to eat. We passed a couple of very expensive restaurants and finally found a McDonald's restaurant. By then we were famished so the food tasted wonderful. The youth hostel was quite inexpensive compared to hotels, but it was very cramped. The four of us had to sleep in bunk beds in one tiny room. If someone was using the small washbasin, there was not enough space for anyone else to stand up! Notwithstanding, we slept fairly well.

After the typical continental breakfast, we went looking for Hermann Peisker's goldsmith shop. Trevor had taken a picture of it in 1979. Another Herman Peisker, born in Australia, was Gwen's uncle and a missionary for the RLDS Church. The Peiskers had originally come from Prussia and Leipzig, and we thought the Swiss family might be related to Gwen. When we finally found the place, it was closed.

Just as we were about to leave, a light came on and the door was unlocked. Two ladies were working there, one of whom was Frau Peisker. Trevor explained in German why we had come and showed her a paper Gwen had brought, giving the birthdate and location of the Peiskers back in Prussia. The lady did not know much about her late husband's family tree, and Gwen was quite disappointed that our inquiry led to a dead end.

We next headed for Lucerne in the lower Swiss Alps. Trevor purposely chose the back roads because they were more scenic and beautiful—with lush, green alpine pastures and snow-covered mountains in the background. The narrow houses were nearly all two, three, or four stories high, with steep gable roofs so the snow would slide off rather than crush the roofs with its weight.

Lucerne was one of the most beautiful places we saw on the whole trip. The city was built on the end of a lake where the river evidently was dammed up years ago by an earthquake. We walked over several covered pedestrian bridges that crossed the river. They were all decorated with flowers and really made a pretty picture. Then we ambled through the riverside shops and markets; Gwen bought a small, beautifully made Swiss clock.

On our way to Zurich, we noticed a large number of vineyards on the hillsides. However, we wondered what the large patches of bright colors on them were. When we got closer to them, we saw that the grapes had yellow and blue covers over them to protect them from the birds. We did not stop in Zurich, the monetary capital of the world. But as we passed through, we saw many tall buildings—including the Swiss banks.

We drove via St. Gallen on our way to Lake Constance, which is the largest lake in Switzerland and borders on Germany. It used to be a big joke to say that you knew someone who was a captain in the Swiss navy—because

Switzerland is completely landlocked. But that joke came to an end during World War II, when the Swiss built a few patrol boats to guard against the Germans. In fact, the father of one of Trevor's schoolmates in Australia was in the Swiss navy during World War II. I do not know if they have any patrol boats now, but for a while that joke certainly went flat.

We had to pass through a portion of Austria to get back into Germany. None of the border guards examined our passports; some asked a question or two, and others just waved us through.

Back in Germany, we travelled on and on and on. When we came to a town, Gwen and I would give a sigh of relief and think, "Good! Now we're going to look for a bed." But we kept going and going at a rather frantic pace—after all, there was so much to see—until even Trevor was tired out. We finally stopped at the Landgasthof (Country Guest House) Hirsch in the Bavarian village of Betzigau. Although not cheap, it was certainly good to have a hot shower and a bed.

The next morning we drove to Füssen and the nearby castles of Hohenschwangau and Neuschwanstein (the "fairy tale castle" seen so much on posters). Martin Luther had sought refuge in Hohenschwangau when he was being persecuted by the Catholic Church. King Ludwig II of Bavaria ("Mad Ludwig") lived in Hohenschwangau while his new dream castle, Neuschwanstein, was being built under his watchful eye. Both castles were set in spectacular scenery on the edge of a lake at the foot of the towering Bavarian Alps. Beautiful large pine forests surrounded the castles. Tourists of all nationalities were there by the thousands.

Neuschwanstein was certainly imposing; it could be reached only by a very steep, winding road. We were dreading having to walk up the hill; but fortunately we found a horse-drawn carriage that seated about 16 people and was pulled by two very strong draft horses. Trevor and Lori decided to walk up the hill to get some exercise, but Gwen and I were happy to ride in the carriage.

After touring that castle, we headed for another one. We drove quite a distance through mountainous terrain before we arrived at Ludwig's summer residence, Linderhof. Although it was much smaller than Neuschwanstein, it was even grander on the inside. It was incredibly elaborate with a number of beautiful crystal chandeliers. There was hardly any wall space that wasn't covered with gold-plated brass ornaments or original murals. I said to Gwen, "I wouldn't want to live in a place like this—it would get on my nerves."

Trevor pointed out Ludwig's primitive but ingenious air-conditioning system. Ice-cold water from a spring behind the residence gushed down the hillside in a large trench and cooled the air above it. Bordering hedges channeled that air into the open windows of Ludwig's bedroom at the bottom of the hill. We were glad that Trevor had been to Linderhof on two previous occasions and showed us that, since our tour guide had not mentioned it. We were also told that the first electric light system in Germany was installed at Linderhof. King Ludwig was a friend of the famous composer Richard Wagner, who used to spend time at Linderhof. Ludwig had the Venus Grotto, complete with a small lake, built inside a hill at Linderhof just for viewing a personal performance of Wagner's opera *Tannhäuser*.

At the nearby town of Oberammergau, famous for its wood carvings and the passion play performed there every few years, we were able to admire the beautiful carvings that adorn the town. South of there we visited another picturesque town, Garmisch-Partenkirchen. Many of the Bavarian, Swiss, and Austrian towns had tall houses with window boxes filled with colorful geraniums and other flowers. The outside walls of many buildings were covered with interesting murals depicting various subjects. Such towns were delightful to drive through.

Back on the German autobahn, we sped toward Salzburg, Austria, the home of Wolfgang Amadeus Mozart. On a narrow alley in downtown Salzburg, we saw the house in which he was born. We also visited the house where he composed much of his beautiful music.

Salzburg is the setting of one of our favorite movies, *The Sound of Music.* Gwen and I went on a bus tour, which took us to the places made famous by the movie. We had a humorous guide, and the tour was very enjoyable. The scenery was absolutely beautiful. It was interesting to see the differences between reality and the movie. For instance, in the opening scene of the movie Julie Andrews sang, "The hills are alive..." on a hilltop. Then she heard the bells of the abbey and ran down the hill to it. In reality, the hill where she was filmed was 15 miles from the convent, so she must have had quite a hike to get back so quickly!

We then joined Lori and Trevor, who had wandered around the city while we were on the tour. Unable to find suitable accommodations in the city (even the youth hostel was full), we drove out of Salzburg into some beautiful mountain country, where there were some scattered farms in the valleys. We found a farmhouse that took guests for a very reasonable price. It was in a lovely rural setting, with green pastures nearby and snow-capped mountains in the background. On a hill not far away was a little village with an onion-steepled church, characteristic of the Byzantine architecture of the area.

The farmhouse was typically Austrian, with the barn adjoining the back of the house. That provided extra warmth during the winter, and I suppose one got used to the smell. Outside was a cement trough with four cans of milk in it. Nearly ice-cold water from the hills ran through the trough—a wonderful way of keeping milk cool until the truck came to take it into town. It was very efficient and cost them no money for cooling.

The family spoke only German, so Trevor translated for us. The next morning, when Trevor was otherwise occupied, I was able to learn quite a lot about the farm by using my hands to talk with the farmer. For example, when I pointed to the barn and used my hands to indicate milking, he showed me the barn and his beautiful cattle feeding in stalls. The family prepared a delicious country breakfast—exactly what we were hoping for. The milk and eggs were produced on their farm, and the butter and plum jam were homemade. The people were most gracious and friendly, making us feel like honored guests and family at the same time. They even came out and waved good-bye as we left.

The four of us toured Obersalzburg, the massive fortress on the mountaintop overlooking the city. We rode a cable car up to the castle and enjoyed a glorious view of Salzburg. We also visited a museum, which contained objects dating from the medieval ages to World War II. I was especially interested in the old-fashioned pumps, which were apparently effective in pumping water to the castle.

Next we drove to Bertchesgaden in Bavaria, a beautiful village on the banks of a mountain stream. Bertchesgaden is best known for Hitler's retreat, the Eagle's Nest, which we saw perched on a nearby mountaintop. We stopped where Hitler's bodyguards had once had their barracks. Some of the buildings were later converted into the General Walker Hotel for U.S. servicemen.

Trevor took us to a beautiful lake called the Königsee. The mountains were so tall and the lake was so deep and narrow that it looked just like the fiords of Norway and Milford Sound in New Zealand. A boat took us to a church called St. Bartholomew's at the far end of the lake. At a certain spot on the trip, the engine stopped suddenly; and one of the crew played a trumpet briefly. The reverberations and echoes caused by the mountain rock faces and the surface of the lake were absolutely magnificent.

The following day we arrived in Nuremberg, which had been mostly destroyed during the war. The old part of the city is surrounded by heavy stone walls with watchtowers. Although the walls showed the scars of battle, they survived the Allied bombing fairly well. On many buildings there was still evidence of pockmarks made by shrapnel or bullets. Some places we could see the faded letters *LS* or the word *Luftschutzraum* (air-raid shelter).

We went to the huge stadium where Hitler held his famous (or infamous) Nuremberg rally of 1934, which is often shown in documentary footage. The arena had stone seats around the outside and a large central area, where thousands of people could stand. Trevor said that at least 200,000 people had been there for the 1934 rally. I was able to stand on the platform where Hitler had been; and I thought, "What a wonderful experience it would be to stand here and preach the gospel to that many people!" At the stadium we visited a museum about the Nazi concentration camps and remembered the wicked history that was made as Hitler was preparing the hearts of the people for world conquest. We thank God that Hitler failed.

In the nearby city of Fürth, we tried to locate Bud Clarkson, whom we had known in South Carolina before he came to Germany with the U.S. Army. He was not home, so Trevor just slipped a note into his mailbox.

We then drove north toward the large city of Hannover. Along the way we came very close to the border with East Germany. Gwen wondered what kept the East Germans from escaping through the forests and at night. Trevor explained that an electrified barbed wire fence, minefields, and watchtowers with guards and dogs ran along the whole border. Not many people were willing to risk their lives. It made us realize just how wonderful it is to live in a free land like America, and how important it is that we keep that freedom. However, that was September, 1989. Just two months later the Berlin Wall came crashing down, and the borders we saw were soon opened.

After a quick stop in Hannover for dinner (pizza), we continued on to Hamburg. The sun had set a little before 8 o'clock; but due to the far northern latitude, even by 9:45 the twilight had not completely faded. It was most fascinating to us.

The next day we continued north, passing through some beautiful farming country in northeastern Germany. At Puttgarden we caught the large vehicular ferry *Deutschland*, which took us across the strait to the island of Zealand in Denmark—a journey of about an hour. The ferry was almost like a big ocean liner or cruise ship. Everyone got out of their cars and went up on the decks to visit the many cafes and shops. Trevor, Lori, and I explored the ship, while Gwen relaxed in a comfortable seat and enjoyed the view on a beautiful sunny day.

As we approached land, we watched the coast of Denmark appear to rise out of the water and get closer. It was quite a thrill to be another Sorensen back in the land of his forefathers. I could tell that Trevor was excited because he kept asking if I was enjoying the trip, and "Aren't you glad to be here, Dad?" and "Wouldn't Grandpa Sorensen have loved this?"

The border officials waved us to go through, but Trevor very thoughtfully asked one of them to stamp our passports. The man graciously obliged, so all four passports have *DANMARK* on them. We can prove that at least our passports were in Denmark!

We drove on the island of Zealand toward Copenhagen, passing through some lush farming country on the way. In some areas our view was obscured by smoke because the farmers were burning off the residue of harvested crops in preparation for replanting. Before long we reached the factories and buildings of the capital city. Copenhagen is old, dating back to the 10th century. While it is quite a large city, it was not very busy on the day we arrived because it was Sunday. We checked into a new youth hostel. Although the rooms had bunk beds like the hostel in Basel, at least Gwen and I had a room to ourselves.

That afternoon we enjoyed some much-needed rest while Trevor and Lori caught up on their laundry.

On Monday we drove into the city and looked for a travel agency to take care of our return trip to America. After parking the car, we had to walk a lot. That was particularly hard on Gwen because many of the sidewalks and streets were cobblestones. Her feet started to hurt, and soon she was limping.

Not finding a travel agency nearby, I asked a passing woman if she could speak English. She replied, "Yes, a little," which seemed to be the stock reply to the question —even though she, like most Danes we met, could speak English fluently. We even heard Danes talking to each other in Danish, then (without missing a beat) switch to English for a while, then back to Danish!

We were amazed to learn that the woman was on her way to work—at a travel agency! She invited us to follow her. I told her my name was Sorensen, which she said was a common Danish name. We already knew that—Trevor had shown us a phone book with many pages of Sorensens. At the agency—named Spies—we made reservations for a flight from Amsterdam to London and confirmed our booking from London to Kansas City.

Trevor showed us the famous statue of the Little Mermaid, but I was not overly impressed with it. In the neighboring park we passed a fountain with great mythical bulls snorting water and kicking up spray as they pulled a Norse goddess in a chariot. I thought *that* was impressive! Then we went into the courtyard of the royal palace, where the guards were wearing scarlet uniforms and large bearskin busby hats.

I spoke to one of the royal guards, who was standing straight and not moving a muscle. To my surprise, he answered me in fluent English. I did not expect that because the Grenadier Guards at Buckingham Palace in London are not allowed to speak or react to tourists. After a short conversation, I thanked him and left. By then Gwen's feet were really bothering her. We went to Magazin, the largest department store in Denmark, for some lunch and relaxation. While Trevor and I left on an errand and to get the car, Gwen and Lori partook of the most effective therapeutic treatment for many women—they went shopping!

Leaving Copenhagen, we drove west across Zealand and caught a car ferry going to another island. Along the way we noticed several large three-bladed wind generators. I assumed that it must get quite windy across those islands, although on that day it was sunny and calm. We crossed over a large new bridge to Jutland, the mainland part of Denmark. Grandpa Sorensen came from northern Jutland.

As we approached the German border, Trevor thought that we should spend one more night in Denmark and spend the last of our Danish money. Stopping at the large Danish town of Aabenraa, we drove into the nearby countryside to the youth hostel, which had the luxury of a shower and bath in our room along with the usual bunk beds. After getting settled, we drove into town to find a place to eat. We had learned from experience that a good way to see a new town was to get Trevor to look for a restaurant. He eventually found an excellent one.

After a good night's sleep, we set out for Holland via Germany. We passed through Hamburg again, this time in daylight so we were able to view the extensive harbor full of large ships. Soon we were past Bremen and into Holland. We could see why the Netherlands is called "the lowlands," because it was partly below sea level. The land, crisscrossed with canals from which it was irrigated, was absolutely lush. Many Dutch houses were so beautifully painted and kept that they looked almost like dollhouses. We learned that the Dutch maintain their old windmills mostly for tradition and as tourist attractions—the government has to subsidize their operation.

In the north we drove along a huge dike which protected the land from being inundated by the North Sea. From our vantage point we could see the North Sea on one side and the Ijsselmeer (Zuider Zee) and lowlands on the other. The difference between the ocean side and the land side must have been about 40 feet. The sea breaks through occasionally. The last break was nearly 40 years ago. The Dutch allow a certain amount of sea water into the inland sea to maintain the correct salinization (salination) level to preserve the indigenous flora and fauna. It was all a tremendous engineering accomplishment.

At Leiderdorp near Amsterdam we went to the home of Ton Peschier, whom Trevor had known at the University of Kansas many years before. We met his wife, Mieke, and two young children, Bart and Judith. Trevor and Lori stayed the night with them, while Gwen and I went to a nearby hotel. We thought we were going to have a good night's rest. However, due to the noise from a wedding party, we got very little sleep.

Early in the morning Trevor took us to the airport, where we caught a British Airways flight to London. From the air we had a good view of Amsterdam, the dikes, and all we had seen from the ground. Before long we arrived at London Gatwick Airport, where we boarded an American Airlines DC-10. We trusted that the Lord would see us safely home, and He did.

The plane took us over the English and Irish countryside, then across the Atlantic. It was quite a thrill for us to see Greenland. The view was spectacular. The rugged coastline and great mountains were covered with ice as far as we could see. There were some little houses grouped along the coast. Out from the shore we saw hundreds of icebergs, which looked as if someone had shaken a salt shaker over a dark blue tablecloth.

The plane turned southwest over the Labrador coast and headed for Dallas-Ft. Worth. There we boarded a plane for Kansas City. Our great adventure in Europe—where we saw 10 countries in 14 days—was coming to an end. What a wonderful trip!

▾ Vivian, the farmer's wife and daughter, Lori, and Gwen at bed and breakfast farmhouse near Salzburg, Austria

CHAPTER 14

Twilight Years

We were home from Europe only two days before we flew to Detroit, Michigan, for a Restoration retreat with about 200 people present. It was a marvelous experience; we finally arrived home again happy but tired.

About a month later Gwen and I went to Tulsa, where I conducted a week-long preaching series, which was very well attended. I lessened my speaking appointments for the worst of the winter, but even then I still had quite enough to keep from getting rusty.

In January, 1990, we traveled 950 miles to Mobile, Alabama, where we stayed with George and Camille Givens and I administered to the sick and preached—much to the joy of the Saints there, who were quite isolated. We also stopped at Tuscaloosa, Alabama, and visited a high priest, Brother Homer Humble, and his wife.

In Mississippi on the way home, we were almost involved in a terrible accident. We were only about 100 yards behind a van and a pickup truck which slammed into each other on a two-lane highway. We had to dodge debris scattered across the road. Both vehicles went off the road and into a deep ditch. The man in the pickup was killed. The other man's leg went through the windshield, and he was tangled up with the steering wheel. We later learned that he died as well.

We were very thankful to the Almighty for our protection. A half minute earlier, and we could have been part of the accident. Because we were the only eyewitnesses, we stayed until the highway patrolmen came. They were extremely grateful to us for waiting; many people would have left, not wanting to be involved.

In early February Gwen complained of pains in her chest for two mornings, as well as being very tired and enervated. The doctor told me to take her immediately to the hospital in Independence, fearing that she might have a heart condition. After many tests, the doctors there determined that it was not a heart attack, but a pneumonia virus. Gwen spent nine days in the hospital.

The RLDS World Conference occurred in April, 1990, but Gwen and I were not delegates and did not attend. The major event of the conference was the groundbreaking ceremony for the new temple. It was rather amazing that one of the main Kansas City television stations gave the RLDS ceremony a scant 30 seconds of coverage. On the same day they gave the Buckner Restoration Branch, one of the "splinter" groups, 105 seconds of coverage on the groundbreaking ceremony for its new church building.

Gwen and I drove to Lamoni, Iowa, in late April, where I went fishing with Carl McGuire on Saturday afternoon and preached to a large Restoration group at Decatur City on Sunday.

In May we were saddened to learn of the death of my sister Silvia by cancer. She was 71 years old. Silvia was a fine lady and always trying to do good for someone. We were especially thankful for the way she had helped give good care during Mother's last years. Her smiling face and sense of humor would be greatly missed.

Gwen and I attended John McGuire's graduation in May. The ceremony was held in the RLDS Auditorium, a favorite graduation location for many of the high schools in the Independence area. He was the first of our grandsons to graduate from high school, and we were happy for him.

On the other hand, our hearts grieved for Marvia's boys. We had recently learned that Marvia and Terry were getting divorced. Her teenage boys particularly needed a loving, strcng father and united home to nurture them.

During the summer of 1990, Gwen and I attended six reunions. The first was for the Central Missouri Restoration Branches at El Dorado Springs. I preached most of the sermons for the 145 registered, plus visitors. The second reunion was at Wilburton, Oklahoma, with 425 registered, 125 of whom were children. The children responded very well with prayers and testimonies at the prayer meetings each morning. I had the evening preaching services. Gwen spoke to the women and the senior high group. The next reunion was at Excelsior Springs, Missouri, with 252 registered. That was followed by the Decatur City reunion held about 20 miles north of Lamoni, Iowa. After that was a reunion at Woodbine, Iowa. Then we went to Michigan for our sixth reunion. Altogether I was privileged to preach and bring ministry to more than 1,000 people during those six reunions.

One Sunday evening in July I preached to approximately 1,100 fundamentalist Saints in the William Chrisman High School auditorium in Independence. It looked like a sea of faces in front of me. I felt very inadequate to minister to so many hungry people, but the Lord used me to preach a much-needed sermon about truth.

Gwen received a letter from her brother, David, along with some tapes and Messianic Jewish newspapers, which were most interesting. It gave us some knowledge of the great crisis that was shaping up in the Middle East and how the thousands of Russian Jews then migrating were being absorbed into Israel.

Although David had been baptized into the RLDS

Church as a boy, during his youth he had abandoned the church and traveled west to central Australia to become a drover (cowboy) in the outback. After so many years of rejecting Christianity and its precepts, he had a conversion experience. It was wonderful to see the transformation in his life. David was still very religiously inclined and had joined the Assembly of God Church. Later in 1990 he went to Newcastle and took care of Marvia's boys while she was away for two months in Sydney with her work. He was a good influence on the boys and would not put up with too much nonsense.

Trevor accepted a job as an aerospace project engineer with Bendix Field Engineering in Alexandria, Virginia, near Washington, D.C. In mid-August he and Lori loaded their belongings in a U-Haul truck and drove from Houston to visit with us on their way east.

In September Gwen and I flew to Michigan for a Book of Mormon Day at Port Huron. Approximately 300 people attended, and we had a very fine experience. We bore our testimonies of the truthfulness and need for the Book of Mormon, and others shared recent archaeological finds. There had been some wonderful discoveries recently in Central America and Mexico, which we felt substantiated the claims of the book.

The next month Gwen and I flew to Florida, where we had two weeks of rest at a condominium at Cocoa Beach, just south of the Kennedy Space Center. Michael Gatrost, the son of an old friend of mine, Lyle Gatrost, allowed us the use of the condo. It was wonderful to spend a relaxing time at the beach. As an added bonus, we were thrilled to see the night launch of a rocket from Cape Canaveral. The noise was deafening, and the exhaust lit up the land almost like daylight. While we were in Florida, I preached at a retreat in Orlando.

In December we spent two weeks in Texas, where the

Saints treated us kindly. I was very busy preaching almost every night and also twice on the Sundays we were there. The first week we were in Houston, where we stayed with Wilbur and Loma Hole. They took us to see the main items of interest in that huge, modern city. One place of particular interest to us was the IMAX movie theater. The screen was six stories high and 80 feet wide. It made a trip down the Grand Canyon most realistic and breathtaking. We also saw *The Dream Is Alive*, an IMAX film about the space shuttle in which Trevor appeared several times when he was working in Mission Control. We were so excited about it that we went back to see it a second time! The Holes took us for a delicious seafood dinner in Galveston, where we saw some of the oil rigs in the Gulf of Mexico.

We were then taken north to Bryan, where we stayed at the home of Moe and Betty Hair. Our final weekend in Texas was an activity for priesthood and wives at Marlin. We had a wonderful time and reveled in the open-hearted hospitality of the Texas Saints. We returned to Houston and stayed overnight at the home of Les and Sue McGuire, who had attended some of my preaching services the previous week. The next day they drove us to the airport for our return flight.

About that time we heard that some of our Australian friends believed we had started our own church. Let me clarify that neither Gwen nor I removed our names from the rolls of the RLDS Church. However, I refused to preach and teach certain things I felt were departures from the truth. We were attempting to hold to the everlasting gospel and finding great joy in so doing.

In February of 1991, we received quite a shock when it was discovered that Gwen had cancer of the colon. Beth recommended Dr. Ron Turner, an elder, for the surgery, knowing him to be an excellent and careful surgeon. He removed a piece of colon and the tumor. The specialist who talked with us after the surgery recommended a special new chemotherapy treatment to kill any cancerous nodes. He said that with the treatment, Gwen had a 50-50 chance of surviving. She agreed to chemotherapy, which she received every week for a year.

In April Brother Norman Melling came from Australia to see for himself the conditions that prevail here in the church. He learned that several men had organized "The Restoration Church of Jesus Christ of Latter Day Saints" and ordained eight apostles to make a majority of a quorum of 12. I could not and cannot support them because I have had no spiritual confirmation of the truth of the movement, which was started by a supposed "inspired" document delivered by Norman Page. Later our old friend, Marcus Juby, became the president and "prophet" of that church. Their movement included many of our old friends from the Carolinas—Doyle Launius, Ed Geiersbach, Leman Johnson, and others. Norman Melling, Neville Churchill, and some other Saints in Brisbane eventually joined that church—even though I warned Norman of my misgivings about it.

In May I taught a priesthood class, and the following weekend I flew to Dallas to attend a priesthood retreat. Gwen and I attended the Central Missouri Restoration Branches' reunion at El Dorado Springs in mid-June. The following week we drove to Oklahoma, where we enjoyed a rich experience at the Wilburton reunion. More than 400 people were there, including 195 youngsters from three months to 18 years of age. I preached all the sermons but one and really enjoyed the opportunity to witness for my Lord.

In July, 1991, as we were returning from the Wilburton reunion, we were involved in a traffic accident on the busy Will Rogers Turnpike near Miami, Oklahoma. I saw a car on a bridge and slowed down, thinking that it was moving slowly. By the time I realized that it was not moving, I could not swerve to the left since a truck was coming and could not go to the right because we might go through the bridge rails into the river. Despite heavy braking, we slammed into the car. Fortunately we had our seat belts on. That and the good Lord, I am sure, saved our lives. We were taken by ambulance to Miami Baptist Hospital, where we were examined and X-rayed. Gwen suffered multiple bruises, and I sustained one broken rib.

I phoned Bill McGuire from the hospital, and he and his friend Mark Sevy drove to Oklahoma in Mark's huge van. While we were waiting for them to arrive, some members of the Baptist Church took us from the emergency room to a nearby recovery house owned by the hospital, where they kindly fed us a meal and gave us a place to rest. When Bill and Mark arrived, they hoisted our car onto a trailer they had brought. Then they made a soft bed for Gwen in the van and had me lie on an extended bucket seat for the 160-mile trip home.

Our car was not worth repairing, so the insurance company paid for a replacement. Although we did not have serious injuries, I determined that I was not in love with broken ribs—especially when I sneezed.

Just in time to cheer us up from our pain and sorrows, we received some joyful news. On July 19, 1991, our first granddaughter, Angela Nicole Sorensen, was born to Lori and Trevor in Virginia. We had waited a long time for a granddaughter after the six grandsons who were born to our daughters. According to a proud and doting father, Angela was just beautiful.

Later that same month I flew in a small plane to Marlin, Texas, with Dr. Milo Farnham for a special weekend event for priesthood and wives. It was 600 miles away, and the flight took less than four hours. Gwen had been invited, but she was still too bruised from the car accident to go.

In August she and I attended a reunion near Detroit,

Michigan, where I had the main preaching load. There were 275 in attendance. We had a fine experience at the reunion, which was held at the Salvation Army grounds. Unfortunately, the kitchen and dining hall had burned to the ground just a few days earlier; but the Saints rallied, and neighboring camps loaned us some necessary equipment. The day before the reunion, Dick and Joyce Wilson had taken us into Canada, where we toured a portion of southern Ontario.

Also in August the Restorationist Saints bought a very large church and an attached three-story school building in the heart of Independence. They planned to open the school for private education with religious instruction included. At the first service in the church, named the Waldo Restoration Branch, about 1,000 people were in attendance.

I continued to provide ministry to the area, including preaching at Bates City, Grain Valley, Chilhowee, Odessa, Oak Grove, Marshall, Harrisonville, Warrensburg, Lexington, Hill Cumorah, South Crysler, Center Branch, and South Branch in Missouri; and preaching series at Sperry, Oklahoma, and Iola, Kansas.

After living in what we had planned to be our "retirement home" at Oak Grove for 13 years, we finally moved into a house on Beverly Road in Independence at the beginning of September. Although we loved our five-acre property near Oak Grove, with its beautiful pond full of fish, the magnificent trees, and the gardens that bore so much wonderful produce for us, at 75 I was getting too old to care for it. By moving to Independence, we were close to Beth and the hospital and closer to where Gwen was receiving her weekly chemotherapy treatment.

Hoping to sell to a family of Saints gathering to Zion, we did not immediately put our Oak Grove home on the market. To keep the insurance on the house, it had to be occupied—which meant that once a week I had to drive to

Oak Grove and spend the night in the house, even during the winter. That lasted until we finally put the house on the open market in mid-1992. It was soon snapped up, and we sold it in July.

In late September of 1991, Marvia arrived from Australia for a month. While she was here, Trevor, Lori, and Angela came from Virginia. That was our first chance to see our delightful little granddaughter. It was also good to have Beth, Marvia, and Trevor together again. We had a special blessing service for Angela at the Hill Cumorah Restoration Branch in Independence. Lori's parents, Ellis and Marilyn Thatcher, came from Houston for the service. I prayed the blessing and was assisted by Brother Houston Hobart, who said that he had never seen such a pretty baby. We were certainly proud grandparents! Marvia sang a beautiful solo, which had been written years earlier by Gwen's father. What a delightful experience! Marvia later flew to Virginia to visit with Trevor, Lori, and her new niece.

As the colder weather set in, I started to produce a new set of missionary slides on video tape. I recruited local artists to help me. We printed the text with computers and laser printers, so the lettering looked very professional.

In March of 1992, Gwen finally completed her chemotherapy treatment. The doctors reported that it was successful, with no sign of cancer in her body.

Even though we were no longer on an acreage, I nevertheless planted a garden. It produced a good crop of peas, tomatoes, asparagus, swiss chard, lima beans, corn, and New Zealand kumuras (sweet potatoes). I also spent time in my workshop in the basement, building a bookcase as well as working on the missionary tapes.

During April we went to the Floods' house to meet the Australian delegation to the RLDS World Conference. The fundamentalist RLDS or "Restorationists" now numbered several thousand in the Center Place. During conference week they met in the Waldo church with a different speaker each night. There were more than 800 people present for each service, including the night I preached.

A Tahitian lady, Tatehau, stayed in Independence after the conference for some scheduled heart surgery. Just as Tatehau was beginning to get drowsy for the operation, Beth, who was the assisting nurse, started to sing *"Tiona nehe nehe"* ("Zion the Beautiful") in Tahitian. Tatehau joined in with her and just managed to complete it before she succumbed to the anesthesia. The doctors and nurses were surprised and thrilled to hear Beth singing in a different language.

One of the activities I especially enjoyed that summer was when I visited the Foundation for Research on Ancient America to share my testimony of the Book of Mormon.

In late June Gwen and I once again attended the big reunion at Wilburton, Oklahoma. Near the beginning of the reunion I had what I believe to be the greatest outpouring of God's Spirit to me in all my experience. Later I was directed to present the things that I had seen to the Saints. Tremendous power accompanied it, which caused us to tremble. The beauty of the experience was glorious, and it set the tone for all the prayer meetings that followed.

A month later we attended a "primitive reunion" south of Harrisonville, about 40 miles from Independence, where I preached six of the seven sermons. Despite the rain, mud, flies, and lack of modern facilities, there was a good spirit present.

We next attended the Central Missouri Restoration Branches' reunion at El Dorado Springs. During the week I thought I might be coming down with a virus; I even had to excuse myself for a while during a class that I was teaching. Apart from that, the reunion went well.

The following Monday I went to the doctor for my regular checkup. He noticed my yellow appearance and thought maybe I had contracted hepatitis at the primitive reunion. When the blood tests came back negative, he ordered a CAT scan. It showed a blockage of the bile duct and a small mass near the pancreas. The doctors explored those parts and inserted a bypass for the bile duct. That was done under general anesthetic. When I came to, the doctor told Gwen and me that I had pancreatic cancer which was inoperable. He thought I would have maybe one or two good years left. But as soon as he told us that, I felt I was indeed appointed unto death.

About that time we also learned that Lori was pregnant again, so a new Sorensen would be coming into the world as an old one was going out. After I was released from the hospital, Gwen had knee surgery. That went fairly well, but soon afterwards I came down with a very high fever and was readmitted to the hospital. There was some concern about whether I would survive, so Trevor, Lori, and Angela flew from Virginia the next day to see me. It appeared that the bypass in the bile duct was not working, so the doctors inserted a larger tube. They noted that the cancer was vigorous and spreading and concluded that I would have only a few months to live.

During my stay in the hospital, I experienced both a "code blue" and a "code gray" alert. The code blue came when my heart stopped. Beth was getting ready for a heart case when she heard the code blue call for my room—she ran up five flights of stairs because she didn't want to wait for an elevator. She was puffing when she arrived! But by then the response team was able to get my "ticker" going again, so I was out of immediate danger. The code gray occurred the next day when there was a tornado warning for our area. They had to move patients to the inner halls, away from the glass windows. I felt that I was special to have both a code blue and a code gray during my short stay in the hospital.

One memory I cherish from my time there was the visit by our little granddaughter, Angela. Despite the fact that I looked terrible, all wrinkled and gray like "death warmed over," that sweet little 14-month-old girl held my hand and called me "Pa." She was not at all frightened of me and really seemed to enjoy holding my hand. It was as if she sensed that it was a special time.

Finally I had recovered sufficiently to return home; for a while my color improved, and I gradually regained a little strength. However, we had to cancel plans for a trip to Florida. In early October Marvia came from Australia to see me and say goodbye; we both realized that it would be the last time she would see me. We had some wonderful talks together, and I tried to counsel her about some matters in her life. She was able to stay for only a few days and had to leave before our wedding anniversary on October 17, 1992.

That was our 50th wedding anniversary; therefore, I got dressed up in my suit and tie for the reception at our home. The event had been advertised in the local paper; and many of our old friends stopped by to visit and have refreshments. Trevor, Lori, and Angela arrived for the occasion. Once again little Angela enjoyed her time with "Pa."

Trevor took me to renew my driver's license. Although I knew I would not be driving again, I wanted to complete this life with a valid license. I gradually started to lose my appetite and become weaker. My skin turned pale as the new tube in my bile duct became blocked.

Gwen and I were very grateful for the help of the local hospice and the Center Place Restoration School, which regularly prepared meals for us. They were delivered by Saints from Heritage House. I also appreciated the visits of Houston Hobart, David Bowerman, James Rogers, and the other priesthood members, who came to administer and pray for me.

Realizing that my time was limited, I set out to record my memoirs as Beth had requested me to do many years earlier. I had not found the time to do that previously, except for a few pages. I also wanted to arrange for the completion of my new missionary video project. I gave my slides, tapes, and other material to Brother Dale Godfrey to see if he could put the old sound track to the new videos. He later demonstrated that it would work, which gave me a sense of relief.

Trevor and his family came to visit for Thanksgiving and Christmas. It was good to watch both Angela and Lori getting bigger. Lori's doctor tried to find out from a sonogram whether the baby she was carrying was a boy, but it was still too early to tell. We were hoping that Trevor and Lori would have a son to carry on our branch of the Sorensen name.

Even though I was very weak, it was wonderful to have family around me during those holidays—the McGuires, the Floods, and the Sorensens. It was hard to say goodbye to Trevor, Lori, and Angela when they left the day after Christmas. We knew that it would be the last time I would see them in this life. Personally, I was not perturbed. As Joseph Smith said when riding off to the slaughter, "I am as calm as a summer's morning." One does not like leaving Mother Earth and all one's relatives; but other than that, I was looking forward to a great adventure—when I would "be absent from the body, and...present with the Lord," as the Apostle Paul said (2 Corinthians 5:8).

☼ ☼ ☼

CONCLUSION

Sickness and weakness have brought me to the end of these memoirs, but there are many more wonderful blessings and experiences I have had during my lifetime in the service of my Lord. I am so happy that the Lord has seen fit to use me so much—even in my years of "retirement." He has been more than good to Gwen and me over the years. When we count our blessings, we know that He has spoiled us to pieces.

We have tried to serve Him and keep His commandments, for which He has blessed us. "I, the Lord, am bound when ye do what I say, but when ye do not what I say, ye have no promise" (Doctrine and Covenants 81:3). It is a stupendous thing to bind the Lord—but because of His Word, He is obliged to bless. When we disobey, He is not bound to bless us—although in His great mercy He often does.

I could not conclude these memoirs without mentioning the anguish of spirit that I have experienced as the forces of evil have tried to destroy the Church of Jesus Christ. I have the assurance that Zion will be, as the Scriptures say, and that God's work will be triumphant in the end. "The works, and the designs, and the purposes of God, can not be frustrated, neither can they come to naught" (Doctrine and Covenants 2:1).

To the youth of Christ's Church I leave this admonition: "This is your day. Take full advantage of it, believing all things can be accomplished if you put your trust in your heavenly Father and give Him first place in your heart."

Epilogue

Vivian Charles Richard Sorensen passed away in his sleep on January 13, 1993, just a month before his 77th birthday. His wife and his oldest child, Beth, were by his side. Despite his years of ministry and multitude of spiritual experiences, he did not feel worthy to enter into the presence of God. In his humility, one of his last statements was, "I'll have to call on the Lord for His mercy."

On March 27, 1993, Eric Charles Sorensen was born to Trevor and Lori, thus fulfilling Vivian's wish for a grandson to carry on the Sorensen name.

▲ Celebrating 50th wedding anniversary, October 17, 1992

▼ Thanksgiving dinner, 1992—Vivian (at left) and family (clockwise): Angela and Lori Sorensen, David McGuire, Frank and Ruth Flood, Gwen, Beth, John, Bill, and Richard McGuire

Abridged Index

This index contains names of people, places, and activities. However, it does not necessarily show every occurrence of a person or word.